The Ruling Caste

The Ruling Caste

*Imperial Lives in the
Victorian Raj*

~

DAVID GILMOUR

JOHN MURRAY

© David Gilmour 2005

First published in Great Britain in 2005 by John Murray (Publishers)
A division of Hodder Headline

The right of David Gilmour to be identified as the Author of this
Work has been asserted by him in accordance with the Copyright,
Designs and Patents Act 1988.

2

A CIP catalogue record for this title is available from the British Library

Hardback ISBN 0 7195 5534 5

Typeset in Monotype Garamond by Servis Filmsetting Ltd, Manchester

Printed and bound by Clays Ltd, St Ives plc

Hodder Headline policy is to use papers that are natural, renewable
and recyclable products and made from wood grown in sustainable
forests. The logging and manufacturing processes are expected to
conform to the environmental regulations of the country of origin.

John Murray (Publishers)
338 Euston Road
London NW1 3BH

*To Maurice Keen
and in memory of Richard Cobb
friends and mentors*

Contents

~

Contents

Contents

Illustrations

The author and publisher would like to thank the following for permission to reproduce illustrations: Plates 1, 2, 4, 5, 6, 7, 8, 9, 10, 11, 12, 13, 14, 15, 16, 17, 18, 19, 21, 22, 23, 24 and 26, Oriental and India Office Collection, British Library; 3, the late Lady Alexandra Metcalfe; 20, Xan Smiley; 25, National Portrait Gallery, London.

Preface

~

DURING THEIR BRIEF momentous period of collaboration, Joseph Stalin and Joachim von Ribbentrop agreed that it was absurd that so much of the world should be ruled by Great Britain. In particular, the Russian leader told the Nazi Foreign Minister, it was 'ridiculous . . . that a few hundred Englishmen should dominate India'.[1] He was referring to the men of the Indian Civil Service (ICS).

The statistic alone seems ridiculous. In 1901, when Queen Victoria died, the 'few hundred' numbered just over a thousand, of whom a fifth were at any time either sick or on leave. Yet they administered directly (in British India) or indirectly (in the princely states) a population of nearly 300 million people spread over the territory of modern India, Pakistan, Burma and Bangladesh.

Stalin's grumble contained perhaps a touch of tacit admiration. More explicit praise came from earlier foreign leaders who, like him, had been in search of empires to rule. Bismarck thought Britain's work in India would be 'one of its lasting monuments', while Theodore Roosevelt told the British they had done 'such marvellous things in India' that they might 'gradually, as century succeeds century . . . transform the Indian population, not in blood, probably not in speech, but in government and culture, and thus leave [their] impress as Rome did hers on Western Europe'.[2]

It is not difficult to find foreign eulogies of British civil servants in India, from the French Abbé Dubois, who in 1822 extolled their

xiii

'uprightness of character, education and ability', to the Austrian Baron Hübner who in 1886 ascribed the 'miracles' of British administration to 'the devotion, intelligence, the courage, the perseverance, and the skill combined with an integrity proof against all temptation, of a handful of officials and magistrates who govern and administer the Indian Empire'.[3] Similar tributes can also be found in unexpected places in Britain. Lloyd George, the Liberal leader, lauded the Service as 'the steel frame' that held everything together, while John Strachey, the Labour minister, judged it the 'least corruptible . . . ablest and . . . most respectable of all the great bureaucracies of the world'.[4]

The same words recur again and again, even from Indian nationalists and their newspapers at the end of the nineteenth century: impartial, high-minded, conscientious, incorruptible. The ICS may have had its critics – even within its own ranks – but about its elevated standards there was no argument. N.B. Bonarjee, a member of the Service but also an Indian nationalist, praised 'its rectitude, its sense of justice, its tolerance, its sense of public duty', as well as 'its high administrative ability'.[5] After independence in 1947, the new nations of Pakistan and India each displayed pride in its traditions. While in Karachi a Government pamphlet proclaimed that the Pakistan Civil Service was the 'successor' of the ICS, 'the most distinguished Civil Service in the world', in Delhi the Home Minister, Vallabhbhai Patel, used it as a model for the Indian Administrative Service, a body that played a crucial role in the integration and unification of the new state. Even at the beginning of the twenty-first century retired members of the IAS were recalling the exploits of their British predecessors with almost embarrassing effusiveness.[6]

The high reputation of the ICS was never reflected in the literature of the country where most of its members were born. This was no doubt partly because civil servants do not make exciting characters in fiction, even when they do much of their work on horseback. During the existence of the Raj they sometimes appeared in the novels of largely forgotten authors such as Alexander Allardyce, Flora Annie Steel, W. W. Hunter, Edward Thompson and A. E. W. Mason. More recently they have featured in the fiction of three winners of the Booker Prize, although not in any leading role except in J.G. Farrell's *The Siege of Krishnapur*, a historical novel about the Indian Mutiny. In Ruth Prawer Jhabvala's *Heat and Dust* the civil servant is a hapless figure whose wife has an affair with the local nawab, while in Paul Scott's *The Jewel in the Crown* he is an uncomfortable liberal who disavows his predecessors and is limited to a brief appearance in a single volume of the Raj Quartet.

Scott's work, criticized both by Indian nationalists and by British conservatives, is a brilliant portrait of the Raj in its closing years. Yet it is limited not only in time but also in the range of its British characters, who (apart from some missionaries) are nearly all connected to the Army. Rudyard Kipling painted a fuller and richer picture of the Raj at its zenith, but this too is restricted in scope, mainly because he lived nearly all his time in the Punjab and left India at the age of 23. He also took most of his characters from the military (with a preference for NCOs and Other Ranks), and distributed his civilians in professions as diverse as forestry and engineering. Some of Kipling's few civil servants are strong men, dedicated paternalists obsessed with duty and the welfare of Indians. But others are pedantic or frivolous or impractical. In his story 'Tod's Amendment' he gave a 6-year-old boy more understanding of agricultural tenancies than the Legal Member of the Viceroy's Council.

Although Kipling was the principal chronicler of British India, the most enduring effigy of its administrators was carved by E. M. Forster in *A Passage to India*. The two writers approached the Subcontinent from angles that could hardly have been more different. Kipling was born in India and returned at the age of 16 to earn his living as a journalist in Lahore. Forster had already published most of his novels by the time he sailed for Bombay in search of India and Indian friendships. There was nothing in his background, character or outlook that predisposed him to look favourably on the Raj. Indeed several of his friends in the Bloomsbury Group had abandoned their traditional family links with imperial rule.* They even persuaded one of their members, Rex Partridge, the son and nephew of ICS officials, to change his name to the less regal-sounding Ralph.[8]

---

*Virginia Woolf's uncle, Sir James Fitzjames Stephen, had been on the Viceroy's Council, and her husband Leonard had been in the Ceylon Civil Service. Lytton Strachey was the son of a General in the Indian Army, the nephew of a Lieutenant-Governor and the godson of a Viceroy. Although his two eldest brothers spent their careers in India, and although he himself wrote a dissertation on Warren Hastings at Cambridge, Strachey rejected any idea of an imperial role for himself and even wrote a family memoir without mentioning the Subcontinent.[7]

A Passage to India is a subtle and in certain ways sensitive work, a well-crafted drama with an evocative sense of place and some plausible Indian characters. But its author's loathing of the British in India – a feeling he confessed to in private[9] – turned it into a tendentious political novel, at any rate for many of his contemporary readers. Kipling was fascinated by other men's professions and wrote numerous stories about work; so was Scott, who diligently carried out research into how the British had administered India. But Forster was seldom interested in writing about work; he preferred portraying people at their leisure or in their domesticity in Florence and the Home Counties. He did not see civil servants inspecting hospitals or canals but witnessed them relaxing at 'the Club', where he judged them philistine and stupid. Then he turned them into caricatures. His District Officer, Turton, is pompous and absurd and wants 'to flog every native' in sight as soon as there is a crisis; his memsahibs are even worse, crude stereotypes, compounds of nothing but snobbery and racial prejudice. Their actions are seldom more credible than their characters. Forster makes them react to an obscure incident in a cave as if it had been a minor massacre. They gather at the club and make semi-hysterical suggestions about calling out the Army, 'clearing the bazaars' and sending the women and children to the hills. There is almost nothing believable about the scene at the club or about the arrest and trial of Aziz, where Forster's ignorance of administration and judicial procedure let him down again. Yet these events, described in fiction and depicted in film, form one of the most abiding images of British India.

The principal historical portrait is a kinder one. Fifty years ago, a former civil servant, Philip Mason, published (under the pseudonym Philip Woodruff) his two volumes of *The Men Who Ruled India, The Founders* and *The Guardians*. They are the work of a wise man and a talented writer who wrote affectionately yet sometimes critically of a Service which had on the whole, he thought, justified its reputation for altruism and benevolent rule. Although regularly and unfairly denounced by post-colonial critics as hagiography, it is the work on the subject best known to non-academic readers.

Two historiograpical developments in the late 1970s changed academic attitudes towards the Service. The most important was the publication in 1978 of Edward Said's *Orientalism*, a hugely influential book that spawned legions of disciples, in India and elsewhere, who took it for granted that colonial rule was always evil and colonialist motives were invariably bad. The other was a sudden interest shown by a number of North American historians in demolishing the reputation of the ICS. In 1976 Bradford Spangenberg published a thesis claiming that the Service was obsessed with status and promotion and declaring that, as a result of his 'scrutiny of the characteristics and motivations of British officials', he had destroyed the 'myths' of its efficiency and 'self-sacrificial esprit de corps'. Although his 'scrutiny' generally and curiously eschewed the examination of civil servants' private papers, it was welcomed by other historians equally eager to demonstrate the self-interest and lack of altruism in the Service. It soon became normal to read American studies of British India without finding a decent motive ascribed to officials who had spent a good part of their careers digging canals, fighting crime and organizing famine relief. Even the officers of the Indian Medical Service, men working (with a certain success) to combat malaria, plague and cholera, were accused of carrying out research 'driven by narrowly professional motives' and of trying 'to advance their careers at home by contributing to the advance of a universal medical science'.[10] How contributions to the advance of medical science can be regarded as inherently sinful is something of a mystery. Even odder is the implication that trying to advance one's career is an activity unknown to American historians.

The most significant contributions to the subject since Woodruff are *The District Officer* by Roland Hunt and John Harrison, which is outside my period, and Clive Dewey's *Anglo-Indian Attitudes*, which just touches the end of it. Dewey's study concentrates on two very different figures in the ICS, Malcolm Darling, a friend of Forster who also befriended Indians, and Frank Lugard Brayne, an Evangelical who attempted to transform his district by enforcing sanitary and agricultural improvements. The author took the two men to represent the Cult of Friendship and the Gospel of Uplift, two contrasting outlooks which, he argued, alternated as the dominant British attitude to India between the governorship of Clive and the viceroyalty of Mountbatten.[11]

Paul Scott became so interested in the mechanics of the Raj that he even contemplated writing a non-fictional account of its working routines. He wished that the last British generation in India would stop reminiscing about tigers and elephants and the smell of dung fires, and tell him how their curious administration had functioned. 'How did it *work*?' There was 'nothing more maddening', he told a retired civil servant, 'than the lack of printed evidence of how men like you actually spent their day. From *chota hazri* to sundown. Minute by minute, hour by hour.'[12]

This book does not pretend to explain how the administration *worked*. That would require a study not only of Stalin's 'few hundred' but of the hundreds of thousands of Indian subordinates who were employed in the various different services. But it does aim to show what the senior men did, how they worked and how they lived from *chota hazri* to sundown, from apprenticeship to the Collector's bungalow and, in some cases, to Simla and Government House. It takes them from background and recruitment through their careers to their retirement; it describes their work and their ambitions, their thoughts and their beliefs, their leisure time and their domestic existences. I have attempted to explain why they went to India, what they did when they got there, and what they thought about it all. While mindful of recent post-colonial scholarship, I have tried to be unprejudiced in assessing their strengths and weaknesses, their successes and failures. If I have been incapable of doing so without irony, I hope at least that I have been fair.

My approach has been an individual's on individuals, coming to the institution through its members, not the other way round. That is why some sections deal exclusively with a single official, notably Alfred Lyall, whose life is chronicled from training to retirement. I began doing research on the ICS fifteen years ago, while working on a biography of Lord Curzon, and since then I have come across hundreds of people writing or being written about in private papers. The experience has led me to appreciate the diversity within the structure. Despite my admiration for Dewey's work, I find that few of the people I have investigated fit comfortably into one or other of his categories: most of them have bits of both Darling and Brayne.

No doubt this view places me in Dewey's categories of 'unreconstructed liberal' or empiricist who denies the importance of ideologies and the Zeitgeist. Of course I am aware that there was a civil service ethos imbibed at Haileybury or Oxford and later reinforced in the provincial capitals of Bombay, Lahore and elsewhere. Similar ideas percolated in the clubs and in the secretariats. But always there was the diversity encouraged by diverse circumstances. The experience of Madras was very different from that of the Punjab; men in obscure districts did not see things in the same way as their colleagues in Calcutta. Ultimately officials in India had to live on their own resources, their lives determined by individual temperaments, environment and experience – and by the eternal problems of human relationships.

Note on Spelling and Currency

~

IT IS DIFFICULT to establish a logical and consistent method of spelling Indian names. Old usages sometimes look absurd while new transliterations are often confusing. Consistency, however, has seldom been regarded as important: for the second edition of his book, *The Native States of India* (1910), Sir William Lee-Warner changed such names as Tipoo, Guzerat and Hyder to Tipu, Gujarat and Haidar.

I have tried to avoid such over-anglicized archaisms as Gopal Row Hurry, and for place names I have opted for the version most familiar to most people, for example the old Cawnpore instead of the new Kanpur but the new Jaipur rather than the old Jeypore. As for the problem of choosing which Indian and Anglo-Indian words to italicize, I have followed the practice of the *Oxford English Dictionary*.

Since 1835 the Indian currency had been the Madras rupee, which was divided into sixteen annas. Before 1873 there were ten rupees to the British pound: a rupee was thus worth two shillings. But in that year the value of the silver-based currency began to fall. It was worth only one shilling and sevenpence in 1885 and had fallen to below one shilling and threepence by 1892. From 1899 it stabilized at one shilling and fourpence, or fifteen rupees to the pound.

Glossary of Indian and Anglo-Indian Words

~

ayah   a nanny
babu   (usually pejorative) an English-speaking Hindu clerk
badmash   a rascal, rogue
bhishti   a water-carrier
bania   a Hindu merchant
boxwallah   originally an Indian travelling salesman, later used (as here) as a British businessman in India
burra peg   a double measure of alcohol, usually brandy or whisky
cantonment   a military station
chaprasi   a messenger or errand boy
charpoy   a string bed
chota hazri   an early light breakfast
chowkidar   a watchman or village policeman
chummery   a house shared by bachelors
cutchery   a court-house, sometimes an office
dacoity   robbery by an armed gang
dandy   a sort of hammock on a pole carried by coolies
griffin   a newcomer in his first year in India
hookah-burdar   a servant in charge of his master's pipe
jampan   a sort of sedan chair carried by two pairs of *jampannies*
jirga   a council of Pathan or Baluchi tribal elders
kheddah   the capture of wild elephants
khidmutgar   a servant who waits at table

ma-bap literally 'mother and father' but used to denote a paternalist District Officer

maidan an open space in a town

mali a gardener

mehta a sweeper

mofussil rural areas, 'up country'

munshi a teacher or secretary

munsif a subordinate Indian judge

nabob a rich Anglo-Indian businessman of the eighteenth century

pakhtunwali the Pathan code of honour

patel a village headman

patwari a village accountant and registrar

poodle-faker seducer, ladies' man (usually military)

punkah a cloth fan on a frame suspended from the ceiling and activated by a *punkah* wallah pulling a rope

purdah the curtain screening women from the sight of male strangers; 'in *purdah*' means the state of being secluded

rajput a member of the Hindu warrior caste, mainly found in Rajputana or the North-Western Provinces

rani the wife of a raja

ryot a farmer, usually a peasant proprietor

ryotwari system the settlement for land revenue made between the *ryot* and the government

sepoy an Indian private soldier in the armies of the East India Company and later of the Indian Army

shikar hunting, shooting or fishing

shikari either a hunter or an Indian hired by a hunter to help him find game

syce a groom

tahsil a subdivision of a district

tahsildar a revenue officer in charge of a *tahsil*

talukdar a landed magnate in Oudh

tiffin a midday snack or early lunch

tonga a light, two-wheeled vehicle, usually drawn by ponies

Vedas the ancient, sacred Hindu books

zamindar a large landowner and rent collector in Bengal

zamindari system the settlement for land revenue whereby landlords collected agricultural rents and paid a proportion into the exchequer

zenana the area in a household where the women were kept secluded

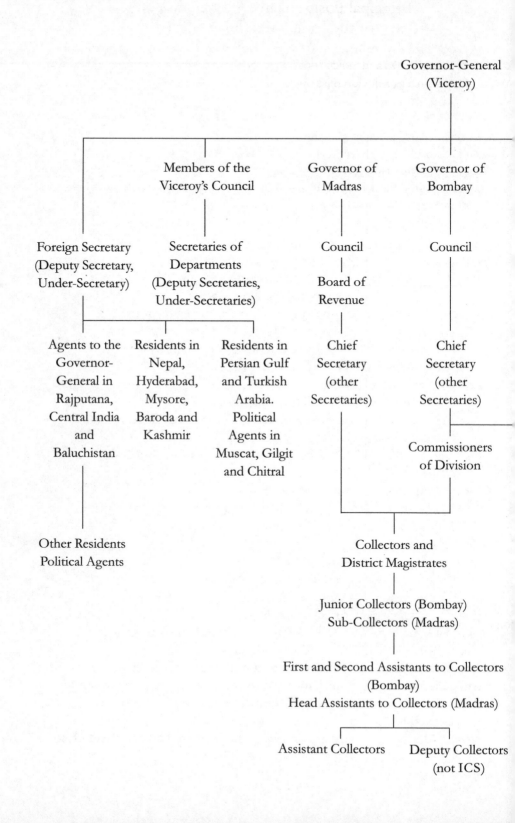

Governor-General
(Viceroy)

Members of the
Viceroy's Council

Governor of
Madras

Governor of
Bombay

Foreign Secretary
(Deputy Secretary,
Under-Secretary)

Secretaries of
Departments
(Deputy Secretaries,
Under-Secretaries)

Council

Council

Agents to the
Governor-
General in
Rajputana,
Central India
and
Baluchistan

Residents in
Nepal,
Hyderabad,
Mysore,
Baroda and
Kashmir

Residents in
Persian Gulf
and Turkish
Arabia.
Political
Agents in
Muscat, Gilgit
and Chitral

Board of
Revenue

Chief
Secretary
(other
Secretaries)

Chief
Secretary
(other
Secretaries)

Commissioners
of Division

Other Residents
Political Agents

Collectors and
District Magistrates

Junior Collectors (Bombay)
Sub-Collectors (Madras)

First and Second Assistants to Collectors
(Bombay)
Head Assistants to Collectors (Madras)

Assistant Collectors

Deputy Collectors
(not ICS)

Principal Positions in the Executive Branch
of the Indian Government, 1900

Note: Legislative and judicial posts have been omitted. So have certain individual jobs such as Salt Commissioner and Inspector-General of Police in Bengal.

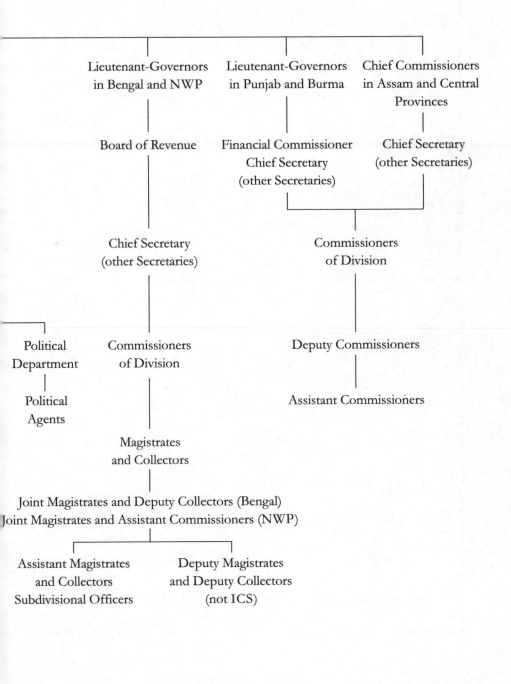

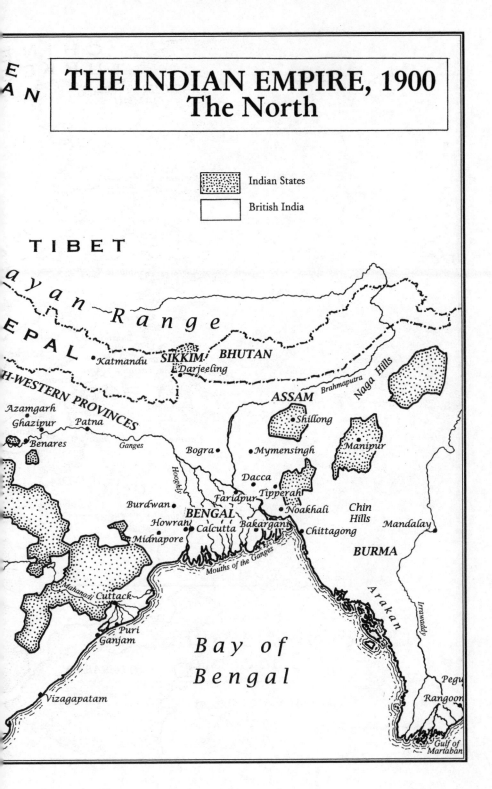

THE INDIAN EMPIRE, 1900
The North

Indian States

British India

TIBET

ayan Range

EPAL

·Katmandu SIKKIM· BHUTAN
·Darjeeling

H-WESTERN PROVINCES

Azamgarh

Ghazipur Patna

·Benares Ganges

ASSAM

·Shillong

Naga Hills

Brahmaputra

·Bogra ·Mymensingh ·Manipur

·Dacca

Hooghly Faridpur Tipperah

Burdwan· BENGAL ·Noakhali Chin
Howrah· Calcutta·Bakarganj Hills
·Midnapore ·Chittagong Mandalay·

Mouths of the Ganges BURMA

Mahanadi Cuttack Arakan Irrawaddy

·Puri
Ganjam

Bay of
Bengal

·Vizagapatam

Pegu·

Rangoon·

Gulf of
Martaban

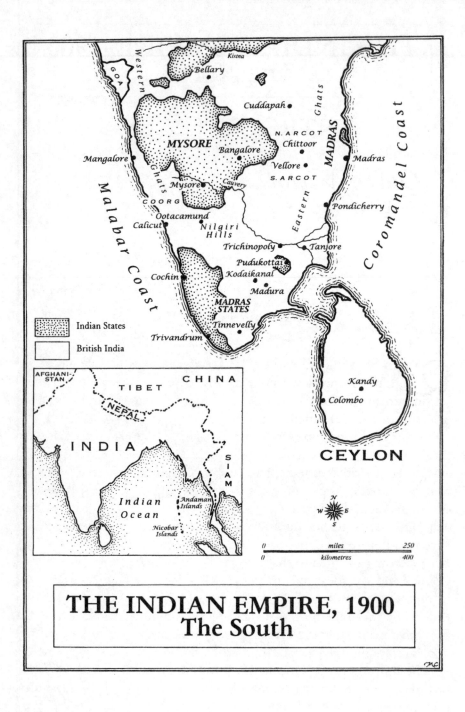

Indian States

British India

THE INDIAN EMPIRE, 1900
The South

INTRODUCTION

Queen Victoria's Indian Empire

~

Maternalism

QUEEN VICTORIA, EMPRESS of India, was a unique figure, a reigning Empress who never visited her empire. Although she sat on her throne for sixty-three years, she never went east of Berlin or south of San Sebastián.

Yet she cared more passionately about her Indian subjects than her three successors, who each visited the Subcontinent, and far more than any previous British monarch. She liked Indians, clerks and servants as well as princes, and employed a few of them in her entourage. Although she had no practical role in the administration of India, she delivered advice to her ministers and dispatched exhortations to her Viceroys. Before his departure for Bombay in 1898, Lord Curzon, her last Viceroy, was urged to shake himself free from his 'narrow-minded' Council and 'overbearing' officials and '*hear for himself* what the feelings of the Natives really are'; he must be careful not 'to trample on' the Indians or 'make them *feel* that they are a conquered people'. Naturally they must realize that the British were their masters, but this 'should be done kindly and not offensively' as had often been the case in the past.[1]

When she became Queen in 1837, shortly after her eighteenth birthday, Victoria knew nothing about India. For her political education she relied on her Prime Minister, the Whig Lord Melbourne, who adored her so much that he remained in office chiefly because it

I

gave him an excuse to go on visiting her. Melbourne steered his sovereign benignly through the first years of her reign, offering her eccentric yet sometimes sage advice which she, who was equally fond of him, carefully noted in her diary. But he did not tell her much about Britain's overseas interests except to remark that the Maoris, though otherwise a fine race, ate people, and that the burning of widows in India was 'not a good custom'.[2]

Her next mentor, her German husband Prince Albert, was understandably even less instructive about the colonies than the amiable Melbourne; from him she learned the austere pleasures of governance while experiencing a very Victorian sequence of childbirth. It was not until the Mutiny of 1857 that she became closely involved with India. In November of that year she happily recorded the widespread feeling 'that India should belong to *me*' and was delighted by the subsequent transfer of its administration from the East India Company to the Crown.* She was also pleased by Lord Palmerston's proposal that the Crown would control appointments to the Indian Army, and correspondingly indignant when Lord Derby's brief Conservative Government placed them under the control of the India Council, a new body presided over by a new cabinet minister, the Secretary of State for India. Eager to establish her influence over the Government in Calcutta, the city that remained India's capital until 1911, she demanded that all important measures should require her consent before they were discussed by the Council, a demand rejected by the Secretary of State who told her she was assuming 'a false position'.[3] Yet she was able to ensure that some of her feelings were reflected in the royal proclamation to her Indian subjects of 1858. The previous year she had applauded the efforts of Lord Canning, the Governor-General,† to restrict retribution to rebels

---

*Although originally set up as a trading organization, the East India Company had administered the British territories in India up until then. Its independence of action, however, had been diminishing ever since the Regulating Act of 1773. Following William Pitt's India Act of 1784, political policy was run by a Board of Control responsible to Parliament.

† Since 1773 the chief executive in India had been the Governor-General, and remained so until independence in 1947. In 1858, however, he was given the additional title of Viceroy to symbolize the fact that he was now the representative of the sovereign. Canning, who was the first Viceroy, preferred it to the older designation, and his successors were usually referred to as Viceroys, although 'Governor-General' remained their only statutory title.

guilty of atrocities and had told his wife that there should be no interference with Indian religions. Now she and Albert insisted on the removal of a proposed passage referring to her power 'to undermine native religions and customs' and its replacement with the declaration that while 'Firmly relying ourselves on the truth of Christianity . . . we disclaim alike the right & the desire to impose our convictions on any of our subjects . . . all shall alike enjoy the equal & impartial protection of the law.'[4]

In 1876 Queen Victoria became Empress of India, though her imperial title did not apply to any other part of her empire, not even Britain. She had long been impatient for the honorific and eventually persuaded Benjamin Disraeli, her second favourite Prime Minister after Melbourne, to arrange the matter through the Royal Titles Bill. The measure was robustly resisted in Parliament and in London society, where the widowed and withdrawn Queen was considered insufficiently active to deserve promotion. The bill was passed, however, and the exultant monarch immediately pressed for a troop of Sikh cavalry to be imported from the Punjab to attend her. She also took to signing herself V.R.&I. – *Victoria Regina et Imperatrix* – even on documents that had nothing to do with India.

The Queen's determination was regarded as rather vulgar and unBritish. Yet it was strange that the ruler of the world's largest empire possessed no imperial title. Russia and Austria had been ruled by emperors for centuries; Germany had just acquired its first, while France had just discarded its second. Besides, the elevation of King Wilhelm from Prussian monarch to German Kaiser in 1871 had created a problem of prestige and precedence. It meant that Vicky, the Queen's daughter who was married to the Kaiser's heir, would one day take precedence over her mother.

Whatever reservations Disraeli and his colleagues may have had, the upgrading was effective both at home and abroad. It helped bring the Queen back into public life after her long mourning and thereby revived the popularity of the monarchy which, despite the scandals involving the Prince of Wales, reached unexpected summits in the years of her Golden and Diamond Jubilees. It also helped turn British attention towards India and provide a stimulus for the new imperialism of the 1880s, reflected in the establishment of the Imperial Federation League and in the astonishing popularity of Sir John Seeley's book, *The Expansion of England*.

In India the effect too was beneficial. The Russian Empire had been galloping southwards and eastwards for decades, absorbing the khanates of Central Asia, and by 1876 Russian troops were within a thousand miles of the Indian frontier. It made what became known as 'the Great Game' sound more equal if a Russian tsar was opposed by an Indian empress. Moreover, it was historically appropriate: there had been great Indian emperors in recent centuries, and a decrepit old man in Delhi had been allowed to keep the title until as late as 1857. Lord Salisbury, the Secretary of State for India, was sceptical of the plan but aware of the need to make it 'gaudy enough to impress the orientals, yet not enough to give hold for ridicule' in Britain. In the end he sanctioned a great durbar in India to celebrate the event, hoping that it would at least obtain the goodwill and co-operation of 'the princely class', the only one, he gloomily observed, over whom the British could establish any useful influence.[5]

The princely class of India was one of the Queen's weaknesses. Curzon complained that its members were all invested with a kind of halo in her eyes and were treated indiscriminately as if they were important royalty. A turban with jewels was so alluring to her that she seemed not to care what sort of character it embellished. She liked the psychotic and irascible Maharaja of Holkar because he sent her a telegram on her birthday. She expressed such concern about the treatment of the Gaekwar of Baroda, who was deposed in 1875, that she had to be reminded by the Viceroy, Lord Northbrook, that the prince's character and behaviour were 'so bad as to render him entirely unworthy of the sympathy' she would 'otherwise naturally feel for a Sovereign Prince who has fallen from his "high estate"'.[6]

In spite of her Viceroys' protests, the Queen encouraged the princes to visit her at Windsor, where they were so petted by the Court and London society that they were often reluctant to return to India and govern their states. The Maharaja of Cooch Behar, a second-rank chief from Bengal, spent much time at Windsor and Sandringham with his friend the Prince of Wales and dreaded returning to Calcutta, pursued by the unpaid bills of Windsor tradesmen, to receive a dressing-down from Curzon. Visits to the Queen were also apt to encourage self-importance. Flattered by the way she allowed him to chat on equal terms with the Tsar and the Kaiser, the Raja of Kapurthala returned to India and promoted himself to the rank of Maharaja.[7]

One prince, who inspired the Queen to pay for his portrait, mixed eccentricity and exoticism with loyalty and conscientious administration. Sir Pratap Singh, Maharaja of Idar and three times Regent of Jodhpur, was an old-fashioned Rajput who came over to England for the jubilees and was the inventor of jodhpurs, the combination of gaiters and riding breeches in a single piece of clothing. Usually adorned by a turban with a miniature portrait of the Queen-Empress set in pearls, he had two great ambitions: one was to die leading a charge of the Jodhpur Lancers wearing Victoria's icon, which was not fulfilled; and the other, which also went unfulfilled, was to wipe out the Muslim population of India. When an English official remonstrated about the second, pointing out that they shared a number of Muslim friends, Sir Pratap replied in his famous pidgin, 'Yes, I liking them too, but very much liking them dead.'[8]

Victoria was not merely interested in the princes or in the trappings of her position at the apex of the Indian feudal hierarchy. According to her biographer, Elizabeth Longford, she had had romantic feelings for 'brown skins' since childhood. Devoid of snobbery and racial feeling herself, she would not allow people to disparage other races or refer to them as black: Salisbury himself was made to apologize for referring to Indians as 'black men'.[9]

When she was about to open the Indian and Colonial Exhibition in 1886, her Foreign Secretary, Lord Rosebery, urged the Queen to inject as much pomp as possible into the event. 'With all the pomp you like,' she replied, 'as long as I don't have to wear a low dress.' She also refused to wear a crown out of doors, a rule she had kept since the death of Albert. Although Rosebery protested that great empires were symbolized by crowns not bonnets, she insisted on opening the exhibition in a bonnet. As Lady Longford observed, 'Queen Victoria's instinct [was] to mother her dark-skinned children rather than to dazzle them'.[10]

On display at the exhibition was a group of artisans serving prison sentences in Agra, who had been brought to London to demonstrate their traditional skills as weavers, potters, coppersmiths and other craftsmen. The Queen was eager to record the appearance of some of 'her more humble Native subjects' (as the newspapers called them) and commissioned the Austrian painter, Rudolf Swoboda, to paint portraits of five of them. Delighted by the results, she then dispatched the artist to India to paint in strong colours and with vibrant brushwork some more of her humble subjects, farmers and artisans, soldiers and peasant girls, young men with dramatic turbans, old men with dramatic beards. The emphasis was on the traditional and the picturesque – as the painter's patroness wanted. But in one picture, called *A Peep at the Train*, Swoboda infused a hint of the modern, a reminder of how the British were changing India: in the bottom left corner of an apparently timeless rural scene, below a Sikh family gazing over a fence, stretches a small section of gleaming rail.[11]

The Queen's maternal instincts towards her Indian subjects took a practical form in furthering the career of one of her Muslim servants, Abdul Karim, who graduated from waiting at table to teaching her Hindustani and eventually becoming the Queen's Indian Secretary with the title of 'Hafiz'. Known as the Munshi, Abdul Karim was regarded by the court as a preening social climber who had excessive influence over his mistress's Indian views. He was also found to have lied about his background, claiming his father was a surgeon-general instead of the apothecary at the Agra jail – a discovery that delighted the courtiers but infuriated Victoria who reacted to their snobbery by reminding them she had known one archbishop who had been the son of a butcher and another whose father had been a grocer. No criticism was permitted of a person she seems to have doted on more than any man in her life after Albert, Melbourne and her Highland servant, John Brown, all of whom were dead by the time Abdul Karim appeared at Court. In her letters to him she signed herself, 'Your affectionate Mother, V.R.I.' and, on advising him about his wife's gynaecological problems, wrote, 'There is nothing I would not do to help you both, as you are my dear Indian children . . . Your loving Mother, Victoria R.I.'[12]

Lord Cromer, the proconsular ruler of Egypt for twenty-four years, remarked after Victoria's death that all her 'Eastern ideas were the Munshi's and were invariably wrong'. During his brief premiership in 1894–5 Rosebery had offered Cromer the viceroyalty and urged him to accept it quickly before the Munshi returned from India; otherwise Abdul Karim might object and persuade the Queen to repudiate the appointment.[13] Rosebery overestimated the power Abdul Karim had over his royal mistress. Although the Munshi may have inspired in her a certain pro-Muslim bias, his influence did not have important or effective or especially negative results. Her fondness for him doubtless fuelled her lectures to Curzon, in which she advised her Viceroy to find a munshi for himself and told him that no people were 'more alive to kindness, or more affectionately attached if treated with kindness, than the poor Indians'. It may have prompted her to argue with a Secretary of State against the hanging of a prince of Manipur for his role in the execution of British officials. And it did encourage her to write to Lady Harris, the wife of the Governor of Bombay, to tell her it was a mistake to tamper with the seclusion of widows and an error to educate Indian men so that they were able to read 'objectionable European literature'.[14] But there was little more to it than that, and in any case the Munshi's views coincided with her own.

It is easy to be sceptical about the Indian popularity of a distant monarch, unheard of by many, her position understood by few, her existence apparent to most people only in the form of solemn statues of bronze or stone portraying an old woman in a crown bearing an orb and sceptre. The popularity of her jubilees is not significant: they were excuses for ceremonial and celebration. But the spontaneous grief and unorganized demonstrations on the day of her funeral in January 1901 require more subtle explanation. She had, as Curzon observed, an 'overpowering effect on the imagination of the Asiatic'. Vast crowds converged on the Maidan at Calcutta, sitting all day without food, little groups holding banners proclaiming sentiments such as 'We poor Mussulmans from Sialdah grieving'. There was no attempt to profit from the day: even the poorest vendors of sweetmeats closed their little roadside booths in honour of the Queen-Empress. Few of the mourners might have been able to explain their presence except as an act of reverence. Perhaps Anne Wilson, a perceptive memsahib, came close to the truth when she noted that Victoria 'was worshipped by Her people in India, who identified Her with their gods, and to whom She was an incarnation of Motherhood'.[15]

Expansionism

The size of British India increased swiftly during the first twenty years of Victoria's reign. At her accession in 1837 it consisted principally of Bengal, the contingent territories known as the North-

Western Provinces,* Madras and the Carnatic coast, a considerable region around Bombay, and smaller areas in Burma, Sangor, Gujarat and Rajputana. It covered nearly half the Indian Subcontinent, and its Government exercised a form of 'indirect rule' over most of the remainder except in the north-west.

At the time of the Mutiny in 1857, Britain's portion had expanded to nearly two-thirds, and all the rest was ruled by dependent princes. Most of the expansion took place in the north-west in the 1840s with the conquests of Sind (an annexation opposed but not overturned by the Government in London) and of the Punjab, which was incorporated into the Empire after the Sikh wars between 1845 and 1849. The remaining territorial acquisitions of Victoria's reign, apart from the conquests of the rest of Burma in 1852–3 and 1885, were achieved without wars. Lord Dalhousie, the Governor-General between 1848 and 1856, employed a method of annexing territory called the 'doctrine of lapse', whereby certain subordinate states would be absorbed by the British if their rulers failed to produce a male heir from their own family. Two of the states thus extinguished were the large Maratha principality of Nagpur and the small state of Jhansi, where the Rajah's widow was so incensed that she later became the chief Indian heroine of the Mutiny. But the most important and – as events proved – most fatal accretion of territory occurred when the King of Oudh, whose family had misgoverned Lucknow and its territory for decades, was dethroned and his kingdom annexed by the Government.

The enlargement of British India was accompanied by significant physical changes, especially in transport. In the hot weather before the coming of the railways, a civil servant travelled to his district by night in a palanquin, a box litter with protruding poles, carried by six men and preceded by a torch bearer holding a gourd full of coconut oil which from time to time he poured on to a torch made of rags.[16] A journey from Calcutta into the North-Western Provinces, which took three weeks by palanquin, could be done a few years later in a day by train. Economies in the duration of sea voyages were almost as remarkable. In 1830 a ship sailing from London around the Cape of Good Hope took about four months to reach Calcutta. By the end

---

*After the creation of the North-West Frontier Province in 1901, the North-Western Provinces became known as the United Provinces of Agra and Oudh.

of the century a boat steaming from England through the Mediterranean and the Suez Canal could drop anchor in Bombay three weeks after departure.

The young and energetic Dalhousie initiated many of the structural changes, including the building of the railways and the establishment of postal and telegraphic services. He was also responsible for the improvement of roads and harbours and for such major irrigation works as the Ganges Canal, which stretches 350 miles from Hardwar to Cawnpore and contains thousands of miles of distributaries. By the beginning of the twentieth century British India had the largest irrigation system in the world, 37,000 miles of metalled roads and 25,000 miles of railways, over half the total in Asia (including Russia east of the Urals). Immense areas had been transformed. At Queen Victoria's accession, Assam had been primarily a jungle: at her death it contained over 4 million acres under cultivation, many of them in tea plantations.

Certain of these achievements – as well as related policies – have attracted arguments between historians. By raising the water-table, canals in some places may have caused the spread of saline deposits and consequent damage to crops. By removing tariff barriers between 1882 and 1894, the British Government did allow Manchester textile manufacturers to undercut the indigenous handicraft industry for a brief period. But in fact saline efflorescence affected a miniscule proportion of the land, and the harm done cannot be weighed against the enormous benefits produced by the multiplication of irrigated land by a factor of eight: by the 1870s the peasantry in the districts irrigated by the Ganges Canal were visibly better fed, housed and dressed than before; by the end of the century the new network of canals in the Punjab had produced an even more prosperous peasantry there. As for British cloth imports, which accounted for only a sixteenth of India's needs, these did not deter Indian entrepreneurs from opening textile factories in Bombay and Ahmedabad or prevent the Subcontinent from becoming the world's fourth greatest cotton manufacturing nation.[17]

The rate of technological change was so fast that an official who began his career travelling around India by cart and palanquin could spend his retirement driving about Kent in a motor car and watch Blériot fly across the Channel. Yet in India, away from the ports and the railways and the irrigation canals, the pace of change was extremely slow. It could not have been otherwise, given the low levels of taxation and expenditure and the British reluctance to tamper with social stability. Any attempt to carry out the kind of social and economic reforms the Meiji regime imposed on its Japanese citizens would have provoked a reaction more violent than the Mutiny. Thus even over so long a reign hundreds of thousands of villages altered little in appearance and not much in material wealth. By 1901 they might have a school and a small dispensary, a few more effective wells, some avenues of trees planted by zealous District Officers in an effort to prevent soil erosion. But little else would have changed, even in the materials used to build houses: beams and clay were only gradually replacing straw sheds.

Anglo-Indians

Benjamin Disraeli famously called India the jewel in the imperial crown. It was a many-sided jewel, a jewel of strategic value, of military power, a jewel which absorbed nearly a quarter of Britain's overseas investment. But it was not a jewel the British particularly liked or one which they wanted to spend much time gazing at. They just liked to know it was in the bank.

The last half-century of Victoria's reign was a period of massive emigration from Britain. Over a million people migrated to Australia and New Zealand; another million went to Canada and South Africa; over three million, mostly Irish, began new lives in the United States. Yet in 1901 the entire British population of India was just 154,691, fewer than the inhabitants of Hull or Nottingham and about a fifth of the number of people living in Glasgow. The vast majority, moreover, were only there to work: few Anglo-Indians had been born in India; even fewer planned to die there.*

In 1901 India had a population of nearly 300 million. Large as the land was, it had few empty spaces to colonize, no vast prairies for grazing cattle or growing wheat. India was not a colony. Its only settlers were a few planters growing tea and indigo; its other permanent Anglo-Indian residents were businessmen concentrated in the larger

---

*During the nineteenth century the British living in India were known as Anglo-Indians while people of British-Indian descent were called Eurasians.

cities. Men went out to India to guard it, to govern it or to make money from it. For nearly all of them it formed the working period of their lives, sandwiched between an upbringing and a retirement in Britain.

Half the British population of India consisted of the Army and its dependants: 61,000 soldiers, about 10,000 women and children, and some 5,000 officers commanding both the British regiments and the 120,000 Indian troops known as sepoys.* Most of the other Anglo-Indians lived in the major cities, about 11,000 of them in both Calcutta and Bombay, 4,000 in Madras, a thousand or fewer in provincial capitals such as Rangoon, Lahore, Lucknow and Allahabad. Even these concentrations were tiny in comparison to the rest of the population: barely 1 per cent of the inhabitants of Calcutta, the capital of the Indian Empire, belonged to the ruling race. And outside the cities and cantonments, with 40,000 Anglo-Indians scattered over an area the size of Europe, the proportion was much smaller. No wonder that the rural population so seldom came into contact with its rulers. No wonder that southern Indians outside Madras and Bangalore might never see a company of British soldiers, whose regiments were mainly stationed near the frontiers in the north; indeed, many might live their entire lives without seeing any Englishman except perhaps an Assistant Magistrate.

While the British presence in India grew slowly in the nineteenth century, its appearance changed enormously. Many of the alterations had taken place before Victoria's accession. The nabobs had departed, along with their concubines and their opulence and the fruits of the pagoda tree. The hookahs or hubble-bubbles had mostly vanished, and with them the *hookah-burdar*, the servant specially employed to prepare the compound of tobacco, spices and molasses which his master would inhale through his water pipe. The nabobs and their sartorial vulgarity had been replaced by men in black frock coats who wished to emphasize their Britishness and to demonstrate the moral and cultural superiority of their civilization. They had come not to revel in the Orient but to improve it – and in the process to limit its revelry.[18]

---

*Before the Mutiny there had been 40,000 British soldiers and 230,000 Indian troops, a ratio of about 1 to 6, but after the conflict it was decided that safety required a ratio of nearer 1 to 2. The ratio of the native population to European soldiers in 1900 was about 5,000 to 1.

The men in black coats virtually extinguished a breed of British administrator. A remarkable generation of Governors, such as Thomas Munro in Madras and Mountstuart Elphinstone in Bombay, had believed that Britain's role in India was not only to govern justly but to educate their subjects so that one day they would be able to govern themselves. They deplored the decision of Lord Cornwallis, Governor-General between 1786 and 1793, to exclude Indians from all the senior posts in the administration, and they insisted that justice could only properly be dispensed 'through the natives themselves'. 'You are not here', Munro told the directors of the East India Company,

> to turn India into England or Scotland. Work through, not in spite of, native systems and native ways, with a prejudice in their favour rather than against them; and when in the fullness of time your subjects can frame and maintain a worthy Government for themselves, get out and take the glory of the achievement and the sense of having done your duty as the chief reward for your exertions.[19]

By the 1820s few people agreed with such views. Evangelical Christians had decided that Hinduism was too benighted to reform – or even to tolerate – and must give way to Christianity. William Wilberforce, the indefatigable opponent of slavery, believed that the conversion of India was still more important than the abolition of the slave trade. In an unlikely alliance with the new spirit of Utilitarianism, the Evangelicals did indeed try to turn India as far as possible into England. While they attacked 'heathenism', the Utilitarians went for the suppression of 'heathen' customs – 'sati' or widow burning, human sacrifice, female infanticide, and the 'thuggee' combination of theft and ritual murder by 'thugs' devoted to the cult of the Goddess Kali. As one historian has pointed out, the two groups complemented each other. 'Utilitarians hoped to improve morals by reforming society; Evangelicals hoped to improve society by reforming morals.'[20] But their achievements were very different: the number of Christian converts was negligible.

The success of the Utilitarian abolitions, which were inaugurated mainly during the governorship of Lord William Bentinck (1828–35), was much trumpeted by subsequent generations and, although they may have exaggerated the numbers of people saved as a result, the reforms were by any standard a humanitarian triumph. But the spirit behind them, the vigorous lack of sympathy with Indian culture that propelled them, prejudiced British rule for the rest of the century. And the man who did more than anyone to nurture that spirit was the Utilitarian philosopher and historian, James Mill.

In 1806 Mill began writing a history of India in six volumes, although he had never been to the Subcontinent and made no subsequent attempt to acquaint himself with the landscape of his work. Nor was his research assisted by any knowledge of Indian languages. Yet Mill was less interested in analysing the history of India than in demonstrating its barbarism and arguing that it could only be redeemed by a system of government based on Utilitarian doctrines; above all, the 'abominable existing system' of Indian law should be replaced by a British system of judicial procedure. Elphinstone, who knew India as well as anyone, found the book offensive and deplored Mill's ignorance and 'cynical, sarcastic tone'. Even the editor of a later edition, H. H. Wilson, thought the *History* was 'calculated to destroy all sympathy between the ruler and the ruled'. Yet this dull and inaccurate book retained a vast and pernicious influence until the Mutiny. It was an important text at Haileybury, the college where civil servants of the East India Company were trained, and it was regarded, incredibly, by the historian Macaulay as the greatest historical work in English since Gibbon's *Decline and Fall*.[21]

The other most influential intellectual on Indian matters was Macaulay himself. He did at least spend three and a half years in India in the 1830s as Law Member on the Governor-General's Council, and he also produced an impressive Penal Code, though this did not come into operation for another twenty years. Macaulay's chief influence, however, was in the field of education, which he saw as the means of regenerating India. And the language of that regeneration, he insisted, must be English. Macaulay's pronouncements were frequently arrogant – notably his claim that 'a single shelf of a good European library was worth the whole native literature of India and Arabia' – but he was on more solid ground in arguing that European science and medicine should be taught with the appropriate vocabulary: English not Sanskrit, the language of Adam Smith rather than the Vedas. Conceding that the British were too few to educate the bulk of the population, he thought they should concentrate on forming a class of 'interpreters between us and the millions whom we govern': it would be a class 'Indian in blood and colour, but English in taste, in opinions, in morals, and in intellect'. Unlike nearly all his contemporaries, however, Macaulay realized this policy would eventually lead to Indian independence. So did his brother-in-law, Sir Charles Trevelyan, a promoter of teaching in English and a future Governor of Madras, who claimed that an independent India, 'endowed with our learning and political institutions', would 'remain the proudest monument of British benevolence'. An empire that educates its subjects in its own constitutional doctrines, and later trains them in its own administrative principles, is of course preparing for its own demise. But it took most Anglo-Indians several generations to understand the corollary.[22]

The Mutiny

The Indian Mutiny of 1857 provided some of the great set-pieces of Victorian historical drama: the massacres at Cawnpore, the relief of Lucknow, the siege and capture of Delhi. It also produced its quota of heroes such as Sir Henry Lawrence, killed in the Residency at Lucknow, Brigadier John Nicholson, shot down while storming the walls of Delhi, and Sir Henry Havelock, whose victories earned him a statue in Trafalgar Square but who died before the year was out.

The most lurid image among the gory tableaux of courage and pain, treachery and slaughter, was the atrocity at Cawnpore where the Nana Sahib's broken promise of safe conduct to the British garrison led to the massacre of the men at a ghat on the Ganges and the murder of the women and children, whose bodies were thrown into a well. Smaller massacres took place at other garrisons where regiments mutinied, but the scale of the reprisals was higher. British troops fighting their way through the rebellious areas did not allow their yearnings for vengeance to be diluted by the pleas of the Governor-General, now mocked as 'Clemency Canning'. According to Alfred Lyall, a young Civilian* in one of the mutinous zones, news

---

*Members of the Civil Service were known as Civilians. Although they all belonged to the same Service, they were historically divided between the Bengal CS, the Bombay CS and the Madras CS. After the Government decided in 1878 that officials could be assigned to different provinces in the course of their career, the presidency names fell out of use and Civilians became generally known as members of the Indian Civil Service (ICS).

of the massacre of British women (accompanied by untrue rumours that they had sometimes been raped) inspired the most 'savage and bloodthirsty' feelings among those who survived. As he told his father, he was not a 'naturally ferocious' person – in fact he turned out to be a poet and historian as well as a Lieutenant-Governor – yet he could have shot down 'any native on the slightest pretext without the least compunction'. After the conflict he was embarrassed that he had felt and expressed such feelings but, as he wrote to his sister, the rebels 'should not have touched women and children if they expected us to treat them according to the rules of civilized warfare'.[23]

The causes of the war have long been a popular nutrient for historians, though few now claim that it was either a simple mutiny by sepoys of the Bengal Army, who suspected they were being issued with cartridges greased with animal fat, or the first round of a nationalist struggle against a foreign oppressor. There seems to have been a general disgruntlement with British rule, from the *talukdars* (landlords) of Oudh, who believed their new rulers were favouring village proprietors, to discontented sepoys frustrated with their career prospects under the East India Company. But as in all revolts, motives were complex and goals diverse. One man may have rebelled because of the cartridges, another may have joined him for the prospect of loot, a third may have supported them because of a grudge against an officer, and others may have followed simply because everyone else in the regiment was doing so.

Much of the violence was an offshoot of the Mutiny and not directed against the British at all. The breakdown of order in the North-Western Provinces led to anarchy and extensive looting. Alfred Lyall spent much of his time helping to defend villages against the Gujars, a numerous caste of herdsmen who took advantage of the chaos to plunder their neighbours. Like other magistrates in the rebellious districts, he was given a year's special authority to imprison and execute murderers. He did hang a number of them – all of them killers of other Indians rather than Europeans – but, like many of his colleagues, he was more bloodthirsty in spirit than in action. Officials cried out for vengeance, he reported, but became 'utterly unable to act when they saw a wretched villain before them begging for his life'. Besides, it was 'much easier to sentence a man' to hang than to superintend the execution, which was part of the duty.[24]

The outcome of the Mutiny was not inevitable. In the end the British prevailed partly as a result of better troops and generalship, partly because none of the major Indian princes, despite certain hesitations, sided with the insurgents, and partly because the rebellion was confined more or less to the central and western sections of the Gangetic plain. There were only brief and minor uprisings in Bombay and none at all in Madras. Hyderabad nearly joined the rebels – and might have stirred up much of the south had it done so – but the loyalty of its ruler, the Nizam, and the skills of the British Resident kept it in line. Most crucially, 'the Punjab held', as the phrase went. The Chief Commissioner, John Lawrence, and his very able and resolute officers, pre-empted revolt there by disarming most of the Bengal regiments (containing 30,000 men) before they had time to mutiny. Aided by the Sikhs, who had no desire to help the sepoys who under British officers had so recently conquered them, he not only prevented the Punjab from making a significant contribution to the rebellion but was also able to send some of his troops to assist in the recapture of Delhi.

The Aftermath

Reflective Englishmen realized that the Mutiny had not been entirely undeserved, that it was not an incomprehensible act of ingratitude towards benevolent and enlightened rulers. They knew that too much had been done over the previous thirty years to frighten and upset the peoples of India. Charles Raikes, a Civilian who had been fighting the custom of female infanticide in the North-Western Provinces, thought it had been a 'fatal error' to attempt 'to force the policy of Europe on the people of Asia'. In Britain the Conservative leader in the House of Commons, Benjamin Disraeli, listed among the 'adequate causes' of mutinous discontent the Government's 'tampering with religion' and its 'destruction of Native authority', especially in the areas annexed through Dalhousie's 'doctrine of lapse'.[25]

Alfred Lyall, who was only 23 when the Mutiny ended, reacted to the victory by despairing of his country's future in India. Britain, he decided, had undertaken a task beyond her strength 'in setting about civilizing and governing Hindustan'. Since the 'whole idea of introducing European civilization' had turned out a 'complete failure', it would be impossible to continue for ever governing as an 'imperial tribe'. Had there ever been an 'enormous nation', he asked his brother-in-law, that had 'abandoned its nationality, and assumed the manners, religion and idiosyncrasy of another nation completely opposed to it at all those points'? Had there ever been a people who became 'reconciled to a dominant race which held all high offices in its hands' and treated its subjects 'with patronizing kindness, professing to teach' them everything? Ireland was a 'thousand times more nearly assimilated' to Britain than India was, yet after 700 years its inhabitants were still conspiring against 'the detested Saxon'.[26]

It was extremely unlikely, Lyall believed, that any people could be civilized and converted by an alien nation's schools and laws and missionary societies. But even if such a miracle did occur, that people would find the aliens' rule even more unbearable than before. Boys in England left school when they were old enough and no longer trembled at the headmaster's frown. So why would an educated and enlightened nation not wish to be similarly free? Would it merely 'read without profit all our literature wherein is set forth how liberty is a priceless boon and how of all things a foreign domination is to be abhorred'? Of course not. Britain's Indian empire would end 'as soon as the natives [found] a Louis Napoleon' to lead them.[27]

British politicians and administrators may have shared some of these feelings but naturally they could not behave as if they did. Since very few of them contemplated the idea of abandoning India altogether, they therefore had to assemble a set of policies calculated to preserve British power, produce a just and stable administration, and do as little as possible to alienate the population. Rewarding loyalty and conciliating the aggrieved were the chief means employed to facilitate the first and third of these priorities.

Before the Mutiny the native states had generally been regarded as feudal anachronisms requiring reform or, when possible, annexation; they were moral as well as physical obstacles to the Indian schemes of Mill, Macaulay and Dalhousie. But in 1857 their chiefs turned out to be crucial allies of the paramount power. Jung Bahadur, the de facto ruler of Nepal, sent thousands of Gurkhas to help the British in Oudh and was himself present at the relief of Lucknow; Sikh rajas provided forces for the campaigns both in Oudh and in the Punjab; and in Rajputana the Maharaja of Jaipur placed his army at the disposal of the British, while the Maharaja of Bikanir personally took the field on their side. All these and many others were showered with honours, money, forfeited estates and multi-gun salutes. The Most Exalted Order of the Star of India was established in 1861 to gratify the Indian aristocracy, although senior British officials including the Viceroy were also pleased to wear the robes and insignia of the order. Of more significance was Canning's reversal of Dalhousie's policy on the princes' rights of adoption, and the Queen's reassuring proclamation that she desired no further extension of her territories.

Conciliation required some specific measures aimed at buying off the disgruntled and powerful; the *talukdars* of Oudh were pacified by Canning's promise that their villages would be restored and the taxation on land reduced.[28] More generally, conciliation took the form of what one Civilian called 'religious indifferentism', a policy of not interfering with the customs of a religion unless they conflicted with the principle of religious equality.[29] Again Victoria's proclamation had been reassuring on this point. Only exceptional circumstances would now induce the Government of India to legislate against customs that most officials and many westernized Indians found repugnant. As a very young journalist on the *Civil & Military Gazette* in Lahore, Rudyard Kipling railed at the Government's refusal to outlaw the custom of allowing elderly Brahmins to marry child brides. Yet it was not until 1891 after an 11-year-old wife had died following sexual intercourse with her adult husband, that the Government – to much Hindu fury – raised the age of consent from 10 to 12.

Some Evangelicals believed that the Mutiny was God's punishment for Britain's lethargic efforts to convert India to Christianity: the correct response to the conflict was to double their efforts rather than abandon them. Dozens of missionary societies from Germany, the United States and many other countries as well as Britain descended on India to help them – but with pitiful results. Bishop Welldon of Calcutta, who was so out of touch with India that he could not understand why Queen Victoria was a more popular figure than Jesus Christ, believed well into the twentieth century that a Constantine would rise up from among the princes and redeem the Subcontinent for Christianity.[30] But after the Mutiny almost no one in Government retained either the hope or the desire to convert

India. Britain's task, as Kipling argued, was to 'save bodies and leave souls alone'.[31]

Although religious tolerance became a crucial feature of post-Mutiny policy, it was not accompanied by any greater degree of racial intimacy. In fact the conflict led to greater aloofness from Anglo-Indians. Partly from fear and partly from an enhanced superiority complex – they had after all defeated an enemy that vastly outnumbered them – they removed themselves more and more from the people they governed, withdrawing to the 'civil lines' in the towns, fleeing in the summer to the hill stations of the Himalayas and the Nilgiris. The British had become convinced of the inferiority of contemporary Indians. Lord Mayo, one of the best of the Viceroys, might regard this as a basis for conscientious paternalist rule. 'Teach your subordinates', he said, 'that we are all British gentlemen engaged in the magnificent work of governing an inferior race.' But in practice such a standpoint was more usually employed to exact subservience. Ten years after the Mutiny, the Civilian Henry Cotton recalled, his superiors were telling him to assume a patronizing attitude to Indians and to ensure that they showed him due deference.[32]

Changes of policy and attitude were accompanied by changes to the structure of government. The administrative functions of the East India Company were abolished along with its Board of Directors in London. In India the Governor-General, or Viceroy as he was now usually known, continued to govern through his Council. But he could be overruled by the Secretary of State in Whitehall, who was responsible for the actions of the Indian Government to the Cabinet and to Parliament. In turn the Secretary of State could be overruled in matters of finance and legislation by the Council of India, a body consisting mainly of retired officials who met under his chairmanship at the India Office. And all of them could be overruled by the Prime Minister and the Cabinet.

These changes were embodied in the Government of India Act of 1858 by which the British Government completed its slow absorption of the East India Company's political role. But other important reforms were made in the years before and after the Mutiny. In 1853 patronage in the Civil Service in India was abolished and replaced by open competition; in the same year an Indian Legislative Council was established, although this was revoked and entirely redesigned eight years later; and in 1861 legislation provided for the establishment of High Courts in Calcutta, Madras, Bombay and Allahabad.

Until 1836 the administration of British India had been divided between the three 'presidencies' of Bengal, Madras and Bombay, all headed by Governors, of whom the senior one (Bengal) was the Governor-General. In that year the North-Western Provinces were separated from Bengal, placed under a Lieutenant-Governor and in 1877 amalgamated with the chief commissionership of Oudh. With the expansion of the territory under British control, it was recognized in 1854 that Bengal needed a Lieutenant-Governor of its own, who had to co-exist uncomfortably with the Supreme Government in Calcutta in the winter but who could escape to Darjeeling in the summer when the Viceroy was in Simla. A fifth province, the Punjab, was established in 1849, first under a Board of Administration and then under a Chief Commissioner who was promoted to Lieutenant-Governor in 1859. A sixth, the Central Provinces, was added in 1861, a seventh, Lower Burma (to which Upper Burma was attached in 1886), the year after, and an eighth in 1874 when Assam was given a Chief Commissioner. By the time that Curzon enraged the Punjab Government by severing the North-West Frontier Province from its territory in 1901, British India consisted of nine provinces, and various parcels of territory in Rajputana, Baluchistan, Coorg near Mysore, and the penal settlement of the Andamans and Nicobars.

In the Victorian period all the main administrative posts (and most of the judicial ones) were occupied by members of the Indian Civil Service except for the viceroyalty and the governorships of Madras and Bombay which were chosen by the British Government.* There was a good case for excluding the top post

---

*There were a few exceptions to this. Bombay had three Civilian Governors, Sir George Clerk, Sir Bartle Frere and Sir Richard Temple, all of whom were a success. Madras would have had one, Sir James Thomason, if he had not died on the day the Queen signed his appointment at Balmoral. The ICS produced a solitary Viceroy, Sir John Lawrence, who was brought back from retirement in England after Lord Elgin died in 1863. The strangest case was that of Macaulay's brother-in-law, Sir Charles Trevelyan, a Civilian from 1826 who had gone on furlough in 1838 and was persuaded to remain in London by the offer of a job in the Treasury. In 1859 he returned to India as Governor of Madras, a post from which he was recalled for his public opposition to the policy of the Finance Member of the Viceroy's Council, but two years later he was sent out again, this time to occupy that very post in the Government of India.

from the Service: so much of the Viceroy's work consisted of persuading the Government in London to back his policies that it was an advantage for him to have had political experience at Westminster. But the restrictions on the chief positions in Madras and Bombay were an anomaly that made no sense and could be justified only by appeals to history and the British addiction to precedent. As administrative posts, the governorships were no more important than the lieutenant-governorship of the North-Western Provinces, which had a larger population, but they were older and carried privileges which almost everyone in India, from the Viceroys to the junior Civilians, wanted to abolish. While the Governors were appointed by Royal Warrant, assisted by an Executive Council and given the privilege of direct communication with the Secretary of State, the Lieutenant-Governors were appointed by the Viceroy, had no Executive Council and were not allowed to correspond with the Cabinet minister.

There were several disadvantages to this system. Braced by their licence to complain to Whitehall, Governors of both provinces liked to assert their independence from the central Government and dispute its policies. Awarded higher salaries and longer gun salutes than the Lieutenant-Governors, they also tended to be self-important, much concerned with questions of protocol and etiquette: Sir Arthur Havelock, a Governor of Madras, spent an extraordinary amount of time affirming his right to have a band play 'God Save the Queen' in whichever area of the presidency he visited. But the greatest drawback was the lack of ability shown by men with no experience of India who had been sent out as a political – or in some cases familial – favour to a member of the Cabinet. Lord Wenlock, a nephew of the Duke of Westminster, had no obvious qualifications for the governorship of Madras and was criticized by the Viceroy, Lord Elgin, for his lethargy in the post. Lord Sandhurst, a brother-in-law of Earl Spencer, was an even less suitable Governor of Bombay: previously regarded by his brother officers in the Coldstream Guards as 'incurably dense', he was considered by officials in his presidency to be almost illiterate. Not all Governors were of such quality: Lord Ampthill, Havelock's successor in Madras, and Lord Northcote, Sandhurst's replacement in Bombay, were able administrators. But the general standard provoked repeated calls for the governorships to be abolished. In his newspaper in 1887 an angry young Kipling mocked Sir Mountstuart Grant Duff, the outgoing Governor of Madras, as a 'discredited failure' and proof of the 'extreme necessity of giving bloated presidencies' Lieutenant-Governors from the ICS.[33]

Justifying Imperialism

Kipling's target, Grant Duff, was an intelligent man in the wrong post. An intellectual, a Liberal MP and the Under-Secretary for India in Gladstone's first Government, he accepted Madras on realizing there would be no place for him in Gladstone's second Cabinet. India quickly diluted his liberalism, a process continued by the Prime Minister's support for Irish Home Rule, and he ended up as a Liberal Unionist, an ally of the Conservatives.

In 1885 Grant Duff drafted a memo for the new Viceroy, Lord Dufferin, setting out the 'two diametrically opposite views' on the nature of British rule in India.

> One school says 'You are here to educate the natives to govern themselves. That done, you have only to go about your business.' The other school says 'No man knows the secret of the future; but for practical purposes you must act as if Great Britain were to govern India for all time, doing nothing which in your judgement has any tendency to undermine the foundations of British power.'

Grant Duff left Dufferin in no doubt that he was a member of the second school. Liberal principles were all very well for an independent nation but must be abandoned even by Liberals when ruling another people. Britain's role in India had been to 'create and uphold an enlightened and beneficent despotism', run by men trained in the spirit of Liberalism and free government. Its ends – doing 'everything for the people' – were Liberal in the true sense and yet would be defeated if the British allowed any material power to pass out of their hands.[34]

The Gladstonian Liberals were vaguer and more subtle than this. They subscribed to the idea of imperial trusteeship: in the words of John Morley, Gladstone's disciple and biographer, the British were in India 'to implant – slowly, prudently, judiciously – those ideas of justice, law, humanity, which are the foundation of our own civiliza-tion'.[35] If Morley was unspecific about how to achieve this, his leader was even more so. 'My own desires are chiefly these,' Gladstone told Northbrook after appointing him Viceroy in 1872, 'that nothing may bring about a sudden, violent or discreditable severance, that we may labour steadily to promote the political training of our native fellow-subjects, and that when we go, if we are ever to go, we may leave a good name and a clean bill of health behind us.'[36] The phrase 'if we are ever to go' revealed that the Liberals had no clear idea about their eventual goal in India: they were as unwilling to rule it as an autocracy as they were to relinquish it altogether. Gladstone sent out a later Viceroy, Lord Ripon, with instructions to associate more Indians with the administration; but by contrast with his Irish policy he did not pretend to know where this would lead. Like Morley, he did not believe democracy could be transplanted to a non-Christian society and for that reason insisted that Indians should not be given 'unbounded' freedom.[37] Gladstonian liberalism had no real answer for India.

It was much easier to be a Conservative, to believe like Lord Mayo that Britain should hold India 'as long as the sun shines in heaven', to do everything in one's power for the good of the people, and to make no concessions to the idea of self-rule.[38] As Mayo himself demonstrated, a Tory could be a more radical champion of the Indian peasantry than a Whig like Northbrook. Yet unlike the Liberals, he and his fellow Conservatives did not have to worry about whether to apply their party's principles to India. Most of them shared the views of Sir James Fitzjames Stephen, the distinguished jurist and Law Member of Mayo's Council, who stated bluntly that the Indian Government was an absolute government which could never represent native principles of life unless it wanted to represent 'heathenism and barbarism'.[39] The Conservatives' one ambition for the Government was for it to be what they already thought it was, a benevolent, beneficent and effi-cient autocracy. Nothing should be done to change its essential character. Wilfrid Scawen Blunt, who was simultaneously a Tory candidate and a supporter of both Irish and Egyptian nationalism, visited Bombay in 1884 and was warned 'very strongly and very earnestly' by the Governor, Sir James Fergusson, 'about the danger of exciting the native mind by appearing to sympathize' with any grievances. The Government of India, Fergusson reminded him, was 'a despotism of a paternal and beneficent character, which was day and night working for the people's good, and any agitation would only impede its efforts'.[40]

Few Victorian imperialists would have claimed that Britain held India solely for the benefit of the Indians; and the 'non-official' Anglo-Indians, the businessmen and planters and other traders, were said to regard the sentiment as a 'loathsome un-English piece of cant'.[41] It was indeed hard to deny the great economic, strategic and military value of India; without it Britain's position in the Far East and in Australia and New Zealand would have been too fragile to sustain. And it was difficult to pretend that British rule rested on consent: co-operation perhaps, but co-operation exacted with bayonets in the background by a nation at its most self-confident, a nation displaying what Stephen (who has been described as the 'only real nineteenth-century precursor of Thatcherism') called 'the masterful will, the stout heart, the active brain, the calm nerves, the strong body'.[42] Yet conceding the coercion and the self-interest did not dent the Victorians' belief in the righteousness of their rule. To their critics they paraded their roads and railways and canals, their system of justice, the medical and sanitary improvements, the (slight) increase in rural prosperity, the incorruptibility of their administration and, at least after the Mutiny, a Pax Britannica frayed to any significant degree only on the north-western frontier. In similar vein, as one able but reactionary Civilian of the twentieth century remarked, it was 'ridiculous and meaningless' to talk about the people of India as 'downtrodden slaves'. The British 'yoke' amounted to 'little more than keeping the peace internally and protecting them externally'.[43]

Gilbert Murray, the Regius Professor of Greek at Oxford, claimed that 'at home England is Greek. In the Empire she is Roman.' In fact she aspired to be Greek in some areas of the Empire and Roman in others. The white dominions were encouraged to take after the old self-governing Greek colonies, while the non-white possessions such as India, Jamaica and later the African colonies were to be ruled like Roman provinces. The experience of the brief Athenian Empire, which had shown 'the fatal effects produced by democracy run mad', was a warning, wrote Lord Cromer, of how not to run a 'sane Imperial policy'.[44]

It was not surprising that British administrators should compare themselves to Greeks and Romans: for a majority of them the main subjects of their education had been Latin and Greek. Most of the Oxford graduates in administrative posts in India had studied Classics because it was considered the best preparation for public life. Latin's 'hard logicality and economy of words', so it was alleged, taught 'good judgement and precise language', while the lessons of Roman history, thought and conduct were regarded as universal. Most instructive of all, the works of the Greek philosophers, Plato and Aristotle, provided justifications for rule by an elite: Plato's 'guardians' inspired the title of the second volume of Philip Woodruff's history of the ICS.[45]

British officials had begun to think of themselves as Romans by the end of the eighteenth century; and the classical architecture then in fashion in Calcutta and Madras suggests awareness of certain similarities. But there could hardly be a greater contrast between Thackeray's fat official, Joss Sedley, and the Roman centurions in Kipling's work. The era for classical resemblance is the late Victorian, when scholars and statesmen delighted in distant analogies. The Roman Empire was smaller and less populated than the British, its 100 million subjects in Trajan's time spread (according to Victorian historians) over an area of 2½ million square miles, while Britain's Empire at the beginning of the twentieth century consisted of 440 million people dispersed over 11½ million square miles. But the growth and shaping of the two empires, the compulsion to occupy territory to prevent another power taking it, had multiple similarities. Sir Alfred Lyall, among other things an historian in retirement, discerned them especially in the formation of the empires' political and military frontiers. Denying that Britain's evolution had much in common with contemporary colonial powers, he predicted that future historians would regard the British Empire as a successor to Rome, 'a second remarkable illustration of the force with which a powerful and highly organized civilization can mould the character and shape the destinies of many millions of people'.[46] The distinguished pensioner was rather less astute than the young pessimist writing after the bloodshed at the end of the Mutiny.

The late Victorians did not spend much time justifying their Indian rule because its benefits seemed obvious. They could admit mistakes and recognize failures. Few of them would have denied that famine relief had sometimes been tardy and inadequate; most of them would have accepted that the policies which led to the Afghan wars were disastrous. But the overall performance seemed cause for ample self-congratulation. Sir John Strachey, one of the most successful Civilians and, like his friend Stephen, an authoritarian liberal, believed that 'a greater or more admirable work' had never been 'conceived in any country' than that undertaken and in the process of accomplishment by Englishmen in India.[47] Curzon was equally certain that either Providence or the laws of destiny had called Britain to India 'for the lasting benefit of the human race'. He admitted that the British often made 'great mistakes', that they were 'sometimes hard, and insolent, and overbearing', but he believed that no government in the world rested on 'so secure a moral basis' or was 'more fiercely animated by duty'.[48]

There were of course voices in Britain and elsewhere that contested the morality of a nation being ruled by foreigners. The imperialists' response to them was both ingenious and ingenuous. India was not a nation, and the British were not really foreigners – at least not more so than the Subcontinent's other rulers. Strachey was the most strenuous proponent of these views: 'We have never destroyed in India a national government, no national sentiment has been wounded, no national pride has been humiliated; and this not through any design or merit of our own, but because no Indian nationalities have existed.'[49] Anthropology buttressed such views. One of the science's dominant figures in India, the Civilian H. H. Risley, argued that, although the peoples of the Subcontinent could be broadly divided into seven different groups, there was 'no national type' and consequently 'no nation in the ordinary sense of the word'.[50]

Such assumptions encouraged the historian Seeley to make the more dubious assertion that 'India had no jealousy of the foreigner, because India had no sense whatever of national unity, because there *was* no India, and therefore, properly speaking, no foreigner'. Alternatively, India could be regarded as a vast continent of foreigners. A Bengali in Delhi was as much a foreigner as an Englishman in Rome. A 'Native of Calcutta', claimed Strachey, was 'more of a foreigner to the hardy races on the frontiers of Northern India than an Englishman' could be. As Lyall pointed out, a good deal of the territory conquered by the British had possessed 'no long-seated ruling

dynasties or ancient aristocracies' – which helped explain its comparatively easy subjugation. But even some of the existing native states
were ruled by unassimilated 'foreign' dynasties. The Hindu population of Hyderabad was governed by a Muslim prince backed by an
army of Arab mercenaries. The so-called Maratha states of Gwalior,
Indore and Baroda had a combined population of 6½ million; but
apart from the rulers and their followers, they contained no
Marathas.[51]

Another justification for British rule was provided by the conviction that India would fall apart if left to itself. 'To suppose', said
Strachey, 'that the manlier races of India could ever be governed
through the feeble foreigners of another Indian country, however
intellectually astute those foreigners may be – that Sikhs and
Pathans, for instance, should submit to be ruled by Bengalis – is to
suppose an absurdity'.[52] The departure of the British would lead to
the disintegration of India, the establishment of rival states and the
certainty of anarchy and civil war. Conveniently for the British, this
view was backed by some Indians. Talking to General Roberts in
1884, Sir Madhava Rao, a former Minister of Baroda, scoffed at the
cry 'India for the Indians': 'you have only to go to the Zoological
Gardens and open the doors of the cages, and you will very soon see
what would be the result of putting that theory into practice. There
would be a terrific fight amongst the animals, which would end in the
tiger walking proudly over the dead bodies of the rest.' When
Roberts asked who the tiger was, Madhava Rao replied, 'The
Mahomedan from the North.'[53] *

One unexpected source of support for this view came from a
couple of French intellectuals, Paul Boell and Leroy Beaulieu, who
believed that the departure of the British would be a disaster for
India and for civilization in general. 'The question', wrote Boell,
who visited the Subcontinent at the beginning of the twentieth
century, 'is not whether England has a right to keep India, but
rather whether she has the right to leave it. To abandon India would
in truth lead to the most frightful anarchy. Where is the native
power which would unite Hindoos and Moslems, Rajputs and
Marathas, Sikhs and Bengalis, Parsees and Christians under one

---

*In 1893 the Civilian A. R. Bonus found a Madrasi who used the same image. 'Open all
the cages in the zoo,' said the man, 'and you'll see the result of "India for the Indians".'[54]

sceptre? England has accomplished this miracle.' Quoting Boell and Beaulieu at the end of his essay, *Ancient and Modern Imperialism*, Cromer was able to conclude that any premature 'relinquishment' of 'the torch of progress and civilization in India' would 'almost certainly lead to its extinction'.[55]

I

Old Boys

~

Dolphin Families

'CERTAIN FAMILIES', WROTE Kipling in his story 'The Tomb of His Ancestors', 'serve India generation after generation as dolphins follow in line across the open sea.' He mentioned some, such as the Plowdens and the Rivett-Carnacs, whose service was spread over three centuries: one Plowden, a judge, was still there in the 1940s, glad that Britain had fulfilled its destiny and purpose and was ready to allow Indians to govern themselves.[1] And he invented one of his own, the Chinns, who knew it was their duty to send their sons out to India, whatever talents they might or might not possess. A 'clever Chinn' went into the Civil Service; a 'dull Chinn' entered the Police Department or 'the Woods and Forests'.

It was common for three generations of the same family to spend their careers in India. Often there were four, sometimes five, occasionally six. A number of Anglo-Indians could boast that both sides of their family had been in India for over a century. The Scottish Wedderburns proclaimed that the ICS had become 'a sort of hereditary calling' in the nineteenth century, replacing the hereditary calling of the previous century which had been to fight for the Jacobite cause and be executed for treason. Not that the ICS was a much safer choice: William Wedderburn joined it in 1860 shortly after his brother and sister-in-law and their child had been killed in the

Mutiny. Later in his career he responded to another Scottish 'calling', joining the band of radical Civilians who supported Indian nationalism and collaborating with another brother, a Member of Parliament who took up the cause of representative institutions for the Indians. After his retirement Wedderburn served two terms as President of the Indian National Congress.[2]

English supporters of Congress were a rarer breed of Civilian, but one of them, who also became its President, came from a family that followed Indian careers for six generations in a direct male line. Sir Henry Cotton's great-grandfather was a Director of the East India Company, his grandfather, father and son were in the Madras Civil Service, he himself was a Bengal Civilian, and his grandson joined the Political Department. Yet there was nothing cosy or sentimental or particularly rewarding about sons following fathers in the profession. It was not like inheriting an estate or entering the family firm where they could be groomed by their parent. The structure of an Indian career meant that sons hardly saw their fathers once they were no longer infants. Sir Adelbert Talbot, the Resident in Kashmir, retired in the same month that his son Addy came out to start his career in the ICS. Henry Cotton's grandfather served in Madras from 1801 to 1830, retiring a year before his son went out to the same presidency where he served for thirty-one years. In the only period when two generations of Cottons were in India for a few years at the same time, they were living at opposite ends of the Subcontinent, Henry in Assam and his son in Madras. The family epitomized 'The Exiles' Line', the poem in which Kipling portrayed 'the soul of our sad East' as it is carried back and forth between Britain and India in the ships of the P & O Company.

> Bound on the wheel of Empire, one by one,
> The chain-gangs of the East from sire to son,
> The Exiles' Line takes out the exiles' line
> And ships them homeward when their work is done.

Families did not operate only in generations. Siblings were often working in India at the same time in a variety of services. One brother might be in the ICS, another in the Army, a third in the Indian Medical Service, and their sisters might be married to a missionary, a planter and a 'boxwallah', or businessman. While Charles Bayley's father was in the Bengal Cavalry, one uncle was a Judge of the High Court in Calcutta, and another became Lieutenant-Governor of Bengal. Keeping the Bengali tradition going (it had been begun by his grandfather who had been Acting Governor-General in 1828), Charles ended up as Lieutenant-Governor of several of the province's truncated portions, Eastern Bengal and Assam in 1911, and Bihar and Orissa in 1912.

Even the Bayleys were not among the most numerous families serving in India. Five Dennys brothers were in the Indian Army, a sixth in the Indian Police and a seventh in the Public Works Department, while their sister successively married two Civilians. John Lawrence was one of five brothers simultaneously working in India; John Nicholson was one of four brothers who died there. All the Nicholsons and all the Lawrences except John were soldiers. The Lyall brothers showed more variety. Alfred and James reached the top of the ICS as Lieutenant-Governors, but the youngest of the four was a slack, hard-drinking subaltern at Secunderabad, while the eldest, who had resigned his commission to become a tea planter, abandoned his wife and children and left them to the charity of his Civilian brothers.

The most powerful pair of brothers in the Raj were not Alfred and James Lyall, who were never in a position to act in combination, but Sir John and Sir Richard Strachey. An ancient though modestly prosperous landed family from Somerset, the Stracheys sent thirteen members from four generations to work in India, filling almost every post in the administration from Acting Viceroy and Lieutenant-Governor downwards. While John was a Civilian who rose to be Finance Member of the Viceroy's Council and Lieutenant-Governor of the North-Western Provinces, Richard went to Addiscombe, the East India Company's military academy, and joined the Royal Engineers. His energy and talents (he was also a scientist and a geographer) won him unusually high promotion for an Army officer, and he became Secretary of the Public Works Department, Inspector-General of Irrigation, President of the Famine Commission and Acting Finance Member when John returned to England for an eye operation.* The brothers so dominated the administration of Lord

---

*His sons, however, inherited neither his talents nor his enthusiasm. The eldest, Dick, twice failed the entrance examination to the Military Academy at Woolwich; the next, Ralph, failed his Army medical; and the third, Oliver, gave up his plan to take the ICS exam because he preferred to become a piano teacher. Lytton and James, the fourth and fifth surviving sons, refused to go anywhere near India.

Mayo that they were known both as Castor and Pollux and 'the Strachey Raj'. They might have been even more powerful had they been supported by their brother William, who had joined the Civil Service a few years before John in 1838. But William returned home after five years without much to show for his service except the conviction that the only 'trustworthy' time was Calcutta time. He set his watch accordingly and lived by it for the remaining fifty-six years of his life, eating breakfast at tea-time and living most of his life by candlelight.[3]

No family, however, contributed as much to British India, at least in sheer numbers, as the Lochs of Drylaw. George Loch died in his thirties in 1788, ill and depressed after family debts incurred supporting the Jacobites forced him to sell his estates outside Edinburgh. Perhaps he would have been less depressed had he been able to foresee the success of his four surviving sons: two were Members of Parliament (one was also Chairman of the Board of Directors of the East India Company), one became an admiral, and the fourth, William, who died of 'bilious fever' aged 38, was a senior official in the Bengal Civil Service. Thirty of George's male descendants spent their careers in India, six in the Civil Service, many of the rest in the Army. A majority of William's descendants followed their ancestor out to India for four successive generations. They included Civilians, doctors, tea planters, indigo planters, cavalrymen, artillerymen, Gurkha officers, Political Officers, sappers and engineers. Only a handful of mavericks dissented: one left the Royal Navy to become a Benedictine monk, while another, inspired by seeing *Aida* in Egypt, studied under Leoncavallo (the composer of *I pagliacci*) and became a music teacher. A later Loch maverick, whose father took his wife's name, was Tam Dalyell, who became a Labour MP, Father of the House of Commons and an indefatigable critic of British foreign policy.[4] But he was only 14 at the time of Indian Independence.

Exile Backgrounds

By the end of Queen Victoria's life Civilians were being recruited from a broad variety of social backgrounds in Britain and from a somewhat narrower selection in India. But at the beginning of her reign, when they were still nominated by directors of the East India Company, the social diversity was much more restricted. A great many civil servants came from Anglo-Indian families; and most of these were relations, godsons or sons of friends of directors of the Company. Their backgrounds tended, therefore, to resemble those of their benefactors. Before 1853, when it was decided to throw the Service open to competition, five Civilians out of six were the sons of Anglo-Indians, clergymen or landed gentry.[5]

The political reformer John Bright famously claimed that the British Empire was a 'gigantic system of outdoor relief for the aristocracy of Great Britain', a remark that was endorsed by others with specific reference to the favours that were supposedly bestowed on 'younger sons'.[6] It was not, however, very accurate. Younger sons may have served in the Army in India, though not in Indian regiments, which would have kept them there for life, but in British ones stationed for limited periods. Later on, younger sons might go out and farm – and make nuisances of themselves – in East Africa. But their imperial exploits do not amount to very much. Older sons and fathers did of course achieve things as proconsuls, as Viceroys of India or Governors-General of Canada, but the real administration of the Empire was overwhelmingly middle-class.

The India Office lists of the nineteenth century contain a smattering of honourables and baronets, though seldom in exalted positions. Yet even these cases do little to support Bright's claim. William Herschel, the Collector of the Hooghly district outside Calcutta, did indeed inherit a baronetcy. But he was not a landed squire. His grandfather had been a brilliant astronomer, knighted for his immense telescopes, his catalogues of nebulae and other star clusters, and his discovery of Uranus, the first new planet to be found since prehistoric times; his father was created a baronet for his astronomical work on stellar parallax and the Southern Hemisphere. William himself also made an important scientific contribution: in the course of his affable rule as a District Officer in Bengal, he became the discoverer and pioneer of fingerprinting.[7]

A more typical baronet was Sir Richard Temple, the eldest son of a Worcestershire squire with an Elizabethan house who belonged to the same family as Lord Palmerston, Lord Dufferin and the Duke of

Buckingham. Temple was educated at Rugby, where he and his friends 'lived just the life . . . depicted' in *Tom Brown's Schooldays*, and where he regarded its headmaster, Dr Arnold, as 'among the greatest people' he had ever known. A political life in Britain strongly appealed to him; and in due course, after a successful and energetic career in India, he pursued it – with less success. But he chose to go to the Subcontinent partly because his mother was a Rivett-Carnac, one of Kipling's dolphin-like families, and partly because his father's second marriage and enlarged family required economies in Worcestershire.[8]

One of the strongest Anglo-Indian connections was with the Anglican Church. Throughout the Queen's reign the clergy produced not only a large number of Civilians but also a disproportionate number in senior posts. The Lyalls' father and his siblings reflected the blend of Anglicanism and Anglo-India. The eldest brother was an MP and a director of the East India Company, another was in the Indian Army, a third joined the Navy, a fourth was an influential Dean of Canterbury, and the fifth (the father) was another clergyman. Yet the blend was evident only in Alfred's immediate family. Elsewhere the Church had a virtual monopoly. His maternal uncle was a clergyman and so were the husbands of four of his maternal aunts; five of his first cousins on his father's side were also clergymen, and so were two of his brothers-in-law.* Perhaps it was not surprising that sometimes, in the heat and solitude of India, the Lyall Civilians should have yearned for a parsonage or a canonry. Alfred, who gained a reputation for seeing every side of a question and for arguing each case with equal persuasiveness, thought a canonry would have given him time to write books and meet other intellectuals. But it would not have prevented him from reading Darwin and Renan, writers who reinforced his inherent scepticism and helped turn him into an agnostic, a position from which in distinguished retirement he influenced many of his younger relations

---

*Alfred Lyall's maternal ancestry was not entirely monolithic. His mother was a Broadwood, the family of piano-makers, and her mother was a Comyn, another clan ruined by its Jacobite sympathies, whose ancestor, the 'Red Comyn', was murdered by Robert the Bruce in a Dumfries church in 1306. The Lyalls themselves had come from the Scottish Borders, but Alfred's upbringing in the Home Counties had smothered any attachment to his ancestral roots.

and thus helped de-convert one of the most Anglican families in England.[9]*

Early Victorian India contained a great many Irishmen, nearly all of them soldiers. At the time of the Queen's accession Ireland provided almost as many soldiers in India as the rest of the United Kingdom put together. But during the first half of the nineteenth century only one Civilian in twenty was born in Ireland, and he was almost invariably a Protestant from the north. Up there too there was seldom any connection with the aristocracy. John Lawrence's father was the son of a mill-owner in County Derry, while his mother was the daughter of a clergyman from Donegal. His successor as Lieutenant-Governor of the Punjab, Robert Montgomery (the grandfather of the Field Marshal), was the grandson of a wines and spirits merchant from Londonderry. Like the Lawrence brothers, he was educated at the undistinguished Foyle College before going to Haileybury.

The Scots had a more prosperous presence in early nineteenth-century India. Sir Walter Scott referred to the East India Company as 'the Corn Chest for Scotland where we poor gentry must send our youngest sons as we send our black cattle to the South'.[10] Here again it was the 'poor gentry' not the aristocracy who sent out their younger sons: the three Campbell brothers who joined the Bengal Civil Service were not children of the Duke of Argyll but members of a Fife family in such decline that all their great-uncles had gone to seek their fortunes in America or the Ottoman Empire.[11] Numerous Scots served in the regiments of the East India Company. Many others worked as merchants in Bombay, while in the 1850s industrialists from Dundee set up Calcutta's jute industry. Thanks to Henry Dundas, who managed to control patronage both in Scotland and in India in the Government of the younger Pitt, Scots were also well represented in the Civil Service.

After the Lochs, the Scottish family most drawn to the 'corn chest' were the Macnabbs, who sent five generations to feed from it. James Monro Macnabb, a civil servant of the East India Company, was the son of a surgeon working in India at the end of the eighteenth century who amassed a fortune sufficient to buy an estate in

---

*Not including his sister, Sybilla, who in 1889 left her husband, the Canon of Canterbury, and entered a Roman Catholic convent in York.

Perthshire for his old age. James Monro, who retired as a Commissioner at Agra in 1833, also made money in India but lost it in the collapse of Alexander's Bank in Calcutta and was forced to sell the estate. Earlier in his career he had performed the memorable service of teaching the young Thackeray to read. After the death of the boy's father Richmond, a Collector of the East India Company for whom Macnabb had worked in Bengal, James Monro took William Makepeace back to England and during the voyage ensconced the 5-year-old in a coil of rope to prevent him escaping his lessons.[12]

All three of James Monro Macnabb's sons went to India, the two eldest as Civilians in the Punjab, where they became Commissioners, the youngest as a subaltern to Meerut, where he was killed in the Mutiny. The middle brother, Donald Macnabb, was a linguist who enjoyed disguising himself as a Pathan. Certainly he would never have given away his real identity by the smell of alcohol on his breath, for he regarded taking a 'peg' as a 'pernicious habit'. A pioneer of irrigation, he paid for his first canal out of his own pocket, which thus justified its subsequent name, the Macnabbwah Canal.[13]

James William Macnabb disobeyed his brother's advice by allowing himself three small whiskies a day but still rose to become Commissioner of Delhi. Three of his sons also went to India. One became a Commissioner in Burma and a writer on tribal dialects and customs, another became the leading official – Agent to the Governor-General – in the native states of Central India, and a third, Archibald, ended his career as Financial Commissioner of the Punjab. At his retirement Archibald returned to his family roots, living in Perthshire and managing to have himself recognized as the 22nd Chief of Clan Macnab. In doing so, he dropped the second 'b' of his surname, becoming A.C. Macnab of Macnab, a process which required more complicated mutations of his wife's name. From Alice Macnabb Macleod of Macleod in 1943, she was transformed into Alice Macleod of Macnab of Macnab in 1954.[14]

The Haileybury Spirit

In 1800 the Governor-General, Lord Wellesley, the eldest brother of the future Duke of Wellington, decided that the teenage recruits to the East India Company's Civil Service should have some special training in India; until then they had been required to do no more than understand a set of merchants' accounts. So he set up the College of Fort William in Calcutta with the intention of educating all young Civilians for three years in general matters of law and ethics, and in various Indian subjects including languages, history, religion and law. Unfortunately, as was his custom, Wellesley made the decision without receiving permission from the Company's directors in London; and they, as was their custom, reacted to such insubordination by deciding to thwart him. They duly cancelled the scheme, allowing Fort William to remain simply as a language school for Bengal Civilians until its abolition in 1854.

The directors did however recognize the need for an East India College in England and established one in Hertford Castle in 1806, moving it to new buildings at nearby Haileybury three years later. The second premises, with a 'Cockney Grecian' façade of porticoes and Ionic columns, was built by William Wilkins and resembled that architect's most famous building, the National Gallery, except that it lacked Trafalgar Square's paltry dome and pepper-pot cupolas. Behind the façade was an ugly quadrangle of dingy yellow brick, but the surrounding countryside was sufficiently sprinkled with charm and literary allusion to induce nostalgia among Old Haileyburians in India. They recalled a plunge into the River Lea, 'immortalized by the pen and angle of Isaac Walton', and riding along the high road where Cowper's John Gilpin galloped madly from Edmonton to Ware.[15]

All candidates for Haileybury were nominated by the Company's directors, and by the time of Victoria's accession they had to be at least 17 years old. Ideally directors were supposed to look around them at worthy families – those that had proved themselves over generations – picking here an intelligent boy with administrative potential for Haileybury, choosing there a 'high-spirited' muscular type, a 'good example of the English country gentleman', and sending him to Addiscombe. Some certainly took selection seriously: one director, who had been to Merchant Taylors' School, found his nominee by asking the current headmaster to recommend his most suitable pupil. But nepotism, even if exercised to select the most talented nephew, was the custom. Sir George Campbell, a Scottish Civilian who believed that English could be spoken correctly solely by people born in Scotland, observed that only in 'rare cases' did the directors do more than pretend to look for the best candidates.[16]

By the end of the Victorian period men were joining the Civil Service for a variety of reasons, including altruism and adventure. But at the beginning the incentive was in most cases financial, especially for the candidate's family. Salaries were good, and so was the pension – £1,000 a year irrespective of position. Nominations were seldom refused because reluctance from a nominee was usually overcome by his family. John Lawrence wanted to follow his brothers to Addiscombe and thence into the Indian Army; he was furious when his family's benefactor only offered Haileybury, and he had to be coerced into accepting a career as a Civilian.[17] But at least Lawrence had wanted to go to India in some capacity. The Aberdonian G. R. Elsmie was an only son quite content to stay at home until a nomination was unexpectedly thrust on him: the title of his autobiography, *Thirty-five Years in the Punjab*, reveals the consequence.[18] But the most unlucky nominee may have been J. H. Rivett-Carnac. In spite of belonging to that most Anglo-Indian of families, he had no desire to go to India. 'Much taken with the blue-and-gold coats of the attachés' he had seen in Europe, his ambition was to become a diplomat. His father had initially favoured this career, intending to reserve the two nominations he had secured for his younger sons. But when it was announced that the old system of patronage was about to be abolished – before the younger boys were old enough to qualify for its final years – he insisted on inflicting a nomination on the aspiring attaché.[19]

One of the few boys to be given the option of refusing an uncle's patronage was Alfred Lyall. Indeed both his father and his tutor at Eton advised him to reject Haileybury and gain a scholarship for King's College, Cambridge, an institution designed by its founder, Henry VI, for the further education of Etonian scholars. It is not clear why Alfred did choose Haileybury and India, but his innate restlessness and curiosity are reasons at least as plausible as the one he gave his mother on arrival in Calcutta – that he 'came out here for money'. Characteristically he spent much of his time in India wondering whether he would have been better off in Cambridge.[20]

Before going to Haileybury the candidates had to take some oral and written examinations at India House in London's Leadenhall Street. They sat papers in History and Mathematics and were made to construe passages from Greek and Roman authors as well as translate from the original Greek of St Luke's Gospel. Although candidates were admonished for such slackness as using 'happen' instead of 'come to pass' in their scriptural translations, the tests were fairly undemanding, and there were not many failures. The Company directors may not have been always scrupulous about selecting the ablest boys as their nominees but they did not want to risk the humiliation of choosing ones too stupid to pass the qualifying exams.[21]

Admission to Haileybury did not, however, guarantee competence or suitability for an Indian career. Some students were so lazy and inept, especially in the learning of oriental languages, that they were removed from the College and sent to India as cornets in the Company's cavalry. A few others, the 'ne'er do wells', were kept on, tolerated and treated leniently by professors unwilling to risk their careers by sacking relations of the men who paid their salaries. Known as the Company's 'bad bargains', they went to India and 'never mended'.[22] They were, nevertheless, greatly outnumbered by good bargains. For all the inadequacies of the Haileybury system, its best graduates were at least as good as those produced by open competition.

The aspiring Civilians were required to spend two years at Haileybury, their time divided into four terms of twenty weeks. There they had to study mathematics and natural philosophy, classical and general literature, law, history and general economy, and those oriental languages relevant to their Indian province. As in other British establishments, much emphasis was placed on classical languages, in this case Sanskrit, Persian and Arabic. A student destined for the North-Western Provinces in the 1850s still had to pass exams in Persian (as well as Hindi) because, although it had been replaced as the language of the Company's courts in 1837 – and substituted by vernaculars – a knowledge of Persian was regarded as indispensable for an understanding of Urdu and Bengali, languages partly derived from it. Similarly, Arabic was taught because it was the 'repository of the Mahometan faith' and the key to other languages such as Pashto and Sindi, while Sanskrit was recommended because among other things it was 'the storehouse of the Religious Ceremonies of the Brahmin' and 'the mainspring of the daily avocations'.[23]

Even brighter pupils found the concentration on classical languages rather futile. Lewin Bowring, who joined the Bengal Civil Service in 1843, won several prizes at Haileybury for Persian, Sanskrit and Hindustani. Yet on arrival in India he found his proficiency in these languages was 'nearly useless'.[24] The abrasive George Campbell was even blunter. After a decade's experience in India he concluded that Sanskrit was no 'more useful to an [Anglo-] Indian magistrate than a knowledge of the tongue of the ancient Germans would be to a modern [English] Commissioner of Police'.[25] As a result, Civilians had to spend much of their early time in India studying the vernaculars and passing further exams before they were capable of appearing in a court and understanding what was going on.

Haileybury had some talented professors, notably Thomas Malthus, the economist and demographer unluckily best remembered for his theory that population growth would always outstrip increases in the food supply. But the level of education was generally low because discipline was lax and most boys were only interested in 'scraping by'. From India Alfred Lyall wrote that his brother James need not bother to attend Haileybury lectures as the place was 'one well organized humbug'; and James Mill, whose personal contribution to the low level was the use of his *History* as a textbook, was appalled by the dissolute behaviour of this 'assemblage of young men'.[26] The memoirs of John Beames, an intelligent and sceptical Civilian, caustically expose the defects of a place that seemed to combine the faults both of school and of university.

At eight in the morning, recalled Beames, the students rushed to chapel, many of them wearing only a nightshirt under a gown or overcoat. Afterwards they returned to their rooms for breakfast which often turned into parties with 'tankards of beer or claret'. Breakfast was followed by smoking a pipe and dealing with tailors and other tradesmen who had arrived from Hertford. At ten o'clock the bell rang for lectures which lasted for two hours on some days, three on others. The studious minority known as the 'steadies' took notes; the others yawned, drew sketches of the teachers and fooled about. After a lunch of bread, cheese and beer, they were free to do what they liked. The oarsmen went to the river, the cricketers went to their cricket pitch, the 'steadies' went for a 'solemn constitutional' along the lanes, and the 'fast men' either slipped off by train to London or else clattered off in dog-carts to play billiards at Hertford or Ware. Dinner took place in Hall at six followed by evening chapel at eight. Then the 'steadies' retired to their rooms and read far into the night, most of the others sat about drinking and singing, and at about two in the morning the 'fast men' returned very drunk from Broxbourne Station after catching the last train from Shoreditch. The College employed a Mr Jones to prevent students from going to London, but he was easy to elude at Broxbourne, and in any case the penalties for visiting the capital were not great. The usual punishment for missing chapel or returning too late was writing out 'lines' of Latin and Greek. This would indeed have been a bore for the 'fast men', but fortunately there were a number of people in the neighbourhood willing to do it for them at the rate of a shilling per hundred lines of Latin and half-a-crown for the same quantity of Greek.[27]

Beames was a witty and irreverent man who spent much of his free time sketching and reading Tennyson. He may have exaggerated the delinquencies of his contemporaries: no other comparable record of college japes exists. But he did not exaggerate the inadequacy of Haileybury as an institution established to prepare young men to be administrators of the Empire. The lectures might deal with Indian subjects, but nobody ever discussed such topics. It was considered 'bad form' to talk about India or simply allude to the fact that the students were all about to go there. Even a professor with experience of the Subcontinent felt it superfluous to tell his pupils what their lives as distant officials would be like; they would find out soon enough for themselves.[28]

At the end of their second year the students took another set of exams for which the only real incentives were gold medals and other prizes and the desire not to come last of the thirty or more places in the year. Their one remaining task, apart from buying their kit and booking their passage, was to sign the 'Covenant', a somewhat archaic document from the end of the eighteenth century which, in return for a substantial salary, made the Company's new civil servants promise not to trade on their own account in India nor 'accept corrupt presents, or make corrupt bargains'. Shortly before their departure some of them went to India House to say farewell to the directors. The most senior of their employers, recalled Richard Temple, 'earnestly adjured [him] to cherish a lively regard for the Natives of India'.[29]

Civilians invariably admitted they had not been well educated at Haileybury, agreeing with Beames that it was 'rather a farce as far as learning was concerned'. They recognized they had learned little about India and only a smattering of the languages. Nostalgic Old Boys might persuade themselves that the 'general tone of the College was good', although the unsentimental Beames recalled that the 'discipline was shamefully lax, and the moral standard very low'.[30] But all agreed – even Beames – that the College fostered a powerful *esprit de corps* that served them well in the vicissitudes of imperial service. The camaraderie of the river or the cricket pitch or even of the pipe and the tankard of claret allowed men to get to know each other and measure their merits and defects. As Lord Salisbury recognized when Secretary of State, the great advantage of Haileybury had been 'the close friendships formed there, which softened the rivalries of after life and secured devoted instead of perfunctory co-operation'.[31] Relationships formed in the yellow-brick quadrangle could affect the running of an entire province. Under the commissionership of his cousin Temple, Rivett-Carnac was able to arrange for the most talented Haileyburians of his generation to assemble at Nagpur and organize the administration of the Central Provinces.[32]

Outsiders understandably found Haileybury's *esprit de corps* excessive and even claimed that the phrase was a euphemism for 'caste prejudice'.[33] It was certainly an exclusive spirit, creating an unnecessary divide between Civilians who had been to the College and those who after 1855 entered the service through intellectual merit. The groups even tended to segregate in the Calcutta clubs, the College men joining the Bengal Club while the new recruits went with Army officers into the United Service Club. Haileybury was closed in 1857, but its Old Boys seldom doubted their superiority over the 'competition wallahs'. Forty years later they were still holding their exclusive reunion dinners at the Grand Hotel in Charing Cross.

2

Competition Wallahs

~

The Career Opened to Talent

NAPOLEON'S IDEAL OF '*la carrière ouverte aux talents*' took some time to be exported across the Channel. Talent did not supersede patronage in the British Civil Service until Gladstone's order-in-council in 1870 established that entry into the Departments of State should be by open competitive examinations except in the Home Office, which adopted the new system in 1873, and the Foreign Office. Talent could not compete with wealth in the Army until 1871, when the same Liberal Government abolished the purchase of officers' commissions. And without private means or outside support, it could not enter Parliament until 1911, when MPs first received salaries.

Yet in India talent was encouraged to enter the Civil Service rather earlier. In 1853 the British Government opened recruitment to competition; the following year a committee recommended how the competition should be arranged; and a year later the first examinations were held. The reform did not originally envisage the abolition of Haileybury, but the survival of the College was soon deemed incompatible with the new system, and it was closed at the end of 1857. Its final year was a talented one, the graduates including James Lyall and John Beames.

The principle of the reform was clear. Selection by merit would be more efficient and more just than selection by patronage. The 1854 Committee, headed by Macaulay, still wanted 'gentlemen' to run the Indian administration, but it wanted gentlemen educated at Oxford and Cambridge rather than ones randomly chosen and herded together at Haileybury. Its most influential member, Benjamin Jowett, the future Master of Balliol College, claimed that the ICS would be a fine career for 'the picked men of the universities'. It would be the perfect answer for Oxford dons like himself when faced with an undergraduate's 'dreary question' about what line of life he should choose when he had 'no calling to take orders and no taste for the Bar'.[1]

For a few years it seemed that Jowett had succeeded. Between 1855 and 1859 Oxford produced a third of the successful entrants, while Cambridge provided a quarter. Of the thirty-two examinees who passed into the ICS in 1859, Oxford and Cambridge supplied eight each, Trinity College Dublin five, Edinburgh three, Aberdeen, King's London and Queen's Belfast two each, and Cork one.[2] But the triumph of the universities did not last long. By 1863 Oxford and Cambridge between them were providing only a quarter of the selected candidates; in 1870 they produced only one each; and by 1874 three-quarters of the candidates and more than half the entrants had been to no university at all.

Lord Dalhousie had once observed that while a 'member of the Civil Service in England is a clerk, a member of the Civil Service in India may be a proconsul'.[3] By the 1870s Britain's best graduates apparently preferred to be clerks. In 1874 nine of the eleven candidates selected for the upper grade of the home Civil Service were from Oxford and Cambridge. While their preference may have been influenced by Gladstone's recent order-in-council, the decline in popularity of the ICS among graduates can more solidly be ascribed to mistakes made by Macaulay's Committee.

The desire for graduate recruitment had persuaded the Committee to recommend 23 as the maximum age of entry, after which the selected candidates were supposed to spend two years at home doing legal training for their future careers. While Haileybury men might start their Indian work at 19 – and their predecessors even earlier – a new Civilian might not begin his most basic work on the ground until he was 25. Since this was rather an advanced age to be learning apprentice skills (especially linguistic ones), the

Government reduced the maximum age to 22 for 1860 and to 21 six years later. It thus became increasingly difficult for a man to acquire a decent degree and pass the ICS exam before he was too old. Indeed the attempt to combine the two risked failure at both.

The Committee's second mistake was to design an exam that demanded little besides a strong factual memory and a concentrated study of academic texts. Not only was this an inappropriate way of choosing men destined for an active and practical career; it soon became apparent that a university education was not the most efficient means of preparing for one. When a candidate was required to explain the 'chief grammatical changes which converted the Anglo-Saxon into the English of the fourteenth century', he could not discover the answer in his classical studies at Oxford. He had to find such things out either by himself in the vacations or, more usually, in a 'crammer', an establishment in London specializing in preparing candidates for the exam. A.C. Macnabb, the future clan chieftain, failed to pass from Balliol and only succeeded after being 'crammed' for a year at Wren and Gurney, the most famous of these institutions. By the 1860s parents were wondering if there was any point paying for a university education when their sons could pass more quickly and cheaply from a crammer. Even housemasters at Harrow recommended that boys should skip university and go straight to Wren's.[4]* Jowett's grab for the 'picked men of the universities' had resulted in the triumph of the Victorian crammer. Fortunately he worked hard enough – and lived long enough – to see the situation reversed.

The success of the crammers outraged politicians, scholars and of course the Haileybury men. One critic claimed that several candidates of a particular year owed their success to the fluke that, on the morning of the natural sciences exam, their crammer had given them a revision lesson on the subject that came up, the anatomy of the lobster.[5] Another opponent was Matthew Arnold, the poet, critic and inspector of schools, who worked for a time as an examiner. Recalling the experience later, he remarked that he would not have appointed the candidates he had awarded the highest marks because 'they were crammed men not formed men'. The 'formed men',

---

*Charles Bayley, the future Lieutenant-Governor of East Bengal, was an unusual case. Between Harrow and Wren's he managed to squeeze in an education at Heidelberg University.

however, gained only low marks because they had not studied the textbooks on English Literature.[6]

Tinkering with the system, such as encouraging graduates by awarding more marks for Latin and Greek, had no effect. A more radical solution was needed and was duly provided by Lord Salisbury, who became Disraeli's Secretary for India in 1874. Salisbury admitted the merits of competition, accepting that it produced fewer 'bad bargains' than Haileybury even if it also supplied fewer officials with 'exceptional powers'. But he recognized that studying at a college with one's future colleagues was far better than studying by oneself in lodgings in London. To Salisbury it was essential to put the ICS back into the universities either before or after aspirants took the exam. Against the advice of the Viceroy, Northbrook, Salisbury decided that candidates would take the exam at school-leaving age (17 to 19), after which the successful ones would spend two 'probationary' years at a university studying a curriculum that included the languages of their chosen province. The probationers would not obtain a degree but they would benefit from the training and ambience of a university. And they would begin their work in India, combining it with local 'departmental' exams in law and the vernaculars, at the age of 20 or 21.

Salisbury's system was inaugurated in 1879 and lasted until 1892, when higher age limits were brought back for good. Nobody much liked it, least of all Jowett who by the late 1870s had overcome the obstacles set by the previous age limit and was pouring Balliol men into the ICS. He agitated for its repeal, maintaining that the candidates were now too immature, too 'exposed to the temptations of London' and, since they had already passed the exam, too reluctant to exert themselves at Oxford. He was supported by his colleague Monier Monier-Williams, the Professor of Sanskrit, who at the opening of Oxford's Indian Institute in 1884 complained that ICS entrants benefited little from their probationary years because they were so concerned to please their 'exacting' London masters – the Civil Service Commissioners – that they took little part in university life. If the current age limit were to be retained, he argued, probationers should stay three years at Oxford, take a degree and use the Institute as their 'rallying-point and central meeting-place'. They would thus get to know each other in an establishment which, so he proclaimed, would 'promote *esprit de corps* and act like a resuscitated Haileybury'.[7]

Indianization

One of Jowett's chief criticisms of the Salisbury system was that it deterred Indian candidates from taking the exam. Since the 1830s and 1840s Indians had dominated the middle and lower ranks of the Civil Service, acting in their thousands as Deputy Collectors, Deputy Magistrates and subordinate judges. But no Indian had been nominated to Haileybury; no Indian had been a covenanted member of the Company's Civil Service. The civil administration of the Subcontinent had largely been carried out by Indians, but they had been always supervised by a small body of Britons.

The exclusion of Indians from the higher posts, imposed by Cornwallis in the previous century, was officially ended by the 1853 Act which opened the Service to 'all natural-born subjects of the Crown'. But the difficulties facing Indian candidates were considerable. Even if they overcame the problem of expense and the objections of orthodox Hindus to voyages abroad, they had to travel to a distant country and sit an examination based almost entirely on an alien curriculum. There they would doubtless shine in Sanskrit, but that would be scant compensation for the higher marks awarded for Latin and Greek.

Only a very talented student could hope to succeed in such circumstances. During the first fourteen years of competition, sixteen Indian candidates took the exam, with only a solitary success, Satyendranath Tagore, the elder brother of Rabindranath, the poet and future Nobel Prize winner. In 1869, however, four Indians passed, including Surendranath Banerjea,* the future Congress leader, Behari Lal Gupta, a future officiating Judge of the Calcutta

---

*The Civil Service Commissioners removed Banerjea's name from the list of successful candidates after an Indian in London informed them that he had lied about his age. Banerjea responded by engaging a lawyer to apply before the Queen's Bench and argue that the age he had given on matriculation at Calcutta University was computed, as was the Indian custom, from the date of conception rather than of birth. The Bench accepted that Banerjea's birth made him eligible for the ICS, a ruling that was not contested by the Commissioners. The new recruit's career was, however, brief. As an Assistant Magistrate he was considered rather lazy and was dismissed after postponing a case several times and then wrongly passing an order entering the accused on the list of absconding prisoners. It may have been a harsh decision, but the ICS was harsh with any official believed not to be telling the truth.[8]

High Court, and Romesh Chandra Dutt who, besides becoming a Commissioner in Bengal and a Chief Minister of Baroda, was a novelist, economist and historian. But these were all exceptional men. In the twenty years following their triumph, only twelve Indians were successful.

The Secretaries of State in London were embarrassed by the situation and sought ways to rectify it. Sir Stafford Northcote, a Conservative, thought it a 'mockery' to tell Indians 'they might come and compete in Westminster if they like' and suggested a small number of posts should be filled annually from competitive exams in India. His successor, the Liberal Duke of Argyll, agreed that something should be done but was wary of any arrangement that gave educated Bengalis an advantage over the rest of the population, especially the tougher but less socially advanced Sikhs and Pathans of the north.[9] He was certainly not prepared to support a proposal by Henry Fawcett, the Radical MP known as 'the Member for India', who urged simultaneous examinations in London, Calcutta, Bombay and Madras.

The cry for simultaneous examinations was taken up by the nascent nationalist movement, the Indian National Congress appealing for them at its inaugural conference in 1885 and continuing to do so afterwards. But the British Government could hardly accept the demand without accepting a thorough transformation of its role in India and the character of its administration there. The idea of competing fairly with a vastly more numerous subject population may have had democratic attractions but it would have been a strange way to run an empire. One Member of the Viceroy's Council predicted that, since teenage Indians were 'infinitely quicker' at exams than Europeans, the result would be that 'at least half the service would be Bengali'.[10] Even if the Government accepted Dutt's assurance that the nationalists would not demand more than a third of the covenanted posts, it could not contemplate a system that would allow the most educated province of the country to take a majority of places on offer.* The British generally held an uncomplimentary opinion of Bengalis, regarding the Hindus among them as sharp-witted but untrustworthy 'babus', a garrulous and weak-willed people incapable

---

*Seven of the first ten Indian members of the ICS were Bengalis, the majority of them barristers-at-law.

of producing good administrators; their 'incurable vice', according to Curzon, was their 'faculty of rolling out yards and yards of frothy declamation about subjects' they had imperfectly considered or did not fully understand.[11] Yet no one doubted that they would win most places, least of all the National Muhammadan Association which urged that a proportion of ICS posts be reserved for Muslims. The British exaggerated the administrative deficiencies of 'baboodom', but Argyll was right to warn that it would be a 'dangerous experiment to place a successful student from the colleges of Calcutta in command over any of the martial tribes of Upper India'.[12]

Unable to accept simultaneous examinations and unwilling to leave things as they were, in 1879 the Government created the Statutory Civil Service, a body that would annually be awarded about a sixth of the places hitherto reserved for the ICS. Its members would be Indians, 'young men of good family and social position' who would be nominated by local governments and would receive salaries two-thirds the size of those given to the Covenanted Civil Service. The scheme never became popular, however, partly because 'good families' showed little interest in it, partly because members of the new service would remain in junior posts unless they received the special sanction of the Viceroy, and partly because ambitious young Indians were angered by the simultaneous lowering of the age limit for the ICS exam.

Recognizing that the system had failed to satisfy Indian aspirations, in 1886 the Government appointed a Public Service Commission, headed by the Lieutenant-Governor of the Punjab, Sir Charles Aitchison, to 'devise a scheme which might reasonably be hoped . . . to do full justice to the claims of the natives of India to higher employment in the public service'. Aitchison, the cleverest and most successful of the Scottish competition wallahs, advocated the abolition of the Statutory Civil Service and its replacement by a Provincial Civil Service, a scheme that would give men recruited in India slightly more and rather higher posts than they had been able to obtain under the old system. The Bengal Government, for example, would be required to reserve for its Provincial Service the posts of one Under-Secretary of Government, one member of the Board of Revenue, four Collectors, six District Judges and eight Assistant Magistrates.

While the Aitchison Committee rejected the idea of simultaneous examinations in London and India, it pleased Indian nationalists by its recommendation that the age limit for ICS candidates should be raised from 19 to 23, an age that would give them time to get a degree, study in London and compete with British candidates on reasonably level terms. The Government accepted the proposal and allocated entrants a year of special training following the exam. After a delay of some years, the new system came into existence in 1892 and resulted in a significant increase in the number of successful Indian candidates. Whereas the 1880s produced only six entrants from the Subcontinent, the following decade provided thirty-four. Nevertheless the proportion of Indians in the ICS remained low. At the time of Edward VII's death in 1910, only six Civilians in every hundred were Indian.

Incentives

Competition increased the social diversity of the ICS and also broadened the range of incentives for joining it. No longer did a boy have to accept the nomination of a family benefactor; he could now voluntarily apply for a post. Ancestral connections remained important, but family pressure was seldom applied to continue them. Henry Cotton was 'saturated with the associations' of the East India Company but did not feel inclined to follow his father and grandfather into the Civil Service. Nor did his father press him, advising his son to become a civil engineer in England. The pull of India was too strong, however, and Henry ended up as Chief Commissioner of Assam.[13]

Many others joined almost by accident. Stanley Bachelor applied for the Service after Cardinal Manning had told him he was not fitted for the priesthood. Claude Hill's father was dismayed that mathematical incompetence prevented his son from becoming an engineer in the Public Works Department but was happily surprised when other abilities won him a place in the ICS and a scholarship at Cambridge. Frederick Fryer thought his military future assured because his Uncle Charles had arranged with the Commander-in-Chief for a commission by purchase. But a row between his father and Uncle Charles eliminated the commission and forced Fryer to consider an alternative career. He sat for the ICS exam and eventually became Lieutenant-Governor of Burma.[14]

Some went into the ICS because they were encouraged by school-masters or university dons such as Jowett and the Reverend Lionel Phelps, a Fellow of Oxford's Oriel College. Others were tempted by the prospect of pay and sport: W. O. Horne had simple requirements, an open air life with plenty of shooting, and chose the ICS over the Army because the salary was better.[15] But many more, particularly towards the end of the century, went out in a spirit of adventure inspired by the idea of service and a sense of imperial mission. They liked the thought of riding around the countryside dispensing justice under a banyan tree. John Hubback passed into both the ICS and the home Civil Service and had to choose between the two: he opted for India because it offered him the 'prospect of an outdoor life and . . . early responsibility', whereas Whitehall presaged a desk and lengthy subordination.[16]

The growth of imperialist sentiment in Britain in the 1880s, fostered by the drama of such events as the death of General Gordon at Khartoum, was assisted by the fiction of G. A. Henty, Flora Annie Steel and of course Rudyard Kipling, who had established himself as the leading Anglo-Indian writer by the end of the decade. Several Civilians admitted that their Indian careers had been determined by Kipling and Steele. Philip Mason, a later recruit, confessed it had been 'the spicy smells and bright colours of the bazaar' that had drawn him to India. Arriving there for the first time gave him 'a sensation almost of coming home' because he was remembering 'the scents of dust and spices' from Kipling, whose work he had loved as a boy and about whom he later wrote a biography.[17]

India did not lose its allure for the old Anglo-Indian families. The Woodburns, an Ayrshire family of prosperous farmers which had already sent two generations into the Indian Army and the Medical Service, continued the tradition with a competition wallah who became Lieutenant-Governor of Bengal. But in many cases the connection was broken by failure in the examinations. Like another recipient of patronage, the landed gentry, Anglo-Indians were not sufficiently competitive.

The chief beneficiaries of the new system were the middle classes. Clergymen's sons had done well at Haileybury but did even better in the exams, providing over a quarter of the new recruits and a high proportion of Lieutenant-Governors. The next most successful group was the medical profession, which supplied a tenth of the new entrants, followed by lawyers and then by bankers and industrialists combined. Between 1860 and 1874 only 7 per cent of the entrants were sons of Civilians.[18]

For most boys, whether they had gone to crammers or universities or both, the crucial years of their education had been spent at a public school. There they had learned – or at any rate had been taught – the virtues regarded as indispensable for running the Empire. The fagging system taught them how to command and how to obey; the cricket and football pitches taught them about discipline and team spirit; the classroom, with its concentration on history and the classics, gave them an idea of imperial responsibility; and the ambience of the place provided a muscular ethos of courage, endurance, loyalty and self-control. For the administration of the Empire, the formation of character was as important as the cultivation of mind.

Cheltenham College was the leading supplier of competition wallahs, its Old Boys returning in retirement to harangue current pupils about their duty to serve the Empire in one capacity or another. Its fees were about half those of Eton and Harrow and its curriculum concentrated less on the Classics than on the 'Modern Side', which taught subjects more likely to be useful to aspiring Civilians such as mathematics and languages. Cheltenham was followed at a distance by Marlborough, Rugby and the new Haileybury, which opened as a public school in 1862 and retained the imperial associations of the old East India College. Eton, Harrow and Winchester provided comparatively few entrants into the ICS. At a certain level of an Indian career an Etonian education might even be regarded as a drawback: the wife of one middle-ranking Civilian complained that her Anglo-Indian neighbours could not forgive her for the fact that her husband had been to Eton, that both of them read books and that neither had been brought up in a suburb.[19] At a different level it was plainly an advantage. In 1894 the Viceroy (Elgin) and the Governors of Madras (Wenlock) and Bombay (Harris) had not only all been to Eton at the same time; they had all been together under the same housemaster, Mr Warre, to whom they sent a congratulatory telegram on the 4th of June, the school's principal holiday.[20]

The new ICS did not consist entirely of middle- and upper-middle-class men from the public schools. Competition also gave an opportunity to boys from poorer backgrounds who worked their way up through scholarships to grammar schools and universities. About a seventh of the new entrants were sons of farmers, traders, clerks and accountants. Joseph Goudge, a stationmaster's son from Taunton, got into the ICS through a scholarship to Oxford. So did John Maynard, whose widowed mother managed to bring up her children by keeping a school for 'young ladies' on Wandsworth Common. After working as a boy in a Yorkshire mill, Henry Savage went to the Liverpool Institute, passed into the ICS and later married a girl who had worked at the same mill.[21]

Among the chief losers in the competitive system were the Scots, who had been accustomed to a good deal of patronage at Haileybury and before. 'Scotland failed egregiously', reported the *Edinburgh Review* after the results of the first examinations revealed that only one Scot, Aitchison, had passed them.[22] But it was not entirely Scotland's fault. As Edinburgh's Professor of Greek pointed out, several of the subjects examined, including political philosophy and modern history, were not taught at any of the venerable Scottish universities. Not that he thought the Scots should change their ways to suit the requirements: the requirements should be altered to suit the Scots. Unless marks were awarded for fencing and gymnastics, he predicted the ICS would consist of 'a race of pale-faced students' and exclude 'lusty, vigorous, strong-nerved men of action'.[23] The Civil Service Commissioners did not accept his advice, and the Scottish entrants remained few. Although two aristocratic families (the Elgins and the Mintos) produced four Viceroys between them within the space of a century, Scotland's chief contribution to India was its businessmen.

To the consternation of the English, competition seemed for a few years to be a means of substituting the Irish for the Scots. While only 5 per cent of Haileybury's pupils had been born in Ireland, nearly a quarter of ICS recruits between 1855 and 1863 went to Irish universities. Trinity College Dublin was especially adept at preparing candidates, though its enthusiasm was quickly copied by the colleges of the new Queen's University at Belfast, Cork and Galway. But the hibernicization of the ICS soon faltered. From the mid-1860s the average Irish contingent dropped to between 5 and 10 per cent.[24] As in Scotland, the chief cause of this was exam failure.

Irish Protestants outnumbered Catholics in the ICS in inverse proportion to their numbers on the island: by about four to one. In both communities middle-class entrants predominated, but several of the outstanding Irish Civilians were from poorer backgrounds. Richardson Evans, who had to retire early from the Service for health reasons, was an orphan whose grandfather had been a cobbler and whose father had owned a bookshop patronized by the Evangelical clergy of Cork and its surroundings.[25] Two Catholics who both became Lieutenant-Governors were from modest rural backgrounds far from Dublin and Belfast: Antony MacDonnell was brought up in a village in Galway, while Michael O'Dwyer was one of fourteen children raised on a farm near Tipperary.

Irish enthusiasm for the ICS and other imperial services baffled Irish-Americans at the time and continues to confuse post-colonial historians. Edward Said's claim that Irish people could never be English any more than Cambodians could be French is a simplism that denies complexities of motive and loyalty and even history.[26] At a personal level Irish ambivalence was well caught by Richardson Evans's response to a stranger's question, 'Are you a Cork man, Sir?' Yes, he answered, 'half with pride at being one and half with pride that I had been taken for an Englishman'.[27] At a political level it was reflected in simultaneous enthusiasm for the Empire and for Home Rule. A follower of Parnell could talk about the 'great and noble Empire' in the same speech in which he denounced the 'unjust and tyrannous system of government in Ireland'. One prominent nationalist, Frank Hugh O'Donnell, wanted Home Rule throughout the Empire but under an Imperial Parliament at Westminster.[28] Yet there was nothing intrinsically Irish about such positions. 'Local patriotism' combined with loyalty to the Empire was a blend found all over the pink-coloured portions of the globe.

Petty, unimportant, mildly racist prejudice against Civilians from other areas of the British Isles existed in all constituent parts of the United Kingdom. Englishmen might refer to MacDonnell as 'our Fenian friend'; Alfred Lyall might mock Aitchison as 'a God-fearing, hot gospelling, Presbyterian Scot'; Irish and Scots might claim a uniquely Celtic sympathy towards Indians unshared by hard-hearted Saxons.[29] But there seems to have been no discrimination against any group: O'Donnell's brother Charles James could become a Commissioner despite repeated insubordination and censure from his superiors. At a time when most Englishmen were opposed to

Ireland ruling itself, they were employing Irishmen to govern other people. In 1886, when Gladstone's first Home Rule Bill was defeated, there were five Irishmen on the Viceroy's Council. In the 1890s, the decade of his second Bill's rejection, seven of the eight Indian provinces were at one time headed by Irishmen. Only the Bombay governorship was unhibernicized.[30]

Candidates

The Civil Service Commissioners were peculiarly stiff-necked people. They ruled by precedent; they never forgave transgressions. If a candidate broke the rules, however unluckily, he was dismissed from the competition. One boy was rejected because his tutor was two days late in producing a necessary certificate. Another suffered the same fate because he thought he had to send his certificate *on* rather than *before* 1 April. When a senior official at the India Office questioned the rulings in these cases, he was told by the Commission that 'we live by rules in this office and cannot afford to break them'.[31]

Each year the Commissioners announced subjects for examination and described the procedures to be followed by successful candidates. In 1875, for example, papers could be taken in English composition, English language and literature, and English history; in the language, literature and history of Greece, Rome, France, Germany and Italy; in mathematics and five natural sciences; in moral sciences, that is, logic, mental and moral philosophy; and in Sanskrit and Arabic language and literature. No subject, however, was compulsory.

The candidates sat their exams at Burlington House in Piccadilly. A few weeks later, after learning the results, the successful ones returned to London to be medically examined, to choose their province and to sign a document promising to use their 'utmost diligence' in preparing themselves for their future examinations. They would then spend two years on probation in Britain, a time during which they would be 'examined periodically, with a view of testing their progress', in Sanskrit, the vernacular languages, law, political economy, and the history and geography of India.

In an average year rather more than 200 candidates competed for about 40 places. The ratio of five or six to one dropped in the 1890s and then stabilized at about four to one at the end of the century. Naturally we know more about the successes than the failures, especially about those who astonished themselves by passing. In the interval between his morning and afternoon French papers, Richardson Evans visited St Paul's Cathedral and, so certain was he of failing the exam, abandoned the evening paper in order to return and climb to the top of the dome. He passed ninth of the fifty successful candidates.[32]

Success in the exams did not give men immunity from the Commissioners' inquisitions until they had reached India two years later. The next hurdle was the medical examination. If a man was pronounced unfit on the day of the test, he was disqualified even if his doctor assured the Commissioners he would recover his health within months. A touch of cruelty was added by the insistence that the medical should take place after the competition rather than before it. Candidates were thus obliged to go through all the expense and labour of the exams before their health could be assessed. One boy, E. P. Eardley-Wilmot, had been a fine sportsman, a member of the cricket and football Elevens at his school, and so healthy that he had been on the matron's sick list only once in seven years. He passed the ICS exam at the first attempt but was turned down on account of a 'slight irregularity of action' in a heart valve caused many years earlier by rheumatic fever. The 'irregularity' had no effect on his athletic life – he went on rowing and playing cricket into middle age – but the doctor's verdict, against which there was no appeal, ruined his career.[33]

Choosing a Province

The number of recruits required each year was determined by the Government of India. The provincial governments told it how many they needed, the Government did the sums, and the Secretary of State in London added two or three for contingencies: a medical failure, a probationer deciding to take another job, or perhaps a man changing his mind because his fiancée refused to go out to India.

Successful candidates were given the choice of province according to the position they had obtained in the open competition. The highest placed went where they wanted, the lowest filled the vacancies spurned by others. The North-Western Provinces and the Punjab were the most favoured destinations; the least popular was Madras followed by Bombay. After the 1875 exam sixteen of the top twenty entrants chose the NWP or the Punjab. When Reggie Partridge passed high into the ICS in 1881, his local newspaper in Devon assumed he would go for the NWP and congratulated itself that a 'Tiverton man who comes of good stock' would be ready 'to put things straight and keep them in order'. When his younger brother George passed low into the Service, it was considered inevitable he would go to Madras and become a 'Mull' (because in the south he would drink mulligatawny soup). The regularity with which the southern presidency received the least promising recruits eventually persuaded the India Office to assign probationers at its discretion and to ensure that Madras would obtain a few of the better entrants.[34]

Iris Butler, who was brought up in the Punjab, recalled in old age how she had 'rather despised a girl whose father was a Madras Civilian'.[35] The feeling was common and was naturally resented. Why Madras became so unpopular is not obvious, except that in its development it had been left behind by Calcutta and Bombay and was a very long way from both. The city itself was spacious and attractive, a mixture of Greek Classical and Victorian Indo-Saracenic; the provincial hill stations, the summer resorts of Ootacamund and Kodaikanal, were among the most agreeable of such creations; and the landscape was the India of the Victorian picture books, the country of lagoons and palms and paddy fields, of red soil and white coasts and dark-skinned smiling natives. Besides, the province could be administered in a leisurely way without much difficulty. The people were less subversive than the Bengalis, less violent than the 'martial races' of the north-west.

But the place had its disadvantages. The shooting was usually bad, the climate was always enervating, and the death rate for Civilians was higher than average. For an ambitious official its chief drawback was its position as an administrative backwater from which he was unlikely to be plucked and awarded a post in the central Government at Calcutta. The result was that the idler members of the ICS gravitated towards what became popularly known as the 'benighted presidency'. One of its Governors admitted that the province had certain officials who were 'eccentrics' and 'bad bargains'; the secretariat gained the reputation of being the most dilatory in India; and the District Officers were demonstrably less aware of what was going on in their districts than their colleagues further north. When Elgin went south to visit his friend Wenlock, he was depressed not only by his old school chum's failures but also by the 'inferiority, speaking generally, of the Madras official'.[36]

Bombay was almost as unpopular a destination for Civil Service recruits as Madras, and for much the same reasons. Civilians in the presidency could not aspire to the governorship of their own province, they were rarely chosen for posts in the Government of India, and they were in almost permanent dispute with Calcutta over questions of financial autonomy and interference from the central bureaucracy. But they did not share Madras's consciousness of inferiority; in fact they believed, erroneously, that they formed the most efficient administration in India. Yet whatever its drawbacks, Bombay was a vibrant place, its growth stimulated by the opening of the Suez Canal in 1869, its wealth displayed in an eclectic but splendid concentration of Victorian Indo-Gothic public buildings. The province also offered scope for diverse enthusiasms. While lepidopterists could revel in one of the highest and most varied densities of butterflies in the world, cricketers could be assured of finding a pitch close at hand. One cricketing enthusiast was Lord Harris, a Governor who earned an unjustified reputation as the 'father' of Indian cricket. In fact he did little to promote the sport among Indians, believing that the 'phlegmatic Anglo-Saxon' would always perform better than the 'excitable Asiatic'. But he did play cricket with Englishmen, insisting on remaining in Poona to participate in a match in 1893 when he should have been in Bombay trying to end Hindu-Muslim riots in the city.[37]

Ambitious ICS recruits aimed for the north, Bengal as well as the Punjab and the North-Western Provinces. The appeal of the Punjab owed much to its frontier life, to its history under the Lawrences, to the paternalist policies of a Government with grand schemes for building canals and improving agriculture. Bengal appealed to the more sedentary and calculating. This vast province of over 70 million people contained the imperial capital and the personal contacts useful for advancement. If a Secretary of the Government of India needed an Under-Secretary from a provincial administration, a candidate working close to him in Calcutta had more opportunity to impress than his equivalent in the benighted presidency over a thousand miles away. The same was true of higher posts appointed by the Viceroy. Bengal could usually count on providing about half the heads of Departments: of India's seven Home Secretaries in the last quarter of the century, no fewer than five came from Bengal and the other two from the North-Western Provinces.[38]

Despite the attractions of Calcutta and the prospects of promotion, the NWP was considered to have several advantages over Bengal. The climate was drier and healthier: a man was less likely to die on the spot or be forced by ill-health into early retirement. Shooting and pigsticking were plentiful. So was social life, much of it provided by British officers and their families quartered in garrisons such as Meerut and Cawnpore. Civilians liked the inhabitants, their language and their masculinity, which they compared favourably to their counterparts in Bengal, and they admired their towns, the Mughal monuments of Agra, the decadent beauty of Lucknow, the Hindu pilgrimage centre at Allahabad built at the confluence of the Ganges and the Jumna.

Apart from Calcutta, Bengal was much less alluring, a province bereft of comparable cities and monuments and cantonments, a place of almost constant humidity, a land consisting mainly of rice fields and villages and so many enormous rivers that travel was usually difficult and invariably slow. A Civilian in the North-Western Provinces could see the advantages of postings in any division from the hills of Kumaon to the ghats of Benares. A Civilian in Bengal saw only disadvantages the further east he was sent from Calcutta. Chittagong was regarded as a sort of penal station for insubordinate Civilians, a place so damp that one's books rotted and one was lucky to escape from it without breaking down.

A further hazard for a Bengali Civilian was the possibility of being forcibly transferred to Assam or Burma if there was a shortage of volunteers for these provinces. The occasional official who went to Assam by choice because he liked frontier life was greatly outnumbered by men who regarded it as a perilous and undesirable exile, a place where Anglo-Indian society consisted of truculent tea planters and where the danger of being killed by hostile tribesmen was greater than anywhere else. Resentment at Assamese postings became so strong that it was eventually agreed that anyone who served in one for five years could return to Bengal and receive a better job.

British (or Lower) Burma was administered by Deputy Commissioners, some of whom were Civilians from Bengal although most
were military officers. In 1881, however, the province began to
recruit its own civil servants, generally from those who had been near
the bottom of the list of entrants, and a few years later Civilians were
brought in from other places to assist in the administration of the
newly conquered Upper Burma. Some bravely trumpeted its advantages, the cheap cheroots, the good polo, the magnificent scenery,
'the novelty of the unknown', the 'infinite possibilities' of development and the absence of 'wrangling' nationalists and 'rival religions'.[39] Another blessing was the lack of caste and purdah, which
allowed them to mix more easily with a friendly and attractive people.
But others regarded Burma as 'a place of banishment, a dismal rice-
swamp' or 'howling paddy-plain' where the sun seldom shone. The
climate was unhealthy and debilitating, especially in Upper Burma
and Arakan, and the mosquitoes were so bad in some areas that even
the cattle were put under nets at night. The province had a higher
casualty rate for Anglo-Indians than any other, and women were
particularly vulnerable. Mortimer Durand refused the Chief
Commissionership because he did not want to expose his family to
the climate. Alexander Mackenzie accepted the job, but his first wife
died there, and his second became so ill that she had to be sent away.[40]

Jowett's Triumph

Under Salisbury's scheme successful candidates for the ICS were
expected to spend two years at one of the approved universities.*
Most of them chose Oxford, where fifty-five of the current seventy-
eight probationers were studying in 1884. If they wished, they could
stay an extra year and take a degree, but they would not retain their
annual grant of £150 and they would start their service junior to the
contemporaries who had gone to India ahead of them.

During their probationary years recruits had to take two 'periodi-
cal' exams and a final one at Burlington House that determined their
seniority in their chosen province. They also had to attend court

---

*King's College London, University College London, Oxford, Cambridge, Edinburgh,
St Andrew's, Glasgow, Aberdeen and Trinity College Dublin.

cases and write reports of what they had seen in the criminal, civil and police courts. Although Richardson Evans from Cork received permission to report from the Assizes of Tralee, most went to the Old Bailey, where they learned the principles of procedure and evidence, and Marylebone and Bow Street, where they observed the duties of a magistrate. Further tests included another medical and a riding exam at the Royal Artillery Barracks at Woolwich. In an uncharacteristic display of leniency, the Civil Commissioners allowed entrants a second chance if they failed to pass the riding test first time.

The probationary curriculum was academic rather than practical. As at Haileybury, no one discussed India or told students anything about their future work there.[41] What they learned about the Subcontinent came from books, lectures and language study. Which languages to teach was the most difficult issue for the India Office and the provincial governments to resolve. Throughout the time of their probation, the entrants had to study the chief vernacular of their chosen province; in their first year they were forced to learn one classical language (Sanskrit, Arabic or Persian), and in their second they could choose between a classical language and the second vernacular of their province. This system was uncontroversial in the presidency of Madras, where Telugu was the main vernacular with Tamil the second. But a problem arose in the North-Western Provinces where Hindi was regarded as the principal vernacular although Urdu, written in a different script, was the language of the courts and the public offices. In Bengal Hindustani was adjudged the chief vernacular, although in thirty of the province's forty-four districts the language spoken was Bengali. And in Bombay Hindustani held the same position although it was spoken mainly by Muslim noblemen and was not used in the courts, the revenue administration or in official correspondence. More important for a Bombay Civilian was a knowledge of Marathi and Gujarati, although even these proved useless if he was sent to the westernmost part of the presidency, Sind, where the language had Persian and Arabic roots, a different script and an alphabet of fifty-three letters. The result of this confusion was that many Civilians turned up in their first district largely ignorant of its language.

Few university dons made much effort to welcome the probationers. Phelps of Oriel was an exception, an Oxford eccentric who encouraged undergraduates during long Sunday walks, gave them introductions in India and kept up a long correspondence after- wards.[42] But at another Oxford college Evan Maconochie discovered that 'the attitude of the Dons was one of more or less benevolent neutrality' towards students unlikely to bring their institution sport- ing or academic glory.[43] The situation at Cambridge was no better. Probationers there found themselves so left out of university life that they resorted to setting up their own club for discussions and debates, an institution which required its members to dress up in a purple blazer, the pocket of which bore a tiger's head wearing a smoking cap.

Oxford owed its pre-eminence as a university for administrators almost entirely to the vision and persistence of Benjamin Jowett, a great classical scholar who spent fifty-seven years at Balliol, becom- ing its Master in 1870 and Vice-Chancellor of the University in 1882. Jowett's interest in India was inspired by two of his brothers who died there, one in the Army, the other in the Medical Service. He worked closely with Florence Nightingale, an enthusiast for social and economic reforms in India, and they corresponded over issues such as sanitation and land tenure. Men who wanted to do 'great and permanent good', he declared, should go and do it in India. When a former pupil went out to Calcutta as Law Member on the Viceroy's Council, Jowett told him he had 'one of the most desirable positions in the world', one that gave him 'a real opportunity of benefiting the natives of India'.[44] Jowett bestowed some benefits himself, cam- paigning for Indian recruitment to the ICS and encouraging Indians to come to his college. Of the first thirty-three Indian undergradu- ates at Oxford colleges, twenty-two went to Balliol.

After the ICS exams Jowett wrote to the successful candidates suggesting they spend their university years at his college. By 1880 Balliol was housing half of all probationers, twice as many as Cambridge and the other Oxford colleges put together. The Master was accused of poaching, but in most cases he had no need to poach. Although all his family had gone to Cambridge, Harcourt Butler went to Oxford simply to be under Jowett; at Christmas in Lucknow a few years later, he was reading the Master's sermons to his brother Montagu. In any case Jowett's ambitions for the ICS went beyond Balliol. In 1853 he had urged that the Civil Service should consist of 'the picked men of the universities', and nearly forty years later, when the Salisbury system was abolished and the age limit raised to 23, he had his way. In the last years of his life over half the ICS recruits were Oxford graduates, and another quarter had been at Cambridge.*

Jowett's Balliol was a kindergarten for politicians and diplomats as well as for colonial officials. It produced one Prime Minister (Asquith), three successive Viceroys (Lansdowne, Elgin and Curzon), and a large number of ambassadors and Cabinet ministers. Yet Jowett, an enemy of zeal, did not force careers upon his pupils; his skill was to identify a talent and encourage its possessor not to waste it. When he told Lord Lansdowne in 1868 that his poor degree did not altogether do justice to his talents, the new graduate replied that he was 'too fond of the society of jolly dogs' to work hard. But the gentle remonstrance did the trick. The jolly dogs were put in their kennels, and Lansdowne embarked on a public life that lasted over fifty years and included the posts of Under-Secretary for War, Under-Secretary for India, Governor-General of Canada, Viceroy of India, Secretary of State for War, Foreign Secretary, Chairman of the British Red Cross, Chairman of the Trustees of the National Gallery and Lord-Lieutenant of Wiltshire. Had it not been for Jowett, Lansdowne later recalled, he would have done little with his life.[46]

Contemporary Verdicts

Competition wallahs seldom enjoyed the approval of their elders in India. In the 1870s, the heyday of the crammer, they were regarded as bookworms without knowledge of the world. 'They neither ride, nor shoot, nor dance, nor play cricket, and prefer the companionship of their books to the attraction of Indian society.' Such was the verdict not of an elderly Haileyburian but of Lepel Griffin, one of the ablest of the first batch of competitive entrants.[47]

Later on, when the age limit was raised and the recruits were graduates, they were dismissed not as ignoramuses but as know-alls, men with fixed ideas who could deal with papers and records but not with people. They became a target in contemporary and by now seldom-remembered novels. In *The Old Missionary* W. W. Hunter has a

---

*The pattern continued after his death in 1893. Between 1900 and 1914, 47 per cent of entrants were from Oxford and 29 per cent from Cambridge.[45]

Lieutenant-Governor grumbling about competition men coming to Bengal with their heads full of ideas and expecting him to find the money to carry them out. The Collector in Alexander Allardyce's *The City of Sunshine*, Mr Eversley, scoffs at the new recruits with all their Latin and Greek: one might 'as well put the country under a commission of schoolmasters at once'. Eversley himself has 'never been able to make a hexameter in the whole course of his life' but predictably he is a master of Eastern vernaculars and knows more about the 'habits and feelings of the Bengalees . . . than any officer in the Lower Provinces'.[48]

Admirers of the Haileybury product thought it more important that an official should be a cricketer and 'the champion of bullied fags' than that he should have got a Double First at Oxford.[49] They looked down on the new breed of Civilians as milksops, too weedy to stand the climate and so unathletic that they could not shoot or even ride properly. Sir James Fergusson, the Governor of Bombay from 1880 to 1885, complained repeatedly that the 'pallid victims of the crammer' fell sick, went off their heads and were generally lacking in stamina. Besides, their inability to ride was 'ludicrous': one of his officials, who clearly had not earned a genuine 'certificate of equitation', would not go out riding without servants walking either side of his horse to catch him if he fell off. Thirty years of competition, he claimed, had proved the need to bring back Haileybury.[50]

Fergusson exaggerated. As a landowner of 21,000 acres who listed his recreations in *Who's Who* as 'hunting, fishing, shooting, yachting, cycling', he may have given sporting prowess an excessive rating. In any case competition could throw up athletes from all backgrounds: Henry Howard, a scholarship boy from Aldenham Grammar School, twice won the 'Inter-Varsity Mile'. Nevertheless the Civil Service Commissioners plainly made a mistake in establishing almost exclusively academic criteria for success in the entrance exams. Their curriculum was an inadequate preparation for men who were going to spend half their year in a hazardous climate and the other half riding around the countryside. The District Officer needed to be a strong and healthy figure who could ride unaided by servants. During his career he was bound to have to display some physical skills, quelling a riot, directing fire-fighters, hunting down a man-eating tiger. Alfred Lyall did not owe his survival in the Mutiny to his Eton scholarship but to his bravery, agility and endurance.

One competition wallah, who had been to both Eton and Oxford, complained that the Haileybury men looked down on him and his colleagues not only because they could not apparently ride or shoot but also because they were assumed to be 'of low birth and vulgar mind and manners'. Predictably this view was shared by Fergusson, a product of Rugby, Oxford and the Grenadier Guards (with whom he had fought in the Crimean War), who observed that their manners were 'not suggestive of the drawing room'. Less exalted figures agreed with him, finding the new Civilians 'argumentative, conceited, insubordinate' and 'very underbred'. When requesting a transfer of Civilians from the NWP, even Lord Northbrook asked for 'good men who can *ride well, and have good manners,* besides a sufficient amount of brains and common sense'.[51]

In the 1860s one Secretary in the Government of India suggested to John Lawrence that Civilians nowadays were sometimes men of 'low moral tone'. The Viceroy replied brusquely that he had not met 'any men of the Competition school of bad or even doubtful character'. But questions remained about their suitability. Even Charles Trevelyan, who had championed the cause of competition in the Haileybury years, felt that Indians preferred to be governed by gentlemen rather than by 'sizars and servitors'. In her novel *On the Face of the Waters* Flora Annie Steel has 'one of the Rajah's people' grumbling that they were 'not to have Sahibs to rule over' them now but the sons of any low-born Englishman who had learned enough at college. By the end of the century even Indians were complaining in the newspapers that the Sahib was not what he used to be. More serious allegations were that modern Civilians were less authoritative and also less kind to the people they ruled. Even William Wedderburn, a competition wallah, later Radical MP and enthusiastic supporter of Indian nationalism, thought the Haileybury system had maintained a 'certain atmosphere of friendly sympathy' with Indians that had been dissipated by the new class of ambitious academic bureaucrats from families unconnected with India.[52]

Critics of the British competition wallahs were unlikely to be more generous in their estimate of their Indian colleagues. Indeed the faults of the native Civilians were magnified versions of those of their English contemporaries. They were even more bookish and even less sporting. Despite twenty years of 'consistent trying', one Indian Civilian was depressed to find himself described by his

Commissioner as 'an enthusiastic but poor shot'.[53] The problem of assimilating with the British administration was as great as joining it in the first place. In the next century Indian candidates were more defiant about their dual loyalties, denouncing British imperialism at the Oxford Union while studying for the ICS; in some notorious cases, such as Aurobindo Ghose* and Subhas Chandra Bose, they abandoned them altogether, travelling respectively into the philosophy of cosmic salvation and into nationalist politics and an eventual alliance with the Japanese. But their more timid and less numerous predecessors of the late Victorian decades had to adopt the British administrative ethos without having had the advantage of acquiring the ethos of the public schools. The temptation was to become more British than the British, 'to adopt the European mode of life *in toto*' and talk about 'going home on furlough' when they went on holiday to England.[54]

Kipling satirized this type in his story, 'The Head of the District', creating an Indian Civilian with 'much curious book-knowledge of bump-suppers, cricket-matches, hunting-runs, and other unholy sports of the alien'. But he did not depict the tragedy of a man who socially belonged to no world, having left one and being unable to enter the other. One Civilian from Madras went to school in England, then to Wren's crammer and finally to Oxford. Enjoying English social life, he expected to have it replicated in his district in India: instead he found his candidature for membership of the local club withdrawn under threat of blackball from non-official members of the British community.[55] Exclusion from the club was both a personal humiliation and a hindrance to a Civilian's work, because it was often there, over a drink at the bar after a difficult day in court, that problems could be sorted out and annoyances removed.

The *Imperial Gazetteer*, an official publication, declared that the 'natives of India [had] on the whole shown greater ability in the discharge of judicial than of administrative functions'. It was a blunt but valid judgement. Although there was a good deal of corruption among the subordinate judiciary, Indian Civilians were regarded as fair and trustworthy judges. Like their British counterparts, they were impartial and honest, one observer noting that the difference

---

*Sri Aurobindo could not openly turn down the ICS without upsetting his family. He therefore contrived to disqualify himself by failing the riding test.

between them was that the British 'inclined to robust common sense' while the Indians, 'with their subtle minds, explored nice distinctions of law and judicial precedent'.[56]

In the late nineteenth century Indians were not regarded as effective District Officers by their British colleagues. Their circumstances were of course extremely difficult. A Hindu Magistrate would be distrusted by the Muslim community, especially on days of religious processions which often led to riots. A Bengali would find it difficult to assert himself outside Bengal; and even in his own province he would not have an Englishman's authority and self-confidence to keep the peace or exact obedience. He was also considered – at least by the British – to be less brave and less energetic. Elgin was 'sincerely sorry' to report that Indian Civilians broke down in moments of crisis. Curzon refused to appoint more of them to senior posts because they were unequal to emergencies and 'rather inclined to abdicate or to run away'. One young British Civilian was asked to oversee a military base camp used for the Sikkim operation because, among other reasons, his Bengali predecessor 'just hinted' that he was frightened of the tribesmen from the North-West Frontier who were working there as mule drivers.[57]

Kipling's 'Head of the District' was a fictional Bengali who ran away from the Frontier as soon as there was trouble with the tribes. But he was inspired by a real Bengali who explained to the Government that his subdivision in Bengal had been too 'disturbed' for him to make an adequate tour of it. It was difficult, commented Kipling in the *Civil & Military Gazette*, 'to conceive the frame of mind of a man who could put down on paper such a humiliating avowal of cowardice'. Ordinary shame, he felt, should have counselled 'a fabrication in some way less injurious to the Babu's character as an official'.[58]

Overall the competitive system received a good many negative verdicts. But had it been as bad as its opponents claimed, it would have been more comprehensively reformed. Few people apart from Fergusson suggested abolishing it and bringing back Haileybury. Besides, the critics were almost invariably older men who in many cases had been part of the previous system. They grumbled rightly about some things and wrongly about others. But much of it was the natural grumbling of an older generation being superseded by younger men and a different world. The Haileybury Civilians had tramped around India on their feet, making their decisions on the spot and seldom going home on leave. The competition wallahs travelled by rail, waited for instructions by telegraph, and took advantage of the Suez Canal to make more frequent visits to Britain. The times had changed more than the men.

Most people would have concurred with Lord George Hamilton, the Secretary of State, who observed in 1898 that the new ICS had 'fewer bad bargains, and fewer geniuses'.[59] They would also have conceded that, whatever the drawbacks, the general standard of ability was now higher. Even the Secretary who complained to the Viceroy of the 'low moral tone' of some of the new men, had not 'the smallest doubt that as regards an average of ability and efficiency the existing system' was better than the old one. Lawrence, a Haileybury man to his boots, 'quite agreed' that it was 'superior'.[60]

3

Griffins

~

Voyages

BEFORE LEAVING ENGLAND, griffins* had to buy sensible clothes for their years in India. This was an expensive business, for they received no clothing or travel allowances, and also a perplexing one on account of the extremes of temperature in some provinces and the differences of climate between all of them. Walter Lawrence bought an outfit that might have been appropriate for Madras but turned out to be useless in the Punjab. A further complication was caused by the absence of uniforms until near the end of the nineteenth century, when levee dress was adopted for very formal occasions. While an Army officer had clear guidelines about assembling his kit, a Civilian had to be prepared for every grade of formality and informality in hot and cold weather.

As London tailors seldom had personal experience of Indian conditions, griffins were better off asking advice from friends and relations who had gone out before them. Alfred Lyall was definite about what his brother James should *not* bring: warm socks, nightcaps,

---

*According to General George Pearse, 'A griffin in India is a person who has not been in the country a year and everyone during that time is anxious to teach him the ropes.'[1] That incomparable glossary, *Hobson-Jobson*, suggests that Gryffyn was an early corruption of Griffith and may originally have been 'used abroad to designate a raw Welshman'.

dressing-gowns and white cotton gloves ('a fearful abomination'). Alpaca coats and flannel shirts were essential, as were good-quality guns and saddlery, because riding and shooting were 'the only pleasures' he would have in a country district. For those without an elder brother to turn to, Anne Wilson, a Civilian's wife, compiled *Hints for the First Years of Residence in India*. Her prodigious clothing list includes tweed suits, flannel suits and Assam silk suits, as well as an evening dress coat, a frock coat and 'for informal occasions' a dinner jacket. It was better, she advised, to bring out an iron bath from England than to buy a zinc tub in a bazaar. Another useful purchase would be a tea basket with a tin case large enough to take cold chicken or sandwiches on railway journeys.[2]

Civilians seldom returned to England until furlough was due after eight years in India. The anguish of departure, intense in any case at the prospect of not seeing parents and siblings for so long a time, was thus aggravated by the knowledge that they were also saying goodbye to grandparents and other people whom they would never see again. Alfred Lyall wept after going to say farewell to an uncle who plainly did not have eight more years to live.

Since the average age of marriage for professional men was 31, it was rare for a griffin to depart with a wife. But it sometimes happened, though more often he would leave behind a fiancée, either because he could not afford a wife on his early years' pay or because of family pressure. John Beames's father had hoped his son would marry an aristocrat's daughter and refused to sign the security bond required by the East India Company unless John promised not to marry his fiancée Ellen until he had been in India for two years. The promise was made and kept but did not prevent the couple from marrying in the end. Nor did it destroy Beames's affection for his father. 'Our hearts were too full for words,' he wrote, recalling the moment when father and son embraced on the deck of the P & O steamer at Southampton. A few minutes later he heard the old man's stentorian voice shout 'God bless you!' from the pier head as the ship steamed down towards the Solent. They never saw each other again.[3]

The earliest Victorian route to India went around the Cape of Good Hope, usually touching Gibraltar, the Cape Verde islands and Ascension in the Atlantic, and crossing the Indian Ocean via Mauritius to Ceylon, Madras and Calcutta. By the time of Beames's departure in 1858, ships traversed the Mediterranean via Gibraltar and Malta to Alexandria; there the passengers disembarked, took a train to Cairo and crossed the desert in an omnibus pulled by mules while their luggage went by camel; at Suez they boarded another vessel that brought them to their destination via the Red Sea and Aden. After the opening of the Suez Canal in 1869, the whole voyage could be made in one boat that took about three weeks to reach Bombay, though the journey was even quicker if travellers went by train through Europe and joined their ship at Marseille or Brindisi. Most people went out on P & O vessels because they were the quickest, but they were also the most expensive and their food was usually worse than on other lines.

The Mediterranean route offered a minor solace to distraught parents. If their boy dawdled in France or went round by Gibraltar, letters could reach him at Marseille and, via the Brindisi mail, at Port Said. After saying goodbye to his son Hopetoun, whose mother had died when he was a baby, the retired Civilian Sir Henry Stokes accompanied the boy's aunts, who were 'in a dotty condition', to a shop 'and made a pretence of buying marmalade or something'. Afterwards he sat down and wrote to a son whom he had had to send home as a baby and whom he had only ever known during the three years between his own retirement as the senior Civilian in Madras and the departure of a boy who, thirty-seven years later, occupied the same position.

> I write this in the hope that it will reach you in Marseilles and cheer you on your way. You may be sure that all the good wishes that love could dictate follow you from this side. You have never given me any cause for displeasure or anxiety and I have no fear for the credit of the old name in the old service to which I was so long proud to belong. I am glad now that you have gone to Madras. Your poor mother would be proud and happy if she could see you now. Her early death was the greatest misfortune which could have happened to both of us . . . I am done now and my chief desire is to see you buckle to [work] . . . It will repay you in honest pride, whether you reap reward of other kinds or not . . . I don't want to sermonise but only to tell you how work was my salvation in my troubles . . . We were all very lonesome after you left . . .[4]

The voyage was a succession of new experiences for young men who in most cases had never crossed the Channel. Those who set off from Southampton or Plymouth were seasick in the Bay of Biscay; those who crossed France visited Versailles and were seasick in the Mediterranean. At Malta they encountered the glare of bright sun on white buildings which made them feel 'queer in the head'. The pre-Canal recruits had their 'first real glimpse of the East' at Cairo, where they saw the Pyramids and heard the muezzin's call to prayer. Their successors experienced it at Port Said, where the ship stopped, picked up the mails and took on a pilot to negotiate the Canal. The port, 'that picturesque but abominable refuse of humanity', attracted and appalled. It contained 'the worst blackguards of the world' who enticed naïve griffins into their 'exceedingly noisome gambling dens'. But it was also a herald for what some of them were seeking, poinsettias and the East and the romance of the desert. And for those who were a little homesick, there was the solace of watching a cricket match played on coir matting on the beach.[5]

Conditions on the ships became more luxurious towards the end of the century. Travelling out in 1857, Henry Beveridge had only salt water to wash in; he and his successors also had to put up with the smells and sounds of livestock. There was little entertainment on board, although in the Mediterranean P & O helped reduce the length of the days – or rather the nights – by advancing the clock by twenty-five minutes every morning before breakfast. Beveridge read Gibbon, but other griffins combated boredom with concerts and whist and games such as deck quoits and hopping races and tugs of war between Oxford and Cambridge men. Unable to ride or row or run about, many felt 'flabby and cramped' by the end of the voyage.

There were inevitable hazards among the other travellers, such as members of the Plymouth Brethren (a sect active in India) giving unrequested lectures while passing Mount Sinai. But most passengers were Anglo-Indians, generals and judges and their wives, a few doctors, a superintendent of police, 'a bevy of fair maidens' going out to be married or to search for a husband. Griffins often travelled with friends from their year at Haileybury or Oxford but, unless they were assigned to the same province, they were unlikely to meet again until they were on leave or in retirement in England.[6]

The ships slowed down after Port Said, taking eighteen hours to pass through the Canal so as not to wash away the banks. The heat became 'something fearful', and griffins began to think they had let themselves in for an 'unpleasantly warm job'. When the temperature in their cabins reached the nineties, passengers abandoned them and slept on deck.[7] A coaling stop at Aden, dirty, dusty and almost treeless, did not encourage their appetite for the East, though small boys entertained them by diving for coins, and Yemeni Jews bargained over ostrich feathers. But Ceylon was exhilarating, especially if the travellers had time to take the midnight mail up to Kandy through swarms of fireflies and wake up to their first view of tropical scenery, palm trees and paddy fields, tea gardens and mountain torrents.

First Impressions

First impressions of Calcutta were usually favourable, the buff-white classical buildings combining with the long rows of shipping to give it a plausible claim to be the 'second city of the Empire', a title disputed by Glasgow. If it did not quite live up to its reputation as 'the City of Palaces', its Maidan was magnificently English, 'Clapham Common, Hyde Park and Sandown Park all in one'.[8] Equally English was the transformation of its principal street, Chowringhee, in the second half of the nineteenth century. From a parade of handsome pillared mansions it became a bustling, largely red-brick thoroughfare of shops and offices and hotels.

The sight of Bombay was equally imposing, at least in its Victorian Gothic heyday. No wonder Indian finance was in a bad condition, wrote one griffin to his mother, when the city had a palace for a post office and a cathedral for a railway terminus.[9] Less impressive was the arrival at Madras, which did not have a pier before 1861 and where steamships lay at anchor outside the surf, dispatching their passengers in small boats that dumped them on the beach. But at least the city was green and bright and tropical, and the clubs were good.

The Victorians did not believe in homesickness. The young Curzon, as sentimental as a boy as he was as a man, believed it was a physical illness and congratulated himself that, miserable though he was on his first night at boarding school, he had experienced no actual desire to be sick.[10] Few griffins admitted to homesickness in their letters home. Dismayed by the society of rough and heavy-drinking tea planters in Assam, a young Civilian might yearn for the panelled walls of his Oxford study. From the Punjab cantonment of Ambala, an ill and disheartened John Maynard might confess to his mother that he pined for a London fog or an Oxford Scotch mist. Yet such men stayed. Within a few weeks of his arrival, Maynard predicted he would be home the following Christmas. But when the time came he had no regrets about staying in India. He could have been dreaming up schemes for the regeneration of mankind in the fire-lit glow of his college rooms, but now he had an active life in which he might achieve something beyond dreams.[11] It was a common feeling. The exhilaration of responsibility, the realization of the power and potential to do good, were – at least in the early years – effective antidotes to nostalgia for home.

Haileybury men destined for northern India started their careers in Calcutta. There they were required to study the languages of their chosen province and pass two exams before being sent out to a district in Bengal, the Punjab or the North-Western Provinces. On arrival in the capital, they reported to the Secretary of the Board of Examiners, found themselves rooms in an agreeable boarding-house and quickly entered Calcutta 'society'. Their new status as apprentice administrators was immediately displayed by the acquisition of a horse, a groom, a dog and a personal servant or 'bearer'.

Calcutta was an easy place to 'learn to swagger', observed a missionary who had just graduated from Oxford: even a British bank clerk was a sahib who drove a dog cart and abused his servants.[12] A 20-year-old Civilian ranked much higher in the social scale than a bank clerk. He belonged to a service whose members were known as 'the Heaven-born', people often resented by other Anglo-Indians for their clannishness as well as for their wealth and social position. Civilians were paid better than their only social equals, Army officers, and were thus the most 'eligible' of bachelors. 'Worth three hundred dead or alive' was a saying that reflected in pounds sterling both their initial salary and the pension they would bequeath their widows. Griffins in Calcutta were thus alluring prey for ambitious women with unmarried daughters. 'Mamas angled for us', recalled John Beames, thrusting invitations on him and his colleagues to dinners, balls, lunches and garden parties.[13]

The life of a Haileybury griffin in Calcutta was pleasant, idle and expensive. Arriving in March, as the city warmed up in earnest, Beames followed a routine of tea on his veranda at six, a ride on the Maidan till seven, then more tea and a smoke with friends till nine when he settled down to a hefty breakfast of fish, mutton, curry and fruit, washed down by iced claret. He then spent two hours on his languages (one of them with a munshi, his teacher) before going out in a gig in the furnace of midday to pay calls on the fashionable ladies of Chowringhee. Tiffin, a similar meal to breakfast, understandably required a siesta which was followed by an evening ride to the Eden Gardens where he and his friends cantered along a turf road before dismounting at the bandstand and talking to ladies in their carriages. Dining and dancing got them through the rest of the day and a good part of the night.[14]

Such a life, varied by shooting expeditions in cold weather, gave little incentive to griffins – except for the more conscientious and anti-social ones – to pass their exams and take up posts in the interior. It did, however, propel many of them into debt. Inexperienced with money yet conscious of high salaries in the future, they splashed out on horses, servants, wine and cards. Youths of 21 quickly found themselves encumbered with debts that took them decades to pay off. Robert Montgomery went into debt on his first day in Calcutta and remained so until he became Lieutenant-Governor of the Punjab thirty years later. Beames himself, who spent eleven idle months in the city, found at the end that he had formed a debt that 'clung' to him and 'harassed' him throughout his career.[15] Whatever drawbacks competition may have had, one indisputable benefit of the change was the decision to steer griffins away from Calcutta and send them straightaway to a district to learn their languages as well as their jobs under the supervision of a Collector.

First Postings

After the opening of the Suez Canal, Bombay superseded Calcutta as the chief port of entry into India. Competition griffins destined for the Punjab, the North-Western Provinces and for the Bombay presidency itself were duly sent there, where they found a letter from the Chief Secretary of their province directing them to report to the provincial capital or else to a civil station, the headquarters of one of the 250 districts into which British India was divided. They were also inducted into the mysteries of Joining Time, complicated regulations based on distance and methods of transport which explained how much time they were allowed to reach their destination.

The districts were theoretically selected according to the merits of the District Officer, known as the Collector or Magistrate in the old 'Regulation' provinces of British India and as the Deputy Commissioner in the newer 'Non-Regulation Provinces' such as Burma and the Punjab. Many griffins undoubtedly owed much to the tutelage and hospitality of a sympathetic Collector. Some also owed a debt to the good nature of the Collector's wife, who might help them buy pots and pans and give them advice about how to deal with their servants: the cook must not be allowed to smoke his hookah or go to sleep in the kitchen; the groom must not be allowed to use the horse's blankets for himself.[16] But their training was rather haphazard and nugatory. Griffins were expected to pick up what they could from others and learn from their mistakes. A Collector could give them some experience of magisterial work or revenue assessment or of looking after the district treasury. But there was little attempt to teach them the principles of administration or to give them practical advice about co-operation between the different services and departments.[17]

The novelist Edward Thompson wrote that one compound was like every other compound in British India, 'this land of repetitions'.[18] There was a certain uniformity about the stations, the style of the bungalows, the layout of the civil lines, the placing of the European quarters upwind and a little apart from the 'black town' so that residents were seldom bothered by the smells of the bazaars even if they could not avoid the occasional sounds of nocturnal tom-toms. The chief difference between them was one of scale. Griffins were sent to stations where the British contingent might number 5 or 500 – or more if it was a provincial capital or cantonment.

Kind Collectors allowed their griffins, now known as Assistant Magistrates or Assistant Commissioners (3rd Grade), to live with them until they found accommodation. Outside the main towns this was almost invariably an unfurnished bungalow with primitive plumbing: the bath water emptied on to the floor and ran out through a hole in the wall covered by an iron grating to prevent snakes from coming in. Where possible, newcomers liked to share with other young men, forming 'chummeries' which reduced both the rent and the solitude. The bachelors in a station tended to dine together and, if it was also a military station like Ahmednagar, with unmarried officers in the Mess of the Bombay Grenadiers. Dining with the military carried an increased risk of a hangover, though officers tended to drink less as the century advanced. The 1840s had seen the abolition of 'wheelbarrows', vehicles stationed outside the Mess in which drunken officers were rolled home by servants to their beds.[19]

Griffins in the Army and the ICS were prone to making gaffes that angered or amused the rest of the station. A subaltern could enrage a senior officer by inviting him to take sherry instead of beer after curry. A griffin 'excited shrieks of laughter' when he saw some vultures near the Collector's bungalow and exclaimed, 'I say, what a lot of turkeys you keep!' So anxious was Malcolm Darling about making a faux pas that he only nibbled his food in case the Lieutenant-Governor asked him a question and caught him with his mouth full.[20] But almost the worst gaffe a griffin could commit was the failure to pay social calls, a custom that required him to visit everyone 'in society' and leave his card (or cards if there was more than one lady in the house) with a servant. No cards might mean no invitations.

British society in a civil station was less varied than almost anywhere else on earth. No one was poor, and no one was very rich. There were no old people and no teenagers; the only children were infants under the age of 7 who had not yet been sent 'Home'. Yet despite its uniformity, 'uninspired by the imagination of youth nor softened by the sentiment of old age',[21] it was an intensely hierarchical society, a hierarchy of officials whose ranking in the order was listed in a Government publication called *The Warrant of Precedence*. A Civilian of eighteen years' standing had an equal status with a Lieutenant-Colonel but was eighteen places above a Major or a Civilian who had been in the country for only twelve years. The intervening places were occupied by officials such as Sanitary Commissioners and Conservators of Forests (1st Grade), Senior Chaplains, Managers of State Railways and Superintending Engineers of the Public Works Department.

The Warrant of Precedence was closely observed even in the *mofussil* (rural areas), especially at rather grim occasions known as 'dining the station'. These events were often planned to coincide with the operations of the Mutton Club, for in most of India for most of the year an animal had to be eaten within twenty-four hours of its slaughter. The Club, whose membership was five or multiples of five, kept a flock of sheep for special occasions to vary the inevitable rural diet of scrawny chicken. The members received in rotation a fifth of the animal, the fore-quarters, the hind legs and the saddle. When it was the turn of the Collector or the District Judge to receive the saddle, they often felt it their duty 'to dine the station', that is, to invite the handful of officials and their wives who made up the Anglo-Indian community.[22]

No one who has left written records of these occasions admits that they were enjoyable. Formality reigned even in the jungle. The presiding memsahib wrote out her menus in Anglo-French and did her *placement* according to the *Warrant*. One griffin recalled that as a result he sat next to the District Engineer's wife at every dinner he went to at his first station. Memsahibs who failed to pay the required attention to the *Warrant* risked a reprimand. One officer, who had been placed as a Lieutenant-Colonel, felt obliged to inform his hostess that he was a 'full Colonel' – to which she gaily replied that by the end of dinner she hoped he would be even 'fuller'. This sounds an uncommonly bright riposte. Alfred Lyall found 'dining the station' a 'gloomy prospect' not because his guests were stupid but because they had the 'art of becoming stupid the moment they appear in "society" – they have a fixed notion that good manners require a series of vapid formal remarks, and that nought beyond must be risked'.[23]

A few fortunate griffins were posted to large stations such as Agra, where they could hunt jackal with the station pack before breakfast, work through the day and go to a party in the evening. Even better was Poona, regarded as one of the best stations in India because of its gymkhana, its society and a climate in which English roses could flourish. It was especially appreciated by Oxford and Cambridge rowing Blues for its river, rowing club and regatta. But Poona society was stiffer than most others, and social ostracism was the consequence of a griffin's failure to pay his midday calls. Happily, however, Poona's bachelor contingent was sufficiently large and gregarious for a newcomer to be able to ignore dancing and the ladies without having to 'live the life of the solitary bull bison'.[24]

Nowhere was Anglo-Indian society more formal and punctilious than in Bengal. In the Punjab a Deputy Commissioner might send a note to his subordinates saying 'Come over and dine tonight'. But his equivalent in Bengal, a Collector, was likely to send written invitations 'requesting the pleasure of [their] company'.[25] Protocol was naturally still more rigid in Calcutta where the Viceroy's ADCs had to work out where the Bishop should be seated in relation to the Chief Justice of Bengal (one place lower) and whether the Commander-in-Chief took precedence over a Lieutenant-Governor (not if the L-G was in his own province, yes if he wasn't). The wives of senior officials staying at Government House were often appalled at the prospect of sitting next to the Viceroy and trying to be 'intelligent, attractive and tactful for sixteen consecutive meals'. The Viceroys and their consorts were equally dismayed. Mary Curzon, a beautiful American who became Vicereine at the age of 28, found herself seated throughout Calcutta's winter season between two of four men, the Lieutenant-Governor, the Commander-in-Chief, the Chief Justice and Bishop Welldon, who himself observed that every senior official was 'pretty well bored to death' by the system.[26]

Yet no one did anything to mitigate a protocol so much more rigid and irksome than it was in Britain. It was as if a society restricted in differences of class, age, wealth and profession, compensated by exaggerating the gradations of official recognition. A society without writers (Kipling left at the age of 23), without students or old people, without painters or actors or musicians, a society which exalted duty and self-sacrifice but undervalued bankers and industrialists – such a society could see itself only in purely official terms, classifying its members by the positions they achieved and the honours they were awarded. It was not surprising that a number of fairly senior Civilians and Army officers – as well as the bon-vivant Maharaja of Cooch Behar – joined the Unceremonials Club, whose main function was allegedly to hold 'Entertainments free from ceremony and conventionality'. The Club's charter proclaimed its intention to 'paint the whole place red', but in fact the only unconventional things its members did were to wear a red cap playing tennis and a red smoking jacket at Club dinners.[27]

The few griffins who liked small stations were intellectuals, who thus had time to read books, and hunters, who could disappear into the jungle. Malcolm Darling preferred to dine in his tennis shirt with a good book rather than dress up for the club and struggle to be polite and 'cheery', a quality much prized by Anglo-Indians.[28] Apart from reading, the chief amusements of a small station were provided by dogs and cards and horses. The game of whist was a treasured staple of Indian life, an enemy of boredom and loneliness, because it enabled a man to spend several hours in the company of three others with whom he might not have anything else in common; a station with only three whist players was a pitiable place. Another staple of small station entertainment was gossip. In a society of twenty or thirty Anglo-Indians no one could be independent or anonymous. Everybody knew each other and was, reported Harcourt Butler, 'intensely interested in the doings and failings of [their] neighbours'.[29] Friendships were made, of course, but they were dislocated by the incessant transfers of officials, men being promoted to new positions or sent to distant districts to officiate for seniors going home on furlough. It was the same with friendship between Civilians and Army officers. No sooner had a man made friends with the officers of the Middlesex Regiment than they were replaced by the East Yorkshires.[30]

The most testing time of the griffin's year was his first hot weather, while his most dramatic moment was the breaking of the monsoon when, after days of burning winds, the rains crashed down with almost unimaginable force and quickly turned the landscape green. The hot weather varied according to province. In Madras hot became hotter; in Bombay and Bengal warm became hot and humid; and in the north cold became very hot indeed. Extremes of temperature reached their peak in Upper Sind, one of the hottest and driest places on earth, where the thermometer ascended from freezing in December to 120° in the summer.

In most places the warm weather started in March, and soon afterwards the punkahs were brought out and white trousers were donned. By late April the griffin was trying to sleep in a temperature of nearly 100° with the punkah-wallahs dozing off as he lay sweltering under a mosquito net that often let the mosquitoes in while keeping the air out. In the 'cool' of the early morning, he found sweat dripping off his elbows as he shaved; drying himself after a bath, he then had to dry the sweat caused by his exertions with the towel.

In parts of Sind the temperature remained at 110° all night and was accompanied by sand flies which could penetrate any net and sting its occupant. Men tried to sleep outside but were kept awake by bats and by the barking of dogs and the shrieking of jackals. In Lahore the young Kipling kept his punkah-wallahs awake and contented with sticky sweet cakes. But even so it was often too hot to sleep, and he became a noctambulist, wandering the alleys and bazaars of the old city, dropping in at opium dens and gambling haunts, strolling with Indians and listening to the tales they told in the men's quarters of their homes.

The hot weather produced a variety of ailments. Kipling himself was often ill with fever and stomach cramps, which he tried to combat with opium. Humidity brought skin infections such as eczema, impetigo and the prickly heat that had men scratching themselves till they were bleeding all over. The combination of muggy weather and prickly heat, observed one young Civilian, turned his station into 'socially the dullest set of people' he had ever met. The ladies never appeared, not even to play croquet or give dinner parties; they lay all day under punkahs.[31] Many places became 'bachelor stations' during this season, for the women had fled to those refuges in the hills which each province possessed. Even a large station such as Lahore, a provincial capital, was reduced to eleven people, Kipling and a few bored officials at the Punjab Club eating 'meals of no merit among men whose merits they knew well'.[32]

Going to the hills was seldom an option for griffins. They were meant to spend their first hot weather in the plains and acquire the habits of working at dawn and sleeping in the afternoon. In Bengal they went to *cutchery* (the court room) at five in the morning. Griffins who had conscientiously passed their language exams by summer found themselves saddled with tasks abandoned by senior Civilians who had gone on leave. While his superiors were up at the Punjab hill stations of Simla and Dalhousie, Michael O'Dwyer, the hardworking griffin from Tipperary, was sent to swelter in Multan and act as Cantonment Magistrate, Magistrate of the district, Treasury Officer, Civil Judge (with limited powers) and Superintendent of the Jail with 500 prisoners.[33] It was a tough apprenticeship for someone who had spent the previous summer at Balliol.

First Duties

A griffin's first months were divided between studying for his departmental exams and doing whatever minor jobs his District Officer assigned to him. In the cold weather the DO might take him on his tour of the district, showing him some of the villages and introducing him to the mysteries of land settlement and revenue assessment.

At the station in summer he might put him in charge of the treasury to learn the system of revenue accounts under an Indian Deputy Collector. In large stations employment might be more varied: Walter Lawrence soon found himself Curator of the Lahore Zoo and responsible for the beautiful Shalimar Gardens, where his friend Kipling organized moonlit parties and tried in vain to fall in love.

Until he had passed his departmental exams, a griffin possessed third-class magisterial powers that allowed him to impose only small fines and prison sentences of up to a month. His first cases tended to be petty thefts and assaults, a man cuffing his neighbour or cutting down his tree, someone's buffalo straying on to someone else's sugar cane and causing blows between the two proprietors. The griffin was aided by a clerk, who helped him understand what witnesses were saying, and by his probationary studies of the Indian Penal Code, the Law of Evidence and the Code of Criminal Procedure. But it was a bewildering and rather dispiriting introduction to India. Sitting in court for hours listening to deceitful witnesses and long-winded pleaders bred a spirit of cynicism and disgust. The experience provoked one disheartened griffin to publish an 'Address to the Wallahs of 1869', a poem suggesting not very seriously that the latest intake of probationers should stay at home and become bank clerks or cobblers.

> All day I swelter in my chair
> Administering the law's redress,
> Bewildered, dazed, provoked to swear
> By perjured 'clouds of witnesses'.
> Lord! how they lie, unmoved by fear
> Of all their million ugly gods;
> I make out scarcely half I hear,
> But then it's lies, so what's the odds?[34]

Griffins often arrived in their first district comprehending a good deal less than half of what they heard. A man destined for Bengal would have to start his vernacular studies from scratch if he was posted to Orissa, a part of the province where neither Bengali nor Hindustani was spoken. Even in a Bengali-speaking district far from Calcutta he would have difficulty in understanding. Richard Carstairs found that the local patois in Tipperah was no more comprehensible to Bengalis from the capital than it was to him.[35]

Languages were an essential part of the departmental exams that a griffin was supposed to pass within his first year. The form of these exams altered over the second half of the nineteenth century, but the content remained based on four subjects: language, judiciary, revenue and treasury. In a typical test a griffin would be handed a police report in English and told to dictate it to a munshi in Hindustani; next he might have to decide three revenue cases after listening to the evidence in the vernacular. Success in the exams rewarded a candidate with a rise in salary and 'second-class powers', which gave him authority to impose fines of 200 rupees and prison sentences of six months, and finally with a Magistrate's 'full powers', where the corresponding penalties were 1,000 rupees and up to two years in jail. Failure was discouraged by the knowledge that seniority was regulated by the results of the examinations, an important consideration in a system where appointments often depended as much on a man's position in the hierarchy as they did on the merits of the contenders.

An Assistant Magistrate with enhanced powers was usually posted to the headquarters of another district, where he adopted the District Officer's routine of *cutchery* in the hot weather and tours of inspection in the winter months. If he was made a Subdivisional Officer, he became the chief civil authority in an area of several hundred square miles. In Bombay and the North-Western Provinces he covered his subdivision while residing at district headquarters. But in Madras and Bengal he was given his own 'capital' in which he acted not only as resident magistrate and revenue officer but also as Sub-Judge, Sub-Jailer, Sub-Registrar and Sub-Treasury Officer. Such independence and authority at the age of 25 could be exhilarating, and it was sometimes claimed that the subdivisional system produced the best officers. But the isolation and austerity of such a post, living in a place where the only other Englishman might be the Assistant Superintendent of Police, where there were no cards or company or newspapers, where the nearest white woman might live twenty or thirty miles away, also produced its quota of dispirited young men.[36] After undergoing 'solitary confinement' in a subdivision, a young Civilian could become enthused even by the amenities of a small station, with its club, its racquets court and croquet two evenings a week with the resident ladies. The prospect of a winter 'week' – an Anglo-Indian institution combining dancing and sport in a provincial capital – was like looking forward to the most exciting kind of school holidays.

Lyall among the Rebels

Alfred Lyall left England in November 1855, shortly before his twenty-first birthday, and nearly drowned before he reached Calcutta. After going ashore at the harbour-less Madras, a vast wave swamped or capsized the boats returning passengers to their ship, and three people were lost. A few days later he arrived at his destination and, following election to the Bengal Club, installed himself in its premises. On a starting salary of 300 rupees a month, he was able to acquire a bearer, a *khidmutgar* (table-servant), a horse and buggy and attendant syce (groom), and a part-time shikari (gamekeeper), who scouted for quail and snipe outside the city. But his Hindu servants soon exasperated him. They cheated him of money and refused to touch his food, insisting that the Muslim *khidmutgar* should fetch him his bread.

Lyall led the typical life of a young Haileyburian in Calcutta. He rode on the Maidan before breakfast, studied for two or three hours in the morning, paid a social call, had tiffin, played racquets, smoked cigars and went out to parties. For a while he enjoyed social life and his bachelor eligibility, but he was soon bored and later referred to the city as a 'dreary vortex of dissipation'. Sometimes he went out by boat and shot snipe in the marshes, but he was soon bored of that too. Boredom and restlessness were his lifelong enemies. He combated them with books, demanding that his mother send him the new volumes of Macaulay's *History of England*, Michelet's *History of France* and indeed 'any other good new book' unless it was written by Dickens, whom he thought had been 'going backwards ever since "Pickwick"' and whom he considered 'unable to write anything but broad farce'. He particularly wanted her to send Voltaire's works, but she, born and married into clergymen's families, refused to encourage her son's innate scepticism.

In Lyall's pre-competition days a Civilian destined for Bengal could choose between the 'Upper Provinces' (i.e. the NWP) and the 'Lower Provinces' (Bengal proper). Alfred chose the first because they offered more excitement and quicker promotion although he hoped he would not be sent to the newly annexed districts of Oudh where, as he perceptively observed a few weeks before the Mutiny, a Civilian was in danger of having his throat cut. The choice determining his study of languages, he engaged a munshi to teach him Persian and Hindi. To his surprise he discovered he could write 'the flowery Persian style' without difficulty, and he passed the first exam within two months. A few weeks later he passed the second after realizing he could with equal facility write Hindi in the 'easy flowing style' required by the Government's examiners. The results qualified him for public service and took his salary to 400 rupees a month. According to the regulations of the time, he would take his last exam, a judicial one, after acting as an assistant in a district court for six months.

Lyall travelled by palanquin to his district, Bulandshahr, a small station in the Meerut division forty miles south-east of Delhi. He enjoyed the experience of being transported in a 'conveyance used thousands of years ago by mighty Rajas of old'. He was pleased also to find that the people of the North-Western Provinces were more backward, more genuine and more attractive than the semi-Europeanized Bengalis he had left behind. A sudden fever made him wonder whether he was about to die, but he recovered and tried to adapt to a hot-weather routine. Accustomed to getting up late, he now put his bed on the veranda so that the cold dawn air woke him just before sunrise. Then he went for a gallop, worked in court between seven and twelve, and returned to eat breakfast and lie torpid in a bungalow where the doors and windows were closed to keep out the burning air. As soon as the sun had gone behind the trees, he opened the door of his human oven and plunged into a swimming bath with the other two English inhabitants of the station.

Lyall spent some of his early months sitting in court while George Dundas Turnbull, the Magistrate and Collector, dealt with cases and occasionally requested his support. But he also had petty cases of his own to try and a part of the district to look after. Despite the solitude and discomforts, he enjoyed his independence of action, his freedom to do his work when he liked. What reconciled him to banishment, he told his sister, was his realization of how much a Civilian could achieve, the great powers he could exercise for the benefit of large numbers of people.

Lyall had his first premonition of disaster during a visit to Delhi in the spring of 1857. Muslims sitting near the Great Mosque looked so savagely at him that he did not dare ascend the long flight of steps to its entrance. Returning to his district, he and Turnbull began disarming Muslim villages, surrounding them with a troop of cavalry at dawn and bullying the leading men into surrendering their weapons. In a mood bordering on nonchalance he wrote home about the 'mutinous disaffection' in the native regiments and told his mother that in a general mutiny the Civilians in isolated stations like his would all be massacred: 'If the company of sepoys here were to rise, nothing could save our throats.'

When the sepoy regiments did mutiny at Meerut, the divisional headquarters forty miles to the north, the three Civilians at Bulandshahr – reinforced by a dozen of their countrymen who had been travelling in the district – barricaded themselves in the Collector's house and waited to be attacked. But there was no attack; and for the moment the local company of sepoys remained loyal. Yet the breakdown of authority quickly led to an eruption of violence in the countryside: Muslims raided Hindu villages, Hindu Gujars plundered Hindu Jats. Identifying the Gujar pastoralists as the principal bandits, Lyall and Turnbull collected a troop of fifteen Indian horsemen and went on to the offensive, riding into Gujar villages and seizing their leaders. In one fight both Civilians shot and killed a mutineer, but usually there was little resistance. Lyall found it 'wonderful to observe what a moral power two white men had over them all'. Writing home between sorties, he admitted he had never enjoyed himself so much in his life. He wished people in England, who liked to abuse Civilians as lawyers and tax gatherers, could see how the outstations in India were being held almost single-handedly by people like him.

When the Mutiny spread to the neighbouring station, all the British abandoned Bulandshahr except the Civilians. Turnbull and his colleagues resolved to save the contents of the treasury, which was guarded by the sepoy company and their loyal troop of irregular cavalry. But as they loaded the treasure on to carts, a large body of armed villagers descended on the town. Turnbull and Lyall with a few horsemen charged and drove some of them off but returned to find another group had attacked from the rear and were busy burning their houses and carrying off their furniture. Meanwhile the sepoys, still guarding the treasure, had turned against the remaining troopers and forced them to flee. In other stations in the province they would then have set upon the Civilians and killed them. Instead they merely disobeyed their orders, marching out of the town gate with the treasure and keeping it for themselves. Forsaken by everyone, Turnbull and Lyall made a successful dash for Meerut, which the mutineers had abandoned for Delhi. Lyall had lost his furniture, his crockery and, worst of all, every one of his books. He retained only his horse, his gun and the clothes he was wearing.

After a few days at Meerut, the Civilians returned with a small band of cavalry but were driven out of Bulandshahr by a force of mutineers under the command of a local Muslim landowner. Lyall went back to Meerut, joined the Volunteer Horse and took part in a number of skirmishes. After the recapture of Delhi in September, he was ordered to join a 'movable column' forming there to sweep the rebels from the country between the Ganges and the Jumna rivers. But he did not remain with it for long. The column's first target was Bulandshahr, which it captured after a pitched battle with artillery, and he and Turnbull were thus reinstated in their posts. Lyall was still, as he put it, in excellent spirits. He did not think he and his contemporaries deserved 'particular praise for facing dangers' because young Civilians had enjoyed the excitement 'after a long grind at office work'. The men to be admired were the older Civilians who had stayed at their posts with their wives and families, men who had made supreme efforts to preserve order and keep their districts loyal. Yet they were seldom rewarded with medals as soldiers were; nor were they thanked for trying to prevent excessive retribution.*

An emergency law made 'absolute despots' of the magistrates in the rebellious districts, giving them a year's authority to hang and imprison men. Lyall duly executed a number of murderers. He believed the British had been 'so insulted and degraded in the eyes of natives by the violation and murder' of their women that vengeance was required for the restoration of their prestige. But he soon became 'soft-hearted', hating the superintendence of executions and regretting his bloodthirsty reaction to the news of the massacres at Cawnpore.

---

*Forty-two Civilians died in the Mutiny. Half of them were murdered; the rest were killed in action or died of wounds or disease. Three ICS officers received the recently created Victoria Cross, two for bravery during the retreat from Arrah, one for slipping through Lucknow in disguise and guiding the relief force to the Residency.

In the middle of the Mutiny, just after his twenty-third birthday, Lyall was promoted from Assistant Magistrate to Joint Magistrate with an increase in salary from 400 to 550 rupees. But there was less magisterial work to do than before the uprising. Petty crime had almost disappeared, and terrified Indians treated him with 'extraordinary servility' and the 'profoundest awe and reverence'. As for the money, this was of limited use because there was nothing in range to buy. Worried about forgetting all his Greek and Latin, he desperately wanted some books: he got 'perfectly furious now and then about not being able to continue a Greek quotation'. But books could not be sent across hostile country. Nor would they come even in peacetime from hostile parents. Frustrated by his mother, Lyall had finally ordered Voltaire's works himself; but the bill was sent by mistake to his father, who refused to pay it. The Reverend Alfred Lyall, who had been advising his son to give up skirmishing, was as worried about his boy's soul as he was about his life.[37]

4

District Officers

~

The Pooh-Bahs of India

INDIA, SAID CURZON, 'may be governed from Simla or Calcutta;
but it is administered from the plains'.[1] He was speaking of the
districts and the men who ran them. British India was divided into
250 districts. These were themselves divided into three or four subdivisions which were sometimes split again into a couple of *tahsils*.
They were also multiplied, a group of between four and seven districts forming a division headed by a Commissioner, which was in
turn joined to other divisions to form a province. Bengal consisted
of forty-eight districts divided into eight divisions. But the key
administrative unit was the district.

The average size of a district was 4,430 square miles – larger
than the combined area of Devon and Cornwall – which at the
beginning of the twentieth century contained an average population of 931,000. The districts of the North-Western Provinces
were usually smaller – about the size of Northumberland – while
those in Bengal were generally larger. The district of Mymensingh,
north-east of Calcutta, had a population of nearly 4 million people
spread over an area the size of traditional Yorkshire. In Madras,
where there were no divisions, the districts were larger still. Several
were more than 12,000 square miles in size – bigger than Belgium
– while the 17,000 square miles of Vizagapatam in the Eastern

Ghats made it larger than Denmark and more than twice the size of Wales.

Small stations contained about half a dozen British officials: the District Officer, a couple of subordinate magistrates, the District Judge, the Superintendent of Police and perhaps a surgeon or engineer. In the old Regulation provinces the DO, the judge and the junior magistrates were members of the ICS. Seven hundred Civilians – about three-quarters of those on active service – were concentrated in Bengal, Bombay, Madras and the North-Western Provinces. Of the 216 ICS men in Bengal, 35 were Judges, 52 were Commissioners or District Officers, and 106 were subordinate magistrates or griffins who had not yet passed their exams. The remainder worked in the secretariat of the Bengal Government and in specialized posts such as Collector of Stamps and Superintendent of Customs. In the Non-Regulation provinces, where Civilians shared administrative posts with Army officers, the ICS presence was lighter. Eighty-six Civilians belonged to the Punjab Commission, and a similar number were divided between Assam, Burma and the Central Provinces. Of the rest on active service, eighteen held posts in the secretariat of the Government of India, while twelve worked under its Foreign Office in the Political Department.*

The key administrative figure was the District Officer,† who held executive power in his district, rather than his superior, the Commissioner, whose role was essentially supervisory and whose territory was too large for him to know thoroughly. Beneath him the DO had the ICS Assistant Magistrates (one of whom after the 1860s might be an Indian) and a couple of native Deputy Collectors from the Statutory (later Provincial) Civil Service. Beneath them he had an enormous office divided into a dozen departments dealing with such matters as revenue, agriculture and education. The departments each had their head clerks and a bevy of record-keepers and other

---

*The numbers varied slightly over the second half of the nineteenth century: these are for 1886. For service in the Non-Regulation provinces, see Chapter 8; for the Political Department, see Chapters 8 and 9.

†The District Officer's title varied according to his province. In Bengal and the NWP he was Magistrate and Collector, in Madras and Bombay he was known as Collector and District Magistrate, and in the Non-Regulation provinces he was called Deputy Commissioner. His role as Collector, covering matters of land and revenue, is outlined in Chapter 5; his duties as Magistrate are described in Chapter 6.

officials, including a 'weeder', who weeded out records without long-term importance, and a 'bundle-lifter', who was in charge of the bundles of files wrapped up in squares of cotton cloth. At the bottom of the hierarchy were scores, sometimes hundreds, of messengers and orderlies, sweepers and water-carriers.[2]

One Civilian compared the District Officer to the Pooh-Bah, the Gilbert and Sullivan character who exercised every function of state except that of public executioner.[3] The DO did not run the railways or the telegraph or the Army – though he had the power to call out troops in an emergency – but he was responsible for almost everything else. Apart from his duties as chief magistrate and principal revenue officer, he was in charge of the police, the jail and the law courts, as well as the treasury, the excise and the records. He was in overall charge of forests, roads, schools, hospitals, fences, canals and agriculture. He tried, with some success, to persuade people to accept vaccination; he attempted, less successfully, to apply sanitary regulations to villages. He was responsible for law and order, government property and the implementation of new laws. He was Chairman of the District Board and of any municipalities; he managed the Government's and Wards' estates – that is, property belonging to minors, women and people mentally unfit to run them. And on top of all this he had to keep himself accessible, to allow people to come and sit on his veranda and 'pay their respects' and hand in their petitions.

It was a life regulated by inspections: inspections of dispensaries and distilleries (if there were any), of the subdivisional and registration offices, of the twenty or so police stations that covered his district, of the treasury, where he counted the notes, and also of the jail (though the health of the prisoners was the responsibility of the civil surgeon). Such a workload demanded steady routine and careful delegation. As a Collector in Orissa in 1873, John Beames started his day in *cutchery* by listening to petitions, most of them plaints in criminal cases which he passed on to his subordinate magistrates. Then came the police charge-book containing the murders, burglaries and other criminal cases sent up by the various police stations. Beames took some of them to try but passed the majority over to the Joint Magistrate. Next, after passing orders on miscellaneous matters such as ferries or cattle-pounds or the promotion of officials, he interviewed the head clerks of his departments who brought him their papers on stamps, salt, road tax or whatever, waited for their orders and then left. Afterwards he replied to letters from the Commissioner and other officials, a process much interrupted by Deputy Collectors requesting guidance. Following a quick tiffin with the Joint Magistrate and the Superintendent of Police, Beames dealt with his revenue officials and then called for petitions concerned with his duties as Collector. After dealing with them, he went home for a cup of tea and received rajas and other local dignitaries. Such a day, which usually managed to include a ride, a visit to the club and some work on his book on Oriyan grammar, was only made possible by a concentrated routine and a rigorous supervision of his subordinates.[4]

Protectors

District Officers all over India shared a similar set of responsibilities. But each province was different and each imposed an additional set of duties relating to conditions unique to its own territory. In the Punjab, where several million acres of semi-desert were irrigated from the 1890s, Civilians sometimes became Colonization Officers. After the canals had been dug, after a plan for roads and railways and villages had been made, ICS men were brought in to settle the area and organize the new communities of Sikhs, Hindus and Muslims. It was their task to select the colonists and ensconce them on square agricultural holdings of seventeen and a half acres in size; and it was their responsibility to ensure that these fragile and artificial communities remained peaceful and became prosperous.

In much of Bengal the chief problem was an excess of water. There was no need to bring more to a land through which so many great rivers and their channels sliced their way. The Brahmaputra was especially capricious, washing away villages, flooding fields and flushing out snakes from their holes. Sometimes it changed course so violently that a village suddenly found itself on the other bank. The district of Faridpur was formed by shoals of the Ganges which the river had abandoned; the area of one of its subdivisions was perennially unstable, increasing by 250 square miles in a single decade. Among the District Officers' most complicated tasks was the need to keep abreast of 'alluvial accretion', to visit all *chars* – islands formed when a river changed its course – and to decide to whom this very fertile new terrain belonged.[5]

Many districts contained mixed populations, Hindus and Muslims, nomads and peasants, Rajputs and Jats. But some also contained aboriginal tribes whose way of life had been little affected by the previous 3,000 years of Indian history. A majority of the Bhils, a hill people inclined to steal each other's wives and cattle, lived outside British rule, in Rajputana and the princely states of Central India. But as some of them inhabited the northern districts of the Bombay presidency, crimes committed there had to be investigated by ICS magistrates. It was clearly futile to try aboriginals according to the Penal Code or the Code of Criminal Procedure, so more flexible methods had to be devised. Every two years, therefore, a Bombay magistrate and a colleague from the Central Indian Agency held a border court to which they summoned the Bhils and settled the prices of the women and the rate of compensation.[6]

The British were not usually as sensitive in their dealings with tribal peoples. A large district in west Bengal, the Santal Parganas, consisted of plains inhabited by Bengali and Bihari cultivators, and hills populated by Santal aboriginals with bows and arrows. All of it was treated in the same way, subject to British courts and regulations which the Santals did not understand. Nor did they understand the concept of borrowing and interest or the way Hindu money-lenders used the courts to seize their property for non-payment of debts and thus turned many tribesmen into virtual serfs. They believed the land belonged to the people who lived on it and warned several times that they would rise up to defend their rights. As nobody listened to them, in 1855 they brought out their bows and arrows, rushed down to the plains and killed a large number of people, nearly all of them Hindus. The monsoon interfered with the suppression of the rebellion, and the subsequent repression was somewhat mitigated by the rulers' realization that they had been in the wrong. Victorians were often sentimental about 'noble savages', and the ICS liked the Santals: one Civilian considered them 'far superior in character, courage and honesty to Bengalis'.[7] As a result, the area was turned into a Non-Regulation district under the wise direction of George Yule, a good example of the old-school Haileyburian. The Bengali police were removed, the court system was abolished, along with its array of Hindu pleaders and intermediaries, and the Santals were placed under the direct supervision of British officials with instructions to deal with them according to simple, commonsensible principles of justice.

In all emergencies, man-made crises or natural calamities, the District Officer was expected to take charge and respond effectively. If a fire broke out in a bazaar in May, with the thermometer at 100° and the wind blowing in the wrong direction, there was not much he could do except rush to the scene with some engineers, order the pulling down of houses and hope that the flames would not spread. He was even more helpless in combating those disasters to which the Bay of Bengal was peculiarly prone, a cyclone that could sweep away villages and turn the mangrove swamps brown, a tidal wave that could drown thousands of people, an earthquake that would cause the river beds to rise, obstructing the drainage channels and resulting in ruinous flooding.

The DO was more successful protecting people from the dangers caused by wild animals, one of his few duties that could be a genuine pleasure. A herd of black buck ravaging the village crops gave him the opportunity of some shooting and a change of diet. Wild boar, an equivalent pest, provided similar entertainment, although Anglo-Indian pig-stickers tended to deplore it: like foxhunters, they believed their quarry should be hunted (in this case speared) rather than shot. Less enjoyable was ridding a community of bats or monkeys, or tackling herds of wild elephants on the rampage and driving them back over the border to Nepal. Another distasteful task was shooting rabid-looking pariah dogs, an activity which villagers sometimes objected to on the grounds that the animals protected them from jackals. District Officers had to balance this consideration against the danger of transmitting rabies to humans, a hazard much increased by the introduction of bicycles and the consequent glimpses of appetizing ankles. Shooting crocodiles – and opening them up to find the anklets and nose-rings of their victims – was less controversial, although the reptiles performed a useful function by devouring corpses thrown into rivers by people who, in order to save fuel, had failed to cremate their relatives properly.

About 20,000 Indians were killed annually by wild animals. Some 700 were victims of tigers, 500 of wolves, 300 of leopards, 100 of bears and 30 of hyenas. Such casualty rates once again gave an incentive to Civilians – as well as Army officers and other Anglo-Indians – to go out and hunt them; no one had any compunction about shooting a panther that carried off sheep and dogs or slow-moving old women returning from the fields. Wild animals were also killed by

Indians, who received Government rewards of 25 rupees for a tiger, 8 for a leopard and 2 for a hyena. Yet by far the most common form of death was by snake bite. The venomous Russel's viper was too sluggish to get out of the way and bit anyone who trod on it; in one district of Burma it killed more people than all the other snakes and wild animals put together. Bengal, however, was the province most afflicted by poisonous snakes: over 10,000 people were killed by them in 1878. The Government offered a reward of one rupee for eighteen snakes, and the following year tens of thousands of snake skins were brought in. But the practice was discontinued when it was discovered that natives were breeding them in pits and then killing them and claiming the reward. Another ploy involved wolf skins. One young Civilian found himself paying five rupees per skin for a large number of dead wolves before realizing that the beneficiaries were using the same carcasses over and over again, each time stuffing a newly killed jackal into the ribcage and smearing it all with fresh blood.[8]

Solomons

A strenuous test of a District Officer's skill and judgement was his handling of communal problems in his territory. He had to determine what was and what was not acceptable in the name of religion and tradition; and he had to ensure that the activities of one community did not provoke a violent reaction from members of another. The Government's policy of non-interference in religious matters – except where human lives were being blatantly taken or endangered – was a general guide. Thus the Commissioner of Orissa would not think of discouraging one raja under his control from marrying a new wife on an annual festival, but he did prevent another from continuing his family tradition of killing a man on his coronation: the chief henceforth had to pretend to kill him, and the man had to pretend to die before being taken away and exiled from the raja's territory.[9]

Human sacrifice did not present much of a dilemma, especially when a petition to sanction it on behalf of the Khond tribes arrived on a District Officer's desk.[10] More difficult was the practice of female infanticide, which was widespread in northern India, especially among

Rajput landowners. Since a nobleman could not marry his daughter into a lower caste, and since he could not afford the dowry required to marry her into his own, the solution was to have no daughters. Among some Rajput septs in the middle of the century, there were no female children at all; in many villages boys outnumbered girls by more than ten to one; for eleven generations the princely family at Bharatpur did not allow a single daughter to survive.[11]

In his post-Mutiny mood of conciliating the landowners, Lord Canning had hoped he could tackle the problem by appealing to 'their right feelings and gratitude', by consulting them and asking their advice on what measures might be taken.[12] But ten years later, when the special census of 1870 found that girls still formed less than a quarter of the infant population of the 'suspected clans', a law was passed prescribing special registration of births and special inquests into suspicious deaths. Under the vigilance of the District Officers, the killings largely ceased, though in some cases neglect – or malnutrition – was as effective an agent as murder. Nevertheless, statistics in 1893–4 showed that even in the worst areas 40 per cent of young children were now girls. Yet the policy was much resented. As late as 1897 Harcourt Butler was reporting from the North-Western Provinces that 'the prevention of infanticide is still bitterly complained of by the poorer landlords, who suffer so heavily in the marriage expenses of their daughters'.[13]

One of Butler's earliest duties had been to superintend the vast Kumbh Mela pilgrimage festival, which takes place every twelve years at Allahabad at the confluence of the Ganges and Jumna rivers: he sat on an elephant at the water's edge, watching as a million people washed away their sins. The great problem of the Hindu pilgrimages was the diseases that they spread. William Herschel, a Collector in Bengal, noticed that pilgrims going to the great Jaganath festival at Puri were robust and healthy, but that on the way back, after exposure to damp and bad food and living under trees, they were weak and sick and often dying. He realized, however, that this was not a case for interference: trying to discourage pilgrims would have been misunderstood and regarded as an attempt to subvert their religion. As Lieutenant-Governor of the NWP, Antony MacDonnell admitted he 'preferred to run the risk of the spread of plague rather than prohibit the great fairs'.[14]

Laissez-faire was not an option when a Hindu fair coincided with a Muslim festival. Then, wrote the young Butler, 'we have to take severe measures to prevent riots, riding at the head of the procession, with warrants ready signed in our pocket. It is sometimes ticklish work.'[15] One dangerous moment was Muharram, the first month of the Islamic year, when Shia Muslims commemorated the martyrdom of Hussain, the Prophet's grandson, by parading night after night with banners, torches, drums and music. A Civilian's work could be especially ticklish if the lunar calendar made the festival coincide with Dasahra, a dramatic pageant in which masked Hindus enact episodes of the *Ramayana* before burning vast effigies of demons vanquished by the god Rama.

Communal rioting increased towards the end of the nineteenth century. The spread of British rule, and the consequent loss of Muslim authority, had contributed to a revival and strengthening of Hinduism and a resurgence of Brahminical emphases on purity and pollution. One manifestation of this was the creation of cow protection societies, which may have begun as animal welfare groups but were soon in the forefront of a political anti-Muslim campaign. Militant Hindus were sent into the countryside to preach against cattle slaughter and to incite people to intimidate its practitioners and to boycott their businesses. 'Kine-killing' became an increasingly serious issue in the north of India. One Civilian was surprised to find that in Kashmir, an overwhelmingly Muslim state ruled by a Hindu prince, there were several 'life-convicts' who had already served eight or nine years for killing cattle. Another came across a Hindu kine-killer covered in a sheet and holding the tail of a cow which the Brahmins of his community had forced him to take to the Ganges and there bathe and purify himself of his sin.[16]

The anti-kine-killing campaign was specifically aimed at the festival of 'Id al-Adha during which Muslims killed an animal to commemorate Abraham's offer of Ishmael (his son by the bondswoman Hagar) on the sacrificial altar. They did not need to sacrifice a cow: a sheep or a goat or even a camel would have sufficed. But since a cow was held to be the equivalent of seven sheep or goats, poor Muslims often clubbed together to kill one. The continuance of this long-established practice so inflamed Hindu revivalist feelings that riots took place and people were killed in Bombay, Bihar and the North-Western Provinces. At the Islamic festival of 1893 thousands of Hindus rioted north of Benares in Azamgarh, confiscating cows, beating Muslim weavers to death and refusing to disperse until they received undertakings that no sacrifices would take place. Although men from the lower castes participated in the violence in Bihar and the eastern NWP, the movement's impetus came from the higher castes and wealthier classes such as the Chauhan Rajputs, who were among the arch-practitioners of female infanticide. Victims of the violence may have been puzzled by the contrast between the Rajputs' eagerness to sacrifice their own daughters and their determination to prevent the sacrifice of other people's cattle.[17]

Loath though it was to intervene in communal disputes, the Government was forced to act. Adhering to the principle that in religious matters customs should be permitted and innovations banned, the Viceroy, Lord Lansdowne, declared that the slaughter of cattle for sacrifice and food would never be prohibited. But to lessen the offence to Hindu susceptibilities, the killings should be done in a private place, and the carcasses 'should not be hawked about or exposed' to view except in a licensed shop.[18] The offence, however, was not greatly lessened, and the cow protection movement enjoyed a violent resurgence after 1910.

Both communities were provocative, even as foreign immigrants in Burma: a Civilian recounted that in 1893 Muslims had sacrificed a cow close to a temple in Rangoon, that Hindus of the town were 'ready to make mischief', and that both sides were 'spoiling for a fight'.[19] In the more traditional battleground of the North-Western Provinces Harcourt Butler noticed that even rich Muslims liked to sacrifice cows, perhaps two or three of them, to annoy their neighbours. Hindus would then react by diverting their processions to mosques, placing a pig's head by the gate and blowing conch-shells during the hour of prayer. It was the duty of the District Officer or his subordinate magistrates to make sure that a procession did not get out of hand. They might attempt this by trying to limit the number of participants and the hours during which it could take place; they could ban musical instruments or draw a chalk line across a road near the mosque and forbid Hindus to step over it. As a last resort they could station armed police outside a temple or a mosque. But such measures were not always necessary. At the end of the nineteenth century the mere presence of a white District Officer was still often enough to forestall a riot.[20]

Nuisances

To the million inhabitants of his district the DO seemed an omnipotent figure, an almost independent ruler capable of deciding their destinies. And his powers were indeed wide-ranging and profound. But his subjects did not see how fettered he was by invisible bureaucrats, how much of his time was spent compiling reports to satisfy his colleagues in the secretariat. Each District Officer had to prepare the magisterial returns by the end of the year; then he had to do the revenue returns by the last day of March, the end of the financial year. The 'report' was the crucial administrative document of British India; nothing important was supposed to be done without it. Unlucky junior Civilians were entrusted with the compilation of their province's administration report, a chore that took them about three months and ended in a volume of some 500 pages consisting mainly of statistics. But since everybody was frantically writing their own reports, people seldom had time to read anyone else's.[21]

The District Officer's routine was often upset and his workload increased by other demands from the Government. Sometimes he was required to entertain a Viceroy, to organize a visit with inspections and fireworks and triumphal arches. Sometimes he was forced to become a host to foreign royalty, for even an Orléans prince during the Third Republic had sufficient kudos to demand that the Government supply him with elephants to ride and tigers to shoot at.[22] Royal visitors from Britain, such as the Prince of Wales and the Duke of Connaught, needed even smarter entertainment, and the jubilees of the Queen Empress had to be marked by a durbar in the district that included sports, a release of prisoners, a dinner for the poor, a children's fête and general festivities with fireworks, illuminations and a magic lantern.[23]

From time to time a District Officer was called on to assist the military authorities on a grand scale. In 1864 John Beames was informed that the 'whole of the left wing of the Bhutan field force' would pass through his district and that he 'must feed them and find carriage for their baggage and ammunition'. As he was also informed that he would 'not be forgiven if a single soldier or a single bag of grain [was] delayed for a day', he quickly went to work to collect 8,500 bullock carts (nearly all the carts in his district) plus 4,500 pack bullocks and 80 elephants for use in the jungles where there were no roads.[24]

But the DO's most time-consuming extra-curricular work for the Government was the decennial conduct of the census, enumerating the entire population of India, its religions, castes, tribes and occupations. It was also one of his most difficult. Conducting the 1891 census in the North-Western Provinces, Harcourt Butler found people reluctant to respond with accurate information because they believed the count presaged increased taxation. In Bengal Nicholas Beatson-Bell came across more curious suspicions: inhabitants of Burdwan believed that the census was being conducted so that every tenth man would be sold into slavery and that houses with numbers on them would be put up for auction.[25]

Neither Haileybury nor the competitive curriculum had helped train its students in Christian religious duties. Civilians were nevertheless expected to perform religious ceremonies in places without resident clergymen: one of them nearly always had to officiate in the Sind town of Hyderabad because the rest of the local chaplain's parish lay on the other side of the Indus. If the station had no church, the DO or the Judge would read prayers in the Circuit House on Sunday afternoons. They married people and buried them. One Civilian, who as Acting DO became ex-officio Registrar of his district, even married himself to a Burmese girl, a proceeding strongly deprecated by the Government.[26]

Religious fervour diminished in the years following the Mutiny. After 1857 there were few Lieutenant-Governors like the Evangelical, Sir James Thomason, who himself conducted 'divine service' in his camp when on tour. Organized Christianity no longer played much part in the lives of men who spent half the year touring their districts without seeing a church or a priest. Alfred Lyall complained that the Service contained some 'dour Low Churchmen with a strong Scotch flavour', and the Evangelical tradition reappeared in the figure of Frank Lugard Brayne, a zealous Commissioner in the Punjab, but religious enthusiasm was rare among late Victorian Civilians. One admitted that he and his colleagues cared 'little about dogmas and doctrines' and would have agreed with Kipling's fictional Assistant Collector who thought 'one creed as good as another'.[27] They certainly did not think that India could be converted to Christianity or even that conversion was a desirable goal.

After Thomason, Civilians rarely had much time for the missionary societies. They might respect their schools and admire their

The District Officer on tour: Henry Cotton dispensing justice in Bengal

The India Office (*right*) and the Foreign Office (*left*) from St James's Park, London

Government House, Calcutta, headquarters of the Indian Empire

Simla, summer capital of the Raj

Lord Mayo (*seated, third from left*), Viceroy 1868–72, with senior officers and staff at Peshawar, 1870

Lord Dufferin, Viceroy 1884–8, with Councillors (*seated*) and Government Secretaries (*standing*) at Simla, 1888
Standing (*left to right*): Sir Edward Buck, unidentified, Sir Antony MacDonnell, Sir Mortimer Durand,
Donald Mackenzie Wallace (Dufferin's Private Secretary), General Sir Edwin Collen, unidentified, Robert Pemberton
Seated (*left to right*): Sir Charles Aitchison, Sir Andrew Scoble, General Sir Frederick Roberts (Commander-in-Chief),
the Viceroy, General Sir George Chesney (Military Member), Sir Charles Elliott, unidentified

Sir Alfred Lyall, Lieutenant-Governor of the North-Western
Provinces 1882–7

Sir John Lawrence, Viceroy
1864–9

Sir James Lyall,
Lieutenant-
Governor of the
Punjab 1887–92

Sir Lepel Griffin and his entourage at the Chichai waterfall

dedication, especially the commitment of missions working with lepers, but they abhorred the chief purpose of their presence in India –
the proselytization of the natives. Many regarded missionaries as
'pestilential mischief-makers' whom they would have liked to expel
from the land. They were both amused and angered by the ratio of
achievement to trouble caused as a result of missionary endeavour:
the missionaries made very few converts but upset a great many
people. Indians did not mind them sermonizing in churches or
teaching in schools, but they regarded it as unreasonable and aggres-
sive when they stood on street corners preaching at Hindu fairs and
festivals: the young Gandhi 'would not endure' the way that missionaries used to stand near his school, holding forth and 'pouring abuse
on Hindus and their gods'. They also resented the conversions,
which were usually made from the lowest castes and often as a result
of nutritional bribery. A convert might feel that by his adoption of
Christianity he could no longer pollute a Brahmin by touching him.
But since the Brahmin did not agree, violence sometimes broke out
between Hindus and converts, forcing magistrates to hurry out and
calm things down. Another provocative consequence of conversion
was the attempt by missionary societies to change the Hindu laws of
inheritance in favour of new Christians. The Government, more perceptive about the dangers of tampering with religion, refused to do
so, Curzon angrily rejecting the idea that 'the law of property and
inheritance [should] be broken down in order to provide an incentive
to Christian conversion'.[28]

Missionaries were not the only difficult Europeans. There were
ladies who bombarded Civilians with letters about the ill-treatment
of domestic animals. There were tramps, especially near stops on the
Bombay-Calcutta railway line, who turned up at the Magistrate's
house where they received a square meal and an escort to the nearest
station. And there were 'loafers', men who differed from tramps
because they did not like to beg and they did not like officials. They
were Englishmen who had 'gone downhill', men who slept by day
and drank by night, men who knew the bazaars and their customs in
the way that Kipling knew them. They were often people who had
deserted from the Army or left their ship at Calcutta; sometimes they
found service with a native prince and tried to fleece him. As Daniel
Dravot and Peachey Carnehan, they were immortalized by Kipling in
'The Man Who Would Be King'.[29]

The most obstreperous Anglo-Indians, however, were the planters of tea and indigo. These men led a lonely existence on their plantations in Assam or eastern Bengal or in the south in the Nilgiri Hills. Beames regarded them as a 'rough, rowdy bachelor lot', while Cotton observed that they drank a great deal of Bass beer and 'brandy pawnee'. They were often violent to their coolies and intimidating to Civilians: one tea planter threatened to shoot any official who tried to inspect his tea-garden. A District Officer was expected to defend peasant cultivators against the rapaciousness of the indigo planters, and to protect coolies from the exploitation of the tea men. Some such as Beames managed to do so. Others, overawed by the 'rough, rowdy' crowd of heavy drinkers, found it impossible to do their job without the co-operation of their fellow Anglo-Indians. Miscarriages of justice were often the result. Surveying the situation in Assam in 1901, Curzon recorded his outrage at the leniency of sentences imposed on planters found guilty of assaulting their coolies.[30]

Ma-Bap

District Officers lived solitary lives, spending year after year in small stations interspersed by an occasional month in the hills and sometimes by spells in the secretariat of a provincial capital. They saw few male compatriots and even fewer female ones. Most of them endured a debilitating climate, living half the year in extreme heat, sapping humidity or monsoons; sometimes they died or were invalided home or finally retired in broken health. Their work was hard, their achievements under-praised. They were like Kipling's official fighting a Madras famine who flushes with pleasure when his superior tells him his work is 'not half bad'.[31]

Yet few District Officers envied their colleagues in the home Civil Service commuting to their office on the 8.15 from Surbiton. Their work was hard, but there was little chance of getting bored. India may have had its monotonies: Army officers could spend years in the same barracks with the same set of men doing the same set of training exercises. But a Civilian's work was always varied. Even the unenthusiastic Lyall was on the whole glad that his chosen 'trade' was 'government on a rather grand scale'. At any rate it was preferable to doing 'mercantile or legal drudgery in England'.[32]

A Civilian's life could be exhilarating in thought as well as in action. It provided what John Buchan called 'a sense of space in the blood'. It gave men 'the joy' – in Beames's words – 'of feeling that one is working and ruling and making oneself useful in God's world'. Officials were sustained by adventure, by responsibility, by the sense that both physically and mentally they were always being tested.[33] As one retired Civilian put it in verses describing a ride of inspection one morning in the Punjab,

> I know that the world was on my shoulders
> And for just this reason my heart was light.[34]

Young Magistrates were often astonished to discover what power they possessed, what potential for good and evil they had in dozens of spheres over thousands of lives. For most of them it was compensation for what they had left behind in England. At the age of 24, reported W. Francis to his old Oxford tutor, he was in charge of 4,000 square miles and more than a million people. The work was 'real and satisfactory', he added, 'so one can't complain that one has nothing to devote one's energies to, or that one's wasting one's life'.[35]

Alfred Lyall compared the powers of a District Officer to those of an Intendant of a province under Louis XIV: both officials thoroughly ruled their districts, both corresponded with a centralizing government, and both shared similar executive, magisterial and financial duties. He also claimed that the head of a district was the best post in India: one could become a 'much higher official but never a greater potentate'.[36] Civilians were transferred too frequently in British India, but District Officers themselves tended to stay longer than their Assistant and Joint Magistrates. Few remained as long as James White, who spent eleven consecutive years in the district of Broach, but it was accepted that they should stay quite a few years, to get to know the people, to get to know the dialects, to be able to pick the right subordinates and place them in the right places. If they did these well then they might deserve to be called *Ma-Bap* ('Mother and Father'), the traditional appellation by which their Indian subjects addressed them when seeking help or submitting a grievance.

A Civilian had few greater satisfactions than to return to his district after many years and observe the improvements initiated by himself and continued by his successors. In 1877 Donald Macnabb revisited his old charge in the Punjab where he had dug (and paid for) the first canal. Then it had been 'for the most part a howling wilderness' where 'the lower men were all burglars and the shop-keepers receivers of stolen goods'. Now the canals had created an area of splendid crops and avenues lining new roads. Now cattle theft was rare, smallpox had all but disappeared, and the criminal villages were apparently devoid of criminals.[37] A few years later the more jaundiced and left-wing John Maynard tried to explain to his mother the nature and atmosphere of the ICS achievement.

> What a strange world this is, with its troubles and its dissipations, its heroisms and its sordidness; and how utterly unlike anything that English people imagine. I don't think Kipling shows you the heroic side of it unless you can read between the lines. It is so unexpected that ugly pallid bilious men and women in squalid houses and among dusty dull flat surroundings should do great things in the very midst of their querulous discontents and unideal aspirations. Probably there never was so strange and painful and wonderful and uninviting an existence lived since the world began to spin. History should do something for us for we have neither credit nor sympathy from our fellow-countrymen now.[38]

5

Campers

~

Touring the District

UNDER A TREE sits a young man at a wooden table. Fresh-faced and fair-skinned, he is wearing riding boots and a light, khaki-coloured coat. He has taken off his sola topi and placed it beside him. At his feet sits a wire-haired fox terrier with a rough white coat and brown V-shaped ears; in the background a bay Arab mare is being rubbed down by a groom. Behind him, at the door of a large, newly pitched tent, stand two *chaprasis*, Government messengers in red coats and gold sashes. On the ground near the table a trio of Indian clerks sits cross-legged with inkhorns and bundles of paper. A little further away a larger group of men have congregated, litigants and petitioners, policemen and their prisoners; they are awaiting their moment to be brought before 'the Presence' and to discover their fate.

It is as good an image of British India as any because for half the year it was the reality. The amount of time Civilians had to spend touring their districts was stipulated by the provincial governments. In Bengal, where the level of land revenue had been 'permanently settled', they were obliged to go on tour for only 120 days. But in areas where reassessments of revenue required regular inspections of crops, the Assistant Collectors often had to spend seven months in camp, setting off in early November and timing their return to their station just before the monsoon broke at the beginning of June. The 'ideal Settlement Officer' was away for even longer, never coming 'in from camp till the monsoon blows his tent away, when he swims into headquarters holding an umbrella over his records'.[1]

Seven months under canvas, seeing hardly a British soul and speaking hardly an English word, could be an ordeal for unmarried Civilians. But most of them enjoyed it, as Evan Maconochie did, for 'the feeling of always being in the open air, the constant change of scenery and faces, the nature of the work and the feeling that you are doing something for the people about you even if it is in a very small way'.[2] Going on tour was the only means of getting to know a district and its people, who talked more freely in the open about their needs and grievances than they did in an office in front of native officials. And it was good for a Civilian to leave his station, where he had spent the summer as a magistrate dealing with criminals, and go out into the countryside and see what Harcourt Butler called 'the orderly elements of the population' or 'the permanent and more agreeable side of oriental life'. Many years later, when he had become Governor of Burma, Butler reflected that 'the world seems full of hope . . . when one is in the jungle'.[3]

Methods of transport varied from province to province. In the Punjab the official, his tents and his baggage were conveyed by camels. In the foothills of the Himalayas, on the northern edge of the NWP, he might choose to walk himself but hire mules or Nepali porters for his baggage and perhaps a Tibetan pony for his wife. But in many districts of Bengal animal transport was useless – as indeed the motor car was later on. Civilians usually toured by boat or on foot using rope bridges, both of them hazardous methods when negotiating rivers full of crocodiles. Conditions in much of Burma were similar: officials went on tour in a rice boat with rowers, taking no tents and staying in monasteries and police stations.

The most common means of transport, however, was by a cart drawn by two bullocks. It was also the slowest, the vehicle travelling at two miles an hour on straight flat roads. Even Assistant Magistrates on their first cold-weather tour set off in style with about eight carts carrying their servants, tents and utensils. A Collector or a Commissioner might muster twenty-four carts, his exodus including a shorthand writer and secretary, a sub-assistant surgeon, two mounted police and several clerks as well as his personal servants.

The slowness of transport meant that many things had to be duplicated. While the Civilian sat in judgement outside his first tent, a wagon-train carrying his second lumbered off toward the next camp so that it would be ready for him in the mango grove when he cantered up in the evening. His sojourns lasted two or three days near most groups of villages and about a week by the headquarters of a subdivision.

The Government usually provided the young Civilian with two tents and a couple of *chaprasis*, who acted as his middlemen with the outer world. Together with the tents came a dining-table and four chairs, a tea-table and a sideboard, a bed, a stove and a zinc bath, a folding stand with a brass basin, and a striped cotton rug. But the official had to bring his own dog baskets – or charpoys if he had greyhounds – and his own plates and cutlery. Most bachelors ate and drank from enamel, a habit frowned on by memsahibs who considered it 'not pleasant to look at, nor palatable to drink out of, as the cup becomes too hot'. White china, however, which was its alternative, was more expensive and unlikely to remain undamaged for very long.[4]

The Civilian was more dependent on his servants on tour than he was at the station. The cook might bring a supply of potatoes but had to forage for other vegetables from the nearest village. He also bought meat from the local bazaar, though the chicken was so scraggy and tasteless that some people found it inedible without Worcester Sauce (a concoction that came originally from India not Worcestershire). A sight of the village butcher's, headquarters of the village flies, was also unappetizing, and sometimes encouraged officials to keep sheep in their camp and have them slaughtered when needed. In the Punjab in cold weather mutton could be hung for as long as a week, which ensured that it was relatively tender. Another problem was the supply of cow's milk, which was so unreliable that Civilians often preferred to take goats or buffaloes on tour with them.[5]

*

At dawn the official in his tent drinks a cup of tea and is on his horse as the sun rises, cantering along a road of rammed earth with (if it is riding country like the Punjab) a group of native officials on ponies. A District Officer on tour is especially reliant on the hierarchy of

Indian officialdom. The senior figure is the *tahsildar*, who is a magistrate with second-class powers and is also (except in Bengal) in charge of the revenue. Below him is the *patel*, the village headman who collects the revenue, the *patwari*, who keeps the village records and accounts, and the *chowkidar*, the village policeman. But the crucial official in any subdivision – even if it contains a junior Civilian – is the *tahsildar*: the District Officer gives the orders, and the *tahsildar* carries them out.

The DO and his retinue ride (or walk or row) through the countryside. They inspect roads and trees and above all the state of the fields. Farmers ask for remission of revenue because drought or a hailstorm has ruined their crops, or perhaps in an eastern district because wild elephants have eaten the local rice store. The party enters a village of brown earthen houses and talks to the *patel* and the *patwari*. The District Officer inspects the school and the dispensary. He asks questions about wells and irrigation and the state of the water supply. Sometimes he is prevailed upon to give first aid; occasionally he forces a sick person to go to hospital. When he has finished his business, the group remounts and rides to the next village.

By eleven o'clock he has finished his inspections and is back in his camp. He has a bath in his zinc tub and a large meal, a sort of late breakfast or early tiffin. By now the party of petitioners has congregated at the edge of his camp. First the Civilian tries the magisterial cases and sends the policemen and their prisoners on their way. Then he listens to the petitions, to the parties in a boundary dispute, to one man who wants a liquor licence, to another who wants a saltpetre licence, to a third whose wife has run away with her lover and taken his money with her. In some cases he adjudicates; in others he tries to persuade the parties to compromise. In any event he hopes the business won't go on too long. He has been working since dawn and would like to have the last hour of daylight for himself so that he can wander off with his gun and shoot a bird for tomorrow's supper. Out of the corner of his eye he is watching demoiselle cranes with their weird cries floating in flocks above the river. He is wondering whether to go down to the marsh after snipe, which are small and difficult to hit, or to go into the forest after jungle-fowl or even a black buck.

Nightfall finds him beside his campfire, tired and hungry but content. He is glad he is not a bureaucrat in Lahore or Allahabad.

He loves the open-air life, the cold dawns and the warm noondays; he loves the sounds and smells of the human countryside, 'the drowsy music of the Persian wheels' in the wells, the smoke of the villages, the 'wholesome smell of unleavened bread'. But he also loves the natural countryside. It has its drawbacks, the paucity of wild flowers in the plains, the shrill ascending shrieks of the brain-fever bird as it proclaims the advent of the hot weather. Yet there are few sights more attractive than a flock of emerald chestnut-headed bee-eaters, few sounds more beautiful than the fluty whistle of the golden oriole or the song of the fan-tailed flycatcher. The forests of the Western Ghats are a paradise for lepidopterists, while the strange music of a thousand frogs consoles the spirit: to some listeners the sound is 'more soothing than the song of birds'.

The Civilian pushes back his folding chair. He is anticipating his supper, a dish of scrambled eggs (known as 'rumble-tumble') and a brace of roast quail which he shot the previous evening. India is a strange country. He can love and hate it many times in the same year, sometimes in the same afternoon. And that goes also for its people. They can be the most craven, irritating and mendacious beings in the world, especially in towns and above all in the magistrates' courts. But out here in the countryside they are charming and helpful and amazingly long-suffering. He sips his brandy peg and feels very paternalistic just now: he is determined to protect his people from the tyrannies of overbearing landlords and greedy moneylenders. Yes, it is decidedly better to be out here in the open than in the secretariat with those bores and their reports and that wretched *Warrant of Precedence*.[6]

Assessing the Land

Land revenue, which had been the main source of funds for the Mughal Empire, provided the Government of India with about 40 per cent of its annual income. At the end of the nineteenth century it produced some 210 million rupees, while Customs, Excise and Stamps brought in 140 million, the Salt Tax yielded 75 million, and sales of opium 40 million. The chief items of expenditure were the Army, which accounted for nearly half the total (244 million rupees), followed by the administration (140 million) and public works (68 million).

Two systems with several variants were used to collect the land revenue. In Bombay and most of Madras the Government had systemized the existing *ryotwari*, whereby it made separate agreements with peasant proprietors who paid rent on the value of their land. In Bengal and most of the north it employed the *zamindari*, usually using local landlords to collect the rents and to pay a proportion into the exchequer.

In most places the land was reassessed every thirty years or so to take account of its changing condition. But in Bengal itself the *zamindari* settlement had been declared permanent and unalterable as early as 1793. This error not only deprived the Government of profits from increased productivity: it also imposed a class of rentier landlords on the peasantry. Lord Cornwallis, who had established the Permanent Settlement with the backing of Pitt's Government, hoped the *zamindars* would be transformed into paternalistic English squires who improved their land, looked after their tenants, built some roads and carried out the duties of local administration. Instead they usually turned out to be absentee landlords who performed none of the duties expected of them except to collect the rent. They certainly did not build roads.[7]

Settlement work was carried out by young ICS officers except in Bombay, where it was entrusted to the Survey Department, and Bengal, where there was no assessment. The prosperity of a district might thus depend largely on their judgement: few people could do more harm to so many – without using violence – than a Settlement Officer who overassessed his district. A rough rule, as one griffin was instructed by his uncle, was to make the assessment not 'so low as to encourage sub-letting nor so high as to discourage thrift and progress'.[8] The margin of error was quite small, but officials could be overruled by their Settlement Commissioner or by the province's Financial Commissioner, to whom farmers had the right to appeal. Assessments are generally agreed to have been too high at the beginning of the nineteenth century but to have been lowered to a reasonable level some time before the end.

A settlement was preceded by a forecast report from a District Officer intended to supply the provincial government with enough information to decide whether a new assessment was necessary. If it was, a Settlement Officer was appointed for about three or four years to assess a district of some two or three thousand villages. He rode around from hamlet to hamlet, surveying the crops, studying the soil, examining titles to land and the system of tenure. He was accompanied by surveyors who measured the fields with chains and theodolites and who dug holes in the earth before classifying the soil. Another member of the party was the local *patwari*, who had a large linen map on a vast scale – 64 inches to the mile – which showed even the tiniest parcels of land. A Settlement Officer was always inspecting and checking things, the state of the wells and the irrigation systems, the survey and entries in the field register, the health of the cattle, the accuracy of boundaries as depicted on the enormous map. One calculated that in the course of his work he and his assistants had had to dispose of 60,000 disputes about boundaries, inheritance, shares, mortgages, leases, sales, tenancies and transfers of property.[9] Officers also had to compile an assessment report on what they proposed to do, and later a settlement report, often several hundred pages long, on what they had done.[10] It was an immense labour, but most of them agreed with Walter Lawrence that there was

no work in the world like that of a Settlement Officer in India. He is always fighting for the people against the Government, who want more revenue: against the Forest Officer, who wants more forest and cares little for cultivation: against the money-lenders, who want more land: and against the privileged classes who want something for nothing.[11]

Harcourt Butler spent seven years as a Settlement Officer – an unusually long time – assessing two districts and part of a third in Oudh. The first required close examination of nearly a million acres of agricultural land where three rental systems were in operation: cash rents (the easiest to operate), appraisal of standing crops (the most difficult to judge) and division of the grain heap on the threshing floor, the most annoying and time-consuming because it led to pilfering and because handfuls of grain had to be taken from the heap and given to any holy man who judged this a convenient moment to pass by on his way to the temple. Butler found Brahmins the worst cultivators and most troublesome tenants. Their higher castes refused to touch a plough and then insisted on lower rents so that they could afford to employ a ploughman, and the traditional fighting castes were almost as eager to avoid labour.[12]

The District Officer was officially 'concerned with all matters affecting the condition of the peasantry'. But there was not much he could do to improve that condition while the Government favoured feudal magnates such as the *talukdars* of Oudh and the *zamindars* of Bengal. Before the Mutiny things had been different. Settlement in the North-Western Provinces had been largely carried out by Robert Bird and James Thomason, Civilians of immense energy, deep religious faith and profound hostility towards the local landlords. Thomason, Lieutenant-Governor of the NWP for ten years from 1843, was an interventionist who aimed to advance village communities by vigorous policies on education, irrigation and land settlements in their favour: he built an engineering college for Indians at Roorkee, and he did more than anyone to dig the Ganges Canal and make the Grand Trunk Road. A driven man, who even as L-G spent the cold weather touring his province in tents, he was admired by Dalhousie and inspired the new generation of Punjab administrators. But whereas the Mutiny enhanced the reputation of the Punjab officials, who had after all saved the Empire, it virtually destroyed those of Thomason and Bird, whose 'levelling' policies were blamed for the alienation of the landlords of the NWP.[13]

Canning insisted on a reversal of policy in the settlement of Oudh in 1858–9: more than 22,000 villages, some 95 per cent of the total, were placed under the jurisdiction of the *talukdars*. The Viceroy believed, like Cornwallis before him, that this class was inherently loyal and ensured stability in the countryside. The *talukdars*, he admitted, were 'rather rough diamonds', but so long as they were 'treated like gentlemen, and with confidence and patience', they were 'wonderfully tractable and apt to learn'.[14] Treating them like gentlemen did indeed keep them loyal, but the policy of not interfering with their affairs allowed them to exact the extortionate rents they needed to fund lives of pomp and extravagance, to build gaudy houses and to parade around the countryside at the head of intimidating hordes of retainers armed with stout iron-tipped clubs.

Not many Civilians sympathized with the feudal magnates; nor were they admirers of other exploiters of the peasantry such as money lenders and grain dealers, whom Butler regarded as the 'curses of the country'. But there was little they could do about them until and unless they reached positions in the Government where they could influence legislation. Antony MacDonnell, who throughout his career tried to improve 'the condition of the peasantry', had to wait until he was Revenue Secretary of Bengal before he could devise and guide the Bengal Tenancy Bill through the province's Legislative Council in 1885. Later, as Lieutenant-Governor of the North-Western Provinces, he received an extension of his office from Curzon so that he could 'round off [his] life's work in India' with a Tenancy and Land Revenue Bill.[15]

Similar moderate pro-tenant acts were passed elsewhere in the second half of the century, provoking landlords to complain that they had been deprived of their 'old customary right of enhancing rents'.[16] During the same period the magnates were also deprived of the obligations which they had failed to discharge properly: police powers, the village watch and administration of the roads were all transferred to Government officials. Meanwhile peasants received some protection from predatory moneylenders by legislation such as the Deccan Agriculturalists Relief Act of 1879 and Curzon's Punjab Land Alienation Act of 1900. Michael O'Dwyer, a later Lieutenant-Governor of the Punjab, saluted the second piece of legislation for having prevented 'the finest body of peasantry in the East' from becoming a 'landless discontented proletariat'.[17]

Limited funds and limited time made it difficult for most Civilians to play very active roles in agricultural improvements. They could give personal demonstrations of the usefulness of the wheelbarrow or exhort peasants not to waste cow-dung by burning it. It was difficult, however, to persuade them to plough the dung into their fields if they could not suggest an alternative source of fuel. A number of energetic Civilians did try to bolster the agricultural economy of their districts, but they were not always successful. William Halsey arrived as Collector in Cawnpore in 1865 and immediately persuaded the Municipal Committee to set up a model farm that invested in imported pigs, a buffalo bull, an Arab stallion and Leicester sheep; the experiment failed after four years because the inhabitants refused to break their habit of buying meat in the bazaar. In the Punjab two generations later, Frank Lugard Brayne instructed village headmen to buy iron ploughs instead of wooden ones. When these were found to be too heavy for the local bullocks, he bought expensive Hissar bulls which died during droughts and were in any case too large to manoeuvre in the small fields of the district.[18]

The problem was that ICS officers were expected to be experts on everything but were trained to be experts in nothing except certain aspects of law, political economy and Indian history. In an unusual departure the Bombay Government sent E. C. Ozanne to England to take a short course at the Agricultural College at Cirencester. He thus returned well-suited to become the head of the newly formed Bombay Agricultural Department in 1883 where he promoted a dairy industry and new methods of cultivation.[19] But generally it needed a vigorous central Government headed by a Viceroy such as Curzon before any significant improvements could be made.

Famine and Disease

The Indian Government's famine policy was seldom consistent, and as a result its record was a mixed one, ranging from the very success-ful to the wholly disastrous. After the monsoon had failed in Orissa in 1865, Civilians there warned the Bengal Government of a possible grain shortage and suggested that rice should be imported in case of famine. The provincial secretariat replied that such a policy would be 'a breach of the laws of political economy', in other words, an inter-ference with the law of supply and demand, and the following February the Lieutenant-Governor, Sir Cecil Beadon, visited Orissa and assured himself that the grain stocks were adequate. Within weeks of his departure famine began in earnest. One Civilian only realized its gravity when he found an old woman in his bathroom apparently eating his soap. A ship was finally chartered to transport rice from Burma, but its arrival coincided with the monsoon, which prevented it from landing its cargo on a coast without a harbour. At the same time floods frustrated attempts to bring food into a prov-ince without railways. Partly as a result of what Lord Cranborne, the Secretary for India, called the 'fetish' for political economy, nearly a million people died of starvation and consequent disease.[20]

In February 1874, after a seven-year absence from government, Cranborne returned to the India Office as Lord Salisbury just in time for the next famine in parts of Bihar and Bengal. No mistakes were made this time on the humanitarian side. Vast (and, as it turned out, excessive) quantities of rice were imported from Burma, while con-secutive Lieutenant-Governors (Campbell and Temple) directed successful relief operations, distributing food to the sick and elderly, and providing work, mainly road and railway construction, to the able-bodied. In a single extraordinary concession to the 'fetish', Lord Northbrook, the Viceroy and Free Trader, refused to prohibit the export of rice *from* Bengal at a time when he was importing several hundred thousand tons of rice *into* Bengal. Thus, as Campbell later recalled, 'the strange spectacle was seen of fleets of ships taking rice out from the Hooghly and passing other ships bringing rice in; often, no doubt, the same ship brought one cargo in and took another away'.[21]

The lack of casualties and the quantities of wasted rice persuaded the next Viceroy, Lord Lytton, to deal very differently with the subsequent famine that ravaged much of the south between 1876 and 1878. The Governor of Madras, the Duke of Buckingham, was determined to save human life at whatever cost. But Lytton, whose policy was 'to avert death from starvation' as cheaply as possible, condemned his extravagance and sent Temple to the presidency with instructions to restrict relief works and reduce food rations to the needy. Later he himself visited the relief camps and complained that they were 'swarming with fat, idle, able-bodied paupers'.[22] He managed to miss the millions who were dead or dying. Parsimony in famine policy, combined with an expensive and pointless war against Afghanistan, were the main features of an irresponsible viceroyalty.

Previous droughts had resulted in a number of local initiatives. Following the Guntur famine of 1833, Arthur Cotton irrigated the arid tracts of the Godavari delta and spent thirty-four years building dams and canals in the Madras presidency. After a lesser crisis in 1868, the 108-mile-long Agra Canal was dug to provide famine relief in the North-Western Provinces. But it was the tragedy of 1876–8 that led to the establishment of a general Famine Commission under Richard Strachey and the consequent adoption of a Famine Code. The Code, based on Strachey's very thorough report, made recommendations for preventing future crises and gave guidance for action in the event of a monsoon failure and a rise in grain prices. Further irrigation works and closer access to railways were designated for areas prone to drought; District Officers were given instructions about the distribution of food and the organization of relief works; tax remissions were authorized and loans were to be made available to farmers trying to recover from the drought.[23] The Code, together with a substantial sum the Government set aside annually as Famine

Insurance, persuaded many people that the problem had been solved. Such complacency was erased by the famine of 1896–7 in which the Viceroy, Elgin, displayed a lack of awareness reminiscent of Lytton, and by a still greater one in 1899–1900 that even the energetic Curzon struggled to contain. At least the Government was now more generous with aid: by the spring of 1900, 5 million people were receiving relief at the cost of £8,500,000, a gigantic effort reflected in a decline in the mortality rate to only just above the average. Three years later James Sifton, a griffin who rose to a governorship in the 1930s, described the state of tension that a famine threat instilled in Civilians during Curzon's rule.

> We are beginning to look anxiously for rain now. Only about ½ inch has fallen since I came out, and if the storms don't begin in about a week, we shall be scouring the district looking for any traces of scarcity. The one thing that a lieutenant-governor can be 'broken' over is a badly-managed famine. So he has everything cut and dried for an emergency. Every year a detailed plan for possible relief works in every district is made out by the engineer. The surveyor marks out the total area and maximum of population liable to famine. And the magistrate keeps his eye on the price of food and sends a fortnightly return on the subject. And if there is only a suggestion that the cattle or the children in any part of the district are looking thin, the magistrate flies off and usually takes the Commissioner too.[24]

Whatever shortcomings the Government may have had, famine duty brought out the best in the ICS. Shaken by the Orissa calamity, the then Viceroy, Lawrence, had announced that the District Officers' duty was to attempt to preserve every life in their districts. And all reports indicate that they did so tirelessly and uncomplainingly. One Civilian, the Collector of Firhoot, stayed at his post while his wife was dying of breast cancer; another returned to Nasik eight months before the end of his furlough and arrived just in time to bury his predecessor, who had died of bubonic plague. Hermann Kisch discovered that, of all the Bengal Civilians seconded to Madras to fight the 1876 famine, he was the only one whose health did not break down. The ICS was not the only service that suffered casualties in the fight. A memorial at Jubbulpore in the Central Provinces commemorates the five Civilians, two subalterns, one police officer and one engineer who died in the struggle to save lives in the 1896–7 famine. A decade later eight Government officials died in a famine in the former North-Western Provinces.[25]

Kisch also had to deal with the Bihar famine of 1874, six months after arriving in India for the first time. He had no idea 'how to dig a good tank [reservoir], or build a grain store, or to store grain so as to avoid injury from damp or heat'. He learned quickly. Within a month of his posting to Tirhut, the griffin had built fifteen Government grain stores and opened twenty-two relief works; he was employing 15,000 people daily and feeding 3,000 more for free.[26]

The principal problem for officials was the physical one of getting food to the afflicted areas. Railways by themselves were not the solution. Wagonloads of grain might be left rotting at a depot because there was inadequate transport to take the food to the villages. In districts where people were starving, the bullocks were unlikely to be sufficiently fit to pull heavy carts. Even if they were, they would have to be fed from their loads because famine areas obviously possessed no fodder. And even if these difficulties were overcome, there was always the danger that the carts would be looted by hungry robbers as they lumbered towards their destination. Those places where grain did not arrive often saw an increase in petty crime. When John Beames was sent to Ambala, he found the large jail crammed with people who had openly committed theft so that they would be sent to prison and get fed.[27]

A Civilian's problems did not end even after the provision of food and relief work. Kisch had to deal with Brahmins who would not eat boiled rice and who would rather die than dig a tank with common coolies. They would pray, they told him, but not work.[28] Other sufferers were reluctant to accept charity because they believed it entailed conversion to Christianity. Northbrook, who successfully managed the famine of 1874, found an even more bizarre example of resistance. The people of one district, he informed Queen Victoria, prostrated themselves before a Civilian and, 'although evidently in distress, prayed not to be relieved, protesting that they were not starving and needed no help'. They had heard, apparently, that the Government favoured emigration to Burma and, 'believing the Burmese to be cannibals with enormous mouths', they thought the administration 'had a plan to fatten up the people first & then ship them off to Burma for consumption'.[29]

One of the finest famine administrators was the abrasive MacDonnell, an Irishman without charm or humour but with much drive and pugnacity. Detested and admired in similar measure by his subordinates, he was regarded by Curzon as the ablest of the senior Civilians. MacDonnell established his reputation by his famine work and a report on relief operations in the 1870s; he consolidated it as Lieutenant-Governor of the North-Western Provinces during the famines of the 1890s. He gave District Officers discretion to spend money in emergencies without waiting for permission and told their supervising Commissioner to impress on them 'their personal responsibility in regard to starvation deaths. The system is ready and they have the funds. They cannot be held free of blame if starvation deaths occur.' Known for his sympathy for tenants' rights as well as for his ability to cope with emergencies, MacDonnell was acclaimed even by the generally hostile nationalist press.

Both Elgin and Curzon realized that the key ingredient of MacDonnell's success was co-operation not coercion. As Curzon explained to the Secretary of State, he 'invariably sends for the local leaders, gets them on his side, makes them put their names to a document embodying his policy, and thus at the same time carries through what he wants and remains free from attack'. This method was especially successful in Cawnpore in 1900 when riots broke out after five people suffering from bubonic plague were removed to a plague camp outside the town. Troops were called out after the camp was burned down and several policemen had been killed, but MacDonnell quickly arrived and ordered them back to barracks. He then sat down with local leaders and discussed the plague regulations before issuing modifications and posting them around the town. Cawnpore soon returned to normal, and only the ringleaders of the riot were punished.[30]

Cholera was an old and usually lethal scourge. Bubonic plague – the Black Death of the Middle Ages – was newer to India and thus even more terrifying. It arrived in Bombay in 1896, soon hit Poona and two years later spread to the north. Since no one then knew how it had arrived (in fact by rats in ships coming from Hong Kong) or how it could be treated, panic spread even more quickly than the disease itself. Except in Bombay, where the Army took charge, District Officers were put at the head of emergency committees consisting of doctors, sanitary commissioners and inspectors of hospitals. They and their assistants descended on towns and villages, sending the infected population to emergency camps, pouring white-wash over the house walls and perchloride of mercury on to people's possessions. In his second year in the ICS Montagu Butler found himself in charge of emptying ten plague-stricken villages and providing huts, wells, shops, food and rudimentary hospitals for their inhabitants.[31]

Civilians dealing with plague and cholera behaved even more courageously than they did on famine duty, living among the victims, burying the corpses after the sweepers had fled, and sometimes catching and dying of the disease themselves.[32] But in their anxiety they were inclined to be a little overzealous, and their heavy-handed measures caused resentment and led to rioting. Indians were outraged by personal inspections by doctors, by British troops searching their houses for suspected plague cases, and by restrictions on how and where their dead should be buried. When an Assistant Collector in Surat ordered that a maximum of fifteen mourners should take a corpse to a distant mosque, he was defied by 3,000 Muslims who insisted on accompanying the body to its last resting place.[33]

British officials justified extreme measures on the grounds that 'native agencies' were so incompetent that they were doing nothing to prevent the plague from spreading. An officer of the Army Medical Service advised W. C. Rand, the Assistant Collector of Poona, to use only British troops to conduct house-to-house searches for hidden plague corpses. He did so, restricting Indians to the role of interpreters to explain to the population what the Army was doing. Shortly afterwards Rand and a colleague were assassinated by Hindu revivalists who claimed that the anti-plague precautions outraged the religious susceptibilities of the people.[34]

Such feelings were widespread. When the Collector of a district in Bihar proposed at a public meeting that urban committees should be formed to supervise sanitary measures, a Hindu speaker condemned the proposal as useless because God had sent plague among them as a consequence of their sins: all that was required for the disease to disappear was that Hindus, Muslims and Christians should respectively obey the teachings of the Shastras, the Koran and the Bible. In Bihar and the east of the country, where the plague was weaker but the outrage was almost as strong as in Bombay, officials were ordered to show restraint: if the Bihari people believed the Government was trying to kill them with disinfectants, then they must not be compelled to use them; if they thought that pouring Condy's fluid down wells did not purify the water but turned it into poisoned blood, then the fluid must not be poured.[35]

Still further east, the fear of riot paralysed the Bengal Government of Sir John Woodburn, who refused to follow the example of Bombay. He did not move people or segregate them or force them into hospitals; in fact he did virtually nothing except disinfect rooms in which deaths had occurred, a posthumous precaution to which nobody objected. His circumspection was fostered by the Bengalis' belief that they were not suffering from plague but from endemic fever. Curzon muttered that Woodburn was an 'amiable, weak-kneed, sensitive, obstinate old gentleman' who hated being interfered with and would do anything 'to keep in with Native sentiment'. But since the Lieutenant-Governor's remedies seemed no more ineffective than the opposite ones pursued by Bombay, Curzon for once did not interfere with the policies of a subordinate. Even so, his private opinion was that the Bengal method was 'the abnegation of all authority'.[36]

Jungle Wallah

The Government of India had its own Forest Department,* but Civilians were expected to look after the forests of their own districts. For some of them trees became a passion. One Irish official regarded pruning a branch almost as tantamount to amputating an arm: while making a road, he would either divert it to save a tree or, if this was not possible, leave the tree standing in the middle of the road.[37] Most Civilians were less sentimental but they recognized that the preservation of woods was crucial to the economic and environmental health of their districts.

Benjamin Heald, the Deputy Commissioner of a district on the

---

*In the nineteenth century this department was mainly run by German experts, who were regarded as more scientific and knowledgeable than British arborists. Three Germans, Dietrich Brandis, William Schlich and Berthold Ribbentrop, were successively Inspectors-General of Forests from 1864 to 1900. Despite his later Germanophobia, Kipling made a sympathetic character of a German forestry official in his story 'In the Rukh'.

Irrawaddy, was sent on special duty to areas where Burmese villagers were cutting down forests so quickly that vast quantities of soil were being washed away by the rains. The result was that, in place of streams irrigating their land, torrents now hurtled on to the plains and inundated their homes. Heald's duty was thus 'to protect the villagers against themselves'. He calculated how much of the forest they required for their necessities – the acreage needed for grazing their cattle, for gathering frogs and snails and other food, for supplying bamboo for their house walls and leaves for their roofs – and closed the rest for long periods, especially during the season of forest fires.[38]

William Henry Horsley, a Civilian from 1870, spent much of his early career as a forest settlement officer, demarcating the woods of the Bombay presidency. The work delighted him, for he enjoyed neither books nor society. He was 'fond of a hard bodily exercise, of a good horse and a good rifle'. When he was at Poona, one of the presidency's three capitals, he forced himself to spend 'an hour or two' at balls 'in the hope of rubbing off a little of the jungle rust'. But such occasions bored him as they would 'naturally bore a man who doesn't dance and isn't in love with anyone there'. It was much better to be creeping 'about the jungle all eyes and ears' than 'ambling blandly at a ballroom'. Yet at least Poona had a boat club and a regatta which he could organize; and girls who terrified him on the dance floor sometimes made excellent coxswains.

After his apprenticeship as a griffin, Horsley became a jungle wallah serving two masters, his Collector in revenue matters and the Conservator of Forests in most others. His job was to demarcate forest reserves and to make maps, to inspect jungles and to submit plans and budgets. It was a 'very Bedouin sort of life', extending even to travel by camel, although, since the grass was often eight or ten feet high, he sometimes wished he could have afforded an elephant. But he loved his existence. When offered a deskbound job presaging early promotion, he turned it down because he preferred 'knocking about his jungles in stained brown raiment, rifle in hand, often from early dawn to sunset, eating his breakfasts under a tree by the side of a running stream'. He liked nothing better than to be camping in a remote tribal area: his life he described as 'a kind of prolonged solitary picnic with a certain amount of official correspondence to fill up the hot midday hours'.

Unconfined to a single district, Horsley could work in the plains in the cold weather and move up to the hills in the spring. In the uplands he lived among the Bhil tribal people, who regarded him as a doctor and asked his advice about toothache and other ailments. Lower down, in what he called the 'tame' districts, he occupied himself in preserving old woods and planting new ones of teak and bamboo. He spent his mornings in the saddle, his afternoons in talk and correspondence, and his evenings with a gun in his hand and his greyhounds bounding in front of him.

At the beginning of June, after eight months' travelling on his camel, Horsley would be back in the station, unpacking his panther skins and other trophies and sending them away to be tanned. The District Officer, the Assistant Magistrate and anyone else on tour would return at the same time, just before the rains, and they would all sit down and ask each other what they had shot: 'the talk was tiger almost uninterruptedly'. Then they would wonder how they were going to while away their leisure moments before they all set out again at the end of October. Were there any pigs to stick? Were there any jackals for coursing? Did anyone have good sporting dogs? For the moment the weather was too awful to do anything but play a little light croquet in the evenings. But soon they would have 'a rush after pig' or set the greyhounds at the jackals. And by September they would be able to play cricket or challenge subalterns from the Poona Horse to a race over hurdles.

Horsley was twice seconded for famine work in Bengal but was delighted to return to his forests afterwards. In 1876 he told his father that a promotion block in the Bombay Service would prevent him marrying for a long time: a low salary not misogyny was the cause of his abstinence. But soon afterwards he acquired a wife called Mary and then a baby called Dolly. Fortunately his new family liked forest inspections and hunting expeditions and travelled with him everywhere: in one month they set up camp in fifteen different places. The unambitious Horsley must have been one of the most contented men in the ICS. After eleven years in his forests he told his father that he and Mary were 'very happy' and had 'everything [they] could reasonably wish for'.[39]

6

Magistrates and Judges

~

Crimes and Witnesses

T HE EARLY HISTORY of the administration of law in British India
is a confusion, a narrative of constant changes in the nature of
courts, their functions, the law they administered and the officials
who administered them. But for the work of the Victorian ICS there
are two crucial moments. The first is 1831, when the division of
powers in the districts of the Bengal presidency was fixed: the Judge
became the District and Sessions Judge, but his magisterial functions
– and control of the police – were transferred to the Collector or
District Officer. The second is the period between 1859 and 1861
during which two separate judicial systems – hitherto administered
by the Company and the Crown – were merged under the Indian
High Courts Act. At the same time Muslim criminal law was replaced
by Macaulay's Penal Code, and the Codes of Civil and Criminal
Procedure were put in place.

The Collector and Magistrate had many different functions, but
for his main two he also possessed different personas. He had separate offices for them, staffed by separate sets of clerks who enjoyed
acrimonious correspondence with each other. One District Officer
'used to find drafts of letters from myself as Magistrate to myself as
Collector accusing myself of neglect and delay, and some very tren-
chant replies placed before me for signature'.[1]

Individual magistrates from the ICS or the subordinate services handled the original criminal work. If the police brought in a suspected thief, the magistrate examined the evidence to see if it justified a committal. If it did, then he or one of his colleagues tried the offender in their judicial capacity and, unless new evidence had emerged, they were likely to convict him. It was not a very satisfactory system for a Civilian to combine the functions of detective, magistrate and judge – especially if he had to rely for much of his evidence on the corrupt Indian police force. But at least his judicial powers were limited to imprisonment for two years and a fine of 1,000 rupees. And there was always the right of appeal.

Nothing in a Civilian's life was more difficult, tedious and frustrating than the hours spent trying to analyse fabricated evidence. A vast amount of his time was consumed by people who, no longer able to fight their neighbours without consequences, brought false cases against them instead. One DO noted that in Bengal the word 'straight' also meant 'stupid', implying that a 'straight man' was someone who had 'not the wit to be crooked'. Another, realizing that the ordinary court oath was no deterrent to perjury, made Hindus swear on a bottle of Ganges water and Muslims put their hands on the Koran and swear by the beard of the Prophet. It made no difference. The truth could only 'be dragged out' of a witness by 'a corkscrew of examinations' – and only seldom then.[2]

Delay in a case made the magistrate's task much harder, for it allowed witnesses on both sides to mingle and bargain: 'Witnesses forget what they have seen or change sides and make up their minds to give evidence for the accused instead of against him.' Well-known characters in Bengal were the 'tamarind-tree witnesses' who gathered under the tree outside the court and learned the right lines. Energetic magistrates soon realized that the key to a successful prosecution was to make 'secret enquiries on the spot, when people are off their guard, and not engaged in the pleasant game of deceiving magistrates and ruining their enemies'. As a District Officer, Richard Temple used to 'gallop to the spot and interrogate the witnesses, before their truthfulness should be tarnished, and before they could be instructed by anyone as to what tale they should tell in Court'.[3]

'Galloping to the spot' – or in James Sifton's case bicycling to it – was the best way of getting at the truth. As the young Civilian told his father:

There was a case of assault before me. A said that B's goats entered his garden and spoiled a young mango tree, and as he was driving them to the pound, B came up and assaulted him and rescued the goats. A had made a fairly consistent case, and I was inclined to believe his story was true. But B said he had no goats and A had no mango tree . . . [Deciding to investigate] I got on my bicycle and started off; it was a village of Mohammedans about 5 miles from Bhagalpur. When I got there I found both parties and about 50 of their friends waiting for me. In the garden I found a mango graft stripped of leaves and miserable. But the earth on the top was slightly disturbed. So I called for a 'kodali', a sort of pick-axe spade, and went down to the roots. The underneath soil was soaked with water and the tree had plainly been planted for my benefit that morning. I then looked at the buds that were broken off. The sap was still sticky; and that settled the question of the mango tree. I got hold of two of B's next-door neighbours and asked if B had any goats. They both told me he had none . . . I went home quite satisfied and next day dismissed the accused and made the complainant pay him compensation for bringing a false case against him.[4]

Spoiling a mango tree was an unusually harmless crime in northern villages which – perhaps because of the British belief in the 'mild Hindoo' – enjoyed an undeserved reputation for tranquillity. In much of the Punjab the favourite crimes were robbery, cattle-theft, abduction of women and, in the hot weather, homicide. Next door, in the North-Western Provinces, the criminal season peaked at harvest-time when cultivators made 'desperate onslaughts . . . on each other's crops', and landlords and their retainers clashed with their tenants, the combatants fighting it out with long heavy clubs loaded with iron at the end. Alfred Lyall was astonished at the way these 'tall wiry men' worked themselves up into 'fearful passions, and then go to work, utterly regardless of any legal consequences'. Further east, in Bengal, the people waited for the interval between the harvest and the new sowing when, as John Woodburn reported, 'the whole mass of the agricultural population has leisure to fight out its quarrels and revenge itself on its enemies'.[5]

Adultery was naturally the cause of much violence, although attitudes varied in different parts of the Subcontinent. In the Punjab and elsewhere in the north the consequence was often the murder of the wife and her lover: one of Richardson Evans's early cases was to investigate a Rajput who had murdered his mother and the *zamindar* in whose arms he had found her. Among the more primitive Bhils, however, the attitude was calmer: instead of killing his supplanter, a cuckold wanted him to pay his bride price so he could acquire another wife. At Mandi in the mountains north of Simla, reported one Civilian, elopements were 'the rule of married life', neither party objecting to reconciliation at the end of an affair. But a more common reaction in the rest of India was cutting off the nose of a wife who was unfaithful or suspected of infidelity.* This had the literal logic of having one's nose cut off to spite one's – and one's husband's – face. It didn't matter if the woman was no longer attractive to her husband; she was hideous to other men, even if she managed to get her nose sewn back on. The provincial administrations tried to stamp out this custom everywhere, even in the native states under their jurisdiction. But they had little success. The Bombay Government attempted to persuade its Judicial Assistants in Kathiawar to impose deterrent sentences on nose-cutters. But as one of the officials explained,

> after the first few months no Judicial Assistant ever did . . . He was only the president of a court that consisted of 4 Indian gentlemen besides himself, and they always sympathized with the husband. In the end every Judicial Assistant, including myself, was converted to their view. The peasant had paid a considerable sum of money for his bride, and he expected her in return to be faithful. If she was not, he could not send her away, for he could not raise the money to buy another. He therefore took the only course open to him to ensure her fidelity. He disfigured her.[6]

Conviction and Punishment

Magistrates were expected to achieve a high percentage of convictions in their own courts. If their success rate fell below half, they risked being judged 'weak and sentimental' by their superiors, the District Officer and the Commissioner.[7] But trying a case of elephant theft with 150 witnesses might be too bewildering for anyone to

---

*The origins of this punishment, which has a long history, appear to lie in the ancient Hindu epic, the *Ramayana*. After the giantess Surpanakha fails to seduce Rama and tries to swallow his wife Sita, her nose is cut off by Rama's half-brother, Lakshman.

reach a decision. Cases that went to a higher court before a judge were often even more complicated; and in those places where a jury system had been introduced, the chances of conviction were generally low.

The main problem was the police. They had acquired such a reputation for bringing false cases against people they wanted to put in jail that nobody trusted them, least of all the judges. One judge in Bengal was prone to acquit in cases where police evidence was crucial: if a prisoner confessed, he believed the confession had been extorted by the police; if stolen property was found, he suspected it was a police plant. Even if a witness claimed to recognize the culprit, this particular judge tended to dismiss the evidence on the grounds that nobody could recognize anybody during the confusion of a *dacoity* (a gang robbery). So distrusted were the police that senior judges were given powers unknown to their colleagues in Britain: they could demand to see the police diary containing all the facts and statements on the inquiry.[8]

Juries were present in cases in the High Courts and were introduced into some Courts of Session, though in most of the latter a judge was assisted by 'assessors' whose opinions were not binding. One Civilian recorded that Bengali juries were willing to convict in cases of dacoity and house-breaking with violence but reluctant to do so in cases of forgery and perjury. Another found it was almost impossible to find a verdict against a Brahmin, especially if it was a murder case carrying a capital sentence. When Andrew Fraser remonstrated with an assessor for favouring the acquittal of a palpably guilty Brahmin, the man blamed him and the British in general for forcing him to choose 'between the sin of saying what [he] believed to be untrue, and the infinitely awful sin of causing the death of a Brahmin'.[9]

Executions had to be attended by a magistrate, usually a junior one, whose macabre duty included going to the jail, identifying the right man and fulfilling a last request: in Burma this often meant handing him a coin to pay for his crossing of 'the Burmese equivalent of the River Styx'.[10] Civilians, especially in the Non-Regulation provinces, were sometimes required to carry out additional unpleasant tasks in the cause of deterrence. Ghazis were Muslim fanatics who believed they could reach Paradise by slaughtering unbelievers: after a murder or attempted murder they were therefore executed in such a way that made Paradise unlikely, even if this meant hanging them with a pigskin around their shoulders.[11]

Death sentences could be passed by Sessions Judges but they had to be confirmed by a High Court. Even after confirmation a condemned man could be pardoned – or his sentence commuted – by provincial governments or the Viceroy. Many judges preferred the alternative of transportation for life to the Andaman Islands, a British territory to the south of Burma in the Bay of Bengal. Many convicts disagreed. After the commutation of death sentences on two Bengali murderers – a mother and daughter who had murdered the young second wife of their husband/father – the guilty women beseeched the judge to hang them rather than send them across the seas. When a prisoner sentenced to transportation begged to be hanged instead, George Campbell had to 'tell such a man that the sentence was given him as a punishment and not to please him'.[12]

In one tragic case the practice backfired. Walter Lawrence related how a Pathan killed a man in a blood feud according to the rules of *pakhtunwali*, the custom of his tribe, but unfortunately he did so a few yards inside the frontier of British India. He was condemned to death, which he welcomed, but his sentence was commuted, which he deplored. Furiously he begged for execution and threatened revenge if he was sent over the 'black water' to the Andamans. A few years later, during a viceregal visit to the penal colony, he murdered Lord Mayo, one of the most successful and sympathetic of all Viceroys.[13]

The 'Judgey' Side

The law courts of British India had a massive amount of work to process. Nearly 2 million people were arraigned each year in the criminal courts; and nearly 3 million suits were brought annually before the civil courts.[14] A complex network of judges with different duties and courts with different functions was required to deal with them.

The great majority of cases were tried by Indian judges, by *tahsildars* (second- or third-class magistrates) in criminal justice, and by subordinate judges or *munsifs* in matters of civil justice. A good number of criminal cases came before the magistrates of the ICS but, as they possessed only limited powers of sentencing, the most serious went up to the Sessions Court. Murder cases, for example, were tried by a Sessions Judge, an ICS officer who in his other capacity as District Judge also dealt with the most important civil suits. He had original jurisdiction in serious cases and heard appeals from magistrates and subordinate civil judges in others.

Above the District and Sessions Courts were the High Courts of Calcutta, Bombay, Madras and Allahabad, and the Chief Courts of Lahore and (from 1900) Rangoon. Replacing the Supreme Court and the Company's courts, these had appellate jurisdiction over the civil and criminal courts of the province; they also had original jurisdiction within the municipal boundaries, though minor cases usually were dealt with by the Courts of Small Causes.* The High Courts still stand, vast monuments to the Victorian rule of law garbed in the most extravagant forms of architectural eclecticism, Flemish Gothic in Calcutta, Venetian Gothic in Bombay, Indo-Saracenic in red sandstone soaring above the Esplanade at Madras.

The ICS ran the judiciary at district level. But by contrast with its position in the administration, it did not dominate the highest ranks of the law. It was given a third of the appointments to the High Courts but never the top post, the Chief Justice. George Campbell railed against this limitation, condemning as 'clap-trap' the idea that only trained lawyers – those who had passed through the Inns of Court – were fit for the job.[15] But in fact Civilians, whatever experience they had gained as District and Sessions Judges, were not highly qualified: very few of them had a law degree. The other two-thirds of the bench consisted in equal numbers of barristers and advocates from Britain and lawyers who had practised in India, usually as pleaders of a High Court. These provisions gave Indians a more considerable role in the judicial life of their country than they enjoyed in the executive branch. Canning appointed an Indian judge to the Calcutta High Court as soon as it was constituted; Alfred Lyall did the same in Allahabad as soon as he became Lieutenant-Governor. The British appreciated Indians as judges rather than administrators and encouraged native Civilians to opt for the judicial arm in the middle of their careers. As judges Indians could hardly be a threat to the stability of

---

*In smaller provinces without a High Court, equivalent powers were exercised by a Judicial Commissioner.

the Empire. 'I am not afraid', remarked Sir Charles Wood, 'of being turned out of India by the ermine of the judgment seat.'[16]

About an eighth of the Civilians on active service were judges, nearly all of them in the Regulation provinces. Bengal had 35, including 6 in the High Court and 27 as District and Sessions Judges. Bombay possessed 20, Madras and the North-Western Provinces had 25 each. They were well paid. A District and Sessions Judge of the first grade earned 30,000 rupees a year, more than the Collector, the head of the district, who in the same grade received only 27,000. A Puisne Judge of the High Court had a salary of 48,000 rupees, considerably more than Commissioners or Chief Secretaries of provincial governments.

No Civilians started off in the judicial branch or 'judgey' side as it was known. They all began as Assistant Magistrates in the Regulation Provinces or Assistant Commissioners in Burma, Assam, the Punjab or the Central Provinces. But after ten years or so about a quarter of them, generally the less able and the less energetic, either opted for – or more usually were pushed towards – the 'judgey'. In the Company days, Hunter observed in his novel *The Old Missionary*, 'the District Judges were for the most part heavy elderly gentlemen, who had not made their mark in the more active branches of the administration'. The situation did not change after the introduction of competitive examinations. Magistrates in their late thirties who were deemed to have lost their zest or their health were ruthlessly 'promoted' to a judgeship. In the famine of 1874 the Collector of Bogra was removed from his post and appointed Judge of Rungpore because, although a 'highly educated and most worthy man', he was not – according to his Lieutenant-Governor – 'a man of action, and [was] unfortunately situated as the Collector of a district in time of trouble'.[17]

During the 1870s provincial governments initiated a new policy of forcing Civilians of ten or twelve years' service to choose between spending the rest of their careers as administrators or setting up as judges. Before then there had been a certain amount of flexibility. In 1862 Campbell had sandwiched an acting judgeship in the Calcutta High Court between the judicial and financial commissionership of Oudh and the chief commissionership of the Central Provinces. At a lower level Robert Moss King in the NWP had been allowed to officiate as a judge in the summer and spend the cold weather as a District Officer in camp. But a promotion block, the result of over-recruitment in the 1860s, persuaded provinces to encourage Civilians to opt for the judicial branch; otherwise they might reach early retirement age (twenty-five years' service) without getting beyond the rank of First Assistant Collector.[18] It was a difficult decision for many, a matter of choosing the less unappealing option: spending nearly all the year in a stuffy courtroom or touring villages in middle age, long after the novelty and excitement of camping had worn off. In many cases it boiled down to a question of promotion prospects. By 1884 William Horsley had spent fourteen happy years as a jungle wallah in his beloved forests of Bombay. But now he had a wife and two children to look after – and a promotion block in his way. When two judges in his province died suddenly, he saw prospects opening in the 'judgey' – and accepted a judgeship in Ahmedabad.[19]

It was a strange system to pitchfork a magistrate into a judge's chair without requiring him to have a law degree or any special training apart from what he had picked up in his magisterial work. He might have been placed for a few months under a senior District Judge who could have taught him how to write judgements; he could have been sent to sit with the ICS Judges of the High Court and learn how to draft decisions on appeals. Instead he was made to preside over a Sessions or District Court before he had been able to grasp the intricacies of judicial work. It was thus hardly surprising if an inexperienced judge was tripped up by nimble Bengali lawyers and pilloried in the press for his incompetence.[20]

Yet once a judge had managed to get on top of his work, he usually enjoyed a life of more leisure and less stress than that of a District Officer. He did not tour and he did not go on circuit. His day's work ended with the closing of the courtroom door, while a Collector was conscious that every day ended with a hundred things still to do. The judge had fixed hours and therefore free time for his other interests. Charles Kincaid could work on his three-volume history of the Marathas as Judge of Satara but not when he was working in the Bombay secretariat. While Judge of Tanjore in Madras A. C. Burnell was able to pursue his studies as one of the great Sanskrit scholars of his time. His work on South Indian palaeography won him an international reputation, an honorary doctorate at Strasbourg University and membership of the Royal Danish Society, the Batavian Society and the American Scientific Society. It was quite a record for a Civilian who died at the age of 42.[21]

Yet a judge's life in a small station was lonely as well as sedentary. Magistrates could live in 'chummeries', but the judge could not share with them or with the Superintendent of Police in case they contaminated him with their views on a current trial. Besides, the judge occupied the station by himself during the seasons when the magistrates were on tour and only saw his colleagues in the hot weather. William Horsley once pitied the poor judge at Dhulia, a 'particularly miserable little place' and 'one of the penal settlements' for Bombay's Judicial Department. Ten years later, after he had joined the 'judgey', he found himself posted there, living entirely alone because his colleagues were on tour and Mary, who was pregnant, had temporarily taken the children off to the healthy climate of Poona. In such circumstances judges did sometimes take to drink or even go mad, as one of Horsley's predecessors did in the 1870s. But the phlegmatic former jungle wallah was made of stouter stuff: he regarded Dhulia as 'a first-class place . . . for wearing out old clothes and otherwise saving money to spend in pleasanter places'.[22]

Furore over Ilbert

The powers of the judiciary were not normally a subject that greatly exercised India or indeed Anglo-India. Invasions of Burma or Afghanistan, cotton tariffs, income tax, questions of plague and famine, problems of military indiscipline – all these were capable of stoking passions and creating frenzies. But not usually the law. Yet in the 1880s a Bill aiming to correct an anomaly in the legal system provoked a spectacular case of Anglo-Indian collective hysteria.

Before 1872 all British-born subjects facing criminal charges were tried in the High Courts of the presidency towns. In that year the Code of Criminal Procedure was amended so that they could be tried in places where they lived by British District Magistrates or Sessions Judges; and in 1877 the restrictions on Indian magistrates trying British subjects in the presidency towns were removed. By 1883, when a few Indian Civilians were nearing the ranks of District Magistrate and Sessions Judge, it seemed logical to end the discrimination that prevented them from trying British subjects outside the three major cities. After Behari Lal Gupta, one of the first Indians to pass the ICS exam, had raised the issue with the Bengal

Government, the point was incorporated into a bill named after the Legal Member of the Viceroy's Council, Courtenay Ilbert, the Bursar of Balliol whom Jowett had urged to go to the Subcontinent and to make the most of his 'real opportunity . . . of benefiting the natives of India'.[23]

Lord Ripon, Gladstone's Viceroy who 'rejoiced to say that the effect of despotic power' was to make him 'more Radical every day', saw no problem with the Bill.[24] It seemed logical to him and his Council and to the provincial governments as well. But it was not logical to Anglo-India, especially when Ilbert, a conscientious liberal, suggested extending the Bill to include a broader category of Civilians, Indian as well as British. Businessmen, barristers and other members of the non-official community were indignant, particularly in Calcutta where petitions were organized, protest meetings were held and a Defence Association was set up. Tea planters of Assam were especially outraged. Accustomed to maltreating their coolies – and being dealt with leniently by British magistrates – they now contemplated the abhorrent prospect of a coolie bringing a trumped-up charge against his employer, an Indian magistrate believing it, and the planter going to jail.

Ilbert believed that the furore was not directed against the Bill itself, which was a 'very small measure, but against the policy . . . of admitting natives to the civil service'.[25] Anglo-Indians took a more emotional view. The cry went up that the liberties of British subjects were at risk, that as a result business investment was being threatened, and – most emotive of all, designed to resurrect memories of the Cawnpore massacres – that the Englishwoman was in danger. If Hindus kept their women in purdah – so ran the argument – they should not be in a position to judge free white women. Although senior Civilians – especially the Liberals among them – rejected such views, their wives sometimes disagreed with them. Henry Beveridge, a District Judge whose liberalism and Bengali sympathies may have frustrated his ambitions for the High Court, supported Ilbert. But his second wife Annette, who had gone out to Bengal before marriage to set up a non-denominational school for Indian girls, published a letter in the press denouncing 'the proposal to subject us to the jurisdiction of native judges [as] an insult'. She was not, she claimed, activated by 'pride of race' but by 'pride of womanhood', by resentment at the intention 'to subject civilized women to the jurisdiction of men who have done little or nothing to redeem the women of their own races, and whose social ideas are still on the outer verge of civilization'.[26]

Astonished and upset by the vehemence of the opposition, Ripon floundered about, wondering how to modify the Bill, hoping that the House of Commons and the Government in London would relieve him of the problem and solve it themselves. At the end of 1883, after feverish discussions in the Viceroy's Council, a compromise was found, heavily weighted in favour of the Bill's opponents. Ilbert's more radical proposals were dropped and, while the principle of Indian judges trying British subjects was maintained, it was in practice largely negated by the concession that the accused could insist on trial by a jury, at least half of whose members would be British.

7

Black Sheep

~

Drunks, Debts and a Lunatic

IT WAS NOT easy to pass into the ICS through competitive exams. But once a man was in the Service and had arrived in India – out of reach of the Civil Service Commissioners – it was difficult to throw him out. Almost the only guaranteed cause of dismissal was financial corruption. Criminal offences or the 'grossest kinds of misconduct' would be punished by expulsion, but these were extremely rare. Toleration extended to all but the most serious cases of alcoholism, insolvency, lunacy, incompetence, insubordination and sexual misbehaviour. Demotion by a grade or so was a much commoner punishment than dismissal. During the Mutiny the conduct of William Tayler, the Commissioner of Patna, was criticized as alarmist, panicky, muddled and irresponsible. But he was only downgraded to the level of District and Sessions Judge, and it was his refusal to accept the post rather than his behaviour that led to his suspension from the Service.

Gladstone believed that one whisky and soda a day was sufficient for a man in India. For someone who served claret at his mid-morning breakfasts, this was rather puritanical and unfeeling advice. Most Civilians drank a little more than a solitary whisky (a burra peg), but it is surprising that they did not drink a great deal more. Remarkably few took to the bottle, even District Judges stuck by themselves in a small station while all their colleagues were on tour. Loneliness and insomnia were sometime combated by a 'peg' of brandy, and occasionally a young Civilian encountered a Collector who was 'drinking his brains away'. As a griffin Maurice Hayward stayed with George Waddington, a Collector who was one of 'the last of the old Haileybury' types, 'a disappointed man who had forfeited further promotion by inability to withstand liquor. He was however kept straight by his good and masterly wife.'[1] A Sessions Judge of Poona, Thomas Fry, was not alas kept straight by anyone. Usually drunk on the bench, he invariably summed up in favour of acquittal so that defendants had no cause to appeal, and therefore the High Court had no reason to examine the feebleness of his work. One result was that the Kolis, an aboriginal people from the Konkan coast, were able to form robber gangs that ravaged the northern part of the district with impunity. Eventually the Superintendent of Police reported the matter to the Bombay Government, and an investigation led to Fry's transfer to Satara and temporary demotion to the post of Assistant Judge. After his successor had convicted and transported eighty Kolis to the Andamans, the tribe gave up *dacoity*.[2]

If a griffin left a college bill or some other debt unpaid after leaving England, his creditor sometimes petitioned the India Office for payment. The reply stated that it was 'the invariable rule of the India Office not to interfere in the private transactions of Indian officers'.[3] Misappropriation of funds would have been something to investigate but not personal debts, unless claims were made for the maintenance and education of a Civilian's family.

Even in the latter case the India Office was disposed to be tolerant. Only in 1879, after receiving applications of debts for five years, did the Secretary of State, Lord Cranbrook, demand an explanation from W. A. Howe, a Civilian in the NWP, as to why he was 'wilfully' neglecting to support his wife and family in England. Howe explained that he and his wife had separated nine years earlier, that he had given her the considerable income of £500 – later rising to £780 – for her expenses and those of their children's education, and that she had spent all the money on herself, repeatedly getting into debt and refusing to pay the school bills. The Government of the NWP accepted the explanation and reported to London that Howe had been 'unfortunate in his domestic relations' but was now doing all he could to 'extricate himself from the difficulties in which he

[had] been plunged by his wife's extravagance'. The Secretary of State also accepted the explanation but started to show impatience when unpaid school bills continued to arrive at the India Office. Eventually Howe's health broke down, and he was allowed to return to England on medical certificate to recover his fitness and settle his financial affairs.[4] But none of this affected his career. In the midst of his troubles he was promoted to the post of Collector and six years later took early retirement.

Cases of insanity were quite common among British soldiers and sailors serving in India but were very rare in the ICS. One Civilian certified for lunacy was T. J. Maltby, an Assistant Collector and District Magistrate in Vizagapatam, the largest district in Madras. In 1879 the man's servants noticed that his behaviour was becoming deranged, especially in his obsession with a bandit leader called Chendrayya whom he threatened to shoot like a bear. While travelling through his district in the middle of one night, Maltby shot dead a village headman, wounded a carter and fired at his fleeing bearers under the impression that they were part of Chendrayya's gang and were plotting to murder him. In the morning a group of Indians found him hiding in a fortune-teller's hut and handed him over to the authorities. Brought before a magistrate, Maltby claimed he had acted in self-defence and had killed not a harmless villager but one of Chendrayya's lieutenants. On realizing that his story was not believed, he suspected a conspiracy against him and threatened to go to Calcutta to secure the dismissal of his Governor, the Duke of Buckingham.

After hearing the evidence of numerous witnesses and a surgeon, the Madras Government acknowledged that Maltby was insane and thus unfit to stand trial. It sent him back to England, escorted by a doctor, and, although at Malta he made an effort to jump ship so that he could join his wife and children in Switzerland, he was soon safely in the Broadmoor Criminal Lunatic Asylum. The India Office decided to pay him as if he were on leave with a medical certificate, although little of his salary remained after deductions had been made for his voyage home, his various escorts and his maintenance at Broadmoor. After Maltby was removed from the Service, the Office agreed in principle to pay his wife a pension commensurate with his seniority.

In England Maltby became the responsibility of the Home Office, whose medical officers judged him to be insane and still suffering from mania with delusions. A few months later, however, his wife claimed he had recovered his sanity and should be released from Moorcroft House, a more luxurious asylum where he had been allowed to go on condition his upkeep was paid for by various friends. The senior doctor at the institution reported that Maltby's conversation was rational on all topics except when he was talking about the night of the shootings: nothing would disturb his conviction that he had foiled an attempt to abduct and murder him. Such evidence – supported by Maltby's friends – encouraged his wife's solicitor to apply (unsuccessfully) for a writ of habeas corpus to be served on the Home Secretary, calling on him to explain why his client should not be released. At the same time Maltby himself asked the minister to send him back to India so that he could stand trial and plead self-defence in his actions against 'certain rebels'.

The India Office and the Madras Government realized they had made a mistake in not trying Maltby earlier and acquitting him on the ground of insanity. The last thing they wanted was to send him back to India for trial now: apart from the fuss it would have caused, the difficulty of getting up a case for the prosecution had been exacerbated by the death of Octavius Irvine, the District Magistrate before whom Maltby had originally been brought, who had just been killed by a cheetah. Fortunately their problem was solved by Maltby's escape from his asylum and his flight to Brussels, where he joined his wife and father, who was Vice-Consul in the city. From Belgium Maltby petitioned for his pension – and even wrote to the Queen – but the Secretary of State declined to correspond with 'a fugitive from justice'. Eventually, three years after the shooting of the villager, an Order in Lunacy was made directing payment of her husband's pension, including arrears, to Mrs Maltby.[5]

Incompetents and Malcontents

Governors and Lieutenant-Governors sometimes grumbled that it was impossible to remove subordinates merely because they were inefficient. Grant Duff, the Governor of Madras, wished the Secretary of State would give him 'more power to get rid of men upon proportionate pensions who are thoroughly bad bargains without being criminal'. He had no means, he continued, of 'dealing with harmless idiots except to place them in the Judicial Department'.[6]

Grant Duff's rancour was roused by the knowledge that, despite his intellectual abilities, he was not making a success of the easiest governorship. But his presidency did contain more incompetents than the other provinces. Bombay might occasionally produce a District Judge such as W. Sandwith, a veteran who was persuaded to retire 'for health reasons' when the Acting Registrar of the High Court discovered that he had 67 cases undisposed of and 104 appeals in arrears.[7] But such men were rarities everywhere except in Madras.

Incompetents were seldom sacked but, as in the case of Sandwith, they were sometimes 'eased out' and given the opportunity to resign in circumstances that preserved their dignity and reputation. Informed that there was a problem in the district of Vizagapatam, the Registrar of the Madras High Court went to investigate the activities of the District Judge, E. C. G. Thomas, who happened to be in England on furlough at the time. Appalled to discover that Thomas had for many years neglected one of his main duties – the inspection of his subordinate courts – the Registrar reported him unfit for his post and suggested he should retire while in England. The judge was indignant, but pressure was applied, and he did not return to Madras.[8]

Insubordinates were more difficult to deal with than incompetents because they were usually younger – and more competent. Only the most obstreperous risked expulsion from the Service; milder rebels merely exposed themselves to supersession and demotion. As a young Civilian, H. G. Joseph published a letter in the *Madras Mail* criticizing his Government for its 'unfair treatment' of the Matron Superintendent of the General Hospital. Although he was warned privately by the Chief Secretary that this was a great blunder for so junior an official, Joseph declined to reply or apologize and was subsequently superseded by an even younger colleague for the post of Head Assistant Collector of his district. But his career was not much harmed, although there may have been an element of punishment in a brief posting to Burma in 1886. He died before the age of retirement as a District and Sessions Judge, the post in which most men on the 'judgey' side ended their professional lives.[9]

A different destiny fell to John Wallace, a Madras Civilian who combined incompetence and insubordination to an unusual degree.

After his first six years in India, during which his Collector described his work as 'dilatory and perfunctory', he was briefly suspended because he had not yet managed to pass his griffin's exams. These unpromising beginnings did not assist his promotion; but neither did they deter him from protesting energetically to the Secretary of State that he was being superseded by junior colleagues. In 1877, after he had finally reached the position of Acting Joint Magistrate of South Arcot, he went 'beyond all bounds of propriety and decorum' in his attacks on the judgements of the local Sessions Judge. As a result he was downgraded to the post of Head Assistant, sent to another district and warned that unless 'his future conduct, which [would] be narrowly watched, [showed] decided change and improvement', his position in the Service could not be maintained. Summing up his record so far, Grant Duff observed that he had consistently 'incurred the displeasure of the Govt, first as a careless student, secondly as a careless Asst Collector, thirdly as a careless Asst Magistrate, fourthly as a Joint Magistrate, considered unworthy to hold that position'. He had thus been 'degraded to be Head Asst . . . [and] told that his conduct as Joint Magistrate had been so bad as to create grave doubts as to the propriety of entrusting him with magisterial powers for the future'.

In 1882, by now the District and Sessions Judge at Cuddapah, Wallace once again 'incurred the severe displeasure of Govt' by launching an attack 'unbecoming in the highest degree' on the High Court for overturning one of his judgements. Censured by the Government for this outburst, he reacted by protesting to the Secretary of State and complaining to the Viceroy that he was being kept out of spite in Cuddapah, a 'notoriously unhealthy station', while his juniors were being posted to more attractive spots such as North Arcot and Coimbatore. Cuddapah was indeed an insalubrious place: one Civilian posted there was hailed as 'Lazarus' when he turned up at Madras for Christmas.[10] But if it was the presidency's 'penal station', then it seems appropriate that it should have been occupied by Wallace. The occupant, however, did not see it like this. Furious that his request for a transfer was turned down, Wallace went to see the Chief Secretary, David Carmichael, and accused the man of punishing him because he had given insufficiently generous wedding presents to the Carmichael daughters. Such a 'gross and scandalous insult' was too much for the Madras Government, which finally appealed for his dismissal. Lord Kimberley, the Secretary of State, removed him in October 1883 and granted a reasonable pension. Wallace, however, was not mollified by the money. A decade after his sacking, he was unsuccessfully suing Grant Duff for 'damages for injury to reputation and loss' caused by the 'false and defamatory libel' that had led to his dismissal.[11]

Hibernian Insubordinate

The case of John Wallace demonstrated how far you had to go before you were removed from the ICS. The case of Charles James O'Donnell showed how far you could go without being dismissed so long as you had political friends and you were reasonably good at your job.

O'Donnell's real name was Macdonald, but he changed it to assist the political ambitions of his eldest brother, who entered the House of Commons as an Irish Nationalist in 1874 under the name of Frank Hugh O'Donnell. The name Charles James Macdonald might have reflected the Jacobite side of its holder's Anglophobia but it was too British for a brotherhood that hoped to outflank Parnell in Irish politics. Both men warmed to Britain's Celtic fringe and disliked 'Anglo-Saxons'. They aimed for Home Rule in both Ireland and India, indeed 'Home Rule All round, radiating from the centre of a really Imperial Parliament' at Westminster.[12]

Charles James arrived in India in 1872 and four years later published a venomous attack on the Bengal Government in 'The Black Pamphlet of Calcutta: The Famine of 1874'. Written anonymously by 'a Bengal Civilian', the document derided the famine relief operations of 1874 as 'a demoralizing comedy on which the resources of the Empire have been squandered'. Since the O'Donnells liked to make comparisons between Indian and Irish suffering, and since at the outbreak of the famine Frank had accused the Government of being dilatory in its response, it was inconsistent of them to claim in retrospect that relief had been too lavish and wasteful. But consistency was not a virtue much rated by either of them. In sarcastic and sneering tones Charles James accused the Viceroy (Northbrook) and the Lieutenant-Governor (Temple) of 'prostituting charity', of creating a 'faminist panic' and of instigating 'relief measures [that] were errors of the most egregious description': all Northbrook's 'mistakes were entirely due to [the] ignorance and incompetent counsel' of Temple.[13] It was a strange way for an Irish Nationalist to react to Britain's most successful famine management of the century.

If a junior subaltern had libelled his commanding officer in such a way, he would have been court-martialled. But even after discovering the author's identity, Temple refused to take official notice of the matter, partly out of generosity, partly because he did not wish to give further publicity to such personal invective against himself. O'Donnell's remarkable escape from censure merely encouraged his erratic behaviour. The following year, portraying himself as a friend of the Indian peasantry, he instigated proceedings against a land-owner which the High Court described as 'hasty, injudicious, arbitrary and unjust'. After the Court's reversal of his decision, O'Donnell made some 'insubordinate and disrespectful' remarks 'showing an utter want of appreciation of his position as a judicial officer'. This time he was censured, reduced a grade and sent to a new post 'under the immediate supervision' of the local District Officer, who was 'instructed to keep a strict and careful watch over his work'.[14]

A few months later O'Donnell apologized to the High Court and was reinstated as an Officiating Joint Magistrate (1st grade). But in 1879 he was censured again and transferred to another district for 'endeavouring to foment ill feeling' between the Maharaja of Hutwa and his tenant farmers. The Acting Lieutenant-Governor, Sir Stewart Bayley, criticized him for his 'hasty and insufficient examination of facts' and regretted that O'Donnell's 'energy and ability and . . . interest in the welfare of the people' were not 'combined with sounder judgement'. Unsoundness prevented him from becoming 'a very useful officer'.[15]

That year O'Donnell decided to deploy his potential usefulness in his own country. In September he announced his candidacy for Galway, informing the electors that he was an 'advanced nationalist' and an 'unflinching advocate of tenant rights' whose interests in Indian Home Rule, education and land reform would make him a suitable MP for Galway. But Disraeli dissolved Parliament unexpect-edly in March the following year, and O'Donnell could not get home in time to participate in Gladstone's triumph. The two brothers' political ambitions were further battered by Frank's eclipse in his rivalry with Parnell.[16] Disgruntled, Charles James returned to India ready with a new controversy.

In England O'Donnell had published a second sarcastic and abusive pamphlet called 'The Ruin of an Indian Province', written in the form of an open letter to Lord Hartington, the Secretary of State. The province was Bihar (then a part of Bengal), and the 'ruin' was ascribed to the failure of Sir Ashley Eden, Bengal's Lieutenant-Governor, to promote land reform. This time the targets of the junior magistrate's pen were Temple again, Eden (a 'fettered Hercules'), Bayley (a 'wicked counsellor'), Lytton (the Viceroy alleged to have snuffed out the scheme) and the Government of India (which was 'more than the despotism of Caesar').[17] Anglo-Indian officials were naturally furious that such an attack had been published, especially in the form of a letter to the Secretary of State, whom even Lieutenant-Governors were not allowed to address directly. Antony MacDonnell, who shared many of O'Donnell's political views, considered the indictment 'unfounded', 'ignorant' and full of mistakes and 'clandestine insinuations'. Senior Civilians were further incensed by the way Frank supported his brother's case by asking questions in Parliament and writing inaccurate letters to *The Times*. Claiming that Charles James was 'exceptionally well-informed' on the condition of the province, Frank even asserted that he had 'served through the famine relief in Behar [*sic*] in 1874'. Few people heard the later correction by the Bengal secretariat that O'Donnell had not been 'in or near Behar' during the famine and had not 'served a single day in the province' before 1875.[18]

Eden thought it intolerable that he, ruler of a province of 70 million people, should be publicly ridiculed by one of his junior officials. But the new Viceroy, Ripon, refused his request to remove O'Donnell from Bengal and had the man transferred to another district 'to give him another chance'. In a fresh controversy in February 1882 the Calcutta High Court found O'Donnell guilty of 'serious judicial misconduct in the course of duty', a verdict that led to yet another transfer and a second demotion. This time even Ripon admitted it 'seemed impossible to doubt' that O'Donnell's 'whole conduct could fully justify his removal from the service'. But fearing that he would be a dangerous man if dismissed, the Viceroy decided to keep him in a 'subordinate position until he has shown that he can be safely trusted'.[19] Such was 'the despotism of Caesar'.

O'Donnell did indeed become more trustworthy over the years. Despite his demotions, he was made a Collector in 1889 and nine years later was promoted to Commissioner, a post which a majority of Civilians did not reach. His retirement was celebrated in predictable fashion with the publication of 'The Failure of Lord Curzon', a feeble diatribe written anonymously in the form of an open letter to Lord Rosebery, the former Liberal Prime Minister. In 1906 he finally entered the House of Commons as Liberal MP for Walworth, remaining there till 1910 while loathing his own Government, especially its leader Asquith, whom he resented for his failure to recommend him for a knighthood. In old age he retained his schizophrenic attitudes towards Britain, its people and its Empire. He boasted that he had 'devoted over half a century' to the cause of the Indian peasantry and admitted that membership of the ICS had been the 'pride and joy' of his life: the Service was 'the most perfect engine of administration and justice' that an imperial power had ever evolved. Yet he remained relentlessly hostile to the people who made up at least 80 per cent of that engine: the English. In his autobiography, with its intriguing title *The Irish Future and the Lordship of the World* (1929), O'Donnell argued that it was time to recognize the supremacy of the Celt over the 'Teutonic or Saxon element' in British life. The great Prime Ministers had been Celts, the great generals had been Irish (except Marlborough whose West Country origins made him a sort of Celt) and so were the 'immortal Edmund Burke, Canning and Sheridan'. Indeed the 'Teutonic or Saxon element' was only admirable if it stayed in Germany, a country he considered to be Britain's greatest friend. Opposed to Britain's entry into the First World War, he was still arguing fifteen years later that German atrocities in Belgium had been greatly exaggerated. He even managed to excuse the sack of Louvain.[20]

Anyone examining O'Donnell's career is bound to wonder how the *'enfant terrible* of the ICS' – as the *Pioneer* described him – remained in the Service until he voluntarily retired after twenty-eight years. It is difficult to think of any other bureaucracy in the world – let alone Caesar's – that would have tolerated a junior official who publicly (and in print) criticized two Viceroys and three Lieutenant-Governors, who was twice demoted and three times transferred, and who rudely and openly condemned a High Court for overturning his decisions. As we have seen, the Government of India was a tolerant employer; and as Bayley conceded, O'Donnell was an able official despite his lack of 'sound judgement'. But these factors would hardly have preserved him if Frank Hugh O'Donnell had not been a Member of Parliament. The one thing the Secretary of State, the India Council and the Government of India were always united on was the importance of avoiding awkward questions in the House of Commons. As Ripon tacitly admitted, it was better to keep Charles James in India than let him join forces with his brother and make a nuisance of himself at Westminster.[21]

Physical Justice

'Never strike a native' was Sir George Wingate's parting advice to his nephew Andrew, who set out for India and a career in the ICS in 1869. The young Wingate heeded it, as did most Civilians, for even minor violence or loss of temper could spoil or retard a career. In 1893 a young Civilian in the Punjab was sacked because he had ordered someone to cut the beard of a Sikh subordinate and had then denied doing so. James Sifton, a young Bengal official, was fortunate not to be reprimanded for his habit of 'taking a man by the shoulders and shaking the breath out of him'. It may have had a salutary effect on the man and on onlookers, but the practice was not condoned by the Government.[22]

Verbal abuse could also land a Civilian in trouble. In 1885 a group of Indian litigants entered the court in Dehra Dun while another case was being heard and were ordered to leave by the Joint Magistrate, George Laidman. The Indians' adviser, Andrew Hearsey, subsequently alleged that Laidman had insulted them: in an official complaint to the Lieutenant-Governor of the NWP (Alfred Lyall) which he reprinted in the newspapers, he claimed that this was 'not an isolated case of Mr Laidman's abusing respectable natives in his court'. Hearsey was a former captain in the Army, a hot-tempered adventurer who later, after his son had failed to obtain a job with the State Railways, threatened to revenge himself on the Government by taking a band of disgruntled ex-soldiers to serve in the Russian Army on the Afghan frontier.[23] He was also violent: he once forced his way into the offices of the *Pioneer* and tried to thrash the editor with a horsewhip after Kipling had made a dismissive reference to him in a report on a Congress meeting in Allahabad.

As the matter threatened to become 'a grave public scandal, involving the reputation of a public officer', the provincial Government gave Laidman permission to file a charge for defamation against Hearsey. The case seemed a straightforward one. While Laidman was regarded in Dehra Dun as a fair and courteous magistrate, Hearsey was considered a bounder who had made reckless imputations about an event he had not even witnessed. Besides, while his own evidence was weak, that of his clients was spattered with inconsistencies. But unfortunately, as Lyall observed, Laidman was 'of humble extraction and mean appearance in the witness box, with a nervous tendency to giggle'. Under cross-examination he convincingly denied the allegations of abuse but admitted that during his sixteen years' service he had sometimes used the word *badmash* (rascal) to describe dishonest people. Although this was hardly a serious matter, the new Chief Justice from England, Sir Comer Petheram, seized upon it and, apparently determined to make an example of an ICS magistrate, summed up, according to Lyall, so 'violently, and with great straining of the law, against Laidman' that Hearsey was acquitted. Later Petherman admitted to Lyall that he had mismanaged the trial, but that was of no use to poor Laidman. The unfortunate giggler was twice transferred and died on furlough in 1887.[24]

Laidman was unlucky, and his downfall was unusual. More typical was the case of Nicholas Beatson-Bell and the problems he caused his Lieutenant-Governor, the Viceroy and the Secretary of State. Beatson-Bell was a product of the Edinburgh Academy and Balliol College, clever, enthusiastic, impulsive and muscular. In the winter of 1894, as an Assistant Magistrate on tour in Bengal, he sent word to a village that he needed to buy milk. On reaching the place, however, a native official told him there was no milk there or anywhere nearby and continued in this line even after Beatson-Bell pointed out that he had just passed a herd of cows. Convinced that the man was being provocative and mendacious, the young Civilian eventually lost his temper and struck him. The matter was soon reported in the Indian press, and Beatson-Bell, who apologized and paid a large sum in compensation, was censured by his Government and transferred from the district.

The Lieutenant-Governor, Sir Charles Elliott, and the Viceroy, Lord Elgin, believed that the magistrate had been sufficiently punished for an act committed under 'extreme provocation'. In Whitehall, however, the Secretary of State, Henry Fowler, admitted he was 'very anxious' about Parliament's response to the case and hoped that Beatson-Bell would be more publicly and powerfully censured before the House of Commons reassembled after the Christmas recess. Fowler's anxiety owed something to an earlier case in which the same magistrate had been accused of 'high-handed and oppressive conduct' by a judge. On learning that two *zamindars* had been quarrelling over a piece of land and hiring teams of armed ruffians to settle the matter, Beatson-Bell summoned the landowners, threatened to prosecute them for planning a riot and then locked them in a room for several hours until they came to terms. Everything went well until one *zamindar* repudiated the terms and disclosed the means used to obtain them. Elliott was enraged by the judge's censure of his subordinate's action and told Elgin that Beatson-Bell had saved human lives, that he had done 'the wisest and kindest thing that could have been done', and that he wished all his officers 'would act in the same way, nipping crime in the bud before it occurs, and treating the natives as children, which they really are'. One of the last of the Haileybury men, Elliott was commending a young magistrate for remaining true to the methods of an institution abolished nearly four decades earlier.[25]

Fowler's anxieties about the response of MPs were further increased by two subsequent incidents featuring Beatson-Bell, whose activities were now being closely examined by the nationalist press. Accused by a newspaper of 'beating a witness in Court', the Civilian claimed that the man in question had begun 'to pick his nose in a rude and offensive manner'. Since the activity had been 'a pure piece of bravado on his part to show contempt for the Court', Beatson-Bell had told him to stop and rapped him on the knuckles with a ruler. The witness filed a criminal petition, but this time the District Magistrate sided with the defendant, ruling that 'Gentlemen should not pick their nose in court while standing beside the presiding officer'.[26]

At the same time, early 1895, the newspaper *Amrita Bazaar Patrika* accused Beatson-Bell of inflicting 'blows after blows' on a Deputy Magistrate because he was wearing native dress. The truth was rather different and had nothing to do with the man's clothes. At a gymkhana in his district the burly Beatson-Bell was trying to prevent an

over-enthusiastic crowd from encroaching on a tug-of-war. Failing
to identify Babu Rasik Lal Sen as a Deputy Magistrate and believing
him to be the most obstructive and obstinate encroacher, he shoved
him aside, causing his victim to trip over a bamboo barricade, fall
down a small slope and dislocate his shoulder. Quickly realizing his
mistake, Beatson-Bell found the Babu a trap and drove away with
him to the doctor to have the shoulder set. Rasik accepted his
apology with 'very gentlemanly feeling' and a 'complete absence of
vindictiveness', but it was too good a story for the *Amrita Bazaar
Patrika*.

Four misdemeanours within two years eventually forced Elliott to
do what he 'deprecated above all things': publicly censuring one of
his officers. Beatson-Bell was duly informed that, combined with his
previous mistakes, his 'rash and inconsiderate action' at the gymkhana had 'brought on him the severe displeasure of Government'
because it seemed to indicate a 'habit of rough treatment of natives'.
The young man must become 'more aware of his own size and
strength' and must abstain from using 'physical roughness of
any kind to natives lest the tendency should grow upon him and
produce results which cannot be undone'. A less talented official
than Beatson-Bell might have been dismissed. But Elliott and the
Bengal Government recognized his potential and did not want to
lose him. Nor did Elgin, who repeatedly tried to convince Fowler
that the young man's errors did not 'arise from any unfriendliness or
harshness to natives, but chiefly from a rather rough and boisterous
manner'. Beatson-Bell vindicated their judgement. In 1921 he ended
a distinguished career as Governor of Assam, took holy orders and
spent his old age as a vicar.[27]

The Odd Corruptible

At his retirement dinner in 1898 Sir John Edge remarked that during
his years as Chief Justice of the Allahabad High Court he had
received over a thousand letters, usually anonymous, abusing the
ICS. Yet not one of them had suggested 'even covertly that any
member of the Covenanted Civil Service had acted from any corrupt
motive in any matter'. With this omission the authors of the anonymous letters had thus paid a great if unintended compliment.[28]

Indian nationalist papers endorsed the view that the ICS was 'absolutely above suspicion', that it was 'the high water mark of morality in the public service of the country'. Civilians could be haughty or discourteous but they could not 'be bribed to do anything'.[29] As Carlyle might have put it, they were 'red-brick Incorruptibles' who deserved their reputation, even if it were sometimes trumpeted with a magnificent lack of understatement. When unveiling a memorial tablet to Sir John Woodburn in his parish church in Ayrshire, the Reverend James Williamson declared that:

> What Pyrrhus, King of Epirus, said of the Roman Consul Fabricus, whom he had attempted unsuccessfully to bribe, was applicable to Sir John Woodburn, that it would be easier to turn the sun from his path in the firmament than to turn Woodburn Sahib from the path of stern righteousness and upright judgement.[30]

Yet there were inevitably one or two 'black sheep', Civilians open to an 'illegal gratification', the Anglo-Indian euphemism for a bribe. Even if 99 per cent of the Service were men of probity, that left room for a miscreant to creep into it every three years or so.

The Government of India had strict views about the financial transactions of its officials. Not only did Civilians have to be incorruptible: they had to be above suspicion. They were not allowed any interest, however innocent, in any commercial venture that might affect their professional conduct. If you were the Chief Secretary in Madras, your son could not own a coffee plantation in the presidency; if you were the Political Agent in a native state, your relations could not buy property there. If, like the Madras Civilian James Gribble, you invested in the South Indian Prospecting Association, the best you could hope for was censure, a suspension ordered by the Secretary of State, and early retirement – even if you had already sold all your shares in the company.[31] No one claimed that John Beames's long career had been blemished by the slightest financial irregularity, but the revelation that he had borrowed money from Indians led to his public disgrace, his removal from the Bengal Board of Revenue and his demotion to a division where none of his creditors were living.

Provincial Governors sometimes responded angrily in defence of subordinates whom the Viceroy or the Secretary of State was intent on punishing for minor transgressions. In 1874 Northbrook privately warned Lord Hobart, the Governor of Madras, that he and his Council would probably direct him to relieve George Ballard from his post as Resident of Travancore on the grounds that his sister had recently bought a small piece of property in the state. 'How is it possible to allow him to remain there?' the Viceroy asked: 'in the eyes of the natives' there was no difference between the action of a Resident and that of a close relative.

Hobart, who died of typhoid the following year in Madras, sent a wrathful reply. Ballard was a 'man of great ability' who had served long and well and upon whose character 'not the faintest imputation' had ever been made. Were he and men like him 'to be supposed *a priori* so corrupt and dishonest that neither they, nor any of their relations, may hold the smallest amount of property there without suspicion?' Was the Madras Government, which had taken great care to select the right officer for the post, 'to be over-ruled and censured by implication, not on any great question of national policy, but on an affair of detail and of such small calibre as this?'

In his reply Northbrook told Hobart, who had only been in India for two years, that he was looking at the Ballards from 'an English point of view'. From the point of view of the native states, however, it was necessary 'not only that the British Resident should be upright and disinterested . . . but that he should give no occasion for the suspicion that he has any personal interests, directly or indirectly, in matters of business which come before him'. Matters such as Miss Ballard's property were not 'questions of detail' but issues of 'the utmost consequence' because British rule depended on maintaining 'the high tone of integrity among our civil servants'. The Governor was thus given the choice of removing Ballard or ensuring that his sister sold her land. Since Hobart had no intention of transferring his Resident, he reluctantly agreed to oversee the sale. Ballard duly remained in his post until 1877 when he was promoted to the Board of Revenue. He retired two years later as the senior Civilian in Madras.[32]

Like Beames and Gribble, Ballard may have been foolish but he was not corrupt and he did nothing illegal. A very small number of Civilians, however, were both foolish and corrupt – foolish because bribes seldom remained secret: news of them soon circulated among widening circles of Indians until eventually they reached the ears of the local government. Arthur Atkinson, a middle-ranking Civilian in Madras, excited suspicion by his ability to reduce his debts in quantities far beyond the resources of his salary. John Garstin, a member of the Board of Revenue, went to investigate and found that Atkinson had 'a notoriously bad reputation throughout the Tinnevelly District', the southernmost part of British India. Among other things, he was accused of accepting a bribe from a *zamindar*, of transferring a case (in which the *zamindar* was an interested party) to his own file, and of subsequently finding in his benefactor's favour. Garstin's report led to Atkinson's prosecution and his dismissal from the Service.[33]

The most notorious case of corruption in Victorian India concerned Arthur Travers Crawford, a Bombay Civilian born in 1835 who behaved as if he were living in the India of Clive and the nabobs. As a younger colleague reported, he had 'run away with two women, [had] been separated from his own wife, and during one Poona season lived with two actresses whom he imported from America'.[34] Yet 'society' did not ostracize him either for that or for rumours that he was corrupt. For many years there had been suspicions that Crawford did not 'run straight'. In 1874 he did not get the commissionership of Berar because of suggestions of impropriety in Bombay; and in 1880 Temple, the Governor, described him to his successor as a 'most able officer' whose career in Bombay contained 'circumstances' which should be clarified verbally.[35] But none of this prevented his promotion to a commissionership in his own presidency or recognition of his achievements in the form of a Companionship of the Order of St Michael and St George.

During the mid-1880s Crawford's debts – chiefly the result of women and a large number of children – encouraged him to accept a variety of bribes, loans and advances from certain rajas in his division. The recklessness of these transactions was incredible, and reports of them inevitably appeared in the Indian press. Placed under house arrest by his own Government in the summer of 1888, Crawford escaped from Poona, bolted for the sea and was apprehended in Bombay wearing a false beard. The presidency instigated criminal proceedings against him but then abandoned them in favour of a Commission of judges. To the Government's surprise and dismay, the Commission then acquitted Crawford of the main charges of corruption against him. It was a perverse and unexpected conclusion, but other facts that the affair had brought up – the borrowing of money, the disarray in the division and the attempted flight in a false beard – persuaded the Secretary of State to dismiss him without a pension.[36]

Mr Clarke and Mrs Howard

Sexual scandal seldom damaged careers in Victorian India. Most Civilians did not lead lives about which scandals could be spread; those who did usually got away with them. In the view of Sir Denzil Ibbetson, a Member of Curzon's Council, the Government should not be 'ordinarily concerned with the private morals of its officers, unless they either constitute a scandal which is calculated to bring discredit upon Govt or the Service, or impair the efficiency of the officer as a public servant'.[37] As a result, blind eyes were generally turned to men who discreetly kept Burmese mistresses or pursued love affairs with Anglo-Indian widows or even had adulterous liaisons in hill stations.

Homosexuals, however, would not have been viewed with such tolerance. Sodomy, opined Ibbetson, 'put a man altogether outside the pale' and would have justified his dismissal, 'scandal or no scandal'. Yet homosexual Civilians either sublimated their desires or else gratified them undetected. Sublimation was rarer in the Army, and scandal was more common. On learning of the sexual activities of Sir Hector MacDonald, who had risen from the ranks to command British forces in Ceylon, his fellow general, Lord Kitchener, wanted him court-martialled and shot.[38] MacDonald decided it was preferable to shoot himself.

In 1845 Richard Burton, the future explorer who began his career as a subaltern in the Indian Army, was asked by Sir Charles Napier to investigate the rumour that Karachi possessed three homosexual brothels. With his passion for thoroughness, Burton spent many evenings in these places and compiled an extremely detailed report about the prices and practices of the inmates and their clients. Although the report was meant to be secret, it was read after Napier's departure by officials who believed that only a homosexual could so diligently have procured such data. Burton was not dismissed from the Service, but his Army career was ruined, and in 1849 he left India.

Another area where governmental tolerance did not operate was the native state, where an official's sexual behaviour was particularly open to blackmail and the scrutiny of the local press. In 1887 Shamrao Narayan, the Dewan (minister) of the state of Cambay, alleged that George Wilson, a senior Civilian, had sent his gardener to make 'an infamous proposal', requesting the Dewan to let him sleep with his daughter who, so he claimed, was already the mistress of the ruling Nawab. Although Wilson denied the charge, and a Commission of Inquiry admitted it was impossible to prove, the Bombay Government decided that its official was guilty and sent its judgement home to Lord Cross, the Secretary of State in Whitehall. Cross, however, did not agree with it. Having read 'very carefully' through the case, he concluded that the Dewan's evidence was on the whole 'unsatisfactory and untrustworthy' and that Wilson was 'entitled to be acquitted'. Since Bombay's view that he was not so entitled had already been made public, Wilson's future presented a conundrum. Eventually Cross decided that 'in the altogether exceptional circumstances of the case' the man should be allowed to resign on a pension proportionate to the length of his service.[39]

The following year the Bombay Government was handed another rumpus in a native state, though this time the woman involved was English and quite happy to share the bed of the Political Agent, Colonel Watson. The trouble began when an Indian journalist alleged that Watson was receiving horses and other gifts from the Maharaja of Bavnagar through a Mrs Mills, the Political's mistress, who was staying as a guest of the Kathiawar chief. Tackled on the subject by his Government, which admitted it was 'naturally and properly sensitive about scandals' in the Political Department 'after the Wilson business', Watson adopted a haughty air, deploring the comparison with Wilson, whose conduct had been 'both dishonourable and revolting to natural decency', and refusing to allow his superiors 'to pry into the privacy' of his bedroom. Haughtiness was the wrong tactic. More interested in prying into the possibility of bribery, Watson's superiors found out about the horses and ordered him to return them and 'get rid' of Mrs Mills immediately.[40]

While the Government of India might overlook a Civilian's mistress, it felt it could not disregard an affair between an official and his mistress's young daughter. In August 1902 Curzon received a letter from England from Mrs Georgie Howard, the widow of a Chaplain in the Bengal Ecclesiastical Establishment, who claimed that a member of the ICS had seduced a girl in her care aged 13. Since the age of consent in India was 12 and had only recently been raised from 10, the seduction itself was not a crime, and Mrs Howard's alleged purpose in writing was simply to beseech the Viceroy to raise the age limit again. Letters from purity watchdogs in England were no rarity, but this one was different. It concealed the fact that the supposed seducer, Robert Clarke, had been Mrs Howard's lover, and that the supposed victim was her daughter Dorothy.

Clarke was a young and promising Civilian in Kashmir who claimed that during his five and a half years in India he had never touched a woman. Asked by the Government to answer Mrs Howard's charges, he replied that the clergyman's widow had invited herself to his bungalow in Srinagar on the pretext of looking at his dogs and had seduced him – an operation he allowed this 'nympho-maniac' (as he ungallantly called her) to repeat several times over the next few days. Departing on tour to Baltistan shortly afterwards, he hoped the relationship had 'come to a natural end'. But Mrs Howard and her daughter pursued him into the mountains, to Kargil, to Leh – one of the highest towns in the world – and finally to Khalsi, where they parted at the end of July 1901. During their month together in Ladakh, Clarke admitted that, although they had had separate tents, the 'nymphomaniac' had lived 'more or less openly' as his mistress.

Such openness did not, however, deter Dorothy, whom the Bishop of Lahore described as 'decidedly big for her age and very good looking'. According to Clarke, her 'no doubt inherited tenden-cies' propelled her to sit on his knee and come into his tent in the early morning while he was still in bed. 'She began making overtures and a great deal of kissing and caressing occurred though nothing approaching seduction took place.' On the last night in Khalsi she persuaded him to get into her bed, which he did, though he 'did not stay there more than two minutes' and 'except with her hand she did not touch' him.

In the autumn of 1901, as Clarke was returning to Srinagar, Mrs Howard went to see an old friend of her husband, the Reverend Cecil Earle Tyndale-Biscoe, and told him that, although she and

Clarke had been engaged in the summer, her fiancé had subsequently seduced her daughter. She then asked the clergyman to visit her lover and find out whether he was prepared either to marry her or to give her a lot of money. 'Failing these two things,' recalled the clergyman, 'she would report the matter to the Viceroy': Mrs Howard was determined 'on <u>marriage</u>, <u>money</u> or <u>punishment</u>'.

Tyndale-Biscoe, who ran the Church Missionary School in Srinagar for over half a century, was not a natural go-between. He was more comfortable teaching his pupils boxing so that they could defend themselves against local pederasts. But he duly called on Clarke, listened to his story and then suggested the erstwhile lovers should have an interview in his presence on her houseboat on the lake. Although shaken by the revelation that Mrs Howard wanted to marry a man who had seduced her daughter, Tyndale-Biscoe assumed that in her own relations with Clarke she had been 'innocent and pure-minded'. Mrs Howard, however, soon made it clear that his assumption was ill-founded and in the interview she repeated both the accusation of seduction and the assertion that money or marriage to herself was the only means of reparation. Not surprisingly, the clergyman found her behaviour 'unedifying' and was perplexed by her rejection of Clarke's suggestion that Dorothy should be examined medically to ascertain if she was still a virgin.

Tyndale-Biscoe believed Clarke was telling the truth and 'left the boat morally certain that Mrs Howard had commenced this vile business'. So did the official's superiors on the North-West Frontier, where he had now been posted. The Chief Commissioner, Harold Deane, thought it 'evident that Mrs Howard having failed to secure what she wanted from Mr Clarke – marriage or money – has made up her mind to ruin him'. But the one man who remained unconvinced by Clarke's story was Deane's superior, the Viceroy. Curzon was not concerned that the young official had 'conducted a compromising and discreditable intrigue with Mrs Howard' or that the two of them were 'persons of low moral character'; but he was greatly interested in the question of Clarke's culpability towards Dorothy. His Private Secretary therefore asked the Bishop of Lahore to make inquiries, explaining that the Viceroy was 'loath to believe that there can be in the Service any brute vile enough to be living simultaneously with mother and daughter, conducting a liaison with the one and seducing the other'.

The Bishop replied that Mrs Howard's refusal to allow an examination was a point in Clarke's favour, despite her subsequent change of mind and the revelation that Dorothy was indeed no longer a virgin. But he did believe in the official's guilt on the evidence of some of the girl's letters, which Mrs Howard claimed to have intercepted, and a statement by Dorothy explaining when and where Clarke 'first did anything wrong with' her. The accused denounced them as forgeries written much later on Mrs Howard's instructions. Deane believed him, wondering why otherwise they should have been produced so late (eighteen months after the widow's threats in front of Tyndale-Biscoe) and mocking the statement of seduction which suggested that the action 'took place on a charpoy in a public place in broad daylight'. He conceded that Clarke's behaviour towards the girl had been 'most unbecoming a gentleman', but he did not think he had seduced her or that he should be 'officially called to account for his conduct'.

In Curzon's mind the issue was 'how far extreme and revolting immorality should come under the notice of Government and be punished by it'. Addressing Ibbetson, the Home and Revenue Member of his Council, the Viceroy observed that 'upon the question of truth or lying' the Government exacted the highest standards from its civil servants: if, as he believed, Clarke was lying, then he should be sacked from the Service. Ibbetson, one of the outstanding Civilians of his generation, admitted that Clarke's behaviour had been bad but did not think it merited dismissal: there had after all been no public scandal. His own recommendation was that Clarke's punishment should be limited to an 'entry of the case' beside his 'character roll' which would weigh against him when future promotion was being considered.

Curzon was 'so little in accord' with Ibbetson's view that he decided the case should go before his Council. More letters from Mrs Howard, which revealed that Clarke had offered to pay for Dorothy's education, convinced him of the Civilian's guilt. By now the history of the girl's hymen had become almost an obsession to a man whose premarital past (and indeed his widower future) was littered with 'discreditable intrigues' with married women, many of whom, by his criteria, were no less 'persons of low moral character' than Mrs Howard. Perhaps his current state of married fidelity had made him intolerant of other people's love affairs.

Curzon's Council did not offer him much help on the fate of the hymen. The Military Member, General Elles, agreed that Clarke should be sacked but believed that Dorothy's virginity had probably been taken by someone else: he had known of 'more than one distressing case of European children of this age being seduced by native servants'. Sir Thomas Raleigh, the Law Member, agreed with Ibbetson that the case against Clarke was not proven and suggested that, if Dorothy was capable of offering herself to one man, she was capable of offering herself to others; he had known a case when a young girl, who 'looked perfectly respectable', had 'offered herself to four men in one night'. He was supported by Sir Arundel Arundel, the Member in charge of Public Works, who thought it 'probable that such a girl with such a mother had been seduced by someone else, even by a servant'; he had 'known a perfectly well-behaved nurse seduced by a native servant'. Sir Edward Law, the Finance Member, refrained from recording further instances of depravity and restricted himself to a refusal to 'attach any importance to any statement made by a woman who accuses a man of seducing her daughter and demands as reparation that the man shall *marry herself*, or give her money'.

Curzon had asked his colleagues 'for their opinion and advice' but declined to accept them on receipt. The 'Cabinet' responsible for the governance of a vast area of Asia continued therefore to send each other memos about whether hymens could be ruptured by masturbation and whether the rupture of this particular one by Mr Clarke's finger would amount to seduction. Ibbetson's rather precise view of an event without witnesses was that Clarke 'took indecent liberties with the girl and that he excited her with his finger, certainly on one, and probably several occasions'. But he was sure that sexual intercourse had not taken place.

The Viceroy, who was equally sure that it had, decided that the case should be sent to London for an inquiry by the Secretary of State. Far removed from the prurient hysteria which seemed to have gripped the Councillors in Simla, Lord George Hamilton declined to act on the matter. Apart from anything else, neither Mrs Howard nor her daughter could be compelled to appear or give evidence before an inquiry; and even if they did present themselves, they could not be put on oath. Forced to resolve the matter itself, the Government of India finally decided to reduce Clarke by seventeen places in the combined gradation list of the Punjab and the North-West Frontier. In effect this deprived him of three years' seniority in the Service. Despite this setback, Clarke was promoted to the post of Deputy Commissioner in 1908, but thereafter his career stalled. He retired in the same position in 1923.[41]

8

Frontiersmen

~

The Punjab School

THREE-QUARTERS OF the Civilians on active service were stationed in the Regulation provinces of Bengal, Bombay, Madras and the North-Western Provinces. Apart from those serving in the secretariat of the central Government, the remainder were distributed among the native states, serving as Residents and Political Agents in the Political Department, and in the Non-Regulation provinces, where they worked as administrators in Burma, Assam, the Punjab and the Central Provinces. In all places outside the Regulation provinces administrative posts were shared between Indian Army officers and the ICS.

As Governor-General between 1842 and 1844, Lord Ellenborough had a predilection for military officers in civil employment. His prejudice was negated by Dalhousie who in 1856 insisted that places in the Non-Regulation provinces should be divided equally between the Army and the Civil Service. In 1867 the Civilian element was increased to two-thirds, and the next forty years saw a gradual erosion of the military's role in civil administration. By 1903 Army officers were no longer employed in the Punjab, the province they felt they had created. In 1907 they were excluded from Assam and found themselves confined to Burma and the North-West Frontier. In the Political Department, however, they retained their ascendancy, consistently outnumbering the Civilians in the native states by a ratio of 7 to 3.

All over British India the crucial administrative figure was the District Officer. But in the Non-Regulation provinces, where he was known as the Deputy Commissioner, there was no separation of powers between the executive and the judiciary. The rationale was that these were frontier territories, recently acquired, where simple, direct methods of justice and administration were preferable to the convoluted legal system built up in Bengal and manipulated by the local Bar. Not all such provinces were the same, but the key feature of the Punjab system in the 1850s was the concentration of authority in the Deputy Commissioner: he was not only Magistrate and Collector but District Judge as well. Above him Commissioners were also required to act as judges until 1885, when they were relieved of their criminal work at the same time that the areas under their control were greatly expanded. The still more senior figure of the Financial Commissioner retained both judicial and administrative duties until an even later date. As a judge he disposed of final appeals in cases under the Treasury Act; as an administrator, he superintended the province's taxes, excise, revenues and trade.[1]

The 'Punjab School' was fashioned in the image of the Lawrence brothers, first of Henry, later of John, both of whom permeated the administration with their different tastes and temperaments, their contrasting styles and methods of work. Henry was a soldier who opposed the annexation of the Punjab after the Sikh Wars but became the President of its Board of Administration in 1849. More sympathetic to Indian customs than his younger brother, he was a believer in 'indirect rule' who planned to administer the new province in co-operation with the Sikh aristocracy. Unlike John, he abhorred paperwork: it was 'all nonsense sticking to rules and formalities, and reporting on foolscap paper', especially when one should be 'upon the heels of a body of Marauders, far within their own fastnesses'. The subordinates he wanted were young men who could 'mix freely with the people' and 'do prompt justice, in their shirt sleeves, rather than propound laws, to the discontent of all honest men'.[2] He certainly had a talent for attracting the daring and the self-confident. 'What days those were,' recalled one of them of the late 1840s:

How Henry Lawrence would send us off to great distances: Edwardes to Bunoo, Nicholson to Peshawar, Abbott to Hazara, Lumsden to somewhere else, giving us no more helpful direction than these: 'Settle the country, make the people happy; and take care there are no rows!'[3]

The recollection might stand as an epigraph for the Punjab School. But if it contains a whiff of Henty and fictional valour, it also contains the essential truth. Nicholson could capture a Sikh garrison or subdue a mutinous regiment without firing a shot. Lumsden, who formed and led the native Corps of Guides, was a dashing horseman and the prototype of the Western role in Kipling's 'Ballad of East and West'. Edwardes might have failed in his incredible ambition to convert Peshawar to Christianity but he managed without bloodshed to pacify Bannu, a remote tribal region which Sikh forces had been unable to reduce. As for Abbott, he 'went native' in Hazara and became a patriarchal and much-loved figure among the Hazarawals, whose district capital in Pakistan is still called Abbotabad. And it was not only Lawrence's famous 'young men' who did such things: their spirit inspired their even younger comrades. As a Deputy Commissioner at the end of the Mutiny, James William Macnabb travelled ninety miles across the border of Jammu, disguised as a rich Indian woman, to arrest a senior Maratha rebel.[4]

But Dalhousie was too efficient a Governor-General, too methodical an administrator, to allow his new province to be run for long by such a bunch of audacious and eccentric and often Evangelical pioneers. He wanted an administration more permanent and logical, a province carved into districts run by District Officers and into divisions run by Commissioners. Soon there was no room for Abbott, who was removed from Hazara and sent to run a gunpowder factory in Bengal. Before long there was no room either for Henry Lawrence, who in 1854 was packed off to Rajputana and later to Lucknow where, as Chief Commissioner of Oudh, he was killed in the Mutiny. Dalhousie had created a Board of three officials, including both Lawrences, to govern the Punjab. But the system never worked well. The brothers quarrelled incessantly, and the Governor-General, who invariably sided with the younger one, appointed John Chief Commissioner in 1853.*

---

*Henry carried his disagreements with his brother to his deathbed. His quoted remarks in his last hours attest to his preoccupation with Duty, God and not surrendering, but,

John was a less attractive figure than Henry but a stronger and more conscientious administrator. A Haileybury Civilian averse to the idea of indirect rule, he insisted that India was better off governed directly by British District Officers. He was obsessed by paperwork – and by the importance of never being in arrears – and demanded 'energy and promptitude' in all things. In manner he was brusque and blunt-spoken: even an admiring subordinate described him as 'a hard and in many ways unfeeling man', a chief who gave little praise to his juniors, a leader who always expected his followers to work as hard as he did. When Lieutenant Pearse, an Assistant Commissioner in Bannu, requested an assistant because he was working thirteen hours a day, he received a 'curt, bluff reply' saying that he would only get one when he was working eighteen hours a day, as Lawrence had done at his age in Delhi. John had no time for 'slackers': he insisted that District Officers should remain in the plains in the hot weather and not go up to the hills. Nor could he tolerate a 'cakey-man', by which he meant someone who, besides presumably liking cakes, 'pretended to much elegance and refinement'. On learning that one misguided Civilian had brought a piano out to India, Lawrence vowed to 'smash' it for him: the wretched man was subsequently transferred five times in two years. Most intolerable of all was unpunctuality. The Government of India – and indeed everyone outside the Punjab – recognized the principle of Joining Time, that a griffin was entitled to so many days (depending on the distance) between disembarking at his port of entry and reporting to his province, even if the entitlement was generous and allowed him to dawdle for a couple of days on the way, sightseeing or visiting friends. Lawrence would have none of it. In 1853 James William Macnabb was sent as his first posting to Multan, an unhealthy station where he fell so sick with fever that he was taken to Lahore and nursed by Honoria Lawrence, Henry's wife. During his convalescence she told him that her brother-in-law had sent him to Multan as

---

(cont.)
according to Dr Ogilvie, who was there, his final words were, 'Tell my brother John he is a bad man.' The doctor repeated these to George Clerk, who knew both brothers well. Clerk, who was twice Governor of Bombay, believed that Henry did not intend to imply that John was anything but honest and well-meaning in character but rather that 'in public life [he was] a man of grasping, illiberal and suspicious disposition and a political officer of "bad" or *unsound* views'.[5]

a punishment for taking his 'full Joining Time which no Punjab Civilian was expected to do'.[6]

The spirit of the Lawrence brothers imbued the Punjab Commission long after John had retired to England, returned as Viceroy and finally gone home for good. Officials were expected to be mobile and to travel light, sleeping on a camp bed and ruling from the saddle rather than from a desk or a textbook. Even John's successor as Lieutenant-Governor, Robert Montgomery, a genial man with a passion for trees who was known as Mr Pickwick, had no patience with someone using his full quota of Joining Time.[7] Assistant and Deputy Commissioners continued to drive themselves hard and rush about the country, epitomizing the ideal of the paternalist District Officer. Their ethos is portrayed in Kipling's story 'The Head of the District' in the persons of Orde, who on his deathbed by the Indus remembers that four villages need a remission of rent because their crops have been poor, and of Tallantire, who defeats a tribal rebellion and brings order to the district after the Indian Civilian has run away.

The British were proud of the Punjab School, of its combination of respect for local culture and intolerance of practices singled out in John Lawrence's famous trilogue: 'Do not burn widows/Do not kill daughters/Do not bury lepers alive.' They were pleased too that they were popular with their subjects, especially landlords and peasants, whom they assisted by legislation to prevent moneylenders from acquiring their land. The Sikhs had supported them in the Mutiny, and so had most of the Muslim chiefs, a loyalty that was subsequently well rewarded. By 1875 half the Indian Army was recruited from the Punjab, while a policy of low rents and vast irrigation projects was leading to an increase in agricultural prosperity. So apparently successful was the Punjab system that supporters recommended its extension to other regions. But such a despotism, however benevolent, could not endure for ever: it depended too much on the initiative, the intuition and above all the calibre of its district despots. Gradually over the rest of the century the Punjab came into line with the older provinces. The paternalist spirit survived into the 1930s, but 'rough and ready justice', dispensed by young men in shirt-sleeves, gave way to codes of civil and criminal law; a Chief Court was set up, similar to the High Courts of the Regulation provinces; and in 1885 the District Officer was shorn of his judicial functions and forced to share his despotism with a judge.[8]

All along the Frontier

The name Punjab means 'Land of the Five Rivers' in Persian and originally referred to the area between the Indus and the Sutlej. (In fact there are six if both these are included, the others being the Jhelum, the Chenab, the Ravi and the Beas.) The territory, which is slightly larger than Britain, consists almost entirely of alluvial plain sloping slightly from the north-east down to the south-west. But to the north-west across the Indus rises a very different landscape, a craggy, rock-bound, mountainous country inhabited largely by Pathan tribes. This area, which in the nineteenth century was reportedly capable of producing 200,000 fighting men, formed part of the British Punjab. But administration there was far less peaceful or successful than it was in the plains between the rivers.

Beyond the mountains was Afghanistan, a country and an issue which divided British opinion and determined the Indian Government's policies towards the tribes along the frontier. The issue concerned the advance of the Russian Empire, which had been expanding for four centuries at the rate of 20,000 square miles a year, and the possibility of a Tsarist invasion of India. As Foreign Secretary in 1840, Lord Palmerston argued that, since the Russian and British armies were bound to meet one day, it was best to ensure the meeting took place as far as possible from India instead of 'staying at home to receive the visit'.[9] The 'Forward School' accepted this argument for three generations, demanding British garrisons in Afghanistan and insisting that the policy of 'masterly inactivity' would be interpreted as weakness, an encouragement both to the Russians to invade and to the Indians to rebel.

Opponents of the Forward School, who were led by John Lawrence, dismissed its assumptions. The subject peoples, they argued, would not rebel as long as they were well governed; Afghanistan would be difficult to defend and not worth the trouble; the Russians would be easier to defeat on the Indian frontier, where their lines of communication would be long and insecure, than in the wastes of central Asia. As Lawrence put it when Viceroy in 1867:

Let [the Russians] undergo the long and tiresome marches which lie between the Oxus and the Indus; let them wend their way through poor and difficult countries, among a fanatic and courageous population,

where, in many places, every mile can be converted into a defensible position: then they will come to the conflict on which the fate of India will
depend, toil-worn, with an exhausted infantry, a broken-down cavalry,
and a defective artillery.[10]

The Forward School persuaded the Indian Government to invade
Afghanistan in 1838 after the country's Amir, Dost Mohamed,
refused to exclude Russian influence from Kabul. Since the expedition led to the most complete humiliation in the history of the
British Empire – the annihilation of the occupying army – the
School found its influence reduced. But in 1878, with Lawrence
near death and Lytton as Viceroy, it persuaded a Conservative
Government to authorize another attempt to intimidate the Afghans
and dismember the country. A combination of viceregal and diplomatic incompetence led to an uprising in Kabul and the murder of
the British Resident (Sir Louis Cavagnari) and his staff, but total disaster was averted this time by an adroit political manoeuvre and a
successful military campaign. The British offered the now vacant
Afghan throne to Abdur Rahman, a claimant backed by the Russians,
and promised to withdraw their troops. They thus secured what they
had wanted all along: a buffer state run by a strong, subsidized and
friendly ruler.

The British had now realized that the conquest of Afghanistan
was pointless in aim and almost impossible in practice. But the
Forward School continued to press for an active interventionist
policy in the tribal areas between Afghanistan and the settled districts of the Punjab. It demanded – and achieved – forts, blockades,
the occupation of Quetta and punitive expeditions against recalci-
trant tribes. In 1893 Mortimer Durand, Foreign Secretary in the
Indian Government, negotiated a curious agreement with the
Afghan Amir which gave India a double border. The 'Durand Line'
(which later became the international frontier between Pakistan
and Afghanistan) ran through the tribal areas, eliminating what had
been a 'no-man's land' and dividing it into spheres of influence
loosely attached to Kabul and Lahore. But behind it to the east,
resting for the most part on the Indus, lay the administrative
border. Between the two the tribes lived under British protection
but not as British subjects. They came under the supervision of
Political Agents, not the direct rule of Deputy Commissioners;

their crimes were dealt with according to Islamic law not the Code of Criminal Procedure.

In 1900, during his second spring as Viceroy, Curzon travelled to the north-west and decided that the Empire's frontier policy was seriously flawed. He had been there before, as a traveller and Member of Parliament, and had liked the tribesmen, those 'magnificent Samsons, gigantic, bearded, instinct with loyalty, often stained with crime'. He prided himself that he knew how to handle these men who were as 'brave as lions, wild as cats, docile as children'. You had to be 'very frank, very conciliatory, very firm, very generous, very fearless'. And you had to avoid being provocative by stationing thousands of troops in expensive fortifications in their tribal homelands. He thus pursued a policy of withdrawing regular troops from advanced positions and concentrating them in the rear, while employing tribal forces recruited by British officers to police the tribal country themselves. His way of managing the Pathan tribesman was 'to pay him and humour him when he behaves, but to lay him out flat when he does not'.[11]

The Viceroy realized that the frontier needed not only a new policy but also a new administration. By 1900 the Punjab contained no senior figures comparable to Edwardes or Abbott, men eager to live for years among the tribes: the Chief Secretaries and Lieutenant-Governors seldom even visited the north-west to see what was happening there. Judging the administration to be an instrument of procrastination on border matters, Curzon revived an old idea to create a new province by detaching the Punjab's frontier districts and uniting them to the trans-border tracts between the Indus and the Durand Line. The severance was logical not just for political and geographical reasons: the frontier districts such as Peshawar and Bannu had little in common with the Punjab, ethnic and linguistic differences separating the mainly Pathan tribesmen from the inhabitants of the plains. In spite of the fury of the Punjab Government, the North-West Frontier Province came into being in 1901 and quickly proved a success. Curzon withdrew regular British garrisons on the Khyber, the Kurram and elsewhere and replaced them with tribal levies such as the Khyber Rifles and the Kurram Militia. Although these levies did not behave quite as well as the Viceroy claimed, the once-turbulent frontier remained largely at peace during his rule. In fact the new province, administered by two outstanding political officers, Colonel Deane and Colonel Roos-Keppel, gave little trouble until after the First World War.[12]

The frontier was, as the novelist John Masters observed, 'a betwixt-and-between place, part India, part Central Asia'.[13] Officials stationed along it lived very different lives from those in a native state or in a district of a Regulation province. Their existence was more isolated, more autonomous, more dependent on good relations with the people they administered. Frontier officers did not divide their work between an office and *cutchery* or between a princely court and a Greek-pillared Residency. They moved among the tribes, consulting local khans and village headmen, persuading the relevant *jirga*, or Council of Elders, to settle a problem or end a disturbance. A. E. W. Mason fictionalized the type in his novel *The Broken Road*, creating a character who was 'of no assistance at a dinner-party, but when there was trouble upon the Frontier, or beyond it, he was usually found to be the chief agent in the settlement'.

Frontiersmen were often inspired by the landscape of their work, the rugged mountains, the empty plains, the evenings by the camp-fire and the nights under the stars. They were also usually fond of the tribes. Anne Wilson believed they had a 'soldier's admiration for the valour of their foes' and appreciated the tribesmen for 'their chivalry, their frank, jovial manners, their songs and their humour, and their stoical indifference to danger and death'.[14] There was perhaps a connection between their 'clean, manly, vigorous life' on the frontier and the similar life they had led (at least in retrospect) at public school.[15] Certainly there was something of the camaraderie of the football field in their confrontations with the tribesmen – fight hard and shake hands afterwards – the kind of virile fellow-feeling expressed in Kipling's famous ballad, not in the line where 'never the twain shall meet' but in the rest of the same verse, which asserts that two men of comparable courage and ability can be equals despite multitudinous differences of class, race, nation and continent.

> But there is neither East nor West, Border, nor Breed, nor Birth,
> When two strong men stand face to face, tho' they come from the
>   ends of the earth.

Retired officials liked to recall the courage and courtesy of the frontier, 'where a man could travel a thousand miles on the hospitality of his fellow Moslems'. But they also remembered it as a place 'where the price of a man's life was considerably less than that of a Government rifle'. No tribesman would kill a guest, but those he had not entertained could be shot in the back or in their sleep without compunction. Armine Dew, an officer described by a subordinate as 'an enormous bearded Viking of a man', could never forget the brutality of the frontier, the sights of a bear skinned, a camp follower mutilated, 'a woman with nose and ears freshly chopped off'. It was an untamed territory and also an uncomfortable one. Anglo-Indian officials had no club, no cricket, no Army mess and usually no women. Even at Peshawar, the capital of the North-West Frontier Province, they could not enjoy a game of golf without an armed guard going on ahead to ensure that the bunkers were not being prepared for an ambush.[16]

One of the best frontier officers was Robert Warburton, the product of a highly romantic and dangerous elopement of a British officer and an Afghan noblewoman. Warburton served for eighteen years in one of the most hazardous posts in the Empire, Political Officer of the Khyber, and established such close relations with the Afridis, that most difficult tribe, that he could go 'about unarmed amongst these people'. It was understood by the tribesmen that, wherever he pitched his camp in the hills, 'the greatest enemies might resort to it with perfect safety. No private, public, or tribal feuds were to be carried out on any condition.'[17] Warburton found the Afridis in the hills easier to deal with than their lawless brothers in Peshawar, the only city on the frontier. In 1876 a member of the Punjab Commission made a list of Afridi rural offences of that year which included robberies of camels, goats, donkeys, bullocks and weapons, the occasional murder of a police constable and the kidnapping of three syces of the 11th Bengal Cavalry while they were cutting grass for the regimental horses.[18] But that was nothing to what the urban Afridis could do at Peshawar.

Warburton's first administrative post was Assistant Commissioner in the city. There he discovered that nowhere in India was so open to attack from robbers who were able to enter the station and cantonment from every angle and carry off rifles and whatever else they wanted. The only way for a householder to deter theft was to employ an Afridi thief as his watchman. In Peshawar and its environs Warburton was faced with three major types of crime: cattle poisoning, in which a man might wait for his enemy's buffalo to pass by and throw it a slice of melon plastered with arsenical dough; setting fire to crops ready for threshing, which required merely a slow-burning dung cake and a pinch of gunpowder; and 'murders for revenge, or on account of *zar, zan,* or *zamin* (wealth, women, land)'. The murder season was in the hot weather when people were sleeping outside, and it claimed 90 to 100 victims a year, a figure twenty times greater than the average for a Punjab district. A large majority of these crimes went unpunished. While it was relatively easy to trace the brother who had killed his sister's seducer or the father who had murdered his dishonoured daughter, most of the other homicides went unsolved. So many false trails laid long before the crime, so many false witnesses coached weeks before the trial, so many implications that were just too convenient to be plausible – it was not surprising that the conviction rate was sometimes only 10 per cent.[19]

Baluchi Backwater

Baluchistan, the western bastion of the Indian Empire, was larger yet more sparsely populated than the North-West Frontier. Its Muslim tribes of Iranian origin were mainly nomadic, wandering over plains and deserts as well as uplands. The greater part of it, Kalat, was a native state whose Khan had joined the ranks of subordinate rulers by signing a treaty with the Indian Government in 1854. The rest consisted of three British districts, certain Agency territories which the Government held on lease, and the small native state of Las Bela. From 1877 Baluchistan was administered by an Agent to the Governor-General (AGG) based in the newly acquired garrison town of Quetta.

A scheming official in one of Kipling's early poems sends his lover's husband to Quetta, where he dies from overwork and the climate, while the adulterous couple enjoy themselves in Simla.[20] Quetta did not have much to recommend it apart from a fine cantonment and well-planned Civil Lines. There were no monuments, few facilities and a dearth of society. But officials in Baluchistan came to like the town and its province. One Commissioner returned to Teddington on the Thames and named his last home Quetta. Mortimer Durand wanted to exchange his post as Foreign Secretary, perhaps the most important job in the Government secretariat, for that of AGG in the Baluchi backwater. The tribesmen might be rather uncouth: Curzon did not invite their 'most eligible chief' to the Delhi Durbar because he 'could neither sit at a table nor eat with a knife and fork'. But they were usually well-liked. Malcolm Darling, who joined the ICS in 1903 and was working for both the Indian and the Pakistan Governments fifty years later, liked them above all other Indians for their humour, dignity and kindness.[21]

The early colonial history of Baluchistan is inseparable from the career of Robert Sandeman, a Scottish officer who fought in the Mutiny, joined the Punjab Commission and in 1866 was appointed Deputy Commissioner of Dera Ghazi Khan, a frontier district 150 miles long on the west bank of the Indus. Sandeman was a forceful personality, compared by a colleague to 'one of those Indians or Afghans who in troubled times used to found a kingdom for themselves by strong character and pugnacity'.[22] His first task was to pacify his western border by preventing Baluchi tribesmen from raiding his district and kidnapping its inhabitants. After capturing 200 of these raiders in 1867, he offered their chiefs a deal: if they promised to stop the raids, he would return their prisoners and employ a number of their tribesmen as auxiliaries, men who would act as messengers in areas where there was no post, who would protect survey parties and guard caravan routes, and who would help in the arrest of criminals and the recovery of stolen property. The chiefs agreed, and the 'tribal service system' came into being. Although the authorities were worried about Sandeman's policy, especially his decision to cross the border and visit the clans with a tribal escort, they had to condone it because it worked.

Sandeman was equally successful in his relations with the Khan of Kalat. He acted as mediator between the Khan and his quarrelling chieftains, bringing them to agreement and negotiating a treaty with the ruler whereby, in return for an increased subsidy, the British were able to build railway and telegraph lines across the state. Sandeman's reward was the creation of the Baluchistan Agency and his appointment as AGG. He remained in this post, improving the British position by his policy of 'conciliatory intervention', until his death in 1892. He was perhaps the most independent and uncontrollable of all the Victorian administrators in India, a proconsul absolutely convinced that he was always in the right. Shortly before his death Durand reported that he had become 'more wild and violent than ever': the 'smallest sign of hesitation in applying Sandeman's "policy" to every tribe in India rouses him to fury'.[23]

The Sandeman system seemed simple. You made friends with the tribes, you dealt with them through their chiefs, you paid tribesmen to patrol your communications, you adhered to tribal custom and settled disputes by *jirgas* and not through law courts. You tried to solve all problems peacefully but you kept an effective military force ready and visible; and from time to time you extended your control by the construction of roads and forts. It was an effective autocracy that was accepted by the Baluchis who disputed among themselves over who should have the honour of burying 'Senaman Sahib'.[24] And it was continued by his successor, Sir James Browne, who died at Quetta on the eve of his retirement in 1896.

Yet Sandeman's hopes that his system could be extended throughout the North-West Frontier were not fulfilled. Perhaps his methods depended too much on his own genius. Certainly their success owed a good deal to the clan structure of the Baluchis. The tribesmen in Baluchistan usually obeyed their chiefs so that, as Warburton pointed out, you could rule them if you had the chiefs on your side.[25] But the Pathans were more fractious and independent; you had to win over the whole tribe before you could control it. Sandeman himself had managed to do so with the more amenable Pathans of Pishin and the Zhob Valley, and his methods were copied much further away – with notable success by the French General Lyautey in Morocco. But the Mahsuds, inveterate raiders from Waziristan on the North-West Frontier, might have proved too much for anyone. At any rate they resisted other officers' attempts to apply the Sandeman system and, despite a lull after the establishment of Curzon's new province, remained intractable until the creation of Pakistan.

Plots and Polo in Manipur

The landscape on India's opposite frontier was quite unlike that of the north-west. Five hundred miles to the north-east of Calcutta, between Bhutan and the north of Burma, heavy monsoons inundated the Naga Hills, providing a vegetation of teak and bamboo and dense evergreen forests. The area's inhabitants were mainly head-hunting tribesmen with animistic beliefs. In certain Angami Naga villages a girl would only marry a man who wore a kilt decorated with cowrie shells indicating that he had slain an enemy. Killing a woman or baby in arms was regarded as a greater feat than killing a man because it implied that the warrior had penetrated the enemy's heartland instead of merely ambushing a stray adversary. James Johnstone, a Political Agent in the hills, knew a tribesman who had slaughtered sixty women and children.[26]

By the end of the nineteenth century the British had extended their control over the area, which became part of Assam, and had put an end to the practices of village raids and head-hunting. But to the south they preserved the native state of Manipur, which was populated by peaceful Hindu Methei in the Manipur River valley and by less peaceful Nagas and Kukis in the surrounding hills. The Maharajas of Manipur were generally loyal to the British, who had defended their territory against Burmese aggression, and they allowed themselves to be guided by a Political Agent stationed in the capital.

Not many Anglo-Indians volunteered to serve in Manipur or the Naga Hills because the tribesmen were violent and the climate encouraged malaria. Officials seemed either to die or to go native. Surgeon-Major Brown, the Political Agent at Manipur, chose the latter: it was said that he had lapsed so entirely into 'native ways' that he registered the birth of two of his children by local women on the same day. But British officials more often fell into the other category. Three successive Political Agents to the Naga Hills met violent deaths in the years 1876–8: Captain Butler was killed in a fight with the Lhota Nagas, P. J. Carnegy was shot by his sentry, and Guybon Damant was killed trying to enter a village during the revolt of the Angami Nagas. In spite of malaria, James Johnstone survived his years as Political Agent in Manipur, but his three successors died there within the space of five years (1886–91), one from wounds suffered fighting the Burmese, the second from fever and lack of medical attention, and a third in a botched attempt to arrest a local prince.[27]

Before serving in Assam, Johnstone had been in charge of *kheddah* operations in the jungles of Orissa, catching wild elephants and transporting them to Government depots. Regarded by Henry Cotton as 'one of the finest fellows [he] ever met', he was also one of the toughest and most effective officers in the north-east. He once defeated a panther, cornered in a village house, which sprang from a window on to his back. When sitting in court in the Naga Hills, he kept a pistol in his hand 'in case of any wild savage attempting to dispute' his authority. He was a natural autocrat, a champion of personal government, but he also believed that native rule should be preserved as far as possible. He interfered seldom with the Manipur Government, and then only discreetly. He asked, for example, to be informed about death sentences so that he might advise officials, 'without appearing to the outer world to interfere', that they would be wrong to execute a man for a crime that was not a capital offence under English law. If he heard that a man was about to be executed for killing a cow, a firm but courteous message to the Maharaja brought about a remission of the sentence.[28]

One of Johnstone's successors was Frank St Clair Grimwood, who was much excited by the prospect of living in the birthplace of the polo club: on a previous visit he had played a game with the Manipuri princes on a ground worthy of Hurlingham in London. His wife Ethel also liked the thought of being mistress of a Residency with red-coated servants and a Gurkha escort. In fact their life there turned out to be monotonous and lonely, and the graves of former Agents in the garden were a rather morbid reminder of their isolation and vulnerability. But Frank had his polo, and Ethel had her pets, her garden and nine Naga malis who shocked her by doing their gardening in the nude. She gave them each a pair of bathing-drawers in an effort to 'inculcate decency' but abandoned her programme when she found them using the garments as turbans.[29]

The monotony and tranquillity of life in Manipur were destroyed in 1890 by a palace revolution. The Maharaja had seven brothers, a band divided into three supporters and four opponents, the latter faction including the second in age (the Jubraj or heir apparent) and the third (the Senapati, the Commander-in-Chief). In September the Senapati, who was the ablest and most popular member of the fraternity, decided to remove his weak eldest brother and install the Jubraj in his place. After shots were fired at the windows of the palace, the Maharaja fled to the Residency, abdicated the throne and, with the three brothers who supported him, left the state intending to make a pilgrimage to the Ganges.

Frank Grimwood advised the Indian Government to accept the

coup and was supported by James Quinton, the Chief Commissioner of Assam. It was not the practice of the Government, however, to acquiesce in the dethronement of a subordinate prince who had done it no harm, and a good deal of dithering took place in Calcutta. Eventually Lansdowne's administration decided on an incomprehensible compromise: instead of restoring the Maharaja, it would recognize the Jubraj but banish his right-hand man, the Senapati. It then ordered Quinton to take a column of Gurkhas to Manipur, announce the decision in public, and arrest the Senapati and force him into exile.

The Chief Commissioner was thus expected to apprehend the most popular man in the state, a commander surrounded by his own troops, at a public durbar. On seeing Quinton arrive with such a considerable force, the Senapati became suspicious, refused to attend the durbar and retired to his house in the palace grounds. Grimwood followed him there to persuade him to surrender and go into exile, but the prince refused. Then the British decided to force their way into the palace, which was in effect a fortress with a moat, but withdrew the Gurkhas after being shot at by the Senapati's troops. When the Manipuris went on to the offensive and attacked the Residency, the British called for a truce, and Quinton, Grimwood and three Army officers walked over to the palace to negotiate. But in the now inflammable atmosphere an angry soldier mortally wounded Grimwood with a spear thrust. Perhaps realizing that there was no going back after that, the Manipuris then beheaded Quinton and the officers and returned to the offensive, forcing the Gurkhas and the British contingent (including poor Ethel Grimwood) to abandon the Residency and flee the state.

The British returned, of course, though they limited their retribution to the execution of the Senapati and four others. In earlier times they would no doubt have annexed the state; now they installed a child Maharaja from another branch of the ruling family and henceforth maintained a close supervision of the administration. But the damage to their reputation was huge. While Quinton had made a mess of carrying out his orders, the orders themselves had been absurd. Recognizing the Jubraj but banishing the Senapati was, as Sir William Harcourt pointed out in the House of Commons, like accepting the restoration of Charles II and ordering the execution of General Monck. Even more scathing was the judgement of Curzon who, as Viceroy ten years later, privately described the Manipuris as 'the most good-natured, harmless, though excitable, people in creation, who were only driven into a revolt against us by a series of blunders almost unparalleled in history'.[30]

9

Residents and Agents

~

The Political Departments

IN 1900 THERE were some 680 native states in the Indian Empire containing roughly 63 million people spread over an area of about 700,000 square miles. No one could be precise about these statistics. Those reckoners who included Nepal and Sikkim reached a higher tally; those who excluded some of the tiny states in Kathiawar reduced the total to about 630. Whatever the number, there were huge variations in the sizes and populations of the states. Hyderabad and Kashmir, each with more than 80,000 square miles, were larger than England and Scotland combined. Other states had the dimensions of Hyde Park.

Five of the largest and most important states had direct political relations with the Government of India: Kashmir, Hyderabad, Mysore, Nepal and (from 1876) Baroda all dealt with the Foreign Office and its Political Department. The historic Rajput kingdoms such as Jaipur and Udaipur were grouped together under the supervision of the Agent to the Governor-General in Rajputana, while the Maratha principalities of Gwalior and Indore were placed with 146 other states under the AGG in Central India. Most of the remainder came under the control of the provincial governments, including the Sikh states in the Punjab, Travancore and Cochin in Madras, Rampur in the NWP, and Sikkim and Cooch Behar in Bengal. But the majority of all the native states of India, over 350 of them, were regulated by the Political Department of the Bombay presidency.

The Government's relationships with the states varied from case to case. About forty of them were based on military alliances and treaties made by the East India Company in the early nineteenth century. These and other agreements resulted in differing degrees of autonomy. Many of the minor chiefs of Kathiawar – lords of three villages and a few hundred acres – did not exercise civil or criminal jurisdiction in their territories. The Nizam of Hyderabad, by contrast, could coin money and execute his subjects. Nepal was the most autonomous of all the states (apart from Afghanistan after 1880) whose foreign relations were conducted by the Government of India. Yet while Calcutta did not interfere with its internal administration, it controlled its imports of weapons and refused to let it fight Sikkim or any other state.[1]

Few native states traversed the nineteenth century without experiencing a considerable erosion of their powers. The Government of India had effective control of railways, post offices and important roads in their territories. It exercised personal jurisdiction over British subjects in the states and extra-territorial jurisdiction over the cantonments it built on native soil. And it could, when thought necessary, depose rulers and alter administrations. The evolving nature of the relationships between the Government and the states led to a debate among the British about the status of the native principalities: were they allies or subsidiary states? Even Parliament gave a muddled answer, referring in 1876 to the 'princes and states in alliance with Her Majesty' and thirteen years later changing the crucial phrase to 'under the suzerainty of'.[2]

One Civilian, Lewis Tupper, claimed that by the end of the nineteenth century the Indian princes had become 'vassals' in charge of 'feudatory states', a view echoed by the French *Géographie Universelle* which declared that '*les princes vassaux*' were destined to become '*une grande aristocratie*' like '*les lords anglais*'. Curzon agreed with them, arguing that the native chiefs were not sovereigns and should not be treated as if they were. Wiser and milder men felt it unnecessary to rub the point in. If the chiefs were losing their powers, they should be allowed to preserve the pomp and aura of majesty; no real harm was done if they called their sons princes and put coronets on their notepaper. If rulers no longer possessed full sovereignty, they should be allowed to believe that sovereignty was divisible and that their states were 'semi-sovereign' rather than feudal. William Lee-Warner, the leading ICS expert on the native states, thought it best to leave the relationship between the princes and the Crown 'undefined'. When Curzon tried to define it, the India Council in London objected to 'the policy of minimising the sovereignty of the native states' and 'reducing the Native Princes to the position of mere noblemen'.[3]

The major states and all those under the AGGs came within the orbit of the Political Department of the Foreign Office. Calcutta may have been called 'the City of Palaces' or 'the St Petersburg of the East', but its FO had little in common with Gilbert Scott's vast Italianate palace in Whitehall: it resembled, said Curzon, 'a dilapidated villa in a decayed London suburb'. Nor did the position of the Foreign Secretary resemble that of Palmerston or Salisbury. In India he was a civil servant who, unlike the other Government Secretaries, was not responsible to a Member of the Viceroy's Council but to the Viceroy himself. There were no particular qualifications for the job except, as Northbrook insisted, an ability to speak Persian or Arabic and to be 'a gentleman with good manners and *courteous to Natives*'. Most Foreign Secretaries, such as Alfred Lyall or Charles Aitchison, were men who had worked for many years in the districts. William Cuningham was a rare bureaucrat, a 'steady' man and 'sympathetic with natives', who spent sixteen years in the Foreign Office, working his way up from Under Secretary to Deputy Secretary to Secretary.[4]

Mortimer Durand was Foreign Secretary from 1885 to 1894, after which he resigned from the ICS and, in an unusual career move, joined the other Foreign Office and eventually became Ambassador to Spain and to the United States. His duties at the Indian FO were triangular: he had to run the Political Department, deal with the native chiefs and administer the foreign relations of the Government of India. An annoying amount of his time was spent refuting French claims in Burma advanced by France's Consul-General in Calcutta, 'a troublesome little man' who was 'neither a gentleman nor over scrupulous in his official dealings'.[5] Equally vexing were his exchanges with Anglo-Indian newspaper editors to whom he addressed long remonstrances about their ill-informed opinions and reports. But most of his time was taken up with supervision of the 'Politicals' – the Residents and Political Agents under him – soothing those who had been denied promotion, exhorting others to be kinder to the local ruler, upbraiding the few whose policies he thought were misguided.

It was a demanding job at all times but especially under Curzon who had messengers running all day between Government House and the Foreign Office a quarter of a mile away. Secretaries who sent him a stack of files each evening and observed how meticulously they had been dealt with by nine o'clock the next morning, thought it a 'standing miracle' that he had found time between dinner and breakfast to dispose of them. On perusing the returned files, they were less impressed by his syntactical pedantry, his allergy to split infinitives and his replacement of commas by semi-colons.[6]

The Foreign Office, together with the Bombay Political Department, had a wide arc of responsibilities stretching from Aden to Bushire, up to Kashgar and down to Sikkim. Within this expanse its officials carried out a variety of functions, chiefly administration on the frontier, diplomacy in the native states and consular duties beyond the border. The Foreign Office posts included a Resident in 'Turkish Arabia', another in Bushire in the Persian Gulf, and a Consul-General at Kashgar in Chinese Turkestan.

In the hierarchy of the Politicals the top positions were the Residents of Hyderabad and Mysore who each received salaries of 48,000 rupees, the same as High Court Judges, the AGGs and the Foreign Secretary himself. Below them came the remaining nine Residents and the Political Agents of Bombay, Central India, Rajputana and the two frontiers. Most of the best jobs were in the hands of the Foreign Office, especially after the Residency of Baroda was removed from Bombay's control. Although the western presidency retained a considerable Political Department, many of Bombay's native states were supervised by Civilians from across the border in British India. The Collector of Satara administered not only his own district but five native states as well.[7]

After the removal of Baroda, the most prestigious post in the Bombay Political Department was that of Agent to the Governor (of Bombay) in Kathiawar, the peninsula that juts into the Arabian Sea between the Gulf of Kutch and the Gulf of Cambay. This was a job so complicated and stressful that Lee-Warner was assured by his doctor that he would get an abscess on the liver if he accepted it.[8] Leading a team of just five Assistants, the Agent administered an area with 300 states, 4,000 villages and over 200 bands of outlaws. Some of the states, such as Junagadh and Nawanagar, comprised over 3,000 square miles and were run by a Nawab or a Jan with an eleven-gun salute. Around them was a myriad of tiny states whose square mileage came in single figures. Akdia had a population of 216 living in two square miles.

In the 1860s the Agent, Major Keatinge, reorganized the Kathiawar states into seven classes, with differing degrees of jurisdiction over their citizens, and a number of *thanas*, groups of pseudo-states whose chiefs possessed no legal machinery to try their subjects. In effect this meant that the thirteen first- and second-class states exercised more or less full criminal and civil jurisdiction; and that the six assigned members of the Bombay Political Department managed the running of all the others as well as the *thanas*. Apart from supervising 300 states – and trying to remember where they were and what they were called – the Agent was also in charge of the railways and civil stations. Additional duties included adjudicating in disputes between the states and trying to stop the Hindu-Muslim rioting that broke out in Junagadh and Porbandar in the 1890s.[9]

Kathiawar was administered from Rajkot, where the local Thakur had ceded a couple of square miles in perpetual lease to the Government. Most of the British stationed there enjoyed the peninsula's old-fashioned, semi-feudal ambience, even if they had to employ a watchman from one of the criminal tribes in order to deter his relations from burgling their bungalows. And there was always the consolation of cricket, especially after the establishment of Rajkumar College, one of the 'Eastern Etons', where the sons of local chiefs were taught by a Parsi professional.[10] Nawanagar produced one of the greatest cricketers of all time, Ranjitsinhji, the famous 'Ranji' who played county cricket for Sussex and Test Matches for England against Australia.

Diversity and Disappointment

Competitive examination tended to produce a certain uniformity among ICS recruits; at any rate they usually shared similar academic attainments. But the Governments of India and Bombay were not seeking uniformity among their Politicals. In fact they welcomed diversity. 'We want lean and keen men on the frontier,' said Harcourt Butler, 'and fat and good-natured men in the states.'[11]

Candidates for the Political Departments had to be Army officers under the age of 26 or Civilians with five years' experience; they were also required to be unmarried at the time and to pass a not very difficult exam. As with the ICS, men sometimes joined the Politicals for ancestral reasons. Three generations of Hancocks served as political officers in Kathiawar; Scots, usually defeated by competition, joined the Army instead and produced Politicals such as Sandeman. There was some truth in the claim that the Departments consisted of soldiers with brains and Civilians who could ride and shoot. The career, however, was more popular with the Army than with the ICS. Military officers queued up to join because Politicals received higher salaries and led a more varied existence than a garrison in peacetime. Some Civilians joined because they were restless and wanted to see a little of India beyond their province; more scorned it because, as Ibbetson argued, it was 'better to rule a district than to humbug a Raja'. Yet their decision was not irrevocable; they could opt for the Political for a period and return later to the ICS. Charles Bayley moved several times between the two services before reaching the summit of both as Resident in Hyderabad and Lieutenant-Governor of two provinces.[12]

Aspiring Politicals from the ICS were sent to the frontier or a native state for six months' training; those from the Army spent eighteen months in a district learning about revenue and judicial work. At the end of these periods they were tested on their knowledge of Indian history, the law codes, the treaties with the Indian princes, and a couple of the vernaculars. But 'bookish knowledge' was not a prerequisite for entrance to the Political Department – or for success in that line afterwards. Percy Fitzgerald hated sitting at his desk, repeatedly failed his exams and neglected his judicial work. But as a young man he was good at fighting pirates in the Persian Gulf; and in middle age he had an unrivalled talent for getting on with the chiefs of the Bombay presidency. He retired in 1909 as Agent to the Governor in Kathiawar.[13]

Unhampered by the Civil Service Commissioners in London, the Political Departments could adopt a more practical approach to selecting the right men to fill the various posts of consul, diplomat, Resident or frontier officer. This resulted in a certain amount of nepotism – as it did with Fitzgerald, whose father was Governor of Bombay. But it also allowed personal qualities to outweigh proficiency in exams. And in the circumstances this was sensible. A raja and his court of noblemen were likely to be less impressed by a taciturn scholar from Oxford than by an ebullient officer who was, like them, a sportsman. Besides, the etiquette of Indian courts was so complicated that it was essential to find men who could be relied upon not to make gaffes, men who would remember not to shake hands with women out of purdah but to give a salaam to a Muslim and a *namaste* to a Hindu. They also had to know about uniforms, whether to wear spurs with levee dress, when to put on their frock coat, their Mameluke sword and their white pith helmet with gold spike and chain. Elgin was reluctant to appoint one well-qualified candidate to a Residency because he doubted the man's ability to 'do the social part of the work'.[14]

It is easy to smile at the departments' Secretaries who inquired anxiously about possible recruits: were they good shots, could they ride well, did they have good manners, what was their batting average? But such things were important in the environments in which they were placed. Colonel Bradford owed much of his success in Rajputana to the respect acquired by reason of his horsemanship, his fight with a tiger (in which he lost an arm) and the way he led his men in the Mutiny with only a riding crop in his hand.[15] A Maharaja of Patiala was a fine cricketer, a Nizam of Hyderabad was a great shot, other rulers excelled at these and other sports such as tennis and horse-racing. It was one of the main tasks of a Resident or Political Agent to overcome the natural suspicion of a ruler and his court that the foreign interloper was merely the Government's spy. There were no better places to do this, to gain influence and to establish friendships, than on the tennis court and the hunting expedition.

In the autumn of 1905, shortly after his resignation as Viceroy, Curzon delivered a speech eulogizing the role of the political officers in India.

A good 'Political' is a type of officer difficult to train. Indeed, training by itself will never produce him, for there are required in addition qualities of tact and flexibility, of moral fibre and gentlemanly bearing, which are an instinct rather than an acquisition. The public at large hardly realizes what the 'Political' may be called upon to do. At one moment he may be grinding in the Foreign Office; at another he may be required to stiffen the administration of a backward Native State; at a third he may be presiding over a *jirga* of unruly tribesmen on the frontier; at a fourth he may be demarcating a boundary amid the wilds of Tibet or the sands of Seistan. There is no more varied or responsible service in the world than that of the Political Department of the Government of India. And right well have I been served in it, from the mature and experienced officer who handles a Native Chief with velvet glove, to the young military 'Political' who packs up his trunk at a moment's notice and goes off to Arabia or Kurdistan.[16]

This panegyric would have resonated with a fair number of Politicals. Colonel Prideaux could not have complained of lack of variety in a career that took him from Bombay to Udaipur via Abyssinia, Zanzibar, Calcutta, Aden, Bhopal, Kashmir and Jaipur. Nor could many residents have grumbled that they were desperately overworked. When Harry Grigg became Resident of Travancore and Cochin, a friend told him that a Residency was now (in 1893) 'the only appointment in the Service that could be occupied by a gentleman'. Taking this to mean that the post was 'not only easy but dignified', Grigg agreed with him.[17]

The Political Department suited men with a strong sense of history. Prideaux had the leisure and opportunity to study numismatics and archaeology. Spared the drabness and monotony of a world regulated by the Public Works Department, Politicals felt themselves living in a sort of historical present, places where history was still alive, inhabited by people who lived as they had long lived – without the sense of grievance and inferiority found across the border in British India. Kashmir and Rajputana were the areas most coveted by Politicals. The Resident in Kashmir led an agreeable existence based at Srinagar, moving up to the lovely hills of Gulmarg ('the meadow of flowers') in the summer and gravitating to Sialkot in the Punjab for the winter. Walter Lawrence lived for six years in the Vale of Kashmir, 'unspoiled by railways and roads, innocent of factories and coal, and long streets and concrete houses, sleeping in boats or in tents always pitched on green turf under the shade of plane or walnut trees, and always within sound of running, singing water'. He regarded Dal Lake as 'the most exquisite corner of the world'.[18]

Since its Maharaja did not accept a Resident until 1885, Kashmir could not offer much employment to Politicals. But the twenty states of the Rajputana Agency required, apart from the AGG, three Residents, six Political Agents, the Commissioner of Ajmer-Merwara and a good number of assistants. The princedoms of Rajputana stirred the normally invisible romanticism of Anglo-India like nowhere else. Brought up on the writings of Colonel Tod, whose *Annals and Antiquities of Rajasthan* had appeared between 1829 and 1832, Politicals were enchanted to find themselves in a medieval world of castles, courts, minstrels and dancing girls. Lawrence, who was there before he went to Kashmir, described it as 'the Middle Ages in sepia' and claimed that in Rajputana at least 'the age of chivalry was not gone'.[19] Even so sceptical a figure as Alfred Lyall, who was AGG from 1874 to 1878, was intrigued by the similarity between Rajput nobles and the barons of medieval Germany. 'The chief nobles hunt, drink, and fight when they are not prevented; they eat the wild boar and get tipsy in their castles.' But the fastidious Civilian did not disapprove of them: the last thing he wanted was for all Indians to become like Anglicized Bengalis. He even told his mother, 'I am afraid that we do not alto-gether improve the nobles by keeping them from fighting.'[20]

Politicals in Rajputana had of course to tackle plague and famine and other problems that afflicted the rest of India. But they also had issues of their own which were more fun to deal with: mediation during the siege of a nobleman's castle; operations against brigands preying on wedding processions in the Aravali Hills; even adjudica-tion over whether a small and impecunious state was obliged to maintain an ancient elephant called Ram Pershad. (According to the sentimental Political, it was.)[21] If the problems were old-fashioned, so were some of the officers who tackled them. Lawrence was aston-ished by the quantity of chillies the older Politicals ate – and by their Rajput hairstyles, which were supposed to make them look like tigers. Their ways of dealing with litigation were also sometimes unusual. Lawrence's predecessor, clad in pyjamas, used to meet the plaintiff and the defendant in court at 8 o'clock and then retire to have his bath. Later he returned fully dressed to ask if they had resolved their dispute; if not, he left them while he had his breakfast and then returned at intervals during the morning to ask how they were getting on. If by mid-morning the pair had still failed to compose their difference, he sent them up to the roof to sit in the sun without water until they became reasonable.[22]

Politicals in Rajputana did not have much to complain of. Jaipur might be very hot in the summer but it had a fine Residency and its Maharajas were amenable rulers. Udaipur might be rather isolated but its climate was good and its lake was one of the most beautiful things in India. As AGG, Lyall was given 'a little trouble now and then' by aboriginal tribesmen, 'black and hairy little men with bows and arrows, who have never been anything but wanderers in the jungle'. But he admitted the job was to his taste. He lived in picturesque surroundings, had little to do and yet 'a great deal of authority and very little law with which to do it'. No wonder that frontier offices referred to the Rajputana Agency as the Great Sloth Belt.[23]

Curzon's encomium of their Service would have struck many Politicals, especially outside Rajputana, as overblown. Civilians might believe that their colleagues in the Great Sloth Belt 'spent their time shooting and feasting with Maharajas and tribesmen'.[24] But in western India the life of a Bombay Political was far less glamorous. In Gujarat, where there were no Maharajas, he was virtually a District Officer with similar administrative and magisterial duties yet without the job prospects of Civilians in the ICS or Politicals under the Government of India. Most of the posts open to him were poorly paid and insalubrious. Few officers could stand long periods in Aden or Gujarat without losing their health; some also lost their lives or went berserk. Aden was a kind of penal station for the Indian Empire: Curzon dispatched the West Kent Regiment there for two years without leave because its officers had tried to cover up the rape of a Burmese woman by some of their soldiers. Yet it was also a post where blameless young Politicals were sent to work and forced to live in a squalid mud hovel consisting of three rooms.[25]

Life was not much more comfortable for the august official who combined the duties of Political Resident in Turkish Arabia and HM Consul-General in Baghdad. The Residency was a rented building in a crowded and very dirty area where the principal thoroughfare was twelve feet wide. Its occupant in the 1880s, Colonel Tweedie, complained that from June to October he had to spend the days in its cellars and the nights on the roof, debating whether the 'damp, darkness and vermin of the former [were] worse than the publicity and frequent hot winds of the latter'. He also suffered from a skin disease called 'Date Mark' or 'Bouton de Baghdad' which produced ulcerations on faces, hands and limbs.

Tweedie had a hobby, the study of Arabian horses (about which he wrote a book in retirement), but he was obliged to pursue it by himself. His wife refused to live in a place where, if she went out, she had to ride 'swathed in sheets and veils' on a donkey in case she was mistaken for a prostitute. Not that there were many incentives to go out: there were no Englishwomen in Baghdad because the few European merchants in the city had married local Armenians. Her husband was depressed by her decision although he understood why she had taken it. After one particularly querulous letter to the Foreign Secretary describing his pitiable existence, Tweedie apologized, explaining that one was unable to repress one's feelings 'at the time of consigning one's wife to the monsoon in the Indian Ocean'.[26]

Butler wanted 'lean and keen' men on the frontier. But while the agencies of the North-West encouraged athleticism, they also spawned loneliness, boredom and introspection. Up at Chitral, cut off from the rest of the world until May of each year, the Political Agent, Francis Younghusband, spent the spring of 1894 worrying about his future, calculating the 2,200 hours of study he planned for his furlough and wondering how he could get as close as possible to 'that ideal life of Christ's'. A few months later, after being thrown from his horse and lying unconscious for fourteen hours, he read Tolstoy and decided to leave the Service and devote his life to God. The next year he did resign but he later rejoined and subsequently enjoyed a prominent and conventional career as Political Agent in Rajputana, as Resident in both Indore and Kashmir, and as the leader of the British expedition to Tibet. But the 'other-worldliness' he discovered in the mountains never deserted him. A collision with a motor car in his late forties convinced him that a benevolent God could not exist. This conclusion led him to exalt free love, 'to unite when and how a man and woman please', a freedom he had not yet experienced for himself. (In fact his first fiancée had broken off their engagement when she realized he found it easier to climb a mountain than converse with her.) In subsequent decades he wrote several books about the existence of superior beings on other planets and claimed that a 'World-Leader' on one of them communicated by ether waves to the rest of the universe. When finally, in his mid-seventies, he discovered the delights of physical love, he believed that he and his mistress (who had already had seven children with her husband) were about to produce a 'God-Child' who would be 'greater even than Jesus'.[27]

Duties of a Resident

The most difficult part of a Political's work was his relationship with the chief of the state to which he had been assigned. If the previous ruler had died leaving a child to succeed him, then the relationship usually began as a kind of tug-of-war between the British official and the boy's female relatives.

An infant chief was the most pampered and coddled of human beings, 'kept like a jewel within its velvet case'.[28] Captain Meade, the Political Agent at Baghelkand and Superintendent of Rewah State in Central India, found the young Rewah Maharaja 'wonderfully sharp': he could translate English, do easy fractions and answer nearly every question about the geography of Asia. But he had been 'so coddled by the Maharanis that he did not know how to feed himself. They put the food into his mouth.'[29]

When he was appointed Guardian of the 6-year-old Maharaja of Mysore, Colonel Malleson quickly identified his future enemies as the previous ruler's two widows and the mother of the adopted heir, herself a member of the royal family. All three were illiterate but intelligent and absolutely determined to control the upbringing of the young prince. In this they were supported by some 200 priests, councillors and attendants who milled about the royal palace, stopping from time to time in the central room to worship two cows which were installed there. Malleson found the little Maharaja looking pale and ill, which was not surprising since he spent all his time inside the palace – or in his mother's house to which it was connected. The atmosphere seemed even more unhealthy than the physical surroundings. The boy's mother treated him not as a child but as a king, while everyone else prostrated themselves before him, speaking in the most abject manner, gratifying every whim and anticipating every desire.

Malleson realized it was essential that the prince be educated outside the palace walls by a tutor independent of the court. He soon found an appropriate teacher, a Hindu who spoke excellent English and was a Fellow of Madras University. But the maharanis let loose a deluge of objections. The education could not begin on such and such a day because it was inauspicious, on another day because the moon was invisible, on a third because the boy was ill although his doctor had pronounced him well. Then it was claimed to be humiliating for a ruler to be educated outside his palace. After Malleson insisted, the ladies demanded that he be driven to the appointed spot – a bungalow attached to the Guardian's house – with an escort of thirty-six cavalry, thirty running footmen and sixteen personal attendants. When Malleson pointed out that the current Viceroy, Lord Mayo, seldom drove out with more than four cavalrymen, they were temporarily silenced. But on the agreed day they again demanded the state coach and the running footmen and did not relent until their adversary threatened to report the matter to the Viceroy.[30]

Politicals often acted as Guardians, Tutors and Private Secretaries to chiefs who were minors or who had recently taken charge of their states. The best of them realized that it was important to get the youths away from the stifling ambience of the palace, to teach them how to run an administration and yet to make sure that they did not lose touch with the religion and customs of their people. Younghusband wanted his young charge, the Maharaja of Holkar's heir, to meet the 'right' British people, to be acquainted with their 'manners and mode of life' while remaining a 'good native gentleman' receiving 'religious instruction from the best Hindoo sources'.[31] So balanced an outcome was not always the goal of men who had spent years struggling against the obscurantism of the maharanis. Young rulers, deprived of equals and surrounded by flatterers, were almost bound to be spoilt, conceited and ignorant when they took power at the age of 18. Major Wylie, the Political Agent at Bholpawar, thought it crucial to encourage his charge to join hunts and go pig-sticking, sports where the teenage Maharaj Rana would meet 'manly English gentlemen'[32] as well as Indian contemporaries who did not want to kiss his feet. Perhaps it was inevitable that some Politicals should incite young Rajahs to imitate some of their own ways. They believed they were right, and success rewarded them with agreeable companions. It was reassuring for a young official in an isolated station to find congenial sportsmen among the brothers of the local Nawab, men who came over to play tennis twice a week, were 'great hands at billiards and shooting and, except that they are given to quail fighting and have many wives, [are] very much like Englishmen in their habits'.[33]

The logical result of the Politicals' influence on upbringing – the emphasis on sport and the study of English – was public schools for the sons of princes. These establishments belong to the second half of Queen Victoria's reign, beginning with the foundation of Rajkumar College in 1870, followed by Mayo College (another 'Eastern Eton') for Rajput nobles two years later, Daly College for Central India and Aitchison College for the Punjab chiefs in Lahore. In fact Mayo far outshone Eton in aristocratic ostentation: the young Maharao of Kotah arrived with 200 followers, while the Maharaja of Alwar brought with him twenty polo ponies. As at Eton and other British schools, a great deal was made of field sports – and their importance for character training – and very little was done to prepare pupils for running an administration. Indian colleges also soon matched their British counterparts in the prevalence of illicit drinking and 'unnatural vice', and outstripped them in the scale of truancy.[34]

Indian public schools might not be the right answer for a chief's education but nor, according to Curzon, were British universities. There could hardly be a 'worse education', the Viceroy believed, than somewhere like Oxford where the future chief learned 'to despise his people, their ways and their ignorance'.[35] One elderly Sikh raja predicted that the practice of marrying sophisticated westernized boys to wholly uneducated, untravelled girls would result in a breed of mules. A related problem, as Curzon discovered, was that the chiefs became so enamoured of European ways that they lost interest in the mules' mothers and even in their hereditary states. The Raja of Pudukottai spent most of his time either in Europe with his mistress or in the southern hill station of Kodaikanal where he played tennis, danced with British ladies and hoped to be taken for an English gentleman rather than an Indian chief.[36]

Curzon might rail against 'the category of half-Anglicised, half-denationalised, European women-hunting, pseudo-sporting, and very often in the end spirit-drinking young native chiefs'.[37] But he realized that it was Britain's fault that the category had come into existence. Political officers had been warning of this development many years earlier. In 1888 the AGG in Central India informed the Foreign Secretary that in his zone of responsibility the result of 'an

English training for princely youths' so far was 'sodomites 2, idiots 1, sots 1 . . . [and a] gentleman . . . prevented by chronic gonorrhoea from paying his respects on the Queen's birthday'.[38] Twelve years later Curzon did not spare his sovereign details of the 'frivolous and sometimes vicious spendthrifts and idlers' that constituted such a large proportion of her princely subjects. The Rana of Dholpur was 'fast sinking into an inebriate and a sot', the Maharaja of Patiala was 'little better than a jockey', the Maharaja of Holkar was 'half-mad' and 'addicted to horrible vices', and the Raja of Kapurthala was only happy philandering in Paris. The Viceroy admitted that Britain was culpable for allowing such men 'to fall into bad hands', for condoning 'their extravagances' and winking 'at their vices'. And the ranis often agreed. The mother of one Rajput chief complained that, without an English upbringing, her son would not have found his state too hot, would not have wanted to summer in the hills and would not have thrown away his money on English clothes.[39]

Officials sometimes complained that without a British education rulers might remain in the hands of their priests or their astrologers or, in the case of the Maharaja of Kashmir, a 'menial servant' who had convinced his chief that he was the spirit of a famous holy man and should be obeyed on questions of eating and drinking and transacting business.[40] But they usually recognized that a successful ruler almost always combined western ideas with religious observance and a strong sense of historical tradition. The Maharaja of Dewas Senior might raise the age of consent and introduce compulsory education, but he consulted astrologers on his travel plans.[41] Curzon's ideal ruler was a man such as the ascetic Raja of Cochin, a humane and enlightened chief who combined 'the most conservative instincts with the most liberal views'. The Viceroy also esteemed the Maharaja of Jaipur who demonstrated loyalty to Britain by going to the coronation of Edward VII and loyalty to Hindu tradition by building a temple on his chartered ship and taking enough Ganges water for himself and his followers to last them the four months of their travels. Curzon's favourite among the younger chiefs was Scindia, the Maharaja of Gwalior, who displayed an almost Curzonian zeal for reform and efficiency but insisted on an education in India for his son and heir. Yet while such paragons made things easy for the Government, they made life rather boring for an energetic Resident. Desperate though he was to leave Baghdad, Colonel Tweedie told

Durand he did not want the Residency at Gwalior because there would be 'next to nothing to do, Scindia [the father of Curzon's protégé] having everything in a fine grip'.[42]

In spite of the maharanis and associated problems of a court, the best time for a Political to introduce reforms was during a minority. Under his supervision a Council of Regency would carry them out, while he himself would impress upon the young ruler the importance of preserving them when he came of age. The Resident or Political Agent was also expected to emphasize the difference between private and public expenditure, between the privy purse of the chief and the exchequer of the state.[43] Such things were more difficult when a Political was sent to a place where the ruler was mature and intractable. On being posted to Indore to deal with the mercurial Maharaja of Holkar, Younghusband decided it was more important 'to get on good terms with him rather than to effect "improvements" in the administration'. If he could make himself 'genial and sympathetic', go out shooting with Holkar or join him in other forms of entertainment, then he would have a chance of exercising some influence over him.[44]

Younghusband also realized the importance of getting on good terms with ministers, courtiers and other officials. He was determined not to be interfering or superior but to remember the natives' 'good points and the excellence of their manners, their patience, their spirituality, their intelligence, their capacity for affection'.[45] A crucial relationship for a Political was that with the chief Minister, the Dewan in Hindu and Sikh states, the Wazir in Muslim ones. An alliance between them could become the main axis of administration, especially when the ministers themselves had received a British education. The Resident's task was much facilitated by Dewans as able as Sir Salar Jung in Hyderabad, Sir Sheshadri Iyer in Mysore and Sir Dinkur Rao of Gwalior, though the latter exasperated British officials by frequent expositions on the Art of Government, an art which, according to them, he believed he had invented.[46] The chief problem with such alliances was their tendency to excite the jealousy of the ruler.

If tact was an essential ingredient of the Resident's character, so was an inner toughness, preferably concealed behind a genial countenance. States had after all to be kept in their place: rulers' sons should be dissuaded from calling themselves princes because that implied their fathers were kings; courtiers should not address a

Dewan as 'Your Excellency' because he was 'hardly on a level with Governors and Viceroys'.[47] Ultimate power should be apparent but invisible and ideally unused. When Harcourt Butler said the Political Departments needed 'fat and good-natured men in the States', he really meant that they should be fat and jovial but steely as well. One of the best examples of this type was Colonel David Barr, a very large and rather sedentary man who was sometimes described as the best Political of his generation. He was Resident in Gwalior, Kashmir and Hyderabad – as well as AGG in Central India – and was so successful in these posts that his successors sometimes admitted that their work was very easy.[48] But like most of the best Politicals, his methods were somewhat unconventional, at any rate in the early part of his career. A criminal he was once pursuing took refuge in the fortified palace of a rani, a member of the Udaipur royal family, who refused to surrender him. Barr therefore exploited a Brahmin priest from the same family who went on hunger strike outside her door until she decided that causing the death of a Brahmin would be a worse sin than handing over a criminal.[49]

'The whisper of the Residency', it was said, was 'the thunder of the Durbar'. But not always. Sometimes louder noises from the Residency failed to cause even a rumble in the Durbar. So long as they were not guilty of misrule or of evading their treaty obligations, certain rulers could be as uncooperative as they chose. The Government admitted that if the chief of an important state wanted to bury himself in his palace, there was nothing it could do to dig him out.[50] With a ruler as prestigious as the Maharana of Udaipur, whose family had defied the Mughals, it could do almost nothing at all. On ascending the lakeside throne in 1884, Fateh Singh refused to have a railway to his capital, a decision applauded by the young Kipling because it preserved Udaipur from 'the tourist who would have scratched his name on the Temple of Garuda and laughed horse-laughs upon the lake'.[51] Later the Maharana sabotaged irrigation projects, blocked mining proposals and refused to spend money on education; by the time his reign ended in 1921, the extent of metalled roads in the state was smaller than it had been at the beginning. The British failed to persuade him – alone of all the important chiefs – to provide imperial troops just as they failed to make him replace a sacked Dewan.[52] On ceremonial matters they were equally unable to secure his co-operation. At the Delhi Durbar in 1903 he even defied

Curzon, pleading illness and refusing to leave his railway carriage on discovering that he would not receive precedence over the rulers of more important states. Eight years later, at George V's Durbar, he did it again, claiming to be indisposed on learning that his elephant would be placed behind Baroda's in the procession.*

On Deposing a Ruler

After the Mutiny the Government of India reassured the rulers of native states that annexation was a policy of the past. As the paramount power it was now effectively guaranteeing that they would not be overthrown by hostile neighbours or by rebellious subjects. Yet it had to retain an ultimate prerogative, a latent force of intimidation, if this kind of insurance were not to be taken as a licence for misrule. If it prevented people from rebelling against their rulers, the Government had to accept the obligation to remove grievances that might justify rebellion. It had to retain the right to interfere with administrations and to depose bad rulers.[53]

The decision to interfere was an easy one to take in cases of civil war, insurrection or the collapse of state government. In the state of Alwar in Rajputana the British had to intervene more than once in disputes between the Maharaja and his noblemen.[54] It was more difficult to calculate when 'gross misrule' was gross enough to justify intervention. An official manual identified the moment when it reached 'a pitch which violates the elementary laws of civilization'.[55] But this was not very precise counsel for Politicals who, while frequently reminded that their chief duty was to 'advise', were often hell-bent on reforming abuses. One difficulty was that even corrupt and inefficient rulers were often popular with their subjects. Richard Temple admitted that the British virtues, justice and impartiality, and the British demeanour, frigid and inflexible, were not greatly appreciated by people who did not really care whether the police were corrupt or the courts inefficient. Indians, he believed, got more upset about matters such as 'the non-recognition of caste or class privileges in matters of law and justice'.[56]

---

*In 1921, after thirty-seven years of obstructiveness, the British finally forced Fateh Singh to abdicate in favour of his son.

Mortimer Durand, the Foreign Secretary, disapproved of zealous Politicals who were 'very impatient of evils and annoyances which are by no means uncommon in our native states'. For this reason he transferred Evan Maconochie from Rajpipla and Trevor Plowden from Kashmir. He was particularly critical of Plowden, an 'autocratic little beggar' who had been 'forcing the pace' and 'trying to set the Maharaja aside'. Durand wanted to give the incompetent ruler a chance to atone for his misrule, to let him form 'an administration after his own heart' and to do so with the help of a Resident 'not already convinced of his hopelessness'.[57] The Maharaja did not rise to the challenge and a year later, in 1889, he found it expedient to abdicate for a few years in favour of a Council of State. But the effort was a typical example of Durand's benign outlook.

> I have always felt that what we should regard as our primary object in dealing with the native states is the gain of their goodwill and confidence, not the establishment of a high standard of administration. We must of course put down gross and systematic oppression, because we do not allow rebellion, which is the natural check upon repression, but I do not think it is our business to look too closely into administrative details, so long as the people are reasonably satisfied with their chief and he behaves well to us. We get no thanks from anyone for working up the native states and insisting upon administrative reforms, which political officers are rather apt to do, and to claim credit for doing.[58]

One of Britain's favourite ways of dealing with an errant ruler was to diminish his prestige. In 1876 the Maharaja of Jodhpur refused to attend Lord Mayo's Durbar at Ajmer – the British enclave in Rajputana – because his seat had been placed below those of the princes of Udaipur and Jaipur. As a result he was told to leave British territory, his seventeen-gun salute was reduced, and his punishment was published in the Government of India's *Gazette*. The Raja of Jhabua lost his eleven-gun salute altogether when he allowed a suspected temple robber to be mutilated before he was brought to trial.[59]

Administrative incompetence did not by itself usually result in the deposition of a ruler. After running up a massive debt of 89 lakhs of rupees,* the Maharao of Kotah was deprived of all

---

*8,900,000 rupees or £890,000.

executive power but permitted to remain on the throne. Even when incompetence was combined with 'gross tyranny' and debauchery, as they were with the Maharaja of Alwar in 1870, the ruler might be allowed to retain a seat on a Native Council under a British president. In clear cases of murder, however, the chiefs usually did not manage to survive. The Nawab of Tonk was deposed in 1867 for complicity in the murder of his uncle and several other people. And in 1893 the Khan of Kalat, implicated in the killing of his Wazir and other 'deeds of savagery', agreed to abdicate in favour of his son.[60]

Sometimes the Political Departments of Bombay and the Government of India clashed over the fate of a ruling chief. In the 1880s Bombay Politicals were determined to get rid of the Rana of Porbandar, an important Kathiawar chief who repeatedly promised to reform his administration but never made an attempt to do so. Among his deficiencies were his failure to understand the concept of an independent judiciary and his decision during a famine to keep 'his granaries well filled while his subjects were dying right and left'.[61] The Politicals failed to persuade one Governor, Fergusson, to depose him but succeeded with his successor, Lord Reay. The decision dismayed the soft-hearted Durand who thought the Rana a 'fine old Rajput of most genial disposition and virtuous private life'. Porbandar, he told Reay, was a great friend of the British and 'incapable of disaffection even [when] dethroned'. Consequently he hoped something might 'be done to make the close of the old man's life happier . . . that without restoring him to power we might perhaps let him return to his own country and end his days in comfort and dignity instead of wandering about as an exile'. In a further elucidation of the Durand doctrine, the Foreign Secretary explained that:

In Rajputana and Central India we have many cases of the kind, in some of which the Chiefs behave much worse than the Rana has done. If after repeated warnings they prove to be incorrigible they are deprived of power, and the State is administered for them by a British officer, or a native Diwan, or a Council of Regency as the case may be. But the general course even then is to let the Chief retain his position as titular ruler of the State, with the ceremonial honours and privileges attaching to it, and even if possible to leave in his hands certain limited authority . . . He might perhaps be allowed to see the Budget, and advise on the appropriation of the revenues, and take an interest in certain other political affairs, in short to become a constitutional ruler of a restricted kind, instead of a refugee . . .[62]

Under pressure from Durand, who was supported by his chief, Lord Dufferin, the Bombay Governor agreed to let the Rana return to Porbandar. But he warned the Viceroy that the decision would have a bad effect on other chiefs 'who would be surprised to see us condone prematurely a long-continued career of obstinacy and resistance'.[63]

The most senior prince deposed in the decades after the Mutiny was Mulhar Rao, the Gaekwar of Baroda, one of the highest-ranking states in India. In 1863 he had tried to reach the throne by attempting to poison the ruler, his brother Khander Rao, who as a result put him in prison. Seven years later he succeeded Khander Rao and followed his example of 'gross misrule', alienating both noblemen and farmers and governing with a combination of tyranny and incompetence. Supporters of his brother mysteriously died in prison; women were flogged and abducted for forced labour in the palace; traders and bankers were compelled by torture and extortion to supplement the royal revenue. In 1873, after three years on the throne, Mulhar Rao was warned by the British that he would be deposed unless he reformed his regime within eighteen months. Shortly afterwards Colonel Phayre, the rather tactless and overbearing Resident at Baroda, claimed that the Gaekwar had tried to murder him by persuading his servants to put poison in his sherbet. The Government of India decided to remove Phayre, whom it regarded as obstructive and ill-suited to his job, and replace him with Sir Lewis Pelly, who investigated the attempted poisoning and reported that the evidence implicated Mulhar Rao. Pending a Commission of Inquiry, it then sent troops to arrest the ruler and take over the administration of the state. The Commission, however, could not come to a conclusion, its three British officials (including two judges) believing in the Gaekwar's guilt, its three Indians (including the Maharajas of Jaipur and Gwalior) unconvinced that he had instigated the plot. In the end Mulhar Rao was removed not for the attempted murder of a British Resident but for his 'incorrigible misrule'. Baroda itself prospered greatly during the ensuing Council of Regency and continued to do so under the enlightened rule of the next Gaekwar, a boy adopted in 1875 who attained his majority seven years later.[64]

Temple at Hyderabad

The most coveted Residency in India was Hyderabad, and not just because of the Corinthian splendours of the building or the pay and prestige of the post. Of all the political appointments, it was the most important (covering a vast area), the most challenging (the Nizams were not a notably co-operative dynasty) and the most varied. In addition to the Political's normal duties of dealing with a native government, the Resident had charge of the cantonments at Secunderabad and Bolarum, and acted in effect as Chief Commissioner of Berar, a huge territory in the north of the state which in mid-century the Nizam had been persuaded to 'assign' to the British in lieu of his debts.

In 1867–8 the Residency was inhabited by the redoubtable Richard Temple, a man who served in every province of the Indian Empire except Burma. Judged by his appointments, Temple was the most successful Civilian of all time: he had the best Residency, held two of the top posts in the central Government (Foreign Secretary and Finance Member) and headed three provinces (the CP, Bengal and Bombay). Able, industrious and a shrewd selector of subordinates, Temple more or less created the administration of the Central Provinces, making revenue settlements, establishing an educational department, setting up schools, public gardens, municipalities and local district boards. Alfred Lyall, who worked under him in the CP, marvelled at the way he rushed about every part of his province,

> looks to everything himself, pushes on local improvements, tree planting and cattle-breeding – examines jails and dispensaries, routs out everybody and keeps them at work by incessant circulars and orders. The country is very backward and he is determined to shove it forward – the country resists inertly as long as it can, tumbles back as often as Temple props it up, and when forcibly driven forward runs the wrong way.

Privately Lyall thought officials should be less zealous and meddlesome. His 'real sympathies and tastes' were not with a 'pushing, go ahead' administration like Temple's, and he wished the population of the CP would show more 'spirit' than simply give 'itself up as raw material to be moulded just as energetic officials choose to handle it'.[65]

Temple was much appreciated by his superiors, including John Lawrence, for whom he had acted as Secretary in the Punjab during the Mutiny. He was after all clever, efficient and willing to please. But he was disliked by many of his juniors, who regarded him as vain, ambitious and interfering. To John Beames he was a 'windbag', to Donald Macnabb a 'humbug'. Beames thought it futile to be always dashing about trying to see everything, asking the wrong questions to the wrong people, writing down the wrong answers in a notebook and compiling a 'vainglorious minute' about it all. Beames was too irreverent to have appreciated Temple in any circumstances, but his memoirs explain the personal animosity. After a large dinner in Orissa he made a speech parodying the pomposity and satirizing the career of a man who was then Lieutenant-Governor of Bengal. One of Temple's staff reported the matter to his master, who notoriously lacked a sense of humour, and the parodist's promotion prospects suffered in consequence.[66]

Temple's conceit certainly invited parody. He declared that he had been inspired by Napoleon I to contemplate 'administration conducted with immense energy in a gigantic sphere'. And he coupled this with trying to look like Napoleon III, wearing a beard and moustache that made him resemble the Emperor's caricature in *Punch*. Such vanity seemed inappropriate for a man whose appearance was described as 'grotesque and grisly', a 'positive miracle of ugliness' and – even by the *Dictionary of National Biography* – as 'ungraceful' and lending itself to caricature.[67] In his memoirs Henry Cotton remembered how 'there simmered over his features a perpetual summer of self-content'. Like Curzon, Temple inspired anecdotes and, as with the Viceroy, many of these were untrue. He did not commemorate his success in the Central Provinces by striking a medal depicting himself with the laurel wreath of a victorious Roman emperor. But he did insist that his banquets – what he called 'opening the hospitality of the Residency to all and sundry in the station' – should culminate in a viewing of the watercolours he had most recently painted.[68]

Temple was not modest about his period as Resident, claiming in his autobiography that he had been 'virtually the Atlas on whose shoulders the Hyderabad state rested'. Yet although it rested at least as much on the shoulders of the Dewan, Sir Salar Jung, Temple's role was vital and intelligently played. He remained generally in the background, 'pulling the strings but reserving all the outward semblance of authority to the Native Government'.[69]

At the beginning of the nineteenth century the Nizam had enjoyed close relations with the Resident, James Kirkpatrick, a descendant of Jacobite exiles and the husband of a Muslim noblewoman at his court. Kirkpatrick was genuinely fond of the Nizam, whom he referred to as 'Old Nizzy' and whom he gave presents such as a lioness, a fur cloak and some complicated clockwork. Old Nizzy returned the affection, addressing Kirkpatrick as his 'Beloved Son' and even paying for the construction of the magnificent Residency.[70] But this brief era was succeeded by a much longer one in which uneasy situations continually repeated themselves. As Temple noted after a perusal of the Residency records,

> the isolation of the Nizam, his incapacity for public affairs, his jealousy of the Minister, his belief that the Minister was leagued with the English, the leaning of the Minister on the Resident for support, the endeavour of the Minister to keep the Resident all to himself, to prevent the Resident from communicating with the other nobles of the state, the isolation of the nobles from each other, from the Nizam and from the Resident, the difficulty in finding a possible successor to any Minister; – all these and the like were nothing new, but were applicable to preceding Nizams, and to preceding Ministers, and had been complained of over and over again by successive Residents.[71]

Temple submitted without much complaint to the etiquette of a court that maintained its Mughal traditions right up to 1947. He wrote letters in florid Persian to request interviews with the Nizam; he travelled in an elephant procession to pay his formal respects. He also received official gifts. At the end of Ramadan the Nizam sent a macebearer with twenty-four goats, which Temple divided among his servants; in honour of Queen Victoria's birthday, the Dewan presented him with boxes of fireworks. Temple hoped to abolish one distasteful custom – taking off his shoes in the Nizam's presence – but was told by his predecessor, George Yule, that Calcutta would never sanction the change. The new Resident made no further objections.

After all, the removal of shoes was only a part of court etiquette, not like the kowtow to the Chinese Emperor, which was an admission of inferiority.[72]

The Nizam was a superstitious man, reliant on fakirs and astrologers. He was suspicious of reforms proposed by the Resident, partly because he saw little wrong with his Mughal system of government, partly because he believed – with some reason – that the British were still trying to reduce his power. According to Salar Jung, he thought reform of the judicial system was a 'conspiracy to disgrace the nobility by bringing them to trial before men of lower degree'. Even before Temple's arrival in Hyderabad, he had sent an official to inform the incoming Resident that his subjects would not consent to vaccination. He was even more opposed to the construction of a railway line to his capital, fearing it might prompt some of his rebellious relatives to disgrace him by jumping on a train and rushing off to Bombay. On the subject of municipal filth he was equally resistant. He did not mind if the British Superintending-Surgeon wished to examine the city's rudimentary drains but he was opposed to proposals that the streets should be cleaned. Temple, however, was firm on this issue, pointing out that dirt increased the danger of epidemics. Once he had persuaded the Dewan of the need for improvement, a system of drain-laying and rubbish clearance was introduced.[73]

Hyderabad owed its only sustained period of good government in the nineteenth century not to Nizams or Residents but to the remarkable figure of Salar Jung, who became Dewan in his mid-twenties in 1853 and dominated the state Government for the next thirty years. He transformed one of the most misruled states in India by reforming the bureaucracy, modernizing the revenue system, setting up civil and criminal courts, and creating a proper police force. Yet although he admired British administrative methods, he was determined to preserve the cultural traditions of the court and the nobility. The price of his success was the hostility of the Nizam, who was jealous of his Minister and resentful of the support he received from the British, who more or less forced the ruler to accept him back after his resignation in 1867. The Nizam reacted to their alliance by observing that his Minister must have had British ancestors and telling him to obey the orders of his ruler and not to 'mind whether the kingdom goes well or badly'. He also forbade Salar Jung to leave the city of Hyderabad – rather a severe constriction for the Minister of a state larger than mainland Italy – and insisted that he ask permission before accompanying Temple to a prize-giving ceremony at the Nizam's own medical school.[74]

The Resident claimed he was the Atlas in spite of not having the power to give orders or a voice in the making of appointments. He 'pulled strings' by talking to Salar Jung over breakfast and writing him letters, sometimes several in the same day. These missives were always courteous and sometimes written in Persian. Temple's style was to advise this, to commend that, to recall something else to the Minister's recollection, a somewhat patronizing and laborious method of explaining what was often obvious to a clever and educated man. The Resident 'earnestly recommended' the preservation of the Nizam's forests, the object being not 'to deprive the people of wood' but 'to prevent their cutting it wastefully and to teach them to cut it economically'. A few months later the Minister was informed that it was a mistake to let people cut down young trees because, 'if allowed to obtain full growth', they 'would be a source of wealth to your country. I earnestly commend this to your attention.'[75]

After Temple's departure the British continued to depend on the Minister. In 1875 the Viceroy, Northbrook, observed that 'the improved state of Hyderabad rests entirely on the life of Salar Jung – one man'.[76] But the one man was never a British stooge. Whatever the Nizam might think or say, the interests of Hyderabad were his priority. After making the state stable and solvent, Salar Jung began to assert its earlier status as an independent power in alliance with Britain. He even applied for the restoration of Berar. These developments were so unwelcome to Northbrook's successor, Lytton, who liked the native states to be decorative and deferential, that after the Nizam's death he refused to allow Salar Jung to rule as sole Regent. Instead he saddled him with a co-Regent who had constantly intrigued against him and whose servant had once tried to murder him. The next Viceroy, Ripon, reversed Lytton's policy and allowed Salar Jung to govern by himself. But in 1883 Hyderabad's greatest statesman died after eating canned oysters at a picnic. One doctor at the Residency maintained that he had died of cholera, but the other disagreed. Since no one else had died of the oysters, and the Minister had many enemies, poison was suspected.[77]

Griffin in Central India

Lepel Griffin was even cleverer than Temple and almost as vain. Yet his career was less successful because he had no tact or manners and because his ability was accompanied by curiously erratic judgement. Temple knew how to please his superiors, and his behaviour towards them bordered on sycophancy. Griffin behaved as if he did not care what they thought of him. He swaggered before them, scornful and arrogant, laughing at fools, flaunting his relationships with women in a manner that was bound to excite the disapproval of Anglo-India.

One of the early competition wallahs, Griffin quickly distinguished himself in the Punjab Commission. He wrote three serious works as an official in the districts including one immense volume, *The Rajahs of the Punjab*, before moving to the secretariat in Lahore. He was in his element as Chief Secretary, enjoying both the work and the social life, in which he established a reputation for being witty and flirtatious. In Lahore he wrote clever articles and lectured on Tennyson. In Simla, the summer capital shared by the Punjab and the central Government, he was a leading player in amateur theatricals. A staple of the season was his farce about women's rights, which contained satirical digs at the Foreign Office as well as his famous aphorism about the Government of India being 'a despotism of office boxes, tempered by the occasional loss of a key'.

In 1875 Northbrook described Griffin as 'one of the most promising of our young officers' but warned him, through his Lieutenant-Governor, 'not to let himself be run away in writing to the Press what is injudicious and inconsistent with his position'.[78] One injudicious opinion which appeared in print was his view that Afghanistan was a 'feudatory' of the Indian Government. This did not, however, deter Northbrook's successor, Lytton, from calling on Griffin to help rescue his disastrous Afghan policy. 'After lengthened consideration', wrote the Viceroy early in 1880, he had come to the conclusion that Griffin was the 'one man in India who [was] in all respects qualified by personal ability, special official experience, intellectual quickness and tact, general common sense and literary skill' to conduct the necessary diplomacy in Kabul.[79]

Although Griffin had no tact and little sense, he was in fact successful in Afghanistan. Lytton's successor, Lord Ripon, saluted his 'real diplomatic triumph' and credited him with 'securing the unmolested retirement' of British troops from the north of the country. Since 'such successes [were] proofs of decided ability and of skill in dealing with Natives', the new Viceroy promoted him to the post of Agent to the Governor-General in Central India. Northbrook warned him against making the appointment, arguing that an Agency of 148 states required 'great tact and firmness', especially in dealing with Scindia and Holkar, 'two very troublesome men'. Griffin, wrote the former Viceroy, should be kept in the secretariat and not given 'serious responsibility' in such a wide political sphere. 'Pray make a note of this.' Ripon ignored the advice and went ahead with the appointment. The new AGG 'had faults of manner', he admitted, but he was satisfied that these were 'outward faults only, which overlay sterling qualities'.[80]

Ripon was wrong about the faults being only 'outward', but it was another Viceroy, his successor Dufferin, who had to deal with the misjudgement. Griffin was, as Alfred Lyall pointed out, 'an ass in externals', making a great fuss about getting a knighthood, 'peacocking' before his subordinates 'in the jungles' and presiding over dinner parties with the pomp of a Viceroy. Dufferin was enraged to learn that the AGG's thirst for 'self-glorification' would have cost the Gwalior exchequer £1,000 if a painter commissioned to do a full-length portrait had not died before starting on the job. Like everyone else, Lyall recognized Griffin's 'sterling qualities', his intellect and his knowledge of foreign affairs. But he also realized that his faults were not all 'outward'.[81] Northbrook had been right to advise Ripon to keep him in the secretariat because in a position of responsibility Griffin became a blunderer.

The principal field of the AGG's blundering was Bhopal, which after Hyderabad was the largest state with a Muslim dynasty. An ally of the British since the Maratha Wars, it was ruled for over a century by four women in direct descent. The most remarkable of these was the second, Sikandar Begum, who survived a murder attempt by her husband in 1838 and governed the state as regent or ruler from 1847 to 1868. An administrator and reformer, she was also an archer, a fencer, a polo player and a crack shot. Her daughter Shahjehan, who loved music and aspired to become a poet, preferred indoor activities. One of her lovers was a seller of perfume called Siddiq Hassan, whom she married as her second husband because, as the British were told, it would have been embarrassing for a Begum to have an illegitimate child. She also made the adventurer her Minister and persuaded the Government to give him a seventeen-gun salute and the title of Nawab. Siddiq responded by forcing his wife to adopt purdah (which her mother and grandmother had abandoned) and taking over control of the state himself. He quickly proved to be corrupt, tyrannical and incompetent. Thousands of civil suits remained undealt with; hundreds of people were incarcerated without trial.[82]

On arrival in Central India in 1881, Griffin wrote to Shahjehan listing her husband's misdeeds and demanding that she did something to rectify them. When the enamoured Begum paid no attention, he urged the Government to intervene, advocating the removal of Siddiq's titles and his arrest on charges of corruption and sedition. From the Foreign Office Durand pleaded for restraint and respect for the Begum's dignity. This time Griffin paid no attention. In 1885 he summoned a durbar at Bhopal at which he publicly accused Siddiq of corruption, withdrew his titles, arrested two of his officials and forbade him to interfere further in state affairs. He did not however banish the Begum's consort, an omission he later regretted.[83]

In the aftermath of this event Griffin refused to show magnanimity towards the angry and humiliated Begum. When she wrote to the Viceroy about the selection of a new Minister, the Agent told her she was wrong in supposing the choice lay with her, and that as a matter of fact she had nothing to do with it. Durand remonstrated, deploring such 'asperities of style'. Dufferin was incandescent, telling Kimberley at the India Office that the AGG was 'dangerous, vain, self-seeking, bad-tempered and not a real gentleman'. But Griffin was unrepentant. People on the Viceroy's Council, he told Durand, knew nothing about the native states. Ilbert, the Law Member, 'regarded Bhopal affairs from the point of view . . . of a barrister's basement in Chancery Lane'. He and his colleagues had no idea 'of the infinite intrigue of a native state, the absolute and, to an English mind, the inconceivable duplicity and unscrupulousness of the highest officials from the Chief downwards, the detected falsehoods, forgeries and perjuries, which occasion no shame or remorse'. They simply did not understand that 'incessant watchfulness and firmness [were] necessary to keep people like [Siddiq] Hassan in reasonable control'.[84]

The Begum reacted to her husband's deposition by beseeching

Viceroys and Foreign Secretaries to reverse the decision. When they refused, on Griffin's insistence, she declined to co-operate with the British in any way, a position she stuck to even after her antagonist, whom she accused of a personal 'odium' towards her, had left Central India. She was so much 'on the rampage', reported his successor in 1888, that Durand thought there was no way out of the 'horrid mess' left by Griffin except to depose the Begum or bring back her husband as Minister. The dilemma disappeared with Siddiq's death in 1890, and Anglo-Bhopal relations were much improved by Dufferin's successor, Lansdowne, who criticized Griffin for his intemperate language and delighted Shahjehan by restoring the title of Nawab to her deceased husband. The Begum died in 1901 and was succeeded by her daughter Sultanjahan, a ruler much more to the British taste. In his notes left for his successor, Curzon described her as 'very loyal & anxious to please, takes a keen interest in her administration – a good little woman'. She ruled Bhopal until her death in 1926.[85]

The AGG in Central India was also Resident of Indore, where he lived and where he oversaw the most difficult of all dynasties, the Maharajas of Holkar. There Griffin entertained in his own manner, a combination of pomp and impropriety. Dufferin deplored his 'cynical contempt for public opinion', his 'pleasure in passing himself off as a destroyer of female virtue', and his 'habit of ostentatiously maintaining intimate relations with some vulgar second-rate woman'. Lyall compared him to Louis XIV, always having 'somebody else's wife living with him in state, a reigning favourite to whom everyone must bow down'. When Queen Victoria's son, the Duke of Connaught, arrived to stay, the current Madame de Montespan was a woman who had been married to a Mr Kingscote and engaged to Lord Malmesbury. The Duchess hinted that the lady might absent herself when she lunched at the Residency, but Griffin puffed himself up and replied that, if Her Highness felt unable to meet ladies staying in his house, then he would have to forego the honour of entertaining her. The Duke was furious, complaining to his mother and to Dufferin about the AGG's 'want of tact and proper feeling'.[86] Later in London Griffin was snubbed by the Prince of Wales, a man whose resemblances to the Sun King were somewhat similar.

Even an official more tactful than Griffin would have had difficulties in dealing with Holkar, a ruler whose violence and irrationality were illustrated by his fondness for kicking his attendants in the stomach, harnessing the state bankers to his carriage at the time of the full moon, and indulging in what Curzon called 'wild freaks of which only a lunatic would be capable'.[87] In 1887 the Maharaja decided to attend the Queen's Jubilee in England, but the Government would not let him go unless he left behind his lover, a man called Gopalia. Eventually, after some bargaining, Holkar agreed to travel with Griffin in what Dufferin regarded as 'a most undignified substitution'. At first all went well on the voyage. Away from 'his evil associations', reported Griffin, the ruler was 'amiable and civil to everybody' and after a few days was dining 'in the saloon with credit', drinking champagne and using a knife and fork with skill. But matters went downhill in London. At lunch in the City with Lord Rothschild he was 'as disagreeable as it was possible to be' and he was afterwards 'most discourteous' to officials during a tour of the Bank of England. As Griffin eventually realized, he became 'more *difficile* and morose' the longer he was deprived of the company of Gopalia. He was so desperate to meet his catamite in either Cairo or Constantinople that he even tried to leave London before the Queen had formally received him. Griffin prevented this but finally allowed him to find Gopalia in Venice. While his reports of these travels to Durand suggest the behaviour of a model diplomat, witnesses told the Foreign Secretary that Griffin had mishandled Holkar, exaggerated his misdeeds and behaved badly himself, ostentatiously flirting with women on the steamer. One of them complained that he had turned the issue of Gopalia into a 'personal struggle', trying to destroy him as he had destroyed Siddiq in Bhopal.[88]

Holkar survived Griffin but he could not survive Curzon. His eccentricities became more pronounced over the years and in 1903 he was forced to abdicate in favour of his son, a process that was repeated in both the following generations. In 1925 Holkar's grandson Tukoji Rao was implicated in the murder of a Bombay businessman with whom a former mistress had run away to live. Presented with the choice between abdication and giving evidence at an inquiry, he abdicated in favour of his son. He later married Nancy Miller of Seattle and spent a prosperous exile, paid for by his former subjects, in a château at Saint-Germain and a villa on the Riviera.[89]

Maynard in the Mountains

John Maynard was a very different man from Temple and Griffin. Like them he was a Civilian who did some work in the native states. And like them he stood for Parliament after his retirement and lost an election. But whereas Temple went down as the Conservative candidate in East Worcestershire, and Griffin was beaten as a Liberal Unionist in West Nottingham, Maynard was defeated as the Labour aspirant in King's Lynn. In subsequent elections he lost for the same party in Stroud and East Fulham as well.

Maynard was in some ways a reluctant imperialist. He believed that India needed Britain, at any rate at the end of the nineteenth century, yet he was uncomfortable with the system of 'everything for the people and nothing by them'. Sometimes he longed, as he told his American wife, 'for the fresh breezes of democracy'. While he accepted the 'burden' of imperialism, 'to seek another's profit,/And work another's gain', he disliked the pomp that went with it. Thus his *bête noir* was Curzon, whom he called 'the Peacock' in letters and 'Lord Cursem of Wheedlestone' in a privately published satire.[90] This was an unusual prejudice for a Civilian. While Curzon upset many Anglo-Indians during his viceroyalty, it was generally the mediocrities who resented him: the best of the ICS appreciated his drive and intelligence and the way he got things done.

In 1889, after serving his first three years as an Assistant Commissioner, Maynard was sent up to the mountains north of Simla to act as Counsellor to the Raja of Mandi, the nervous and worried ruler of one of the Punjab's native states. Its capital was a town of slate roofs and mitre-shaped temples with sacred bulls in painted stone at their entrance. Around it were hills of vast forests dotted with villages, water mills, buffalo pens and iron forges. The townspeople were turbaned and Hindu; the hill men had Tibetan features and wore felt caps and grey shawls.

The middle-aged Raja was delighted by his young Counsellor and became embarrassingly dependent on him. He asked him how he should allocate his time, at what hour he should get up, when he should perform his religious worship, and how many cups of tea he should drink. He even requested a manual of daily duties and declared his intention of taking up such hobbies of Maynard's as badminton and going for walks. But the poor man was tormented by religion, the legacy of a Calvinist missionary who had told him that unbelievers were damned. Maynard tried to reassure him that God would not punish a ruler who did his duty to his subjects, but the Raja was not convinced. After much agonizing he decided that if God proposed to punish him for remaining a Hindu, he would tell him, 'Your judgement is of course correct Your Majesty. But I submit that if you wished me to be a Christian, you should have caused me to be born in England. It is not my fault that I was born in India.'

A dead French theologian may have given the Raja nightmares, but the ruler still relied on Brahmins and astrologers to assist him with the daily business of the state, deciding such matters as what incantations should be used to combat a buffalo disease, what to do with a mad but sacred bull loose in the town, how much cow-dung an ex-communicant should eat before he was restored to his caste, or what hour of what day would be auspicious for the Raja to set off on his travels with his 341 camp followers, 50 of them carrying the kitchen utensils. Maynard laughed at the chaos of the state, the comic-opera administration, the pantomime punishment of officials: the Head of the Public Works Department was placed 'on an ass, painted half red and half blue, with his face to the tail, and conveyed in this ignominious fashion to the frontier'. But he took his reform work seriously, concentrating on the reduction of forced labour, which virtually amounted to slavery, and the creation of fixed tenant rights in the land. He did not, however, take a missionary approach to the local marriage system whereby a man could have several wives and a woman could have several husbands, usually brothers. Giving the Minister a holiday and taking over his work for a few days, Maynard found himself dealing with the registration of wife sales, from which the Raja took a tax of 20 per cent of the purchase money. Selling women was not an edifying procedure, but the women did not become slaves and indeed seemed freer than in the rest of India. Elopements, noted Maynard, were 'the rule of married life, and neither party objects to reconciliation when the spree is over'. Mandi was outside the nose-cutting zone of the Punjab.

A year after his sojourn in Mandi, Maynard was sent to the neighbouring state of Suket to assist his Commissioner, George Smyth, in dealing with a less attractive ruler. The Raja was in his early twenties, very fat, very shrewd and terrified that his state was about to be taken away from him. Since he had already received three or four 'final warnings' about his tyranny and misrule, Maynard assumed that he and Smyth were going to Suket to dethrone him. But by previously rushing to Lahore and abasing himself before the Lieutenant-Governor, the Raja had managed to secure yet another reprieve. The Civilians were empowered only to listen to complaints of injustice and to force the ruler to carry out their decisions.

Maynard spent the first week reading petitions and 'examining the aggrieved subjects of the state'. There seemed to be no injustice of which the Raja was incapable, no crime he had not committed, and no section of the population that was spared his tyranny. He dispossessed peasants at will and made those who survived pay their rent before the harvest was ready. He sent landowners to jail, where they sometimes died, and confiscated their estates. Extortion, robbery, torture and murder were all employed to fill the chieftain's coffers. Women were 'seized, and either given as wives to dependants of the Raja or forcibly sold to the highest bidder and the proceeds credited to the state treasury'. One elderly woman complained that a certain Ruldu, 'the chief instrument of the Raja's tyrannies, had seized and sold . . . two daughters-in-law of hers, one of whom committed suicide from grief, and next her only daughter'.

As the inquiry continued, Maynard noted, the Raja's mood swung from 'insolent pride to contemptible and cringing humility'. The young Civilian longed to do something, at the very least to arrest Ruldu on the charge of murdering a prisoner. But the Commissioner, who seemed worn out after nearly thirty years in the Service, was nervous and irresolute, spending 'a whole evening walking up and down, pale and excited and wringing his hands, expostulating and raising difficulties'. Finally his deputy prevailed upon him to arrest Ruldu and put him in handcuffs. Although it was mid-January, Maynard decided to leave Smyth reading petitions in Suket and go up into the snows with his prisoner for a three-week tour of the state. The sight of the sulky Ruldu in fetters beside him astonished the villagers and encouraged them to give evidence of his corruption and tyrannies. After Maynard returned to Suket, he and Smyth wrapped up their business. They finished their cases, issued some proclamations, forced the Raja to comply with their demands and marched their prisoners out of the state. Ruldu himself was banished for ten years.[91]

10

Mandarins

~

Armchairs and Clockwork

Some ninety Civilians, about a tenth of the ICS on active service,
worked not in the districts or the Indian states but at a desk in
Calcutta, Simla or the provincial capitals. Most of these were secretaries of some kind, Under-Secretaries and Chief Secretaries of local
governments, Under-Secretaries and Secretaries of the departments
of the Government of India. Sometimes they were also Private
Secretaries to a Governor or a Viceroy.*

Although the bureaucracy was served by legions of clerks, it was
not an especially bloated one. The departments of state each had two
or three members of the Covenanted Civil Service, except for the
Legislative Department which had one. The larger provinces and
Burma had six or seven Civilians in their secretariats, the Central
Provinces three, Assam two. Secretaries in the Government of India
often rose to become Members of the Viceroy's Council responsible for the same department, a leap equivalent to a Permanent

---

*Other posts outside the districts and the states that were always or generally filled by the
ICS included the Inspector-General of Police in Bengal, the Opium Agent at Benares,
the Salt Commissioner, the provincial Postmasters-General, the Collector of Customs at
Calcutta, the Commissioner of Customs at Bombay and the Collector of Sea Customs
at Madras.

Under-Secretary in Whitehall becoming a cabinet minister. Promotional opportunities in the provincial secretariats varied from place to place. In Bengal and the NWP the Chief Secretary could aspire to membership of the Board of Revenue and even to the lieutenant-governorship. In Bombay, where there was no Board of Revenue, he could become a member of the Executive Council, one of the triumvirate (which included the Governor) that ran the province. And in Madras he could be a member of both the Board of Revenue and the Executive Council. In the Non-Regulation provinces, however, there were neither boards nor councils. The second post in the Punjab was the Financial Commissioner.

While their positions were much sought after, the secretariats did not appeal to everyone. After his adventures in Mandi and Suket, John Maynard quickly became 'sick of a desk and the Secretariat routine' of his new job in Lahore. Another Punjab Civilian, James Wilson, actually resigned as a Secretary to the central Government so that he could return on a lower salary to his province. Membership of the Viceroy's Council was one of the highest positions in India, but it bored George Yule so much that his health broke down. A man described in his obituaries as 'the greatest votary of sport in India', the 'emperor of the spears', the slayer of 'hecatombs of boars' and 500 tigers, was made ill by the sedentary life of Simla. Retirement did not suit him either. A hero of the Mutiny, he died from injuries caused by slipping on an icy pavement in London.[1]

William Horsley refused a job in the secretariat because he did not want to leave the jungles of Bombay. But few junior Civilians rejected such offers. They were usually too frightened of being stuck in remote districts and forgotten; besides, most of them liked a period of respite from solitude and solitary responsibility. They were also aware that it was difficult to get to the top without some experience of the bureaucracy. George Campbell was a rare example of a Lieutenant-Governor who had never served in the secretariat, although he had been a personal assistant to Lord Canning. Michael O'Dwyer was also unusual: he briefly acted as Under-Secretary in the Punjab, but his handwriting was so bad that he was soon sent away to work as a Settlement Officer. He did, nevertheless, become Lieutenant-Governor of his province.[2]

Provincial governments tended to leave their less effective civil servants in the countryside, playing out their time as Collectors and

District Judges. But they liked to rotate their best Civilians between work in the secretariat and administration in the *mofussil*. Henry Cotton closely combined both labours, advancing from Assistant Magistrate to Collector (of Chittagong) to Chief Commissioner of a province (Assam) while in between filling most of the posts in the Bengal Government from Under-Secretary to Chief Secretary via the secretaryships of the Revenue and Finance Departments. Charles Bayley's career achieved a different symmetry, its thirty-seven years divided fairly evenly between the secretariat, the districts and the native states.

Viceroys often insisted that Civilians should have experience of the *mofussil* and the bureaucracy, even if it meant transferring grumbling Secretaries who had just built themselves a house in Simla and did not want to become Commissioners.[3] Sometimes, however, governments noticed that a Civilian showed such aptitude for the secretariat that they could not let him go back to a district. As a young subdivisional officer outside Dacca, Henry Howard had embarrassed the Government by his martinettish behaviour: he had even tried to prosecute an engine driver for blowing his whistle too long as his train approached the town of Narayanganj. Although he improved his reputation as Deputy Superintendent of Police in Calcutta, he did not discover his real *métier* until Curzon, a good selector of men, appointed him Under-Secretary in his Government's Finance Department. Howard then rapidly became one of India's leading financial experts, publishing the much-praised *India and the Gold Standard* and the more esoteric *Bengal Manual of the Sea Customs and Tariff Laws*, and filling the posts of Collector of Customs, Controller of Currency, Acting Secretary of the Commerce and Industry Department, Secretary of the Finance Department and Acting Finance Member on the Viceroy's Council. His career was cut short by the death of his wife, which persuaded him to take his five small children back to London. In retirement he continued to work on financial matters, becoming Controller of Finance at the India Office, Bursar of St John's College, Cambridge, and Treasurer of the university boat club. He also published *An Account of the Finances of the College of St John the Evangelist in the University of Cambridge, 1511–1926*.[4]

Assistant Magistrates plucked from the jungles were forced to make adjustments in their comportment. When Maurice Hayward was transferred to Poona as an Under-Secretary to the Bombay

Government, his superior had to give him hints about etiquette, about taking his hat off, about addressing the Governor as 'Sir' and his wife as 'Your Ladyship' rather than 'Your Excellency'. Under-Secretaries also had to acquire a full-dress uniform in dark blue embroidered with gold, accompanied by a sword and a cocked hat.[5] Their work too required radical readjustment. Instead of dealing directly with people and crops, they spent their time reading reports and writing minutes. They often stayed nine or ten hours in their offices, considerably longer than civil servants in Whitehall.

After working for seventeen years in the districts, Alfred Lyall became Secretary of the Home Department in 1873. He was delighted to exchange jungle work for an office with an armchair surrounded by boxes of papers. The work was not demanding because he found it 'much easier to deal with papers than with men – much more simple to draft orders than to carry them out'. Sometimes he worried that he was in the wrong job because his mind was reflective rather than bureaucratic – and the whole point of his post was that he should not put his own reflections on paper but acquire 'the knack of expressing other people's thoughts in the language which suits their taste'. One day a week he talked to Northbrook about departmental business that interested the Viceroy, and on another he attended the Council, producing papers for its Members to debate: at the end of discussions on home affairs Northbrook would turn to him and say, 'You understand, Mr Lyall, the conclusions at which we have arrived, and you will write accordingly.' And the Secretary wrote accordingly, better than anyone else.

The following year, after he had been transferred to Rajputana as AGG, Lyall recalled that his secretariat work had been 'regular grinding' but that his office had gone 'like good clockwork, and the work fell as grass before a steam scythe'. But out in the western deserts he had once again to 'take . . . in hand the primitive hand scythe, and to labour painfully with confused papers and untrained clerks'. A further drawback of his new job was the incessant interviews he had to grant to people of the states. Such things had not interfered with his routine in the Home Department. As a Secretary, he recalled, he 'used to feel a throb of pure pleasure on coming into a large cool quiet office room, with mountains of papers scientifically filed by a first-rate Head Clerk on each side of an armchair'.[6]

The secretariat 'type' attracted satire. Kipling's Aurelian McGoggin

was 'all head, no physique and a hundred theories', while the
Secretary in Aberigh-Mackay's *Twenty-one Days in India*

> inquired into everything; he wrote hundredweights of reports; he proved
> himself to have the true paralytic ink flux, precisely the kind of wordy dis-
> charge, or brain haemorrhage, required of a high official in India. He
> would write ten pages where a clod-hopping collector would write a sen-
> tence. He would say the same thing over and over again in a hundred
> different ways. The feeble forms of official satire were at his command.[7]

The reality was just close enough for such satire to be effective.
Secretaries prided themselves on the prodigious paperwork they
produced in the forms of notes, minutes and dispatches. 'Curzon will
hassle you secretaries,' an Army officer warned 'Jock' Cuningham on
news of the viceregal appointment in 1898. 'Oh no,' replied the
Foreign Secretary, 'he will be paper-logged in three months.'
Cuningham had misjudged his new boss, who was determined to put
an end to what he described as the era of 'tranquil procrastination'.
Hitherto, the new Viceroy observed, nothing had been accomplished in under six months. 'When I suggest six weeks, the attitude
is one of pained surprise, if six days one of pathetic protest, if six
hours of stupefied resignation.' Curzon was astonished by a system
in which proposals circulated the departments and returned to their
starting point many months later, garnished with an array of minutes
from Secretaries and Under-Secretaries who revelled in dialectics
and had perfected the art of the put-down. 'All these gentlemen', he
complained ungenerously, 'state their worthless views at equal
length, and the result is a sort of literary Bedlam.' Matters that could
have been settled by the relevant officials in a couple of discussions
went unresolved while their files proceeded in a leisurely way around
Calcutta and Simla. 'Round and round', noted the Viceroy about one
of them, 'like the diurnal revolution of the earth went the file, stately,
solemn, sure, and slow; and now, in due season, it has completed its
orbit, and I am invited to register the concluding stage.'[8]
Determined to cut down on minutes, Curzon told Cuningham
that he did not want 'the personal impression or the opinion of
everyone in the Department on everything that comes up'. His subsequent note on the system of minuting, which was distributed to
the provincial governments, resulted in a significant decrease in

the number of official papers. Only one notorious minuter was exempted from its edicts – himself.[9]

Red Tape

The secretariat was generally resented by District Officers who felt that they received inadequate reward for doing the real work of Indian administration. They toiled all year in the plains, through the furnace of spring and the monsoons of summer, while the Secretaries seldom experienced a day of climatic discomfort. The bureaucrats passed the pleasant winter months in Calcutta (or Allahabad or Madras) and, as soon as the punkahs were brought out, went up to the hills, to Simla or Darjeeling (or Naini Tal or Ootacamund). And once they were there, living congenially among their fellow countrymen, they arranged each other's promotions and dictated policies for the DOs. Or so it was believed.

District Officers often complained that Civilians in the secretariat were out of touch with the real India, that many of them went into the bureaucracy with insufficient experience of the *mofussil* and in consequence issued 'preposterous rules and orders' from their capitals. They might 'oscillate between an office stool in Calcutta and Simla' but their experience of India was limited to glimpses of villages from first-class railway compartments and interviews with 'polished native gentlemen, one and all veneered imitations of Englishmen'.[10] Henry Beveridge, a Civilian from Bengal, described them as men who 'bestride the poor land of India like Colossi in touch with it only at the two points of Simla and Calcutta, and sublimely regardless of all that lies between'.[11] What irritated the DOs was the Secretaries' self-confidence, their assumption that they were always justified in imposing their views on the men on the spot. They might have had the 'paper knowledge' of a particular subject but they seldom had the practical experience.

Civilians in the districts were scathing about the 'departmental mind', its reverence for legal symmetry and its distrust of individualism. Up at Simla a Secretary might devise a brilliant and logical rule for the 250 districts of British India. In the plains a District Officer would rage at a bureaucrat who thought that a system suitable for the Hooghly area outside Calcutta might work with the bow-and-arrow aboriginals of the Santal Parganas. In Hunter's novel, *The Old Missionary*, a Commissioner is demoted because 'one of his protests against applying a uniform procedure to races in widely different stages of human society' was 'held to have gone beyond the decorous limits of official remonstrance'.[12] Such demotions may have been rare, but the protests were common. As a young Civilian, Harcourt Butler was quickly convinced that India was not a country for general principles: 'the abstract and the absolute ought to be unknown'. According to him and many others, the growth and centralization of the bureaucracy had made the Government increasingly out of touch with the people. There was 'too much head at Simla and too little heart'. What was needed was 'a little more human sympathy'.[13]

District Officers also blamed the secretariat for the expansion of paperwork that kept them clamped to their desk when they wanted to be out among the people. Before railways and the telegraph, an official had to use his own influence and initiative to govern his district: he could not call for instructions or receive help with any speed. It was thus personal rule in both senses: without knowing the population of his charge, the individuals, the castes, the religions, he could not have done it. But technology reduced his independence. Orders came by telegraph, supervisors came by train, and his scope for action was further restricted in the twentieth century by the advent of the telephone and the motor car. As Hamilton, the Secretary of State, lamented in 1899, 'in place of the old-fashioned official constantly in the open air, and constantly coming in contact with the Natives, we have substituted a bureaucratic class, who are seldom able to leave their offices, and who govern India with a code in one hand and a telegraph wire to the Governor in the other'.[14]

Technological advance was accompanied by a new bureaucratic obsession with gathering information. District Officers now had to submit to the drudgery of clerical compilation. They had to write reports which few people read, furnish statistics which had limited value, and submit returns which were quickly filed and forgotten; if they had any time left over for ideas, these were likely to be strangled by red tape. An additional burden was the expansion of regulations. One Civilian recalled that as an Assistant Magistrate he needed to take just a small volume of rules when he went into camp: by 1913 he had 'to pack a portmanteau with codes and regulations'. Even before the end of the previous century a District Officer in the Punjab was required 'to have at his elbow some seventeen volumes of laws and rules, including three thick volumes of *Acts and Regulations applicable to the Punjab*'.[15] Alas poor Lawrences, so much for government from the saddle.

The chief consequence of all this was that the overworked District Officer was unable to spend enough time outside his headquarters with the people he was supposed to be governing. One journalist from England employed only a slightly fanciful Dickensian image in comparing him to 'a parent who writes treatises on education while the children play in the gutter'.[16]

Promotions and Rewards

Promotion in the ICS, the Judiciary and the Political Department had a variety of sponsors. Provincial governments controlled most of the appointments, bringing Assistant Magistrates into the secretariat, advancing Joint Magistrates to the rank of Collector or District Judge. The Secretary of State was in charge of Crown appointments such as the governorships of Madras and Bombay and the Civilian memberships of their Executive Councils. He also appointed the Chief Justices and the Judges of the High Court from Britain, as well as those Members of the Viceroy's Council who did not invariably come from the ICS: the heads of the Financial, Legal and Military Departments. But the real patron of the ICS in its higher echelons was the Viceroy. After consultation with the Secretary of State, who could veto a selection, he appointed the Lieutenant-Governors and Chief Commissioners, the Secretaries in the Government of India and the remaining Members of his Council. He also chose the AGGs and the occupants of the most important Residencies, though the process was not usually conducted so cryptically or genially as Curzon's legendary appointment of Sir David Barr to Hyderabad. A man who was bald and diffident as well as talented, Barr was persuaded to remind the Viceroy of his existence before the choice had to be made.

He telegraphed to Curzon, who was then in Simla: 'Psalm 132, verse 1', which, being interpreted, read, 'Lord, remember David'. Curzon replied with 'Psalm 75, verse 6': 'For promotion *cometh* neither from the East, nor from the West, nor from the South.' Barr was presumably encouraged, since Curzon was in the north. He telegraphed: 'Psalm 121, verse 1', 'I will lift up mine eyes to the hills, from whence cometh my help.' Curzon rounded off the series neatly with 'II Kings, 2, verse 23', 'Go up, thou bald head.'[17]

Junior promotion in the ICS was usually by seniority. Incompetent Civilians might be overtaken by younger men and left to stagnate in remote districts, but this was a rare occurrence. Most officers rose to the rank of Collector or District Judge unless they had given proof of incapability. Beyond this level, however, promotion was made on merit: a senior Civilian had to earn his appointment as Commissioner or Chief Secretary.

Young officials risked jeopardizing their career by refusing an appointment. When in 1856 William Money withdrew his acceptance of Canning's informal offer of an assistant commissionership, the Governor-General's Private Secretary wrote acidly to inform him that an officer who 'refused honourable promotion' on 'purely private grounds' could not 'claim to be considered as evincing zeal for the public service'.[18] Had Money not subsequently distinguished himself in the Mutiny at the Siege of Lucknow, he would not have become a Collector at the age of 29.

Senior officials were given more latitude to ponder a promotion. Durand, who had pleased several Viceroys, did not suffer for turning down the chief commissionership of Burma because it was a health risk for his wife. Griffin, who had annoyed some of the same pro-consuls (and did not have a wife at the time), was less leniently treated. Dufferin decided that his hesitation about accepting the offer of Burma relieved him of 'all obligation' towards this 'flashy and not very reputable person'.[19] The Viceroy, who was so flushed by his conquest of Upper Burma that he subsequently called himself Dufferin and Ava (the seat of the royal court), was intolerant of officials who complained about their appointments. When Dennis Fitzpatrick, who hoped to be confirmed as Chief Commissioner of the Central Provinces, admitted his displeasure at being sent to Mysore, Dufferin declared that he had treated him 'damned well' and told the complainant he was a 'hot tempered peppery fellow'.[20]

While promotions were generally made on seniority or merit,

other considerations were sometimes involved. The Government of Bengal found it difficult to fill vacancies in Assam without promising volunteers a better posting afterwards. Another obligation was placed upon it by the climate of the Ganges Delta which was so unhealthy that officials stationed there frequently had to be transferred to the drier districts of Bihar to prevent them breaking down. Such transfers, however, were made at the cost of administrative efficiency because Civilians from the Delta, where Bengali was spoken, were unlikely to speak the languages of Bihar.

Most Civilians never worked outside their province. The few who did were men who had managed to attract the eye of some important figure. Lyall owed his promotions to Commissioner and Home Secretary to the enthusiasm of Temple and the judgement of Northbrook. But disfavour from on high could be equally telling. He languished longer than he wanted in his next post, AGG in Rajputana, because Lytton had been informed that in London on furlough Lyall had sniggered at viceregal plans for an 'Imperial Assemblage' in Delhi, an enormous durbar at which Queen Victoria was to be proclaimed Empress of India.[21]

Promotions inevitably caused bitterness among people who did not get what they felt they deserved. There were charges of favouritism and vindictiveness against senior officials on account of their selections. But on the whole these do not appear to have been well-founded.[22] Men who were sent to the so-called 'penal stations' had usually done something to be penalized for. Few first-rate officials failed to get near the top even if they missed out on their ultimate ambition, a lieutenant-governorship. Beames was perhaps unlucky, but then he did annoy Temple and other senior figures, and he had borrowed money from Indians. The only group of Civilians who may have had a legitimate grievance was that small band regarded as 'unsound' on account of their support for Indian nationalism. Henry Beveridge probably missed his promotion to the Calcutta High Court for this reason. Yet it would be illogical to expect an empire to promote employees, however talented, who in effect advocated its liquidation. In any case the supporters of the Indian National Congress did not do too badly. Neither Allan Hume nor William Wedderburn nor Henry Cotton mouldered in a 'penal station'; all of them achieved senior positions in the secretariat at least. Cotton, who was sometimes referred to as a 'white baboo', may have been passed over once or twice in his career, but in the end he spent six years as head of a province before retiring and becoming President of the Congress.

In the days of the East India Company Civilians who went on furlough did not retain their positions in India unless they spent their leave in Australia, Ceylon or South Africa – a bizarre anomaly that few took advantage of. If they went to Britain for a year or two – as almost all of them did – other men took their place, and they had to look for a new post on their return. But after the Mutiny the system was changed so that they retained a lien on their appointment while on furlough. A Collector would go to England, a Joint Magistrate would serve as Acting Collector in his place, and an Assistant Magistrate would be promoted to Acting Joint Magistrate – a process that sometimes made it seem as if everyone in the Service was 'acting' for someone else. In 1861 the departure on furlough of Augustus Fortunatus Bellasis, the Collector and Magistrate of Surat, required the transfer of thirteen subordinate officials down to and including his Acting Second Assistant.[23] Politicals were shunted about almost as often. Other men's furloughs meant that between 1879 and 1885 Colonel Tweedie did three stints in Gwalior, two in Baghdad, two in Ajmer, one in Jodhpur, one on the road between Peshawar and Kabul as Political Officer during the invasion of Afghanistan, and another as Political Officer in charge of Jalalabad.[24] And if an official's departure caused headaches, his return produced several more. Ideally a Collector would come back to India and be promoted to Commissioner or Secretary of Government. But if he returned to the same district, his Acting Collector and several junior figures had to be found new posts that did not look like demotions.

So much movement was disruptive of administration and complicated to organize. It was also demoralizing for officials and their families. Civilians 'acting' for someone else were endlessly expecting a telegram to tell them that they were about to be dislodged and sent to another district. Anglo-Indians always had to be ready to pack and unpack, to buy and sell furniture, to say goodbye to old friends and make the effort to find new ones. They seldom stayed anywhere long enough to see the results of their work.

There was only one thing worse than being moved about, and that was not being moved about because there was nowhere to be moved to. This non-experience occurred mainly in the mid-1870s as a result of over-recruitment in the early 1860s. The deaths of forty-two Civilians in the Mutiny persuaded the India Office to double its ICS intake for three years, a decision that eased the immediate administrative problem but quickly led to a promotion block for those recruited subsequently. By 1875 it had become clear that, without action from the India Office, some Civilians below the promotion block would reach early retiring age (twenty-five years of service) before they had attained the rank of Collector or District Judge.[25] At the moment of retirement a Bombay Civilian might therefore be earning, as First Assistant Collector, a salary of 10,800 rupees compared to a Senior Collector with 27,900 and a Junior Collector with 21,600. After protests from the Civil Service in Bombay and the northern provinces, the Secretary of State reluctantly agreed to make certain concessions. Young Civilians affected by the promotion block were given compensation allowances, and older ones were allowed to retire early on pensions.

Salaries in the ICS were good, higher than in the other Indian services, higher than in the Civil Service in Britain and indeed in any other service in the world. They ranged from 4,800 rupees a year for an Assistant Magistrate to 100,000 rupees for a Lieutenant-Governor. The majority of Civilians, those who ended their careers as Senior Collectors, District Judges or Deputy Commissioners, were earning between 27,000 and 30,000 rupees at the time of their retirement. During their service they subscribed 4 per cent of their pay to a pension fund, and in return all of them – whatever rank they had attained – received in retirement an annual sum of £1,000.

Even young Civilians on the lowest salaries had little difficulty living on their pay so long as they were unmarried and had not got into debt in the Haileybury manner in Calcutta. Hermann Kisch found it 'quite impossible' to spend his income as an Assistant Magistrate in Bengal even though he employed a shepherd, a chicken-keeper, two grooms and three punkah-wallahs.[26] But married life multiplied expenses in a way that could not have happened in Britain. In addition to school fees and the cost of a household, a middle-aged Civilian might have to pay for a place in the hills where his family could spend the hot weather, a place in England where it might stay during visits and school holidays, and a great many tickets on P & O ships steaming between Southampton and Calcutta. As Commissioner of Orissa, John Beames received a salary of 35,000 rupees (just over £3,000 after deductions), but he had heavy debts, a wife and eight children in England, and school fees costing him nearly £600 a year.[27]

In 1870 ICS salaries were slightly lower than they had been forty years earlier although the cost of living had risen over the same period. More serious for Civilians, however, was the subsequent depreciation of the currency. In *The Importance of Being Earnest* Miss Prism instructs her pupil Cecily Cardew not to read a chapter on the fall of the rupee because the subject is too sensational and melodramatic for a young girl. It was certainly an undesirable sensation for men who earned a salary in rupees but spent much of it in sterling. Prussia's defeat of France in 1870 had led to the victors' abandonment of silver and adoption of a gold-based coinage, an event that affected other currencies and had unlucky consequences for the silver-based rupee, which had no fixed value with the gold-based pound. The result was that the rupee, which had been worth two shillings (a tenth of a pound) in 1870, fell to one shilling and seven-pence in 1885 and to below one shilling and threepence in 1892. Although this was an advantage for Indian exports, it was a disaster for Civilians with financial obligations in Britain. A thousand rupees, which had been worth £100, now purchased only £62. Henry Beveridge's salary, which had been the equivalent of £2,640, was by 1886 worth less than £2,000; each pound spent on school fees in England thus cost him thirteen and a half rupees rather than ten.[28] Six years later, the situation was even worse.

Civilians generally reacted to the blow by maintaining their children at school but reducing their own standard of living in India, a course which had the effect of deterring potential recruits to the Service and encouraging early retirement. Since their salary was paid in rupees and their pension in sterling, there was little incentive for Collectors to stay on to enjoy the ever-decreasing extra money. As one junior Civilian reported, 'Most of them say that 700 rupees a month extra [the difference between pay and pension] isn't worth-while when it entails living in a pestilential country, away from your wife and children, and in a post that takes 12 hours work a day.'[29]

Migrations to the Hills

One of the quintessential proceedings of Victorian India was the 1,200-mile spring migration from Calcutta to Simla: the packing up of the files and dispatch boxes of the imperial secretariat, the transport of hundreds of clerks and officials by rail across the Gangetic plain, the journey up a winding road into the hills by bullock cart, mail carriage and tonga, the arrival at a small English town of tin-roofed houses 7,000 feet above sea level and cut off by mountains from the rest of India. Similar journeys were made from the provincial capitals to comparably inaccessible hill stations. The almost miraculous construction of branch lines into the mountains made these expeditions easier around the end of the century, but the migrations remained complicated undertakings. The journey from Allahabad, the capital of the North-Western Provinces, to Naini Tal, the summer headquarters, required one change of trains at Cawnpore, another at Bareilly, and after Kathogodam – where the railway ended – an ascent into the hills by tonga, pulled by Tibetan ponies which had to be changed every three miles.[30]

Kipling understood the attractions of Simla but doubted whether any other nation would have pitched its seat of government a hundred miles from a railway 'on the wrong side of an irresponsible river' and liable – with the collaboration of a steady downpour and the mildest of earthquakes – to be cut off from the land it ruled as effectively as if 'separated by a month's sea voyage'.[31] As Governors-General both Bentinck and Dalhousie had spent seasons at Simla, but John Lawrence was the man responsible for its establishment as the summer capital of the Raj. It was the appropriate place, he argued, because it had one foot in the Punjab and another in the NWP.[32] (It also had a house on a hilltop watershed where rain falling on the north roof swelled the Sutlej and reached the Arabian Sea via the Indus, while rain on the other side flowed by way of the Ganges into the Bay of Bengal.) But its advantages were climatic rather than strategic or geographical. Lawrence claimed he could do more work in a single invigorating day at Simla than in five days of Calcutta's stifling humidity.

Every province had a summer headquarters in the hills except Assam, whose pleasant little capital Shillong was already in the hills. The secretariat in Burma went to Maymyo, 3,000 feet up in the Shan

Hills above Mandalay, where the climate was like an English summer and in spring the place was a paradise of violets and cherry blossom. The Rajputana Agency went to Mount Abu west of Udaipur, the CP officials settled in Pachmari in the Satpura Hills, and the Punjab Commission distributed itself between three hill stations: Simla, where from 1876 the secretariat lived in uncomfortable proximity to the central Government, Dalhousie, where the Commissioner of Lahore did his summer work, and Murree, which brewed the best beer in India.

The Madras Government was rather late in perceiving the attractions of a summer capital. But once it had found one, it was unwilling to go back to Madras. In 1870 the Secretary of State, the Duke of Argyll, ungraciously sanctioned the migration of the Government to Ootacamund in the Nilgiri Hills so long as it did not stay there for more than three months. Ten years later the India Office was complaining that it spent more time in that agreeable spot than it did in Madras.[33]

The Bengal Government was also dilatory about appreciating the charms of Darjeeling. In the 1860s most members of the secretariat stayed in Calcutta during the summer, and Campbell, the Lieutenant-Governor, continued the tradition in the early 1870s, remaining in the city or touring the province in his yacht. He conceded that Darjeeling had splendid views and rhododendrons but he hated the rains and the fogs that followed them. Yet once the narrow-gauge mountain railway had been built in 1880, Darjeeling proved irresistible. As Lieutenant-Governor between 1887 and 1882, Ashley Eden insisted that throughout the summer at least one Secretary must stay in Calcutta and that the Under-Secretaries should go up to the hills one at a time. But by 1886 the entire Government was to be found in Darjeeling: not a single Under-Secretary remained in the capital of the Indian Empire.[34]

While the annual exodus from Madras and Calcutta was much criticized, nobody seemed to mind about the even more complicated arrangements in the western presidency. Each April the Bombay Government moved up to Mahabaleshwar in the Western Ghats and stayed there until early June. Then it went down to Poona till October, when it returned for a month to the hills before re-establishing itself in Bombay for the winter. The extra moves were justified by the heavy monsoon in Mahabaleshwar, which made the houses unsafe and blocked the road down with landslides, and by the heat in Poona in October. But the scale of the itinerary was much smaller than the migrations to Simla and Darjeeling: only the Secretaries and a few clerks took part in it. Moreover, Mahabaleshwar was merely 75 miles from Poona, which was itself only 120 miles from the capital. Four dispatches a day were sent from Bombay, which reached the hill station within twenty-four hours and Poona within six. Besides, unlike the summer retreats in the north, Poona was neither remote nor mountainous nor restricted in space. It had once been the Maratha capital, the base of the Peshwa, and it was the headquarters of the Bombay Army until 1895, when the presidential forces were amalgamated under a single Commander-in-Chief.[35]

The fashion for hill stations prompted a good deal of public and private building. In the 1880s Simla acquired the Town Hall, the Ripon Hospital, two vast new offices for the Army and the secretariat, and the neo-Elizabethan Viceregal Lodge on Observatory Hill. The Lodge was the passion of Lord Dufferin, who inspected it twice daily during its construction and thought it 'beautiful, comfortable, convenient [and] not too big'. His successors and their wives were less enthusiastic. To the American Mary Curzon, the interior was vulgar and hideous, while the outside resembled the sort of building a millionaire from Minneapolis might revel in.[36]

All summer capitals needed a Government House, but Naini Tal acquired three of these buildings within a single generation. The first was too small, and the second became unsafe. In September 1880 the hill station had suffered the worst calamity experienced by such places in the history of British India: unusually heavy rainfall caused a landslide which, assisted by an earthquake that set off a second landslide, pitched the Hotel Victoria, the library, the Assembly Rooms and various other buildings into the lake: 151 people were killed, including 43 Europeans.[37] In 1896 the Lieutenant-Governor, MacDonnell, reported that movement in the foundations was causing alarming cracks in the walls of the second Government House, another neo-Elizabethan edifice, which might as a result collapse at any moment. He wanted to move his administration to a different hill station, Mussoorie, which was higher and healthier than Naini Tal and had more room for expansion. As the current summer capital had no roads or flat space except the Mall and the sports ground, people who did not ride had to be transported by dandy, a sort of hammock on a pole carried by coolies. The slopes were so precipitous that the Lieutenant-Governor compared moving around to 'going up or down like a fly on a pane of glass'.[38] The Government decided not to allow MacDonnell to shift his headquarters in the hills but it did let him abandon his own residence and build a vast new Gothic one with a garden façade dominated by six castellated turrets.

The practice of sending secretariats to hill stations was condemned by people who could not take advantage of such places, by businessmen who had to carry on their affairs in the cities, by newspaper editors who had less news to report, and by an older generation of Civilians who had had no choice but to swelter in the plains. There was much talk of the 'grave scandal', of the 'dereliction of duty' that the exodus entailed, much envious resentment that a bureaucracy 'above the reach of human censure, not to say human observation, amid the cloud-capped mountains and mirth-bearing breezes of Simla', should allegedly give 'itself up body and soul to the *dolce far niente* of the mariners in Tennyson's "Lotus-Eaters"'. The criticism tended to be puritanical. General Sir Henry Durand argued that, even if the premature deaths of three consecutive Governors-General (Dalhousie, Canning and the first viceregal Elgin) had been attributable to the climate of the plains, 'it was the condition on which India had been won, and could only be kept, that men in high place must risk health and life in the execution of duty'.[39] Durand, who was Foreign Secretary twenty years before his son Mortimer held the same post, was himself killed in the execution of duty when an elephant he was riding charged at an arch too low for his howdah. He had just been appointed Lieutenant-Governor of the Punjab.

Journalists were another breed who liked to castigate governments for spending half the year in the hills. Lovat Fraser, a distinguished Editor of the *Times of India* in Bombay, argued that the custom was 'largely to blame for the growing detachment of the British from the people of India'. If a Secretary defended hill stations because he was able to work in them without interruptions, Fraser answered that that was 'precisely why he ought not to be there. If he is helping to rule India he must expect interruptions; he is in India to be interrupted; personal accessibility is a thing that Asiatics greatly prize, and the institution of hill stations denies it to them'.[40] It would perhaps be futile to try to formulate an equation of the benefits conferred on the few by personal access versus the potential advantages to many of a reform conceived in solitude in front of a log fire in Simla. Lyall voted for the log fire, though he admitted the summer capital 'was almost dangerously cut off from the vast country which lies below us and beyond the hills'. So did MacDonnell, who was 'very certain' that legislation could be 'infinitely better' prepared 'with the thermometer at 65° than at 90°'. The imperialist Radical MP, Sir Charles Dilke, defended Simla on the grounds that its climate gave 'vigour to the Government, and a hearty English tone to the State papers issued in the hot months'.[41]

The hill stations were little islands of Englishness, even though they all contained an Indian bazaar. The gardens were planted with ferns and roses and familiar vegetables; the houses were villas and cottages with comforting names. Ootacamund, known as Ooty, had Apple Cottage, Hopeful Cottage, Grasmere Lodge and, more bizarrely, Bleak House and Walthamstow. Darjeeling had Meadow Bank, Orchard Lea, Cedar Cottage, Beechwood, Willowdale and others.[42] The Anglo-Indians have been much mocked for such replicas of Englishness, but they were good for the heart and the spirit. For similar reasons the Romans built Roman villas in Britain, and the Greeks built Greek temples in Sicily. In India most Anglo-Indians spent most of their time in very unBritish landscapes. One should not be too hard on those who tried to create corners in the Subcontinent that seemed entirely British.

The best place of course was Ootacamund. Everyone could find their own type of Britain in Ooty. The most usual comparison was with the Sussex Downs, but Edward Lear thought the place resembled Leatherhead, and an imaginative Civilian compared its rocky end to the Pass of Killikrankie and its hunting end to the Braids Hill in south Edinburgh. Other administrators went for multiple home-based similitudes. To Macaulay, Ooty's landscape seemed like 'the vegetation of Windsor Forest or Blenheim spread over the mountains of Cumberland'. Lytton's blend was even more extravagant: 'a combination of Hertfordshire lanes, Devonshire downs, Westmorland lakes and Scottish trout streams'.[43]

In fact Ooty did not really resemble Britain except to people desperate to be somewhere more reassuring than the temple towns of the south or the landscape of the Eastern Ghats. It looked more like Australia, especially after 20,000 Australian acacias were planted around the lake in the middle of the century. The impression was fortified by the addition of large numbers of eucalyptus trees. One had to be feeling very nostalgic and imaginative to think that even from a distance gum trees looked like Scots Pines.[44]

I I

Life at the Top

~

The Viceroy's 'Cabinet'

THERE WAS NO set route to the top of the ICS. But by the end of the nineteenth century senior Civilians were increasingly following each other through three stages from Chief Commissioner (with a salary of 50,000 rupees) to Member of the Viceroy's Council (80,000 rupees) to Lieutenant-Governor (100,000 rupees). Sometimes, as in the cases of MacDonnell, Mackenzie and Ibbetson, a secretaryship in the Government of India preceded their appointments as Chief Commissioner. John Strachey went through the three final stages but then, at the plea of Lord Lytton, reverted to the Council. He was so captivated by the new Viceroy that he accepted a drop in salary to take the post. His brother Richard was also entranced by their chief and asked him to be godfather to his fifth son, whom he called Lytton. He thus saddled the future debunker of eminent Victorians with the name of one of the least eminent of Victorian Viceroys.[1]

Before the Mutiny the Council consisted of four 'ordinary' Members (including the Governor-General) and usually one 'extra-ordinary' Member, the Commander-in-Chief. Afterwards a fifth Member was sent from Britain to reduce the fiscal deficit caused by the conflict and to reorganize the finances following the transfer of power from the East India Company to the Crown. From 1874, when a sixth Member was added to direct public works, the administration consisted of seven departments, four (Finance, Military, Legal and Public Works) with their own Member, two (Home and Revenue & Agriculture) under the same Member, and the Foreign Office supervised by the Viceroy. The composition of the Council was subject to certain constraints. Three of its Members had to have worked in India for at least ten years, and one had to be an English or Irish barrister or a Scottish advocate of at least five years' standing. After the Mutiny it became a convention that Madras and Bombay should alternately provide one of the three Anglo-Indians, a practice much deplored by Viceroys. In 1886 Dufferin conceded that it was the turn of the southern presidency to supply a Member but asserted that there was 'nobody in Madras at all fit to assume such a position'.[2] Judgements like this reflected the general view of the calibre of the ICS in the south, but they were not always fair. Sir Henry Stokes, the senior Civilian in Madras, was capable enough to be Finance Member, but unfortunately his entire experience of financial matters had been limited to his province.

The Council's workload was unevenly distributed. Ilbert might claim to be a combination of Lord Chancellor, Attorney-General and special adviser to the Viceroy, but in fact the Law Member had only a few hours' work a day outside the short legislative session in Calcutta. By contrast the Member in charge of both the Home Department and the Revenue & Agriculture Department did the equivalent work of at least two Cabinet ministers in London: in one capacity he dealt with educational, medical, sanitary, ecclesiastical and judicial affairs, as well as local government and the police, and in the other he was responsible for forests, land revenue and the agricultural development of the country. Curzon complained that almost the entire administration of the Subcontinent was being run by two people, himself and Denzil Ibbetson, the overworked Member for the two departments. Ibbetson, who was in the middle stage of his rise from Chief Commissioner of the Central Provinces to Lieutenant-Governor of the Punjab, was the ablest member of the Council. But as he was also the frailest, much of his work had to be done by the Public Works Member to prevent him breaking down. Under pressure from Curzon, the India Office agreed in 1905 to have separate Members for the two posts and also to set up a Department for Commerce and Industry.[3]

The Finance Member prepared the budget and was in charge of

currency, banking and taxation. The first holders of the post were financial experts and politicians from Britain, but subsequently the appointment usually went to Civilians. Temple held it from 1868 to 1874 but did not shine in the position. His long-winded speeches in Council and his over-optimistic budget estimates annoyed the Viceroy, Lord Mayo, who often managed to overrule him. The Finance Member was sometimes described as the second most powerful man in India, and occasionally he was. One such figure was Evelyn Baring, who dominated Ripon's Council before being sent to Egypt, a country not technically part of the Empire but which, as Lord Cromer, he effectively governed for the next twenty-four years. Another was James Westland, a forceful Civilian fully aware of his own intelligence: on minuting a Government file, he 'had first to prove to his own satisfaction that everyone who had noted on it already was a born fool'.[4] A third was Auckland Colvin, whose efforts to balance the budget inspired Kipling's 'Rupaiyat of Omar Kal'vin', a brilliant pastiche of Fitzgerald's translation of the 'Rubaiyat'.

> Whether at Boileaugunge* or Babylon,
> I know not how the wretched Thing is done,
> The Items of Receipt grow surely small
> The Items of Expense mount one by one.

The Council met once a week in Calcutta and at Simla under the chairmanship of the Viceroy. It decided all questions by a majority vote, and its decisions, recorded by the relevant Secretary, were called Orders in Council. Members also belonged to the Legislative Council, again presided over by the Viceroy, which met to consider and pass the Government's bills. This was not a very powerful or representative body. Apart from the six Members, it consisted of about sixteen officials, non-officials and Indians, all of them nominated by the Viceroy. In 1892 it was given permission to ask questions and discuss the budget, but its composition made it almost impossible for a Government bill to be defeated.[5]

Members tended to be less applauded than Lieutenant-Governors, especially by Kipling who suggested in the pages of the

---

*A suburb of Simla close to Viceregal Lodge.

Civil & Military Gazette that Dufferin's Councillors transmigrated after death into 'the bodies of the great grey langurs'. In 'One Viceroy Resigns', one of his earliest attempts at a monologue in the style of Browning, he imagined Dufferin describing them to his successor Lansdowne.

> They look for nothing from the West but Death
> Or Bath or Bournemouth. There's their ground. They fight
> Until the Middle Classes take them back,
> One of ten millions plus a C.S.I.,
> Or drop in harness. Legion of the Lost?
> Not altogether. Earnest narrow men,
> But chiefly earnest, and they'll do your work,
> And end by writing letters to the *Times*.

Kipling, a cub reporter for the Simla season, did not know them well enough to judge with such confidence. But he did perceive the defects, the rather narrow, jaded, subservient mentality of men who had spent thirty years in India and aspired to one final promotion.

Unlike Cabinet ministers with a power base in a political party or the electorate, the position of Civilian Councillors was entirely dependent on their chief. If they wanted to become Lieutenant-Governors before retirement, it was wise to be deferential to the Viceroy. After attending the Council at Simla, Lyall (by then himself a Lieutenant-Governor) observed that the non-Civilian Baring was the only Member who showed any zeal: the others were just 'laboriously noting and voting'.[6] A strong Viceroy seldom had difficulty with his proposals at Council meetings. After his first two and a half years in India, Curzon could claim that on only one matter of any importance had there been a division in his Council, and then he had won on a vote of five to two. During that period not a single Government dispatch had gone to Whitehall with a dissentient minute appended. By the end of his long viceroyalty the total number of non-unanimous dispatches was three.[7]

Before Curzon's time, Members were not expected to play a vigorous part in the social life of Simla, where they went for six months to work rather than for a few weeks' holiday. Ilbert, Ripon's Law Member, did much of his business before breakfast and did not want his routine to include after-dinner rides along narrow mountain paths in the middle of the night. Curzon, however, took the view that Councillors received large salaries so that they could live and entertain in a certain style. He told the bachelors among them that they should not economize by living in clubs in Simla and Calcutta but rent a house and fulfil their social obligations. He was also bossy about their clothes. At Levees and State Balls, he decreed, Members should wear white breeches and stockings as ministers did in London and not 'take refuge in the less dangerous but irregular trouser'.[8]

Lieutenant-Governors

Members of Council seldom enjoyed the prestige or received the recognition accorded to Lieutenant-Governors. The high point of Sir William Muir's career was not his last posting as Finance Member to Northbrook but his previous one as Lieutenant-Governor of the NWP, during which he campaigned against female infanticide and established Muir College, the nucleus of that inspired muddle of Hindu, Cairean and Gothic styles that is Allahabad University. A Lieutenant-Governor's term in office was often celebrated by a large building bearing his name, sometimes when he was still in the job. Aitchison's tenure in the Punjab was immortalized by Aitchison College in Lahore, while two of his predecessors were honoured by the construction of the Lawrence and Montgomery Halls in the same city. During Bartle Frere's governorship of Bombay the Frere Hall was built in Karachi 'to commemorate' – as the *Illustrated London News* put it – 'the benefits of his past administration'.[9]

It was logical and desirable that a Lieutenant-Governor should be the leading Civilian of his generation in his province. He would know the people, speak their language and be familiar with their terrain. But problems of timing and availability, combined with some eccentricity in selection, sometimes upset the logic, especially in Bengal. In 1898 the province had an L-G from the North-Western Provinces, Woodburn, while the NWP had one from Bengal, MacDonnell, who complained that Calcutta not Allahabad 'ought to have been the finishing up' of his Indian career. In the early 1890s Bengal had another Lieutenant-Governor from the NWP, Charles Elliott, and after Woodburn's death received one from the CP, Angus Fraser, who had never served in the province before. In the year between the death of Woodburn and the appointment of Fraser, Bengal was ably administered in an acting capacity by one of its own Civilians, James Bourdillon, before he was mysteriously transferred to the Residency in Mysore.

Some of these appointments were plainly inappropriate. Elliott was hard-working and energetic, a man who grasped details but who was too old to start trying to understand Bengal. He was also tactless and antagonistic, defects that seemed magnified when he took charge of the province after thirty-four years of service in other parts of India. Not that familiarity with the territory was a prerequisite for sympathetic rule. There was something to be said for the policy of bringing in outsiders who had not spent the previous thirty years convincing themselves that Bengalis were physical and moral cowards. Both Campbell and Temple enjoyed successful terms as Lieutenant-Governor in the 1870s after spending the rest of their careers elsewhere. Campbell was on furlough in Britain, trying to enter parliamentary politics, when he was offered the appointment. Although he would have preferred to govern the Punjab, he accepted the post and came to Bengal without understanding the language or knowing its people. But he also came without prejudices against its inhabitants and before retirement told a large Bengali audience that he looked forward to the day when a Bengali House of Commons would be sitting in Calcutta.[10]

Appointments to a lieutenant-governorship generated months of speculation beforehand, much anxiety among aspirants, and a certain amount of discreet lobbying. Sometimes the choice was straightforward, as it was when Alfred Lyall was appointed to the North-Western Provinces in 1882. But often there were several candidates. In 1885 and 1886 much conjecture centred on the Punjab succession to the esteemed Aitchison, regarded by Ripon as a 'real good man of the best Scotch type' and by Dufferin as 'the most experienced, the most upright, and the most sensible man in India'.[11] The choice was between three Civilians from the Punjab, Charles Bernard, Lepel Griffin and James Lyall, the brother of Alfred. The industrious and high-minded Bernard, who was a nephew of the Lawrence brothers, had always seemed destined for the post and was the first choice of the Viceroy, Dufferin. But both Salisbury, who became Prime Minister for the second time in August 1886, and Cross, the current

Secretary of State, were unimpressed by his erratic performance as Chief Commissioner of Burma (where he was overworked and understaffed), and it was known that his health was not strong. Nobody wanted the post more than Griffin, who was bored of Indore – which he called 'death in life' – and resentful that he had been passed over for the foreign secretaryship. But he had been left without his main backer after Lord Randolph Churchill, who regarded him as 'one of the most attractive, cultivated persons' he had ever met, left the India Office in February 1886.[12] The third candidate, Lyall, was the least talented of the three, but he had managed not to alienate anyone involved in the selection process. He had never worked in the secretariat and had spent his entire career in the Punjab before his current posting as Resident in Mysore.

Lyall's brother Alfred realized that, if the appointment were made on ability alone, it would go to Griffin. In the autumn of 1885 he believed that his exasperating colleague would 'cut out' James 'if he had the sense to keep his liaisons with certain ladies in the background, to foreswear pomade, and to talk without affectation'. If his brother won the contest, it would be because he was the 'safer' man. In the event Griffin did not try to conceal his liaisons. Lyall saw him in Simla behaving like as 'unblushing rake' with a married lady, Isabella Burton,* and compared him to a 'fine neighing stallion that wants castrating and regular breaking in to harness before you can get any solid steady work out of him'.[13] Nor did Griffin learn to show humility before Dufferin. Not only did he directly solicit the Viceroy for the post: he also pointed out how much he had been admired by previous Lieutenant-Governors of the Punjab and managed to give the impression that he was the only worthy candidate. Not surprisingly, Dufferin thought him 'inordinately vain and egotistical' and told Cross that, while the applicant was 'extremely intelligent', he could not appoint a man with such uncertain judgement and so scandalous a private life. 'It is a great pity that Griffin's considerable abilities should be marred by this [his private life] and other faults, but his vanity and egotism, and his cynical indifference to "*les convenances*", have spoiled an otherwise valuable public servant.'[14]

As Dufferin would not accept Griffin and Whitehall rejected

---

*Mrs Burton was the inspiration for Kipling's witty, cynical and 'honestly mischievous' Mrs Hauksbee in *Plain Tales from the Hills*.

Bernard, the Punjab fell to James Lyall. The Viceroy admitted he was not 'a very brilliant man' but he was 'thoroughly trustworthy', popular with both the Service and 'the native community', and 'one of the best revenue officers in India'.[15] Griffin, who never understood his talent for antagonizing people, was shattered by the rebuff. He subsequently accused the Viceroy of treating him 'with a complete absence of consideration' and recorded his 'deep mortification and sorrow' on realizing that he had not won his confidence. Dufferin regarded this as a 'very nasty and very improper letter' and felt no further responsibility to Griffin, although the Hyderabad appointment was mooted.[16] It was effectively the end for Sir Lepel, who had already shown reluctance to accept Dufferin's compensatory offer of the chief commissionership of Burma. He retired in England in 1889, married at the age of 51, wrote a book about Ranjit Singh, the Sikh ruler, and attempted unsuccessfully to start a political career. Churchill's offer of his Paddington constituency was rescinded when Joseph Chamberlain declined to back the former cabinet minister in Birmingham. After having to wait a decade before he was given an opportunity to contest another seat, Griffin succumbed to the Liberals in West Nottingham in the election of 1900. In his sixties he fathered a son, Lancelot, who also went into the ICS and was a Secretary in the Government of India at the time of Independence.

Proconsular Lyall

Although they ranked lower in the hierarchy and the pay scale than the Governors of Madras and Bombay, the Lieutenant-Governors were more powerful officials. Temple, who moved from Bengal to Bombay, found his new position 'more dignified and more diversified in function, but less potential in reality'. His 'peace', he recorded, now depended on the co-operation of his 'Honourable Colleagues in Council'. The less pompous Campbell put it more bluntly. While a Governor's powers were limited and controlled by his Council, the Lieutenant-Governor was a 'personal ruler with no executive council, but only secretaries and heads of department under his orders'. Yet while they might enjoy their 'autocracy', as Alfred Lyall did in the North-Western Provinces, they sometimes wished they had a confidential adviser other than their Private Secretary.[17]

Energy in an L-G could be important, as MacDonnell demonstrated in his struggle against the famines of the 1890s. But on the whole Lieutenant-Governors had less work to do than Collectors or Secretaries or Members of Council. Most of their duties were supervisory or ceremonial. They tried to ensure that the administration ticked over and that legislation was enacted and made to work. Alfred Lyall's other assignments included opening railways, opening bridges and investing the heir of the Nawab of Rampur, a princely state enclosed by his province. 'Visits to native capitals', he thought, were 'the pleasantest bits of Indian life, something like staying at a large oriental country house.'

Entertainment was one of the most important and time-consuming duties of a Lieutenant-Governor. MacDonnell hated it, although he enjoyed preparing its setting, methodically designing the building and gardens of the new Government House at Naini Tal. Unlike other L-Gs, he thought a more important duty was the restoration of Indian monuments in his province, a priority for which Curzon, an obsessive restorer himself, forgave him his deficiencies as a host. Few other Lieutenant-Governors shirked their social obligations. A successor of MacDonnell, Harcourt Butler, found that his duties on a single day at a Naini Tal 'Week' included giving a lunch at the boathouse (as Commodore of the Yacht Club), a *thé dansant* and garden party at Government House, and a dinner at the Club. A Lieutenant-Governor knew that nothing made him more unpopular than parsimony or inaccessibility. He had to have 'At Home' days with ADCs in uniform at the door ready to receive callers and introduce them to his wife; and he had to give frequent and often prodigious parties even if they put him out of pocket. At the end of the nineteenth century it was said that no Lieutenant-Governor was able to save part of his salary for retirement and that 'only a man of some means' could afford to be L-G of Bengal.[18]

Entertaining local 'society', the bigwigs of a hill station or a provincial capital, might be rather boring and limited. But you did not have to do it every night, and the guests you invited to dinner were not there to plague you at breakfast the next morning. Visitors staying at your house were more of a trial. When Aitchison was touring India as head of the Public Service Commission, he naturally stayed at Government House in whatever province he was currently conducting his inquiries. This meant that during the Commission's visit to the NWP, Alfred Lyall was forced to sit next to Lady Aitchison, whom he found humourless and unlikable, for thirty consecutive meals.

The most unpopular guests were MPs and other 'globe-trotters' who took hospitality from Anglo-Indians and afterwards attacked them in print or in the House of Commons. Kipling satirized the type as the 'Member for Lower Tooting', a gentleman who 'did' India in a few weeks from the comfort of Government House and a first-class railway carriage and then went home and wrote a book denouncing British rule.[19] The Member was hardly an exaggeration. Evan Maconochie, a young Bombay Civilian, complained of MPs who 'come out in the cold weather and, having shot our game, drunk our wine and generally done well unto themselves at our expense, abuse us to [the British public] when they get home and cut us when we meet them in Piccadilly'.[20] Alfred Lyall's bugbear was the radical Tory, Wilfrid Scawen Blunt, who took the offence a stage further. On reading the first of a series of his articles in the *Fortnightly Review*, Lyall observed that his former guest 'abuses us roundly and rather unworthily – for he suggests that all the good hospitality we gave him was rung out of the starved ryot, and that altogether we are a set of incompetent bloodsuckers'.

Lyall became a Lieutenant-Governor in 1882, nine years after he had been Commissioner in West Berar. In the intervening decade he had been Secretary of the Home Department, AGG in Rajputana and Foreign Secretary. He could not at first make up his mind whether he wanted the lieutenant-governorship or whether it would be better to wait for a vacancy on the Viceroy's Council. After accepting the former he characteristically regretted not having chosen the latter. Allahabad, his new capital, was 'grand, pompous and expensive'; it was also lonely because he was now 'such a big man' that nobody dared approach him. At Simla, by contrast, he would have been with his old friends and in the house he had lived in as Foreign Secretary. Altogether he was feeling 'low and remorseful' about his decision.

The situation was even worse at Naini Tal, his summer capital, where he was 'tethered' to a mountain top for five months of the year without congenial companions. Life there was 'desperately dull' and was not improved by the position of Government House, built 1,200 feet above the lake, which deterred people from visiting him. A chronic grumbler, Lyall was bored by his dinner parties in Allahabad, where nobody talked about pictures or music or the 'refinements of civilization'. Fancy dress balls were even worse. 'When one is bilious,' he wrote to his sister Barbara, 'people in wild absurd costumes impress one as lunatics.' But Naini Tal irritated him still more with its frivolity and flirtations and the way women carried on, kissing and displaying their legs in amateur theatricals. Perhaps he was getting old and censorious, he told Barbara, but he did not see how the British could go on governing India by spending a few hours in their office with 'the rest of the day being devoted to amusements entirely among' themselves.

Lyall also grumbled about his duties as L-G, which he found parochial and uninteresting compared to his work at the Foreign Office. But slowly he began to change his mind and even to appreciate his new appointment. He relished his autocracy and believed that 'the immense majority' of Indians had a hatred for 'reformers and improvers' and preferred a 'simple despotism' like his. Provincial governors, he thought, were the 'only strong institutions in the country' because they were autocrats, 'governing in close relation with the people, and thus more or less representing the form of rule natural to the country in its present form'.

As Lieutenant-Governor he was tenacious of his independence: 'I am driving my own coach cautiously and trying to prevent the Govt of India from driving me.' But Dufferin, obsessed by Burma and not much interested in internal affairs, showed little desire to interfere with him. In any case there was not much to interfere with. Lyall rather sauntered through his term of office, amending the Oudh Rent Act, examining the system of land revenue, promoting the odd Indian to the High Court and other places, slowly working on a scheme of local self-government that gave greater powers to district and municipal boards. But he inaugurated no great reforms. Considered a bit indolent by one Viceroy, Ripon, he was highly rated by the next, Dufferin, no demon of energy himself, who considered Lyall 'a shrewd, hard-headed, industrious administrator'. Dufferin accurately described his subordinate's mind as 'philosophical, analytical and pessimist, with a considerable dash of cynicism'.[21]

Towards the end of his term Lyall had become sufficiently fond of the post to accept an extension. Indeed he hoped that his experience of heading an administration might be extended to Bombay or Madras, governorships he would have filled more capably than his successful rivals, Lord Harris and Lord Wenlock. As he grew into his job, he even began to like Naini Tal. He enjoyed walking and meditating on its slopes and he liked camping in its hills when touring nearby. A visit to Simla made him realize that the summer capital of the Raj was less picturesque and more suburban than his own demesne. Naini Tal may not have provided intellectual companions but it gave him time to read books and write articles for the *Edinburgh Review*.* Even when he had guests, he could spend the afternoon under a tree with a novel while they played tennis. Some of them might have noticed he was reading a new writer called Tolstoy, who had just been translated into French (long before he became available in English). Lyall was so excited by *La Guerre et la Paix* that he read it twice in four months and wished he could review it. In between readings he diverted himself with a slightly older writer's *Crime et Châtiment*, a 'very powerful' book, and then devoured *Anna Karenine*, which he had ordered from Paris. 'Having fallen under the spell' of 'le comte's' style, he regarded this as 'far above anything the French [had] lately written'. But he thought it unlikely that the protagonist would have thrown herself under a train. 'To a delicate highly refined woman like Anna the idea of crushing herself under a train before a crowd of people would be too repulsive and disgraceful, not to say ungraceful.' It would have been better if Tolstoy had drowned her.[22]

---

*Some of his earlier essays, written mainly for the *Fortnightly Review*, were published in the first volume of *Asiatic Studies* in 1882. They are elegant and perceptive articles, mostly about Indian religions.

12

Thinkers

~

Readers

C.E. WILD, THE Commissioner of Excise, was described by a colleague as 'a typical [Anglo-] Indian Civilian – a great pig-sticker
and polo-player' who was 'witty and amusing and would clap all
Home-Rulers into jail'. Apart from being sporting and reactionary,
'typical' ICS officers were also said to be philistines, men who did not
care about music or art and who spent their free time at the club
moaning about their work. As Philip Mason, a twentieth-century
Civilian, pointed out, the club was 'philistine no doubt by the standards of Sir Osbert Sitwell', but it provided an important respite, a
place and a time to unwind after a day more strenuous and stressful
than anything habitually experienced by the Sitwell family. E. M.
Forster and other visitors to India saw Civilians in their clubs, heard
them talking, watched them playing billiards, and marked them down
as philistine and insensitive. If they had seen them at work, in court
or out in the open, they might, as Forster himself admitted, have
taken a different view. They might also have been more sympathetic
if they had been familiar with the work of the ICS scholars, men who,
as the historian Anil Seal has pointed out, 'worked to establish much
of the ancient history and ethnology of India'.[1]

The intellectualism of the ICS varied from generation to generation, fluctuating with the changes in the British Government's

policies on admission. Early competition wallahs from the universities were more educated than their predecessors from Haileybury or their successors from the crammers. With the introduction of the Salisbury system in 1879, which sent probationers to the universities, the intellectual level rose; with its abolition, which favoured postgraduates, it rose higher still.

Griffins of the 1890s, half of whom had been to Oxford, were anxious to maintain contact with their past lives and their recent learning. They were eager for news – which crew had won the Boat Race? – and subscribed to the *Oxford Magazine*. They were determined to keep reading so that, as Harcourt Butler put it, they did not become 'groovey' – that is, stuck in a groove – in a country where 'the mind was so apt to become weary and stagnate'.[2] Writing to his old Oxford tutor, Phelps of Oriel, one Civilian said he had taken up Persian and ordered 'a Homer and a Horace' so as not 'to become an animal'; another former pupil read Pater and Keats to prevent himself turning into a stereotypical Anglo-Indian, 'a sort of 1830 Philistine, strong-hearted, curry-eating, self-important and antiquated'.[3]

Members of this generation discovered Kipling, whose first collection of poems, *Departmental Ditties*, and first volume of stories, *Plain Tales from the Hills*, had been published in India in 1886 and 1887. Phelps's many friends and former pupils in the ICS found these so 'capital', 'excellent' and 'true to life' that they urged their old mentor to read them. Evan Maconochie later recalled 'how often in the watches of a tropic night has [Kipling] taken us away from our fever and our troubles into his magic world, and sent us forth again cheered and refreshed and with a clearer vision of the humour and the pathos of the life about us'. Whatever fame he acquired later in life, said Maconochie, Kipling was 'for ever the peculiar and priceless possession of the District Officer'.[4]

Junior magistrates had plenty of time to read novels, especially when they were in camp. There they settled down to read Trollope and Thackeray or went back to the classics to study Plato. One told Phelps that he had read more books in his first two years in India than in any other five years of his existence. Some read as an escape from solitude or uncongenial company: living among the 'half-civilized European tea-planters' in Assam, Percy Lyon regarded books as his 'only solace' and begged Phelps to let him know what new works he should order from Calcutta. The old don received frequent requests from young Civilians 'hankering after new books' and publications 'on the questions of the day'. They did not want just to sit and read Dickens in the jungle: they wanted to keep in touch with what was going on in Britain.[5]

Conditions in India did not assist them. Only men stationed in cities could browse in bookshops or find more than an occasional colleague with literary tastes. Those in the *mofussil* were unlikely to be detained long by the shelves of the club library. 'I care only for books and for talking about books,' wrote Joseph Goudge from a camp in the district of Sitapur. But even when he did have books, there was no 'congenial soul' with whom to discuss Ariosto and Carducci. Readers could order books from Calcutta but often preferred to deal directly with London. Booksellers in India were 'regular fiends', complained one of Phelps's correspondents, 'never buying a book till you have read, discussed and forgotten it in England'. A further disincentive to acquisition was the condition to which books were reduced by insects and the climate.[6]

For all their good intentions, most Civilians did not persevere with their reading of journals and contemporary books. There was not much point finding out about plays at the Haymarket when you had no chance of seeing them, no great inducement to follow the feud between Ruskin and Whistler when you had no means of judging whether the former was right to compare the latter's art to a pot of paint flung in the public's face. As they got older and their duties piled up, Civilians had less time and aptitude for reading: they worked long hours and usually relaxed with games or sports. After nine years in the ICS, Havilland Le Mesurier admitted he could no longer 'tackle any stiff reading': 'even a modern novel' knocked him out, and 'any real thinking [was] out of the question'. Five years later, by now a successful Collector in Bengal, he was unable to 'read as steadily and attentively' as he once did and found himself 'sinking into dullness and absorption in his work'. A contemporary, writing in 1896, told Phelps he had 'firmly resolved' to follow his advice and study Indian history, religion, ethnology and anthropology so as to prevent himself 'growing into an Anglo-Indian bore with no knowledge of anything outside his shop'. He did indeed investigate the ethnology and religion of 'one or two of the rarer races' but then lost his notes and never returned to the subject. Now he was labouring in his office till seven in the evening, taking work home on Sundays, and at the end of the day his brain was 'pulp and only fit for reading the illustrated papers or talking the usual talk of a club smoking-room'.[7]

Some Civilians refused to give up. Malcolm Darling, who in his first posting was seen in court with a volume of Keats, read remorselessly throughout his career, devouring almost every serious writer from Homer to Tolstoy. He had a special bookcase constructed which folded like a trunk so that it could be put on a horse and taken into camp. One piece of good fortune was his appointment as Tutor and Guardian to the Maharaja of Dewas Senior, which gave him the opportunity of teaching his pupil Plato and Aristotle as well as Bagehot and John Stuart Mill.[8]

Even the most dedicated readers realized that they could not devote much time to their books when they were posted to the secretariat: the work was too relentless, the ambience too distracting, and the social life difficult to avoid. Although Arthur Howell was depressed by his transfer from Simla to a commissionership in the Central Provinces, he consoled himself with the thought that he would be able to renew his friendship with his 'old and best friends', Aristotle, Tacitus, Juvenal and Horace. Alfred Lyall and Charles Elliott kept their interests going throughout their careers, especially when they reached the top. In his last spring as Lieutenant-Governor, Elliott managed to get to Darjeeling ahead of his files and was thus able to read a canto of Dante each day with a commentary.[9]

Dante was also a solace to Goudge, the stationmaster's son from Taunton whose wife had died of cholera in India. According to one official, the only cure for a Civilian who could not think about anything but his work was 'to take up . . . an abstruse subject – one that took some tackling but . . . could never be any possible use to you in your profession'.[10] The official himself had chosen Roman Law. Goudge chose Italian literature although he had never been to the country that inspired it. In camp at Sitapur he got up and read Tacitus with his early morning tea, and then, if feeling 'lazy, read a book of Italian lyrics under the sandalwood trees'. From ten past eight he concentrated on files, visitors, telegrams and petitions until tea-time at half past three, when he settled down with Fogazzaro's *Piccolo mondo moderno* before doing some more work and eating his solitary dinner. In the same period he also read Dante, Carducci, Spinoza's *Ethica* in Italian, and the memoirs of D'Azeglio, the sceptical

Piedmontese statesman who suggested it might be more difficult to make Italians than to make Italy. He seems to have had little interest in the art or literature of India but dreamed a good deal of travelling to Rome and Florence when he married again. In retirement at Sandwich he translated *Orlando Furioso* into Spenserian stanzas.[11]

Many Civilians took up hobbies that were useless to their profession, although these were not often as alien to Anglo-India as Fogazzaro and *decadentismo*. They generally became students of Indian subjects, botanists and ornithologists, numismatists and lepidopterists. Some made themselves authorities and acquired international reputations and honorary doctorates. Allan Octavian Hume, known as the 'Pope of Ornithology', spent the enormous sum of £20,000 accumulating a collection of 82,000 eggs and stuffed birds which he donated to the Natural History Museum in London. Enthusiasms were best pursued by individuals not groups. Civilian musicians had a sad time of it, seldom finding a piano in tune let alone colleagues with whom to form a trio or a quartet: about the best they could usually hope for, outside the cities, was to accompany a singing memsahib in the club. As with Indian philosophy, Indian music passed nearly everyone by except Elliott who, when a magistrate, assembled a group of minstrels to recite a lengthy tale of Rajput chivalry called the 'Lay of Alha'.[12]

Scholars

Civilians in India produced a small library of books, but less than half a shelf of this is occupied by works of fiction or poetry. Of all Anglo-Indians, Kipling was by far the ablest practitioner of either form. Among the storytellers of Victorian India he was followed, at a lengthy distance, by Flora Annie Steel, the wife and sister of Civilians, whose novels included a Mutiny saga, *On the Face of the Waters*, Philip Meadows Taylor, a political officer and author of *Confessions of a Thug*, and Henry Cunningham who, as Advocate-General of Madras, wrote *The Chronicles of Dustypore*. The Civilian contribution did not go much beyond a handful of novels by Durand, Hunter and Septimus Thorburn, who wrote two as Commissioner of Rawalpindi, and Romesh Chandra Dutt, who wrote a couple in Bengali about rustic life in his province.

Few careers can have been less conducive to the writing of fiction than the ICS. Alfred Lyall, however, claimed that the problem was not his profession but his temperament. He longed for the energy of 'Trollope & Co' so that he could write three-volume novels, but he knew he would get bored and disgusted with his subject at an early stage. Even after writing a few pages of a review or an essay, he managed to convince himself, quite wrongly, that he was 'becoming a bore'.[13]

Light verse was a much more popular genre for literary Civilians than fiction. Many of them liked to send facetious efforts to the newspapers and contribute to publications such as *Madras Occasional Verse*. A representative figure was Alec McMillan, who did not like India, did not get further than District Judge, and retired as soon as he qualified for a pension. One poem published in the *Pioneer* was his griffin's lament.

> My ruddy cheeks have long grown pale
> Beneath the sun's relentless fire,
> I dare not drink a glass of ale,
> And those damned seniors won't retire.
> Black scorpions infest my shoes,
> Ants batten on my best-loved books,
> And last home mail brought out the news
> My Maud had wed that blockhead Snooks.[14]

A rather loftier lament for a Civilian's exile was written by Lyall in 'The Land of Regrets'. Addressing India, he wrote:

> Thou hast racked him with duns and diseases,
>   And he lies, as thy scorching winds blow,
> Recollecting old England's sea breezes
>   On his back in a lone bungalow;
> At the slow coming darkness repining
>   How he girds at the sun till it sets,
> As he marks the long shadows declining
>   O'er the Land of Regrets.[15]

Many officials must have read the poem with a sense of fellow feeling, a shared experience of loneliness, a similar awareness that they had been lured by the sirens of the East to pursue a career that was not worth the hardships of climate and illness and separation. But the poet claimed privately that the work was 'something of a cynical parody': he had experienced no such pangs himself, he told his sister, except that 'on the whole' he wished he had gone to Cambridge.[16]

Lyall's poetic oeuvre consists of little more than a small volume of eighteen melodious poems, a paucity he blamed on the fact that his 'leisure intervals [were] apt to be invaded by low spirits'. They were also invaded by a feeling of pointlessness even when he was writing essays: nothing, he told his mother, 'seems worth writing, because the more I read the more I find that everything worth saying has been said'.[17] In fact no Anglo-Indian had written poetry with his tone of melancholic reminiscence, a tone usually given to the voices of elderly warriors, 'The Old Pindaree' or 'A Rajpoot Chief of the Old School', men who mourn the passing of their warrior days and their current impotence in a world dominated by the English and the Hindu babus. Such works became very popular, to the astonishment of Lyall, who thought he had written only one good poem, 'Theology in Extremis', a 'soliloquy that may have been delivered' in the Mutiny by an Englishman who, despite his doubts about God and his mercy ('Yet I could be silent and cheerfully die,/If I were only sure God cared') and despite the knowledge that his sacrifice will go unrecorded, decides not to save his life by converting to Islam.

> I must be gone to the crowd untold
>   Of men by the cause which they served unknown,
> Who moulder in myriad graves of old;
>   Never a story and never a stone
> Tells of the martyrs who die like me,
> Just for the pride of the old countree.[18]

It was common for Civilians to contribute articles to Anglo-Indian newspapers, a practice encouraged by the Government so long as they kept 'within the limits of temperate and reasonable discussion'.[19] In fact the limits were frequently broached, but the writers were seldom reprimanded unless they were felt to be jeopardizing official policy. Several young Civilians, including Beames and Cotton, wrote for the *Indian Observer*, a satirical weekly paper founded in

Calcutta in 1870. Cotton was virtually its editor at the time it published 'a particularly clever and offensive attack' on Campbell, the Lieutenant-Governor of Bengal. The normally irascible Sir George reacted not by trying to identify and punish the author but by promoting and transferring several of the contributors to other stations where they found it difficult to keep writing. Cotton, who as Judge of a Small Cause Court had plenty of time to write for the papers, was brought into Campbell's own secretariat and kept busy among its files. Yet while he regarded the Government's tolerance as unwise, he continued to take advantage of its 'great laxity' on this issue. His promotion to Chief Secretary was not prevented by his book, *New India, or India in Transition*, permeated though it is with his nationalist sympathies, or by his comparison of Burmese resistance to British forces to 'Hereward of old in the Fens of Lincolnshire' holding out against the Norman invaders.[20] As the case of O'Donnell demonstrated, a Civilian could write almost anything without losing his job, although too much nationalist enthusiasm might cost him promotion. He could even predict the date of Britain's departure from the Subcontinent, though Judge Hart-Davies's book, *India in 1982*, did give the Empire thirty-five years longer than it turned out to enjoy.

The Civilian as poet or journalist is a less representative image than the Civilian at a table in a remote station compiling gazetteers about his district or grammars of the local language and its dialects. It was natural for Donald Macnabb, who became a Commissioner in Burma, to write a book about a Burmese tribal group (*The Chin: His Manners, Life and Customs*) as well as a *Grammar and Dictionary of the Chin (Haka) Dialect*. One Political on the frontier, John Lorimer, wrote *Grammar and Vocabulary of Waziri Pashto*, while another, his brother David, who became Consul for Kerman and Persian Baluchistan, composed several philological books including *The Phonology of the Bakhtiari, Badakhshani, and Madaglashti Dialects of Modern Persian*. George Grierson's numerous works on Indian languages included *Seven Grammars of the Dialects and Subdialects of the Bihari Language* which came out in eight volumes between 1883 and 1887. But such enterprise was not limited to the derided bookworms of the competition system. Beames, a Haileyburian and sportsman, found it necessary to refresh his 'weary soul' with a daily 'plunge into Sanskrit and Pakrit'. The eventual result was a *Comparative Grammar of the Modern Aryan Languages of India*, a study for which he also had to learn German so that he could consult the relevant German authorities.[21]

Some Civilians wrote out of boredom, isolated in dismal surroundings and needing to demonstrate that they were still alive. After several years in a 'penal' district in the NWP, Charles William Whish was 'seized by an almost uncontrollable desire to come into contact with the outside world in the only method available *viz* by rushing into print'.[22] Most books, however, were the product of genuine intellectual enthusiasm, studies of the folklore of Sind and the religion of the Sikhs, of the history of Assam and the agrarian systems of the Mughal Empire. William Muir's experience of living among Muslims in the North-Western Provinces led him to a study of Islam and the authorship of books on the Koran, the Caliphate, the Prophet Muhammad and the Mameluke dynasty of Egypt. So esoteric were the scholarly passions of John Fleet that a special post was created for him, that of Epigraphist to the Government of India. Although his chief interest was compiling works such as *Inscriptions of the Early Gupta Kings and Their Successors*, Fleet managed to rise to the level of Commissioner, ending his career in charge of the Central Division of Bombay.

Another unusual scholar was Foster Fitzgerald Arbuthnot, a Bombay Civilian from 1853 to 1878. A friend of Richard Burton, he shared the explorer's interest in erotic literature and translated from Sanskrit the *Ananga Ranga*, sometimes known as *The Pleasures of Women*, a fifteenth- or sixteenth-century work which tried to demonstrate how variety in sexual positions could prevent a marriage from going stale. Anyone who read the book, its author had declared, would discover 'how delicate an instrument is woman, when artfully played upon, how capable she is of producing the most exquisite harmony'. Like Burton, Arbuthnot hoped that European men would abandon the 'rough exercise' of a husband's rights and learn some sexual subtlety from the works of Eastern sages. Later the two of them collaborated on their famous translation of a more ancient erotic text, the *Kama Sutra*, which they prepared in India and secretly published some years later in London. Since Arbuthnot's work appeared after his retirement as Collector of Bombay – and even then under the reversed initials of A. F. F. – we cannot know to what extent the Government would have disciplined its author.[23]

One of the most distinguished intellectuals in the ICS was the

Bengali, Romesh Chandra Dutt, who wrote, apart from his novels and translations, histories of ancient India, Bengali literature and the economy of the Subcontinent. One of the most prolific was Charles Kincaid, whose thirty-six books included a three-volume *History of the Maratha People* and *The Hindu Gods and How to Recognize Them*.* But the most prominent 'man of letters' in the Victorian ICS was William Wilson Hunter, a Glaswegian who made his literary name with *Annals of Rural Bengal*, a rambling but sympathetic account of traditional customs in the province. Hunter was not a popular figure in the Service because he was regarded as self-seeking and 'thrifty' to the point of meanness. But his scholarship and prose style were widely admired. After just a few years in the *mofussil*, he was made Director-General of Statistics, a post which enabled him to write not only his Statistical Accounts and his *Imperial Gazetteer* but also books on famine and Muslims and a biography of Lord Mayo. Later undemanding jobs allowed him to increase his oeuvre with books such as *The Indian Empire* and *England's Work in India*. After twenty-five years' service, he applied for an administrative post but was turned down by Dufferin who regarded his skills as 'essentially literary'.[24] When his request for a salary to write a history of India was also refused, he retired to Oxford and produced several more books including his novel *The Old Missionary*, a biography of Dalhousie and a book on the Thackeray family in India.

Hunter's nine volumes of the *Imperial Gazetteer*, which were crammed with details about the land and peoples of India, were directed more at the administrator than at the 'scientific inquirer'. Nothing, he said, was 'more costly to the government than ignorance'.[25] He thus made himself a target for future historians, enabling them to claim that he and his fellow 'orientalists' were not genuine scholars but agents of colonialism who pursued their studies to assist the administration and exploitation of India. Since their knowledge was acquired to fit such an agenda, so runs the argument, it must therefore be false or at the very least slanted: it was 'not disinterested or objective', Barbara Ramusack has claimed, 'but imbricated with political power'. Especially objectionable was their reduction of the

---

*His son Dennis was also an author and a member of the ICS. Born in 1905, he managed to write five novels, a biography of Shivaji and *British Social Life in India* before he was drowned in the sea south of Goa in 1937.

Orient to allegedly over-simplified categories such as 'caste' and 'Hindus', although it is hard to see how either of these can be regarded as concepts constructed by the British.[26]

The logic of all this is perplexing. Scholarship can have diverse aims without being dishonest or invalid. James Mackenna's paper, 'The Rhinoceros Beetle . . . and its ravages in Burma', could simultaneously be useful to the Government, satisfying to the author and helpful to the people of Burma. Anthropologists in the ICS welcomed their dual role. Herbert Risley was pleased that his *Tribes and Castes of Bengal* was not 'a mere scientific luxury, as it might be in Europe', but 'almost an administrative necessity in a country like Bengal'. Denzil Ibbetson advocated study of 'the customs and beliefs of the people among whom we dwell' because ignorance not only deprived European science of necessary material but also meant 'a distinct loss of administrative power to ourselves'. Yet this in itself did not invalidate the science.[27]

The ICS produced a number of outstanding anthropologists, some of whom became university dons in retirement. Among their most important works were William Crooke's studies of the peoples of the North-Western Provinces, George Grierson's *Bihar Peasant Life* and Malcolm Darling's post-First World War books on the villagers of the Punjab. Their scholarship can only be regarded as colonialist literature in the sense that it made administrators better informed about the people they were ruling. Some of Risley's work was different in objective. He advocated the science of anthropometry, in particular measuring different dimensions of the nose, as an aid to identification, one that could be used to catch members of the 'criminal' castes or tribes. As an aid to crime detection it was not, however, very successful and was soon superseded by the science of an older Civilian, William Herschel, the pioneer of finger-printing.

No serious survey of the scholars of the ICS could conclude that they were a body of men who employed their skills to define an Indian 'Other' and create a body of knowledge for the purpose of furthering colonial rule. A few of them, such as Hunter, Risley and Ibbetson, did plan to use their research as an aid to administration – they were scholar-administrators after all. But most were like the German orientalists, who had no colonialist agenda of their own, men motivated by pure curiosity and a desire to learn. Such people investigated in a mood of inquiry, not in the spirit of James Mill trying to find faults that demanded correction. Some might even admire what they studied, the character of the Buddha, the vernacular literatures, the empires of Asoka and Akbar, the architecture of Agra and Fatehpur Sikri. What imperialist use could be made of Fleet's work on the inscriptions of the Gupta kings or Howell's translation of Mahsud ballads or Burnell's catalogues of the Sanskrit manuscripts in the Palace of Tanjore? How, one wonders, are such works 'imbricated with political power'? How do they fit in with Edward Said's theory that 'all academic knowledge about India . . . is somehow tinged and impressed with, violated by, the gross political fact' of British dominion?[28]

Reactionaries

'With all their magnificent qualities,' Northbrook remarked to Dufferin, Civilians 'have strongly ingrained in their minds, excepting some of the very best of them . . . that no one but an Englishman can do anything' in India. Many of them did indeed think 'the natives' incapable of running their own affairs. Even the young Maynard, who hoped and believed that the Indians had a political future, thought the entire structure of administration depended on 'two or three [Anglo-Indians] in each district [who did] the work of a very Atlas'. The educated Indians were no use because they had no political or public virtue, while the rest, 'gentle, simple and dreamy', were 'dependent on Englishmen for everything'.[29]

Walter Lawrence was unusual in suggesting that it was 'not a bad thing to serve under Indians', as he had done as Settlement Commissioner under the State Council of Kashmir. Many of his colleagues would have considered him crazy. One griffin in the North-Western Provinces found no Indians capable of governing 'a wax doll except one or two Mussulmans who have some of the old conquerors' pride and fire still left in them'. A widely held view was that Indians were like children and should be treated as such. Curzon thought them 'a very gentle and sympathetic race' although they were 'often most aggravating', a people who respected two qualities, 'kindness and firmness'. This was the attitude of many ICS officers. They sympathized with the people they ruled and did their best to improve their lives. But the sympathy was often that of a headmaster supervising children who would take a very long time to grow up.[30]

Such attitudes did not presage enthusiasm for Lord Ripon's

reforms – and not simply because bringing more Indians into the administration would ultimately cost the ICS their jobs. The principal objection was that Indians did not want or need liberalism; nor in the foreseeable future could they be ready for democracy. What they wanted and appreciated, wrote Butler in 1891, was 'paternal government, stern, kind, just'. Thirty-five years later, at the end of his career, his opinions had not changed: it was 'ridiculous', he believed, 'to talk of grafting democracy onto a caste system'.[31]

Herbert Thirkell White voiced a widespread Service view when he argued that 'political education' of the people inspired by Western ideas was not part of the British mission: writing of the Burmans in particular, he insisted that the mission was 'to conserve, not to destroy, their social organism'.[32] The lack of representative institutions was generally regarded as a blessing. 'I have a sense of relief', wrote Lord Reay, the Governor of Bombay, 'when I think that here every day we have the power of improving the condition of millions without ever ascending a rostrum to cajole them.' Ripon, whom Reay privately accused of having 'taken no trouble to understand Indian society', was jeopardizing a system that was inevitably precarious and vulnerable to sudden change. As one young Civilian put it, 'Out here one feels that one lives on the crust over a volcano, and regards with distrust anyone who pours water through the cracks, even if it's only for fun, to see what will happen.'[33]

Civilians may have been racially aloof and even dismissive, but they were not racist in the sense that they considered racial differences to be permanent and innate. They believed they belonged not to a superior race but to a more advanced civilization. They might disparage Hindus for their animal gods or for their history of defeat at the hands of comparatively small groups of invaders. They might pride themselves that they possessed the truer religion, the higher morals, the superior arts of government, but they did not claim that they would hold these advantages for all time. Their prejudices had little to do with race or the colour of skin. They were expressions of a self-confidence that may have been unattractive but was perhaps not unnatural in citizens of a prosperous country with a large empire and a long and relatively peaceful history of political development.

Anglo-Indians may have stuck together in civil lines and had holidays together in the hill stations, but most of them were fond of the people they ruled. In addition to servants, whom they tended to treat as naughty but likeable children, they usually appreciated Rajputs, Sikhs, Pathans, hillmen in general, and Coorgs, who lived in 'the Wales of India' near Mysore and who, though nominally Hindu, would eat meat and drink whisky with the Assistant Commissioner. Other generally well-liked groups were peasants, who were admired for their stoicism, hard work and attachment to village and family, and Muslims who, though often turbulent and troublesome, were regarded as more spirited and straightforward than Hindus. Harcourt Butler expressed a common view among Anglo-Indians when he suggested that monotheistic Islam was 'infinitely purer and more elevating' than Hinduism. In middle age Kipling recalled that he had never met an Englishman who hated Islam and its peoples.[34]

It is less easy to find Anglo-Indian sympathy for Hinduism and some of its alliterational practitioners, Babus, Brahmins, Bunnias (merchants) and Bengalis. Griffins sometimes decided that Hinduism was so absurd and incomprehensible a religion that there was no point in trying to understand it. Their early contact with Bengali babus did not impress them either. As a type they seemed to be deceitful, garrulous, servile and lacking in backbone.[35] Some Civilians did not progress beyond such views. In 1905 Bamphylde Fuller was depressed when Curzon asked him to be Lieutenant-Governor of the new, largely Muslim province of Eastern Bengal and Assam. Although he accepted the 'difficult and thankless position', he told the Viceroy he would have preferred to end his Indian career in the United Provinces (as the NWP had become) where he would have been in 'the seats of the patricians instead of fighting with beasts in the arena below'. It was difficult to like the Bengalis, he told Curzon, even when they were Muslims. They seemed to be 'a special kind of humanity, possessing intellect which is untempered by either morality or feeling – except perhaps the feeling of fear'.[36]

Bengalis did have Anglo-Indian friends who appreciated their gentleness, intelligence and love of the arts. But the admiration was often accompanied by exasperation. Much as he liked them and sympathized with their political hopes, Henry Beveridge thought their 'besetting sin' was that 'they will think and talk and talk and think for ever but they will not act'. Yet he was tolerant of their lack of 'truth and straightforwardness'. These were not after all 'Oriental virtues', so it was perhaps understandable that there was a 'preference in the Bengali mind for the milder virtues such as patience and charity'.[37]

Beveridge deplored the fact that relations between the British and Indians were deteriorating in the 1880s. So did some of his contemporaries in Bengal such as Henry Cotton and James Cruickshank Geddes, who blamed the unpopularity of the British on their insistence on living in isolation.[38] The process of racial separation had begun early in the century and had accelerated after the Mutiny. Since they were so outnumbered and had so nearly been beaten, Anglo-Indians felt the necessity to behave like a ruling race, keeping aloof and demanding deference. Puzzled by signs of Indian animosity to British rule, Temple once asked Salar Jung for an explanation. The Hyderabad Minister replied that, although previous rulers such as the Emperor Aurangzeb had been far more tyrannical than the current regime, they had 'with all their faults . . . settled among and amalgamated themselves with the people', something which the British, with all their virtues, had not done.[39] Temple took the point and subsequently argued that the problem with British-Indian relations, the failure of communication between the governors and the governed, stemmed from the fact that they lived separately. Of course not everywhere was the same: racial divisions were gentler in Bombay than in the other presidencies. But almost the only places where British and Indians could really meet on equal terms outside the native states were at meetings of Freemasons and the Theosophical Society. It was not surprising that Kipling liked to escape from officials in Lahore's Punjab Club and spend time with the intercommunal brotherhood of his Masonic Lodge where 'there ain't such things as infidels' among the 'Brethren black an' brown'.[40]

Among Indians there was also a conscious move away from the social interplay that had characterized relations between the races in the days of the nabobs. The more blatant intrusions of the West – the annexations, the missionary endeavours, the abolition of abuses against women* – had led to a Hindu reaction, a certain codification of the religion and a stricter brahminical emphasis on purification,

---

*These included the abolition of sati (1829), the Hindu Widow Remarriage Act (1856), the raising of the age of consent (1891) and the campaign against female infanticide. Some Hindus supported these measures: the Bengali Rammohun Roy fought against sati, while the Madrasi G. Subramaniam Iyer (the founder of the *Hindu* newspaper) and a number of reformers from western India vigorously espoused the right of widows to remarry. But all these policies were passionately denounced by a larger number of Hindu conservatives.

especially in the preparation and consumption of food. This caused problems for those Anglo-Indians who wanted to mix socially and thought that the best way to do so was around a table laden with food and drink. They were consequently discouraged by the refusal of invitations and by visits that could not include even a cup of tea. At the highest levels of society a certain amount of social meshing did take place. In 1872 Northbrook assured Queen Victoria that the 'most enlightened' Hindus and Muslims no longer hesitated to dine with him at Government House. In 1887 Cotton could give a dinner in Calcutta attended by senior Civilians, Congress leaders, British judges, Indian barristers, native chiefs and several members of the Tagore family.[41]

Mixed social gatherings in the *mofussil*, however, tended to be stiff and awkward occasions. After attending 'an entertainment with fireworks given by a wealthy Babu', James Sifton, an Assistant Magistrate in Bengal, reported that at such events he would shake hands with his host on arrival and departure but would not otherwise see him for the rest of the evening. Nor was he able to talk to many other Indians present because the seats for the Europeans were put in an area separate from all the others. His Commissioner's wife, Mrs Williams, gruffly refused to tolerate racial segregation: with 'her masterful way . . . and a complete disregard of her own bad Hindustani', she barged into local zenanas and insisted that the ladies inside them, who were not allowed to appear in public, came to her 'purdah-mishin' parties. Henry Beveridge and his wife tried a softer approach with an 'International Evening Party' for 160 people at their house at Bankipur outside Patna. They solved the eating problem by setting up separate tents for Hindus, Muslims and Christians and by keeping the bandsmen's ham well away from the Muslims.[42]

A Punjabi man told one Civilian's wife that he wished the English sahibs would talk to him about themselves, about what they felt and thought and wanted. The lady replied that they would work for him and perhaps die for him but they would never talk about how they felt. The Maharaja of Dewas Senior told Malcolm Darling, a Civilian who made friendship with Indians the chief object of his life, that 'we might have liked the English but we do not know them'. Yet Indians themselves put obstacles in the way even of acquaintance. The British memsahibs wondered how they were expected to form friendships when Indians would not eat with them, invite them to their houses or allow them to meet – or even discuss – their wives and daughters. The young Kipling articulated a common attitude when he suggested the races should mix socially only when Indian women could be included in the party.[43]

This attitude – 'If you don't let me call on your wife, you shan't call on mine' – may have been a blinkered one, but it is difficult to see what memsahibs were expected to do to rectify matters. Some Civilians admitted that they could not hope to understand India when half of it was closed to them, because the 'confinement of women in zenanas [was] an impassable obstacle to our getting a glimpse of their family life and customs . . . from *within*'.[44] Walter Lawrence said that his chief regret in 'The Land of Regrets' was that he never knew or even met the women of India. When he visited their husbands in Kashmir, he knew the ladies were there, watching from their latticed windows, but he could never talk to them. That 'crippling convention', he claimed, cut the British off from 'the real India', making it impossible for them to understand 'her heart and mind and soul'.[45]

There were other crippling conventions. Justice Banerjea refused Curzon's invitation to go to England for the coronation of Edward VII because he felt that acceptance would make 'his position in his own family circle . . . intolerable' and 'he might never be able to marry his daughters if he were to cross the sea'. The Viceroy did not blame Banerjea, whom he admired, but he regretted that 'caste scruples, religious scruples, social scruples [should] intervene at every point'.[46] Another senior figure, General Roberts, may not have minded that the Maharaja of Travancore had to undergo 'a severe purification at the hands of the Brahmins' after sitting between Roberts and his wife at dinner.[47] But lesser officials did not find it easy to be friendly with a man who would wash his hands and change his clothes after their greeting and then refuse to eat his food if he thought their shadows had fallen across it. Civilians could not be expected to feel warmly towards a Brahmin visitor who arrived on their verandas attended by a servant carrying a bowl of water in which he would wash his hands after the handshake.[48] The British were not in India to be treated like Untouchables.

Reformers

Not all Civilians were happy to play the autocrat, the headmaster of perpetual children, however beneficent they felt their rule might be. If humanitarian paternalism was one aspect of imperial rule, another was the liberal tradition. Political and economic liberalism had brought prosperity and had helped spare Britain the revolutions that broke out in each generation in France. It was thus often disconcerting for young men receptive to this tradition to be confronted by the reality of authoritarian rule in India.

In the settler colonies of North America and Australasia liberalism meant progress towards self-government, elected legislatures and dominion status. In India it meant 'sympathizing' with the 'aspirations' of 'educated natives' and 'associating' Indians more closely with the administration. Ripon made an effort to turn these phrases into practice, and so did his Finance Member, Evelyn Baring, who did not think the Government would 'subvert the British Empire by allowing the Bengali Baboo to discuss his own schools and drains'.[49] But Alfred Lyall's liberalism did not extend to teaching Indians how they might govern themselves or to doing anything very concrete about 'association'. It was 'tremendously difficult', he thought, 'to carry on oriental government on liberal European principles', and the attempt only led to disaffection. The best chance for India lay in educating the landowning upper classes, 'not in bringing forward a crowd of smart pushing young Indians to fill all the professions and compete for everything'.[50] The great mass of India was still feudal and old-fashioned, alien territory for the tiny group of English-speaking lawyers clamouring for rights.

Gladstone, argued Lyall, knew only 'the world of civilized politics' and had forgotten that ultimately British rule in India depended on force. The Prime Minister's policy, which Ripon, Baring and Ilbert were trying to carry out, was 'stirring' up the 'educated classes' to such an extent that there would soon be a movement of 'India for the Indians'. Then the British would 'have to put down their foot and to say "Thus far and no further"', a stance that might result in another mutiny. Nothing, he thought, should ever be done quickly or radically in India. The Ilbert Bill, for example, may have been just in theory but it was unnecessary in practice and badly handled as well: pushing the measure through was 'like setting fire to an important wing of the house to roast a . . . small pig'.[51]

The great questions for Liberals were the more or less eternal ones. Why are we here? What are we doing? Where are we going? Francis Younghusband, a relentless examiner of his own thoughts, listed his preoccupations under the title 'Questions to Investigate'. Was Britain's 'rule ephemeral as Elphinstone supposed or [was] it bound to last?' Should the 'aim be to train the natives so that eventually they [would] be able to rule the country themselves?'[52]

A small group of Civilians agreed with Elphinstone and wished that Ripon had done more to accelerate the ephemerality. One of them was Henry Beveridge who was convinced early on in his career that Indians should eventually govern themselves. But he believed that a transfer of power could not happen in the near future. If the British suddenly left India, they would be behaving like 'a man-stealer who should kidnap a child, and then in a fit of repentance abandon him in a tiger-jungle'. The approach should be gradual, 'Indianizing' the ICS by such means as holding examinations in India as well as London and reserving judicial appointments in Bengal to natives.[53]

Most Civilians preferred not to think of such issues, keeping their heads down and getting on with the job they had been employed to do. But others could not help wondering whether a few people from a small and distant island could go on ruling a vast country with so many layers of ancient, medieval and more recent civilizations. Henry Cotton's view was unequivocal.

> The administration . . . of a great country by a small number of foreign visitors, in a state of isolation produced by a difference in religion, ideas and manners, which cuts them off from all intimate communion with the people, can never exist as a permanent state of things.[54]

Cotton was an unusual Civilian who might have been happier leading the life of a Victorian man of letters, an acquaintance of Tennyson and a friend of the Savile Club littérateurs. In India he was the victim of both his conceit and his integrity. He longed more than anything to be loved by the people of Bengal: his autobiography is full of assertions that they did indeed love him and that, despite 'the imputation of egotism', it was 'no more than the literal truth' to state that he 'left India accompanied by demonstrations of popular sympathy and regret which had never before been accorded to a provincial

Governor'.[55] In his book *New India* Cotton appealed to the Government to make 'a prompt and liberal concession' to India's 'legitimate' aspirations which were becoming ever 'more reasonable and more irresistible'.

> The waves of the ocean of native progress are dashing against the breakwater of English prejudice. The members of the Anglo-Indian community, like the courtiers of Canute, call loudly on the Government to restrain the advancing tide. The Government, insufficiently attuned to the requirements of the situation, unlike Canute, is not yet strong enough or wise enough to turn a deaf ear to their advice.[56]

Such views, which were publicly held and frequently stated, did not slow down his career except during the lieutenant-governorship of Sir Rivers Thompson in the mid-1880s: Thompson's successor, Stewart Bayley, promoted him to Chief Secretary of the Bengal Government shortly after admonishing him for a nationalist speech in Calcutta and ordering him to 'keep a more discreet check on his tongue in future'.[57] But this vociferous enthusiasm for the nationalist cause probably did cost Cotton the lieutenant-governorship in the end. His political views were similar to those of his contemporary MacDonnell, but whereas the Irishman allowed these gently to influence his administration as L-G, Cotton's determination to proclaim them loudly may have cost him the prize his talents deserved.

Cotton attended one of the first conferences of the Indian National Congress in 1886 and served as its President after retirement. But the Civilian most closely involved with the establishment of Congress was the ornithologist Allan Octavian Hume, a talented, arrogant and fractious Aberdonian. Hume's main defect was not his need for popularity but his egotism. As a Secretary to the Government, he proved so obnoxious to Lytton that the Viceroy decided to get rid of him by merging his department and abolishing his post. Embittered by this experience, Hume retired early and tried to set himself up as a kind of Indian Parnell. For nine years he worked as general secretary for Congress, writing pamphlets, organizing committees and turning himself into an agitator so outspoken that even his organization had to rebuke him.

The next most prominent Civilian supporter of Congress was another Scot, William Wedderburn, who annoyed his superiors by

Sir Charles Aitchison and his family at Barnes Court, the Lieutenant-Governor of the Punjab's summer residence in Simla

The Collector's House: Henry Cotton in Bengal

The Judge's House, Bellary (Madras)

The Club, Burdwan (Bengal)

Sir George Campbell, Lieutenant-Governor of Bengal 1871–4 (*centre, with stick*), meets the Raja of Sikkim and his family

Picnic at Darjeeling: Sir Rivers Thompson, Lieutenant-Governor of Bengal 1882–7, sits in the middle of the group

Sir Denzil Ibbetson, Lieutenant-
Governor of the Punjab 1905–8

Sir Charles Elliott, Lieutenant-Governor
of Bengal 1890–5

Sir Mortimer Durand, Foreign Secretary
of the Government of India 1885–94

Sir Harcourt Butler, Lieutenant-Governor
of Burma (twice) and the United
Provinces between 1915 and 1927

Victorious oarsmen at Poona

The Peshawar Vale Hunt

Sir Donald Macnabb's children in the Punjab

Sailing at Naini Tal

Left: Rudyard Kipling by William Strang, 1898

Below: Future administrators: Indian ICS probationers at Oxford, 1921

never losing 'an opportunity of associating himself with native political movements'. The Bombay Government felt that, among other misdemeanours, he had taken 'a somewhat too active part in a project for compounding with the creditors the debt of the Dekkan ryots'.[58] Like Hume, whose biographer he became, Wedderburn retired early, after he had been passed over for promotion, and served as President of Congress in 1889 and 1910. Like Cotton, he became a Liberal MP and, as Chairman of the Indian Parliamentary Committee, a sharp critic of the Salisbury Government.

13

Players

~

Games

IT WAS SAID that the British in India saw every holiday as a chance
to rush out and shoot something. That was not quite true. Some of
them took the opportunity to hunt a jackal or spear a boar or go
down to the river and fish for mahseer or Carnatic carp. Others
formed teams to play polo and cricket or row a race. Physical exercise was taken very seriously in Victorian India. Nobody spent a
holiday indoors playing whist or billiards: those were pastimes for
evenings and the monsoon.

Methods of hunting birds and animals had changed very slowly
since the invention of gunpowder. Indoor games were also evolving
gently, whist making way for bridge, billiards bifurcating from 1875,
its larger branch transfigured into snooker by a young Army officer
in the Ootacamund Club. But athletic or team sports (known as
'games': 'sport' involved bloodshed) changed a good deal both in
their form and in their appeal in the course of the nineteenth
century.

Archery, practised by both men and women, was one of the most
popular diversions of early Victorian India. But by the 1860s it had
been eclipsed by croquet, the favourite recreation of the Viceroy,
John Lawrence. Having spent much of his life dashing about the
Punjab on horseback, Lawrence was bored by riding slowly up and

down the Mall at Simla: it was more fun hitting heavy balls with heavy mallets through very wide hoops. In the town itself the game was played on earthen or gravel courts, but enthusiasts went down to the valley, to a flat piece of land known as Annandale, and played on the grass without boundaries.[1] Croquet's popularity spread throughout Anglo-India because it could be played in small stations by both sexes. Badminton had a similar appeal: in India it was usually played languorously by elderly people in their normal clothes.

Younger and more energetic Anglo-Indians preferred racquets, another game that did not require a large area or a troop of contestants. Rudimentary racquets courts sprang up all over the country, but before the end of the century the sport had ceded its popularity to lawn tennis, though this was usually played not on lawns but on courts of beaten earth. Tennis, which was taken up by both sexes, was 'a very satisfying game', observed one Indian Civilian, because 'one got all the exercise one needed in an hour and a half at the end of a day spent in inspections and files'.[2]

Team games were not often available to Civilians from stations which found it difficult to rustle up enough players for a game of whist. Sports requiring more than four participants needed the right combination of climate, location, topography and population. Rugby never took off in India because the ground was too hard to play on except during the monsoon. Rowing could only take place where there were navigable rivers – which are rare in India – or large lakes, as at Srinagar, Naini Tal and Ootacamund. Oarsmen from all over the Subcontinent flocked to Poona to compete for cups at the regatta on the River Mula, which was wider than the Thames at Hammersmith Bridge. But it was a sport enjoyed only by very junior Civilians. When the 25-year-old Horsley was unexpectedly beaten in a sculling race by a man fresh from England, he was forced to realize 'how India takes it out of a man'.

Polo became a popular sport in the 1860s and was enthusiastically taken up by a number of Civilians. As a Joint Magistrate in Bengal, Beames used to play 'hockey on horseback' every evening with his assistants on small ponies from Manipur. In Manipur itself, Frank Grimwood played the game with local princes before the blunders which led to his death and their exile. But although ICS teams often played the military, they rarely won matches. Not only did an Assistant Magistrate have far less time to practise than a subaltern, but there were seldom four Civilian players in the same place who could train together.

A few Civilians played football: Durand organized a tournament at Simla (later known as the Durand Cup) and at the age of 39, despite 'getting bald and grey', was still playing three days a week in the season. Rather more played golf, although the courses were atrocious. 'If you have a chance,' Crosthwaite told Ilbert, 'learn to play golf. It is a great solace.' Yet the game they most played in any numbers was cricket. Sedentary types in the secretariat might raise eyebrows at the waste of time: Lewis Tupper, the Punjab Chief Secretary, gazed in 'wild surprise' at a junior who asked if he could leave the office on Saturdays at noon so that he could go out and play. But most people were sympathetic to a game that – perhaps like nothing else except a hill station – gave men a sense of release from the Indian grind, a feeling that they were still a part of England, that out there on the pitch they were able not only to enjoy themselves but to display such cardinal virtues imbibed at school as fortitude, self-denial and team spirit. Later the British developed the theory of the 'Empire of Cricket', that they taught their subjects the game so as to unite the rulers and the ruled. But until the end of the nineteenth century they did little teaching and gave negligible encouragement. Cricket was as British a preserve as the club.[3]

It was difficult to prepare and preserve good pitches in India. In places where grass did not grow the wicket was made of matting; even where it did, at least theoretically, the pitch resembled tarmac more than a lush village green in England. Cricket flourished mainly in Bombay, the North-Western Provinces and Bengal. At the Christmas 'Week' in Lucknow, an ICS team confronted La Martinière College and in summer played other matches up at Naini Tal. Two of the best Civilian players reached the top of the service in Bengal, Rivers Thompson and James Bourdillon, the Acting L-G in 1902–3. In the 1870s, when the ICS team in Bengal included Bourdillon, an all-rounder who had captained Marlborough, and Lennie Abbot, a stylish batsman who had captained Cheltenham, it could even defeat the Calcutta Club.[4]

Shikar

The most popular recreation of British India was shikar (hunting and shooting) which could be conducted on any scale from one man and his dog to vast viceregal pageants which involved so many people that the startled game often ran away. The Raj is notorious for its tiger-slaying and its enormous shoots: in 1906 the Maharaja of Bikanir laid on a two-day gathering for the Viceroy, Lord Minto, during which the guns bagged 4,919 sand grouse, a bird which is almost inedible. Yet these occasions were usually limited to Viceroys, Governors and visiting royalty. The ICS had its dedicated hunters such as George Yule, but Civilians seldom participated in such events. Many of them only shot a tiger if it was molesting a village.

The ICS encouraged its members to 'shoot for the pot', to go out in the evening when on tour and bag a brace of quail for the next day's supper. It was believed that Civilians who strolled about their districts with a gun over their shoulder would get to know the people they administered. Those who did not like guns or fishing rods lost an opportunity to learn. 'Many a clue to what a villager is thinking', said Maconochie, 'is gained over a chat between beats or while watching one's float by some quiet pool.'[5]

India abounded with varieties of game that had lived largely undisturbed until the arrival of the British. Vast quantities of duck and geese could be found right across the Subcontinent from Burma to Sind. Snipe drummed in the marshes; partridge skimmed across the fields; black buck careered about almost everywhere. The hunter might have to give his gun a rest in the hot weather, but for eight months of the year he could stalk his way through the seasons of duck, deer, jungle fowl, peacock, snipe, partridge and quail. All areas teemed with targets. Sportsmen might complain that Madras was not as good as the NWP, and that there was no pig-sticking to be had, but up in the Nilgiris a man could still return from a hunting trip with bears, boars, black buck, woodcock, snipe, quail, jungle fowl and a tiger.[6]

One of the most obsessive Civilian hunters was Frank Simson, who wrote *Letters on Sport in Eastern Bengal*. He arranged his life so that he could spend every holiday – Christian, Muslim or Hindu – in pursuit of birds or animals. For him shikar was not a matter of grabbing a gun from the wall and setting off for the nearest forest. The approach had to be scientific, the programme planned, research carried out by himself and his private shikari, preferably a Muslim from the *mofussil*. If he wanted to shoot snipe in the paddy fields, the conditions had to be just right: the rice-crop between a foot and eighteen inches high, the ground a sticky mud covered by about an inch of water. Two days of sun made the fields too dry, two days of rain made the water too deep – and the snipe disappeared.

Simson believed that a serious hunter should not be married. Nor should he live in a place with a racecourse or a 'Mall', where he would be expected to ride up and down with the 'charming ladies of the station'. When he was sent to Noakhali, on the eastern edge of the Ganges delta, a friend told him it was 'a beastly mudbank . . . where there was no society and no doctor, where they made bad salt, and stuck pigs and shot tigers'. Nowhere could have suited Simson better. Although Noakhali was the 'station most heartily disliked by the Service', he volunteered to remain there, serving six years as Magistrate and Collector, because of the quality of the pig-sticking.[7]

For Simson pig-sticking (as it was called in Bengal) or hog-hunting (as it was called in Bombay) was one of the great sports of the world, 'second only to fox-hunting with the best packs in the English Midlands': in 1857, just before the outbreak of the Mutiny, he killed sixteen boars in a single day. 'Galloping after pig' was an extremely dangerous sport. Small groups of riders chased boars across wild country where neither they nor their horses could see where they were going. Horses stumbled into holes and did somersaults; riders and their spears went flying; boars turned and charged, trying to savage their pursuers with their tusks. Participants admitted the cruelty of the sport but justified it by pointing to the damage the animals inflicted on village crops.

The sport was pursued in most of India except Madras, where there were no pigs, and the Central Provinces, which had two drawbacks: the open country was too rocky for horses, and the pigs preferred to stay in the jungle. It was administered by 'tent clubs' with strict rules. Spearing a sow was considered as 'wicked' as 'killing a vixen at home': the Calcutta Tent Club fined its members a crate of champagne if they killed a sow other than in self-defence. The same penalty was exacted from a rider who jostled another or who rode 'across the hog in such a way as to cause him to jink his pursuer'.[8] In the summer, tent clubs held an annual dinner to commemorate the past season and look forward to the next. It was a great 'antidote to hot weather distress' to sit down to a banquet and exalt the sport with songs, speeches and plenty to drink. At the annual dinner of the Bareilly Tent Club, all of whose members were civil servants or Army officers, ten speeches were followed by songs such as 'The Mighty Boar' and 'Over the Valley', written by W. Cruikshank, a famous Civilian pig-sticker who once, on being told that a boar was rampaging about Cawnpore, adjourned his Court, dashed into the street and hunted it down in the bazaar.

> Over the valley, over the level,
>   Through the *dak* jungle, ride like the devil:
> Hark for'ard a boar, away we go!
>   Sit down in your saddle and ride, tally-ho![9]

Coursing with greyhounds and hunting with packs of dogs were more familiar British sports. Coursing jackals and small grey foxes went on in some parts of the Subcontinent, usually in the districts of the Bombay presidency, but it was not a popular sport among Civilians. Foxhounds also operated in Bombay, chasing jackals on the island of Salsette three times a week during the season. Most of the hunts were based in the north-west, at Quetta, Peshawar and Lahore, but there was also a famous pack at Ootacamund. One anglophile chief in Kathiawar aimed to please the Political Agent by importing a pack of hounds and even a huntsman from England. But the project was expensive and a failure. The hunting ruined the cotton fields, and the hounds soon died.[10]

Opinions varied on the merits of jackal-hunting. Simson did not think much of it. The problem with jackals, he observed, was that their scent was bad, they stuck to the villages and, when flushed into the open, they did not run fast enough. Furthermore, when cornered, they bit their pursuers so severely that they put a number of hounds out of action for several days.[11] Hunters on the North-West Frontier disagreed. Up there the jackals gave them as fine a run as a fox in Leicestershire, although the mass of ditches and the lack of hedges made the sport bear more resemblance to hunting in Ireland. Evelyn Howell, a Civilian who was whipper-in of the Peshawar Vale Hunt, recalled with nostalgia the twice-weekly meets as the sun rose, the quality of light on the bare brown hills, and the 'rousing gallop for 20 to 40 minutes over real sporting country'. It was over by ten o'clock so that 'the magistrate and the judge and the political officer [could] go hunting with a clear conscience' and be in their office by mid-morning. Howell, who ended his career as Resident in Kashmir and Foreign Secretary to the Indian Government, wrote 'The Peshawar Vale Hunt Song' (to the tune of the 'Eton Boating Song') and 'Hounds of Peshawar' (to the music of 'Hounds of the Meynell'). He was also a linguist who in retirement translated the *Poems of Khushnal Khan* from Pashto.[12]

The majority of Civilians did not hunt jackals or stick pigs. But most felt compelled sometimes to go out shooting even if they did not particularly like it and were not very good shots. Among those followed in this book who did not conform were Maynard, who refused to shoot, Temple, who preferred sketching, and Cotton, who restricted himself to killing a pariah dog, whose death haunted him for days, and an alligator, whose bellyful of women's bangles released him from feelings of guilt. Lyall was characteristically ambivalent about the matter. He went out sometimes with a gun but did not enjoy it and said that 'no one bored [him] so much as a man who is eternally talking about shooting'. To his mother he confessed to a 'queer secret sympathy for the tiger when alone and with his claws only he defeats men armed with powerful rifles'.[13]

In Victorian India shooting was very much 'the done thing', a proof of manliness, a demonstration of British skill and pugnacity. Men had themselves photographed surrounded by animal skins or with one foot on the carcass of a tiger. They had their trophies stuffed and their sambar stag's head mounted on the wall of the retirement home in Cheltenham. Early competition wallahs learned to shoot in the hope that the Old Haileyburians would not sneer at them as bookworms. It was difficult for men to free themselves from such an ethos. George Campbell admitted it had taken him fifty years to 'emancipate' himself from the 'superstition' that it was 'necessary to a man and a gentleman to take every opportunity of killing something'.[14]

At the end of the century, however, a reaction set in among Civilians, caused partly by the changing social origins of the ICS intake. A man like Maynard, a scholarship boy with left-wing views brought up in Wandsworth, was unlikely to want to emulate Sir George Yule, the Scottish Haileyburian dubbed 'the Emperor of the Spears'. A still younger Civilian, James Moore, observed that among his contemporaries, who arrived in India at the beginning of the twentieth century, people no longer instinctively said, 'It's a fine day, let's go and kill something.'[15] This did not mean that Indian wildlife suddenly became much safer: birds were still shot in large quantities. But men were now less inclined to slaughter large creatures like buffaloes, very easy targets as they lumbered across the fields.

Hills

Mountains were the usual destination for Civilians with a summer holiday. Most men were able to spend a couple of weeks at a hill station unless they were saving up their leave to go home to Britain. It was a necessary part of the annual routine. Officials lay awake in the plains, thinking of Ooty with larks singing on the Downs and the air smelling of eucalyptus, or of the azure lake and the precipices of Mahabaleshwar. Lying on rooftops further north, with the thermometer at night in the nineties, they dreamed of the day when they could exchange their oppressive nights for the cool air of Simla, for blankets on their beds and log fires in the evening. They yearned for the smells remembered from previous years, of the whiffs of sawn wood from the carpenters' shops, of the intoxicating scent of resinous pine needles trodden on a picnic on a sunny afternoon. They longed for the luxury of being able to sit in the sun without worrying about sunstroke.[16]

Besides the scenery and the climate, Civilians from the *mofussil* enjoyed simply seeing people, taking the air on Simla's Mall, sitting in Peliti's Café with old comrades from Haileybury and Balliol, rushing from picnics to tennis to dinners to dances. Those who were married sometimes camped in the deodar forests but usually took the more expensive option of renting a house. Bachelors stayed at the United Service Club, which had five tennis courts, two squash courts, running hot water and the essential soda-water factory. The young Maynard enjoyed staying there because it reminded him of Oxford. There may have been a few 'fogies and martinets who object[ed] to noises', but one could always find someone interesting to talk to in the library or the smoking-room.[17] And even the fogies could sometimes entertain: Kipling was delighted by the sight of a senior Civilian 'tobogganing' down the main staircase on a table top.

Viceroys, Councillors and Lieutenant-Governors tended to scoff at Simla. Curzon, who claimed to like every place in India except his summer capital, grumbled about having to spend half the year on a single hilltop chained to a sort of middle-class suburb. Lyall thought Simla society was 'silly and simple'. Clinton Dawkins, a Finance Member from London, expressed his amazement at the vulgarity and silliness of English people trying to amuse themselves.[18] These were snooty and insensitive attitudes towards people who had spent the last eleven months in the plains, lonely in the cold weather, sick and uncomfortable in the hot months, and desperate for a fortnight's relaxation. Simla's attractions grew in inverse proportion to the amount of time one could spend there and the extremity of the climate in which one lived for the rest of the year. As a young official in the Punjab, Walter Lawrence loved his brief escapes to Simla: the place was healthy and delightful, its society 'the brightest, wittiest and most refined community' he had ever known. But when he returned fifteen years later, living there for half the year as Curzon's Private Secretary, he thought it rather rowdy and frivolous. Feeling middle-aged and disinclined to take part in society's 'high jinks', he preferred to spend his free evenings advancing through a shelf of Dickens.[19]

Bishop Welldon of Calcutta suggested that Anglo-Indians were like 'people dancing under the shadow of a volcanic mountain'.[20] Viceroys might sneer at Simla's pleasure-seekers as frivolous, but it was the frivolity of people under strain, the frenzied gaiety of aliens often unsure why they were in India and desperate to enjoy themselves while they could. The solitude of a small station made serious men look forward to musical fêtes on moonlit lawns, to dances by torchlight under the pines, even to Fancy Dress balls and Alice in Wonderland dinners. The young Lyall used to stay up till daylight after a ball, sitting on a veranda and 'watching, through the smoke of a cheroot, the dawn breaking over the Himalayas'. Civilians on short leave were determined to enjoy themselves, cramming in as many events as possible, dancing with redoubled zest as the time approached for their return to the plains.

Most of them played sport at least as hard as they danced. During the daylight hours Simla was congested with croquet games, polo matches, tennis tournaments and gymkhanas among the pines at Annandale. A speciality at Mahabaleshwar was Badminton Breakfast at the Club with barley water and bacon sandwiches. One of the most frenetic sporting venues was Naini Tal with its two 'Weeks' in the late spring and early autumn. Civilians from the plains and from other hill stations flocked there to join ICS teams and challenge 'the Rest' at cricket, football, hockey, tennis, golf, polo, rowing and – after Saturday dinner at the Club – billiards. At the end of the nineteenth century there was also a September sporting week for women, in which teams were cruelly selected according to marital status. In the competition of 1901 the unmarried ladies, known as 'spins', drew with their opponents at tennis but won the boat race, the hockey and the cricket by an innings.[21]

Middle-aged Civilians often sent their families to a hill station for all or part of the season. This gave 'grass widows' and their daughters plenty of opportunity to dance, to flirt, to become the subject of gossip and to feature as a type in Kipling's *Plain Tales from the Hills*. Iris Butler, the daughter of one Civilian and niece of another,* once managed to dance on twenty-six consecutive nights in Simla. Although that was in the early 1920s, her mother had set a precedent earlier on. Iris's Scottish nanny used to recall her behaviour in grim tones: '*Puir* Mr Montie only up from the burning plains for ten days, and there was your mother out every night and not getting up till late in the morning, and then off and away on some nonsense again.'[22]

Simla's reputation preceded the publication of Kipling's stories and originated during the regime of the flirtatious Lytton, who was himself suspected of adultery there. One priggish young subaltern was reluctant to visit the town in 1885 because he had heard that its 'main occupations' were 'gambling, drinking and breaking the 7th Commandment'.[23] An older officer, General Pearse, recalled Simla's 'frisky young Dames, and a few young fellows full of mischief and devilment'. He remembered also that, while most women dressed their *jampannies* in light costumes to be 'discernible even in a darkish night', those 'who were given to tender meetings by moonlight midst

---

*Montagu and Harcourt respectively. Both ended their careers as Lieutenant-Governors, or Governors as the post was renamed in 1921: Montagu in the Central Provinces, Harcourt in Burma (twice) and the United Provinces.

those dark, umbrageous, pine-lined roads, chose the darkest of liveries for their menials'.*[24] But it was Kipling's tales and the poems in *Departmental Ditties* that set an image of the town sufficiently frivolous and immoral for Curzon to feel obliged to reassure Queen Victoria about the 'unfair and rather malevolent impressions that have gone abroad and have received some colour from the too cynical stories of Rudyard Kipling'.[25] Hunter, who had just retired from the ICS when he reviewed *Departmental Ditties*, praised their author as a 'literary star of no mean magnitude' but suggested he had better things to do than break 'those poor Simla butterflies on the wheel'. He admitted the town's dual nature but insisted that the important side was not the 'silly little world' of the poet's verses but 'another Anglo-Indian world which for high aims, and a certain steadfastness in effort after the personal interest in effort is well nigh dead, has never had an equal in history'.[26]

Anglo-Indians' resentment at their portrayal as frivolous and adulterous prompted Kipling, in the preface to a subsequent book, 'to assure the ill-informed that India is not entirely inhabited by men and women playing tennis and breaking the Seventh Commandment' – an assurance that might have puzzled the ill-informed when they discovered that most of the stories in *Under the Deodars* were precisely about such people. But the writer's fans among young Civilians saw no need for such disclaimers because they regarded the works as an accurate representation of their world. 'The amount of malicious scandal talked is fairly amazing,' one of them reported to his old Oxford tutor, 'and Kipling is much more true to the life in his women-kind than most Anglo-Indians allow.'[27]

Maud Diver, who wrote *The Englishwoman in India* with the purpose of refuting the idea that Anglo-Indian ladies generally misbehaved, claimed that 'the two most insidious' pitfalls for grass widows in the hills were 'amateur theatricals and the military man on leave'; one or other was 'accountable for half the domestic tragedies in India'.[28] A third was the viceregal entourage: Northbrook's son had a liaison in Simla, while Dufferin's heir became so enamoured of Kipling's sister

---

*Women in Simla were transported by a type of sedan chair called a *jampan,* which was carried by two pairs of native *jampannies.* The *jampan* was superseded by the rickshaw around 1880. In Kipling's poem, 'The Tale of Two Suits', a drunken lover, unaware that two Simla ladies have similar costumes for their rickshaw carriers, talks ardently in the dark to the wrong woman.

Trix that he had to be sent home. Lord William Beresford, who won a VC in the Zulu War and was Military Secretary to three Viceroys from 1882, was a particular magnet: his future nemesis was the subject of much speculation, observers in Simla wondering whether he would break his neck with his reckless steeplechasing before he was cited as co-respondent in a divorce case.

Civilians in the secretariat had the opportunity to take part in Simla's 'high jinks' if they were young or, like Griffin, bachelors. Older, married, hard-working ones were – like those left in the plains – more likely to be deceived husbands. Simla society was convinced that Lytton was having affairs with the pretty wives of two of his ICS subordinates, George Batten, his Private Secretary, and Trevor Plowden, the Under-Secretary at the Foreign Office. In fact the Viceroy flirted innocently with both, although, to his chagrin, they 'consoled themselves' less innocently with his ADCs. When Wilfrid Scawen Blunt visited India, Mrs Batten told him not only of her own love affairs but about those of all Simla too. She also began an affair with Blunt which she continued in England when visiting him in Sussex for the Goodwood race meeting.[29]

Scandal percolated through Simla but seldom exploded in a public place. One of the noisiest exceptions occurred just after the First World War when a Mr King, who hated balls, became suspicious about the lateness of his wife's return from dances in the company of his closest friend, a cavalry officer with a reputation for philandering. Late one night in their hotel, he tanked himself up with alcohol, grabbed hold of a poker, burst into the friend's rooms and, on finding his wife in the bed, laid the officer out with his weapon. He then roused all the other guests to witness the shamed wife and the prostrate poodle-faker. 'The poker pokered' was the reaction of Harcourt Butler, who had a taste for lewd jokes and salacious limericks. All three fled Simla, and the officer was sent to a department called 'Remounts', a posting which tickled Butler and made him believe that the Army had a sense of humour.[30]

Furlough

Members of the ICS were entitled to a variety of different types of leave. Although the rules changed several times in the course of the nineteenth century, at the end of it these consisted of privilege leave, special leave, leave on medical certificate and furlough. Privilege leave was effectively the Civilian's annual one-month holiday: 'one eleventh part of the time during which he has been on duty without interruption'. If he wished, he could save up to three months' leave over three years to go to Britain so long as he did not mind spending half his holidays at sea. Special leave of up to six months was granted for 'urgent private affairs', which usually meant going home after the death of a parent or taking children back to Britain after a wife had died in India. Leave on medical certificate is self-explanatory, and furloughs – from the Dutch word *verlof*, meaning leave of absence – were the long vacations spread over the duration of a man's service.[31]

In the second half of the century Civilians were allowed to be away from India for periods of up to two years while retaining their positions on half pay, so long as this sum did not exceed 833⅓ rupees a month. If they retired after 25 years, they were entitled to a pension if they had spent at least 21 of them on active service; if they carried on for the maximum of 35 years, they could spend six of these on furlough. Out of his 34 years' service in India, Henry Beveridge had leave totalling five years and ten months spread over four furloughs, taken every eight years or so, and one special leave to get married in Scotland.[32]

Civilians were allowed their first furlough after eight years in India unless there was an emergency or their province had too many officials on sick leave.* Some did not go even when they had the opportunity. Walter Lawrence never went home in his sixteen years in the Subcontinent, while Beames returned only twice during his thirty-five. Before the Mutiny, when the voyage took much longer, Civilians sometimes spent their entire careers without seeing Britain. Bartle Frere, who retired as Governor of Bombay in 1867, had not seen his homeland since leaving Haileybury in 1834.

Anglo-Indians were naturally excited and apprehensive about their first furlough. There was the liberating ritual of throwing their sola topi into Bombay harbour, though some preferred to wait until they reached Port Said. There was the excitement of the Suez Canal, of the voyage across the Mediterranean, of the arrival at Marseille

---

*Lieutenant-Governors and Members of Council could not take furlough while holding these appointments, but they could have six months' leave on medical certificate.

where they found themselves speaking Hindustani to French porters. They might not enjoy mainland Europe very much because in one direction they were impatient to arrive home and in the other they were demoralized about going back. But the Channel held a permanent enchantment, and so for some did the Tweed, the Severn and the Irish Sea. Going home provoked a confusion of emotions: parents were older and frailer, siblings had become strangers, grandparents were no longer alive. But there was exhilaration too, and comfort, and physical and mental respite. Health could improve almost miraculously. A winter in Tipperary, hunting three days a week, helped cure Michael O'Dwyer of malaria.

Visits to families and friends were only a part of furlough. A sojourn of two years required diligent planning: Civilians needed an occupation, a place to live, an opportunity to do all those things they had been missing in India. After repeatedly postponing his furlough, William Horsley, the amiable jungle wallah from Bombay, admitted he was 'apt to dread the unknown'. And after sixteen years in India, England belonged to the 'unknown'. Horsley was nervous about what he would do there, about how far his money would go, about whether after sixteen consecutive hot weathers he would be able to cope with a couple of English winters. The problem of where to live was an 'inexhaustible subject' of conversation between him and his wife Mary. Since he was in favour of 'country delights' yet she did not want to be 'buried' in the shires, they compromised on Tunbridge Wells.[33]

Young Civilians often spent part of their furlough trying to find a wife.* Older ones were absorbed by the search for suitable schools† and houses for their families. Middle-aged officials tended to settle in Anglo-Indian 'enclaves' such as Cheltenham or Eastbourne or in London in such areas as Bayswater and South Kensington.[34] G. O. Trevelyan listed a few of the 'fresh and pure joys' of the returned Civilian: 'the first sight of turnip fields and broad-backed sheep; the first debauch on home-made butter, and bacon which is above suspicion; the first picnic; the first visit to the Haymarket Theatre . . .'[35] The pleasures were no doubt real, but so were the various disappointments. The weather was worse than he remembered, the cost

*See below pp. 279–81.
†See below pp. 302–5.

of living was more expensive than he expected, the means of transport in London were more crowded and less dignified than he was accustomed to. He often felt a bit bewildered, out of place, out of touch and very much ignored, even by his employer, the India Office, which offered him little encouragement to visit.[36] No one seemed very interested in his exploits so many thousands of miles away.

Most Civilians did not regard furlough merely as a holiday and a family reunion but also as a chance to widen their education and perhaps do something to advance their careers in India and beyond. Many of them who planned to take early retirement did not intend to come home at the age of 47 and just live on their pension. Determined to make up for his lack of university education, Younghusband decided that on his first furlough he would have lessons in chemistry, physics, geography, botany, biology, agriculture, photography and social sciences, that he would look at good paintings, listen to good music, write a book about his travels and above all study religion and great religious men.[37] Lewin Bowring felt that the great void in his life was travel. In 1854 he therefore set off on long journeys through Rajputana, China (where his father, whom he had not seen for ten years, was Governor of Hong Kong), France, Italy and Central Europe (which he toured three times), and the British Isles, where he inspected seventeen cathedrals.[38]

Ambitious officials usually spent a good part of their furloughs in London. Henry Cotton divided his time congenially between playing whist at the Savile Club, watching cricket at Lords and moving in the literary circles of the *Fortnightly Review*, for which he was a contributor. He also wrote his controversial book, *New India*, a vindication of Ripon's reforms and a plea for further measures. A number of Civilians read for the Bar, conscientiously studying law and eating the requisite number of dinners at the Inns of Court. Philip Hutchins, who later became a Member of Lansdowne's Council, spent his first furlough between a barrister's chambers and a cricket pitch and was called to the Bar on his second. G. R. Elsmie, who rose to be Financial Commissioner in the Punjab, enrolled at Lincoln's Inn because he calculated correctly that 'the status of an English barrister would lead to advancement in the judicial line in India'.[39] Called to the Bar at the end of his first furlough, he relaxed during his second and spent most of it in his native Aberdeenshire.

George Campbell, an austere and crotchety native of Fife, did not think that leave – or indeed life in general – was meant for playing. He also read for the Bar during his first furlough but spent most of his time writing the 553 pages of *Modern India*, which was published by John Murray in 1852, followed by the 438 pages of *India As It May Be*, which came out a year later. During a subsequent furlough he decided to go into politics and stand as the Liberal candidate for Dumbartonshire, where he found 'whisky tasting' with electors 'rather trying'. Electoral success would have required his resignation from the ICS, but Liberals in Glasgow thought they had spotted a loser and persuaded him to withdraw from the contest. Campbell then wrote a short book, *Irish Land*, which advocated 'security of tenure and a thrifty peasantry' as the 'best hope for Ireland', and followed that up with a couple of essays on Indian land tenure and Indian revenue and finance. After another attempt to stand for Parliament had failed, this time at St Andrews, he returned to India to take up a wholly unexpected offer, the lieutenant-governorship of Bengal.[40]

14

Husbands and Lovers

~

In Search of a Wife

GRIFFINS WERE NOT expected to go out to India as married men, though they might marry the daughter of a Collector or a Colonel when they got there. Even so, such unions were discouraged during the early years of a man's career. The custom was for a Civilian not to look for a wife until his first furlough. In his twenties his superiors wanted him to be mobile, solvent and unencumbered by a family.

Nevertheless there were no rules or prohibitions. At the age of 21 Henry Cotton married Mary Ryan, an Irish girl of 18 who a few years earlier had been found begging with her mother on Putney Heath. The photographer Julia Margaret Cameron had taken her into her household and later portrayed the pair – he in imperious Byronic haze, she in languishing floral reverie – before they sailed to Bengal. But it was more common to become engaged at home and then wait a few years until exams in India had been passed and salaries had been enlarged. Frank Hudson and John Hubback both left their fiancées behind for three years; the distraught Hudson also left his girl's love letters under his pillow in the steamer. Similarly, Maurice Hayward went out for three years, saved up all his privilege leave and then, assisted by funds from his prospective mother-in-law, returned to England to marry Alice Barber.[1]

Such stories usually had happy endings, the betrothed couples marrying after long separations, although in the case of Henry Middleton Rogers his 'intended' decided to stay in England and become the second wife of the 10th Duke of St Albans. But even happy marriages caused much frowning and head-shaking.

> Down to Gehenna, or up to the Throne,
> He travels the fastest who travels alone.

Kipling may have been writing about an Army man, Captain Gadsby, but young Civilians shared the view, informing each other of the 'dreadful news' when a colleague in the Service became engaged.

> You may carve it on his tombstone, you may cut it on his card,
> That a young man married is a young man marred![2]

'Don't marry till you have five years' service', a senior Civilian warned one young Assistant Commissioner in the Punjab: it would be 'utter ruin to your prospects'.[3] This was not always a sequitur, as the careers of Hubback, Hudson and Hayward – and indeed Cotton – all showed.* But it could affect early promotion: if there was a vacancy for an Assistant Commissioner in Sind, one of the most saddle-bound of posts, it would almost always go to a bachelor. Early marriage invariably made a Civilian poorer and less mobile. As one junior magistrate disapprovingly put it, he inevitably became reclusive and frugal, playing badminton instead of cricket, travelling in a dog-cart rather than on a horse, going to church regularly and spending his money on dispatching his family to the hills.[4] The strain of trying to combine family life and an Indian career often led young men to abandon ambitions to become a District Officer and to apply for a post in the Judiciary.

Civilians who did not find the right girl in India usually waited until their first furlough before making an intensive search for a wife. Such abstinence was dictated by prudence and lack of opportunity rather than by any weird theory that empire builders sublimated their sexual desires in order to conserve the energy needed to build empires. By the time of their furlough, when they were about thirty, many of them were understandably desperate. A few may have risked

---

*Hubback became Governor of Orissa, while both Hudson and Hayward rose to be Members of the Bombay Executive Council.

brothels in the cities, a few more or less discreetly kept native mistresses, and a few had occasional flings with memsahibs in hill stations. But most of them stayed mainly celibate in their most sexually potent decade – and celibate in a very monastic way: not only did Assistant Magistrates seldom have sex, many of them seldom saw women with whom they might have wanted to have sex.

The men on furlough were thus determined to return to India with a wife. Even George Campbell realized that, after writing his books and reading for the Bar, it would be advantageous to 'provide' himself with a mate. For some the search did not take very long: Maynard met the American Alfreda H. Eppes in Egypt on his way home and proposed to her behind a pillar in St Mark's in Venice. Others did not make it their priority and began to panic as the end of their leave approached. After unsuccessfully scouring Dunfermline for a suitable bride, the 32-year-old Henry Beveridge found the 16-year-old Jeanie Goldie in Edinburgh in the final weeks of his furlough. Since she was still at school and too young to marry, he went back to India alone and returned eighteen months later to claim her.[5]

Civilians were usually more methodical in their search than Beveridge. No one could have been less romantic than John Lawrence, who went on furlough to find a woman of good health, good temper and good sense. Referring to this as yet imaginary person as 'the calamity', he looked for her in Bath and, having failed in his quest, went to Donegal and tracked her down there.[6] One of Lawrence's subordinates emulated his single-mindedness. After being rejected by a girl in India, Lewin Bowring was determined to go to England and 'not to return . . . without a wife to share [his] home and halve [his] joys and sorrows'. He did, however, narrow his options in the early part of his furlough by going to Exeter and converting to Catholicism, a move which persuaded him to find a Catholic matron in London who could introduce him to his new co-religionists. Before long he fell in love with Mary Laura Talbot, who seemed to him 'well fitted to adorn an Indian home'. They were married and had two children before Mary died suddenly in Mysore in 1866. Miserable though he was, Bowring claimed that 'God's grace' prevented him losing his composure and allowed him to take his children back to Britain. He went into retreat at Roehampton and, a year after his loss, made up his 'mind to marry again, not only with the view of securing a suitable companion' for himself, 'but also, looking to the future, to find one who could bestow a mother's care and attention' on his children when he retired from India. This prompted another trawl through the Catholic families of London, which was this time unsuccessful, but he did eventually find the suitable companion.[7]

Men such as Campbell, Lawrence and Bowring did not waste time waiting to fall in love. For them suitability was more important than romantic attachment, though doubtless even they would have regarded the latter as a bonus. Their basic requirement was a mate who would manage their households, look after their children and put up with a life of loneliness and moving around. Perhaps they did not appreciate that such an existence – in which men and women had to depend on each other much more than in Britain – was only tolerable if it included a certain romantic flavour. As Kipling wrote in his story 'By Word of Mouth', India was 'a delightful country for married folk who are wrapped up in one another. They can live absolutely alone and without interruption.' Conversely, the Subcontinent was a terrible place for couples who did not get on: it was bad enough for women to have to trail through jungles and across deserts even when they liked their husbands. Quite a few, like Mrs Howe, got fed up, took the children home and spent most of their husbands' salary in England.[8]

Some stayed for the perks or returned when they saw perks in the offing. John Hewett's wife left him when he was in the secretariat but insisted on returning when he was made a knight and a Lieutenant-Governor: the two of them inhabited different wings of Government House in Naini Tal and seldom spoke to each other. Hewett was one of three consecutive L-Gs of the United Provinces who were miserably married. His successor, James Meston, had a wife who could not control her jealousy, while the next occupant of the post, Harcourt Butler, had a wife who even abandoned him temporarily on their wedding day. Butler's marriage did not improve after her return. He confided to his Under-Secretary that, although he had been married to his wife for many years, they had not lived together for more than eight days. Lady Butler gave an order to the same official: 'Mr Lupton, never leave me in the room with Harcourt.'[9]

Courtships in India

Civilians sometimes got engaged in India, but there were not enough Anglo-Indian girls in the country to make this a common occurrence. Occasionally they married the daughter of an industrialist, the owner of a sugar factory in Madras or a manager of the textile mills in Cawnpore, a city rather fancifully dubbed 'the Manchester of the East'. But there were barely half a dozen business communities in India. A Civilian was more likely to be competing for the daughter of his Collector or the local Colonel or – with perhaps less competition – a local missionary. Nevertheless, while his salary and prospective pension ensured eligibility, he would generally be regarded as less dashing than local subalterns who were also in pursuit of their CO's daughter.

Smitten Civilians went through the rigmarole of courtship in a civil station, the morning rides, the games of badminton and lawn tennis, the occasional gatherings in the club with music and singing and sometimes a little dancing. But potential fathers-in-law, who had often brought their daughters out from Britain to look after them and act as their hostess, were in a strong position to sabotage such romances. Lewin Bowring was one of several suitors of a girl who 'sang like a bird', 'rode like an Amazon' and 'won all hearts'; each of them, however, was so deterred by her angry and resentful father, a General, that she never married. Others were daunted by the girls' status and expectations. An Assistant Magistrate in a distant subdivision might be apprehensive about offering himself to the daughter of a Commissioner or Colonel whose life revolved around balls, bandstands and a hill station: William Horsley said he would 'as soon think of proposing to one of the Pleiades'.[10]

Yet such unions took place and, despite the problems of adjustment, they often seemed to work. Mary Esme Talbot, the daughter of the Resident in Kashmir, renounced the charms of Srinagar and Gulmarg when she married a Political, Armine Dew, and spent the next twenty-two years wandering between the frontiers of Persia and Afghanistan, practising her violin in solitude among the myrtle groves.[11] Marital alliances within the Service did not usually entail such an exile. Ambitious young Civilians tended to fall for daughters of successful older Civilians and thereby remain close to the centres of the administration. Lieutenant-Governors often had sons-in-law who rose to a comparable level. The daughter of Robert Egerton, a Lieutenant-Governor of the Punjab, married William Mackworth Young, who became L-G of the same province. John Strachey's daughter married Hugh Barnes (later Lieutenant-Governor of Burma), Denzil Ibbetson's married Evan Maconochie (a future Agent to the Governor in Kathiawar) and Alfred Lyall's married John Miller (who became Chief Commissioner of the Central Provinces and a Member of the Viceroy's Council). The success of the sons-in-law owed little to nepotism: their bride's fathers had retired or, as in Ibbetson's case, died long before they reached the top. But they did perhaps reflect the gravitational pull of a Government House on young men with ambitions to occupy one in the future.

Not all Civilians were married by the end of their first furlough. Some did not plan to marry at all. William Henry Crowe, the bachelor District Judge of Poona, became the target of a Colonel's widowed sister who ingratiated herself by pruning the creepers on his bungalow and, 'in spite of wearing bloomers to the scandal of Poona', persuaded him to marry her.[12] Down in Madras George Partridge decided to marry in his forties not because he wanted a wife in India but because he needed a chatelaine for the small estate in Devonshire which he had bought for his retirement. So charmed was he by his encounter with two married sisters in Ooty that on his next furlough he went to their home in Northern Ireland and successfully proposed to one of their siblings.[13]

Most middle-aged marriages, however, were remarriages. If a wife died, a Civilian either had to take his children home or quickly find them a stepmother. In Poona Horsley reported that it was 'rather common' for a girl fresh from England to be snatched up by a widower with children the same age as herself. When James Macnabb's wife died, leaving him in charge of six children, he married the young sister-in-law of a Major-General and had six further offspring. Not all remarriages had a merely practical purpose. Civilians had often found their twenties so lonely that they could not bear to experience another solitude following their wife's death. Henry Beveridge married again soon after Jeanie died in childbirth at the age of 19. The Anglo-Indians' record for remarriage was held by George Jenkin Waters, a Judge in South India who became known as 'the Bluebeard of the Civil Service'. He buried his first wife in 1823, his second in 1828, his third in 1831 and his fourth in 1833; later he managed to fit in numbers five and six before dying at Brighton at the age of 90.[14]

Mistresses

At the beginning of the nineteenth century British officials frequently had Indian wives and mistresses. Colonel Skinner, the founder of Skinner's Horse, was said to have fourteen wives and eighty children. Sir David Ochterlony, the Resident in Delhi, supplied each of his thirteen wives with an elephant upon which she could accompany him on his evening ride around the city walls. In both Poona and Hyderabad the Residents were married to upper-class Muslim women. James Kirkpatrick in Hyderabad had his children brought up as Muslims wearing local costume and speaking either Persian or Urdu as their first language.[15]

Sexual relations between the races were common right across the social scale and in all ranks of the Army. At Baroda in the 1840s Richard Burton noted that every officer in his regiment had a local mistress who, possessing an 'apparently infallible recipe to prevent maternity', looked after him, ran his household and tried to teach him erotic techniques.[16] But the custom soon declined and within a generation it had vanished from most of India. In the 1870s it was still possible to find an old High Court Judge with an Indian wife, and in the 1850s Colonel Meadows Taylor, the novelist and Political Agent, retained a flourishing harem which included a 15-year-old girl called Tara, whose only duty – apparently – was to 'mull' her master's eyebrows.[17] But such survivals were rare. After the Mutiny open cohabitation was largely restricted to remote areas on the fringes of the Empire in Burma and Assam.

The change is traditionally blamed on self-righteous and interfering memsahibs. Certainly Anglo-Indian ladies disapproved of such liaisons, and of course improved communications encouraged more young women (known as 'the fishing fleet') to come out from Britain and trawl for officers and officials for themselves. But morals and mores had changed among men also, both in Britain and in India. What had been acceptable to the Prince Regent was intolerable to the Prince Consort. What the nabobs had lapped up was no longer appetizing to the Stracheys and the Lyalls.

One place in which the memsahibs had little influence was Burma, where the climate was in many places so bad that several of them died and many more fell ill and had to leave. Herbert Thirkell White's wife, who was at her husband's side throughout the thirty-two years of his Burmese career, was almost unique. The Rangoon Government realized it could not send a married man as Political Officer to the Chin Hills, and it was sometimes unable to find a healthy bachelor suitable for the post. Charles Crosthwaite, Chief Commissioner in the late 1880s and the man responsible for the 'pacification' of Burma, regarded the mortality risk as so high that he counselled his officials not to marry. His successor, Alexander Mackenzie, agreed, suggesting that all British wives in Burma should be advised to leave. He knew what he was talking about. In 1892 his first wife died there, and in 1895 his second nearly succumbed also.

One consequence of the climate was that relationships between British men and native women became as common in Burma as they had once been in India. The attractions of Burmese girls were obvious to any visitor. Blending them with palm trees and temple bells, Kipling immortalized them in 'Mandalay', a poem of great charm and striking inaccuracy: Burmese girls did not wear petticoats or caps or yellow clothes (which were reserved for monks); nor did they kiss their idol's feet or call him either Buddha or 'the great Gawd Budd' (in Burma he was called 'the Gautama'). Among other advantages, the Burmese had no caste and no purdah; their women only married when they wanted to, and divorced when they chose. Nor were there many inhibitions: one junior Civilian reported that in his subdivision the women gambled away their skirts and had to go home naked. According to an investigator on the spot, 90 per cent of the British in Burma had local mistresses.[18]

Lord George Hamilton, the Secretary of State at the turn of the century, took a sympathetic view of such liaisons. Burmese women, so he had 'always understood', were 'most admirable housekeepers' and were 'busy engaging females, with a natural aptitude for the society of men'.[19] But Chief Commissioners, pressed on the subject by the Bishop of Calcutta and a number of crusading women, felt obliged to be less tolerant. This suited the puritanical Aitchison, who tried unsuccessfully to convince the amorous Lytton that Civilians in public relationships should not be promoted. Subsequent heads of the province decided to turn a blind eye unless a liaison created an uproar. Crosthwaite believed it was not the duty of the Government 'to enforce morality', and Mackenzie agreed that it was not his business 'to pry into private life', although he was determined 'to show no mercy where an illicit connection' gave 'rise to official scandal'.[20] A successor, Frederick Fryer, accepted that it was 'out of the question' to 'stamp out concubinage in Burma, human nature being what it is'. He therefore decided not to interfere with his Civilians' arrangements unless they were officially brought to his notice. If that happened – and it often did – he told them they must 'either lead a clean life' or forfeit promotion.[21]

In 1900 Curzon wrote to Fryer about Mrs Ada Castle, the wife of a police officer in Burma, who had inaugurated a 'crusade against impurity'. Although he disliked the 'morbid puritanism' of her letter and thought she must be 'a terror to her surroundings', the Viceroy was concerned that her allegations might be damaging to British prestige. Fryer confirmed that she was a purity crusader, as was her husband Reginald, whom he had had to remove from Pegu after he had attacked the Deputy Commissioner, a now respectably married man who had once had a Burmese mistress.[22]

Mrs Castle focused her attack on an Acting Deputy Commissioner, Walter Minns, who was apparently living openly with two Burmese ladies, one of whom accompanied him on official tours. Curzon knew that sexual relations between the races could not be prevented but he was appalled that they should be conducted so flagrantly. Defending himself, Minns claimed that he had been ill and that the woman had toured with him 'not as a mistress but as a nurse', an explanation which Curzon found 'profoundly unsatisfactory'. The Viceroy would have liked Minns to be denied promotion for a time but, as Fryer pointed out, he was an excellent linguist (he had enthusiastic teachers) and before long he became Deputy Commissioner of Rangoon.[23]

Fryer soon realized it was fruitless to tell his officials to choose between leading 'a clean life' and forfeiting promotion: in almost all cases they resolved the problem by marrying their mistress. In 1903, twenty-five British officials in Burma (including five Civilians) were married to Burmese women, nearly all of whom had previously been their mistresses. Marriage may have been a solution that disarmed the purity-mongers and the Bishop of Calcutta, but it was of no comfort to Fryer. Burmans often approached the mistresses in the hope of gaining favour with the Deputy Commissioner, but they knew that wives were in an even stronger position to help them in exchange for a little bribe. As early as 1895, when he began his rule in Burma as Chief Commissioner,* Fryer had tried to transfer two young Civilians from the province because he suspected their Burmese wives of giving the impression that they could influence their husbands in return for a present. But the Government of India rejected the idea and some years later turned down a suggestion that Civilians who married Burmese women should automatically be transferred. As Ibbetson pointed out, such a rule could have been regarded as an incentive to marriage 'since most officers would consider it a privilege to be transferred from Burma'.[24]

Curzon himself did not think that an official should be taken from one part of the Empire and 'dumped' in another: in any case, there were 'no vacant dumping grounds'. But he did formally request the India Office to issue rules discouraging the practice of marrying Burmese women. After perusing his dispatch on the matter, the Council of India in London declined to do so. One retired Lieutenant-Governor (Lyall) did not see how a man could be penalized for marrying his mistress, while another (Crosthwaite) thought the Government had no 'right to dictate to its officers whom they shall or shall not marry'. The benign Hamilton was relieved that he did not have to act: he had 'always been disposed to make very great allowance for European officers . . . shut off from contact with women of their own race and nationality'.[25]

Anglo-Indians seldom flaunted European mistresses in late Victorian India. Those who did, like Griffin, Watson and Crawford, tended to be risk-takers, men who lived on the edge and attracted notoriety in other ways as well. Civilians did not generally have a reputation as seducers or 'poodle-fakers': it was generally Army officers who went up to the hills and laid siege to grass widows. Of course some of them had liaisons, which were usually conducted discreetly unless one of the parties decided to make an issue of betrayal or breach of promise. But they rarely lasted longer than part of a season in Simla or Ootacamund. Anglo-Indians were transferred too often to be able to enjoy lengthy adulterous relationships.

A major obstacle to infidelity was the lack of privacy. No

---

*In 1897 the post was elevated to a lieutenant-governorship.

Lieutenant-Governor could have an affair without the connivance of his ADCs, who were with him throughout the day except when he was with his Private Secretary. Even a junior official could not have an assignation without the knowledge of his servants unless he and his lover were prepared to risk outdoor sex in the potential company of snakes. Unlike their compatriots in Britain, Anglo-Indians lived in bungalows with open verandas and rooms with four doors and servants who padded about in bare feet.

While affairs could be conducted more discreetly in cities and in the hills, they were virtually certain to be known by everybody in a small station. Flora Annie Steel, the novelist, educationalist and general busybody, recounted in her autobiography how she decided to interfere in 'a grave scandal that was a setting a whole station by the ears'. The District Officer was a married man with nine children; his wife and family were in England; and a predatory 'Becky Sharp', a 'clever little cat', had moved into his bungalow. Since the DO was in the middle of a nervous breakdown, and since unspecified persons in the station were preparing to denounce him to the Government, Flora made a dramatic move. She installed herself in the bungalow with the adulterous couple and made it plain that she would stay there until they separated. As she had taken on the Government on a number of issues and usually won, they did not stand much of a chance. But the 'clever little cat' held out for three days until eventually she caved in, retired to a bungalow specially prepared for her, and twenty-four hours later gave birth to the District Officer's baby. The denunciation was never sent to the Government.[26]

Unfortunately, Mrs Steel was not at hand to avert a tragedy in Cawnpore, where the Collector, James McCallum Wright, married a sergeant-major's daughter and attempted to 'improve' her. He sent her to England to learn manners and hoped she would behave like a proper memsahib on her return. But she fell for a manager of the Elgin Mills and had trysts with him behind a rose trellis between their two compounds. McCallum Wright took to drink and died of alcoholism at the age of 50. His wife died in the same week, although opinions differed over whether the cause was alcoholism or a mismanaged abortion.[27]

Unsuccessful Civilian marriages did not usually end so dramatically. Most drifted into a frigid and uncompanionable lack of communication. In one respect Anglo-Indians were more fortunate than their compatriots at home because they could disguise separation by claiming it was better for their wives to be with their children in England. When they eventually retired, they could then discreetly lead separate lives. This was certainly the scheme of Sir John Grant who, after retiring as Lieutenant-Governor of Bengal, had no intention of resuming married life with a woman who had given birth to two children who were not his. Following pleas from his wife and eldest daughter, however, he rashly agreed to a 'reconciliation' which led to a further three decades of married misery.[28]

Divorce in India was also rare, although it managed occasionally to cause problems for a society governed by etiquette and *The Warrant of Precedence*. In Britain a host could choose his guests; in India official hospitality required invitations to be sent to all who qualified for them, even if these included a divorced woman, her co-respondent, her former husband and his new wife. Lyall was rather amused by such situations. At Naini Tal he wondered whether to extend an invitation to 'a lady who ran away from her husband, was divorced, and then married her husband again'. He did so, concluding that 'her husband knew best'.[29]

Lyall Infelix

During his years as a Lieutenant-Governor, Alfred Lyall suffered a good deal from depression. He used to wake up before dawn and lie in bed with all the errors of his past 'arrayed before' him. The conviction that he had 'made endless mistakes in life' made him feel 'far worse than violent neuralgia'.

Lyall's chief mistake, so he believed, was his marriage to a Dutch girl, Cora Cloete, in 1863. His observation about his brother Walter – 'a married Bohemian is as a red Indian in chains' – was also autobiographical. After two years of marriage he was telling his relations that India was a field for hard work, not a place where he would willingly keep his wife 'if she could stay in England'; it was 'a *man's* country' where travel was 'wretched work for ladies'. A year later he admitted he was 'not sorry' to have a son but said he did not want to be 'hampered' by any more children for the moment. As he planned to concentrate on his work for a few years, he dreaded 'a rapid increase' in his family, 'besides being generally averse to babies and their appurtenances'. He failed, however, to prevent the increase and became the father of two sons and two daughters. The demands of family life and the constant presence of children soon annoyed him. 'The way to get on with a male Lyall', he reminded one of his sisters, 'is to leave him a good deal alone.' After six years of marriage, he was no longer glad he had a son: indeed he wished he had no children at all, a feeling that persisted. In 1886 he told another sister that his 'only wish' was that he had no family, especially no daughters, and that he occasionally considered 'escaping from them by some long foreign travel'. He was 'disgracefully tired of the *vie de famille*' and wanted to 'possess' himself.

After fifteen years of marriage, Lyall admitted to his siblings that he got little pleasure out of life. Success in his profession was the 'sole consolation' for his 'mistake' in marrying Cora. Referring to his wife as his 'misfortune', he wished she would return to England and look after their children. Since they did not get on well and had no prospect of a serene domestic life, he could not understand why she insisted on staying with him. To his sister Sybilla, he complained that 'Cora loses control of herself when she is ill and out of sorts; and there is literally no reasoning with her'. Half his life, he moaned, had 'been wasted by one mistake'. For years he had 'had to work uphill with a drag' on him and without anyone 'to counsel or give' him rest at the times when a man needed such things at home. Later he admitted that a happier marriage might have made him less successful in his career because, as soon as he 'woke up' to his mistake, he threw himself into his work. He also admitted that Cora made a good L-G's wife, enjoying 'her rank and dignities' as the hostess of Government House in Allahabad and Naini Tal. But such things were for him – and doubtless also for her – a limited solace.

In 1873 Lyall had told his sister Barbara that he wished he had 'had some romance to get hazy about': it had been the great failure of his life that he had never experienced one. A few months later he met Rachel, the wife of William Holmes, an Assistant Magistrate in the North-Western Provinces. She was a charming, spirited, inquisitive Irish woman who loved literature, spoke German, read French and loathed the gossipy side of Anglo-Indian society. After their first meeting she inaugurated a correspondence with a request for advice on how she could train herself to be a writer; later she asked him to tell her about himself. As only one side of the correspondence survives, we know merely that he wrote often and sent her stories by Mérimée. Rachel was briefly excited by the prospect of Lyall's appointment as Foreign Secretary – and the possibility that her husband might join the secretariat at Simla – because it would have reconciled her to life in a country where she hated the monotony, the lack of culture, the 'terribly English narrow minds and petty interests'. But Lyall was sent instead to Rajputana, several hundred miles to the south-west, and their relationship became epistolary and literary. 'How I wish you were here,' she wrote from Dehra Dun: she was reading *Far from the Madding Crowd* but wishing she was riding with him in the hills nearby. In French she read Turgenev, a writer who, like her admirer, could see all sides of a question.

In the spring of 1875 Lyall stayed for two days in her house while her husband was away. Her letters indicate that they became lovers. Rachel wrote later that his visit seemed 'like a dream' and that her life had 'been only vague ever since'. 'What a curious thing it is, that getting a sudden glimpse into anyone's life – a continuous vision and succession of pictures for two days – and then presto, the door is shut and there is utter blank.' Many years later Lyall returned to the house and confessed to Barbara that he had spent two days there with 'a beautiful and extraordinarily clever woman'.

After that Rachel read Shakespeare and walked in the mountains and told him she wished he was with her. Four years later, 'as the years slip by and bring no meeting with you or possibility of meeting as far as I can see', she reminded him that they had agreed to meet again one day. A year later, when he had at last become Foreign Secretary, they did, in Allahabad at the beginning of 1881. The encounter prompted Lyall to confess to Barbara that he wished he had 'run away with someone in early life'. It was 'too late to begin now', he added, though he confided that 'a lady' at Allahabad had 'seemed much inclined to propose it'. Rachel was buoyed up by their meeting and by their agreement to see each other again on leave in England. 'Some time,' she wrote optimistically, 'when we have plenty of time (*quel château en Espagne!*).' Waiting for an opportunity to tell him what she had thought and felt about their relationship over the years, she asked him if he was fond of some appropriate lines of Swinburne.

These many years since we began to be,
What have the Gods done with us? what with me,
What with my love?

In September 1881 Lyall left the Foreign Office, went to England and returned the following spring as Lieutenant-Governor of the North-Western Provinces. His papers include a letter to Barbara in which he says he would like to tell her one day about his last meeting with Rachel in London. They also contain a telegram from an official in Benares to his Private Secretary in July 1882: 'Mrs Holmes died this morning.' Six months later, he recalled his visit to the place where she was buried.

> Before I left Benares I went to look at Mrs H's grave – a flat mud surface covers the narrow bed where moulder the remains of one of the cleverest, most sympathetic and handsome women I ever saw – who might have lived a splendid life if she had not, unhappily, come to India, to be struck down in her prime by cholera at a cursed little hole like the Benares cantonment.

The following year he found himself by 'a curious and sad coincidence' staying in the house where he had been with Rachel nine years earlier. Haunted by her memories, he remarked enigmatically that his regret took on 'a very strange colour of remorse' which he would explain one day to Barbara.

Six months after Rachel's death, her husband became Lyall's Private Secretary, the official with whom a Lieutenant-Governor spent most of his working day. Whether Lyall made the appointment for reasons of guilt, sentiment or suitability is unclear. Three years later he reported that Holmes was an excellent Secretary but had become 'utterly enthralled by a kind of *diablesse*' who took 'pleasure in first subjugating and then trampling on him'. Lyall found it 'rather wearisome' that his Secretary was 'constantly wishing [to be] elsewhere than in' Government House, but he was simultaneously grateful that the *diablesse* had distracted Holmes's attention from his teenage daughter, Sophy. Her father was worried about Sophy, whom he suspected of having 'very strong sexual instincts', and he was deeply embarrassed by her obvious passion for his Private Secretary. Although he considered transferring the official, he realized that this would not only be unfair to Holmes, who had done nothing to encourage the passion, but 'would create a scandal all through our gossiping Anglo-Indian society and would damage Sophy irretrievably'. The only course was to keep an eye on things until he retired or Holmes was promoted.[30]

15

Families and Exiles

~

The Shock of Asia

THE EDWARDIAN WRITER Maud Diver calculated that at least half of British women living in India at the beginning of the twentieth century had spent their early childhoods there. In most cases this meant that they had 'been sent "Home" at the age of seven or thereabouts, returning at seventeen'.[1] For them there would have been nothing very daunting about the thought of coming back to India to live as an adult. Many of them had happy memories of a warm, spacious and protected childhood. On returning after ten years to their parents, they usually found that the size and attractions of their family's home had grown: during their absence their fathers had been promoted from Major to Colonel of the Regiment, or from Joint Magistrate to District Officer or Commissioner.

In preceding generations the proportion of British women who had been born in India was lower. More typical than the Commissioner's daughter flirting at Poona was the vicar's daughter caught by a Civilian on furlough, taken from a Berkshire rectory, given a cursory honeymoon, put on a large ship, transported to the Indian Ocean and disembarked while just beginning to suffer bouts of morning sickness.* Usually she had to learn the roles of wife,

---

*In the days when the journey to India took four or five months via the Cape, births often took place on board ship. Richard Strachey's second wife Jane (the mother of

mother, expatriate and Asiatic traveller in the same year. For such a girl, whose destination was an Assistant Magistrate's bungalow, the physical shock of India was often overwhelming: on top of all the upheavals in her life, she was suddenly forced to cope with discomfort and danger, the possibility that she might catch malaria or tread on a snake, the certainty that in the hot weather she would feel as if her head was being fried. Maurice Hayward's wife was appalled to discover that her first marital home had a floor made of cow dung and a cobra outside the door; later she discovered one rat in her chest of drawers and another in her bed.[3]

Many women embraced the challenges of their new lives and enjoyed them, especially the cold-weather tours. But there was no fun in travelling in a bullock cart when pregnant, as often happened when a Civilian was transferred at short notice to another district. While sailing down the Ganges at the end of 1867, John Beames was 'obliged to stop for a time as [his] wife was about to be confined'. After Ellen had given birth to a daughter in the ancient fort of Monghyr, the family resumed their voyage to Calcutta.[4] Jennie Partridge, the wife of a Deputy Commissioner, had one baby on the way to a new posting at Garwhal; she had another the day before her husband disappeared on a month's tour, leaving his wife in a remote and mountainous region where there were no Europeans except the nanny they had brought out from Budleigh Salterton. Desperately lonely though she was, Jennie made a list of all the bright sides:

> 1st Reggie 2nd The dear children 3rd That we all have good health 4th That we can all live together 5th Nurse 6th The delightful climate 7th That Reggie's work is congenial and not trying to his health 8th The comfortable house and beautiful garden 9th That we can put by some money for our dear little children.[5]

New postings were more attractive to Civilians than to their wives. Lyall felt that India would be 'unbearably monotonous' if he was settled in one place for too long. But he admitted that so much moving about was 'hard upon Cora'. Rachel Holmes also found it difficult. No sooner, she told Lyall, had she begun to attach herself to

---

(cont.)
Lytton) was born in the middle of a storm off the Cape of Good Hope in 1840. One of their baby daughters died at sea during the voyage twenty-two years later.[2]

a place, to 'like one or two people a little', to begin 'to get rid of the feeling of utter desolation with which India inspired' her, than she and her husband were moved somewhere else. For men, a transfer meant new challenges and sometimes promotion. For women, it meant packing and unpacking, selling furniture, settling into new homes, finding new servants, trying to make new friends. It meant the abandonment of cherished gardens, the asparagus bed newly dug, the roses ordered last autumn from Calcutta which had only just been planted. If the transfer was to a different climate and vegetation, it also entailed the disposal of much-loved pets. A brown gibbon from Burma could not live by the Ganges at Allahabad.

Anglo-Indian men became busier as they grew older, but the reverse was the case with their wives, especially when the children had gone to England and the nursery was empty. A memsahib in a station in the Bengal *mofussil* had little to do unless she possessed some skill such as painting which she could practise alone. One Civilian's wife found herself the only European woman in the station because the other British officials, the Collector and the Judge, were bachelors. As her husband complained, not only was she denied 'the ordinary feminine diversions of shopping, visiting friends, and making dainty a permanent home'; she was also 'without the traditional compensations India [was] supposed to offer, of regular games, pleasant touring, obliging servants [and] a cheery club'. In the evening the only diversion was tennis, though the pleasure was limited by the fact that they had to play a threesome with the one other player in the station. Although for two months of the winter the weather did 'permit one's wife to be a companion on tour', the travelling conditions in their district were 'so crude' that it was better for her not to come. Thus 'for the greater part of each month all the year round she is left absolutely alone in a trying climate with nothing whatever to interest her except receiving and writing the Home Mail'.[6]

Living in such an environment did not encourage a broadening of minds or a generosity of spirits. Some memsahibs doubtless deserved their savage description by Goldsworthy Lowes Dickinson: women 'with empty minds and hearts, trying to fill them by despising the natives'.[7] Perhaps it was natural for the lonely wife of a Collector, queen of her husband's district, to become rather grand and to look down on others. Josie, Malcolm Darling's intellectual wife, was very snooty about such people 'who would be *nobodies* at home', women who would belong to 'the "Edinboro ladies'" class or even lower'. It was pathetic, she said, 'when a middle-aged woman, who would be in the Morningside set . . . puts on the airs of a *grande dame*'.[8] Perhaps. But perhaps one can feel a degree of sympathy for forlorn women in a distant continent trying to compensate for the lost certainties of Princes Street.

British imperialists are among the most stereotyped of extinct breeds. So are their wives. There were of course idle women in the hills who sneered at Indians, gossiped about Anglo-Indians and salivated over subalterns while their husbands were roasting in the plains. But there were many others who were determined to make India part of their lives rather than regard it merely as the regrettable location of their husbands' work. They painted its landscape, studied its botany, learned some of its languages and sometimes read the *Vedas*. Increasingly, towards the end of the century, they became involved in philanthropic causes such as child welfare and maternity clinics. A number worked for Lady Dufferin's Fund, which the Vicereine had set up to provide medical aid, especially nurses, to Indian women who were denied access to male doctors.

The Memsahibs' Routine

Whatever they did with their leisure, most memsahibs shared certain tasks. They had to make a home, run a household, supervise the health of children and servants, and assist their husband's career by accompanying him on tour (if possible) and entertaining his colleagues in the station. Wherever they were, they had to adapt to the routine of the province and its climate. The calendar was naturally unlike anything they had been accustomed to: in the North-Western Provinces April Fool's Day was the time to hang the punkahs; a week earlier, the mosquito curtains were put up; other times signalled routine practices such as whitewashing the bungalow and renewing the palm-leaf matting.

The wife of an Assistant Under-Secretary in Whitehall might have three or four regular servants to deal with. Her equivalent in India usually had to supervise the hiring and employment of about forty people. Annette Beveridge, who was married to the very unostentatious Judge of Bankipur in Bengal, had in 1882 a staff of thirty-nine, a hierarchy headed by the coachman, followed by the butler, cook and chief nanny, and ending with the watchman, the water-carrier and the assistant vegetable-gardeners. The family's horses alone required six servants, three grooms to look after them and three grass-cutters to go out and forage. Although the size of such staffs suggests leisure and luxury, most of the servants supplied services that in Britain would have been provided by shops or local government. The Beveridges employed a *bhishti* because there was no water supply, a *mehta* because there was no sanitation, a cowman and a fowlman because there was nowhere nearby where they could purchase milk and eggs. And if Bankipur had possessed trams or omnibuses, they would not have needed such a large equine establishment.[9]

Memsahibs were careful to choose servants from the appropriate communities. Cooks and butlers were usually Muslims, although some women preferred to employ Christian chefs from Portuguese Goa. Most other positions, such as gardener, tailor and groom, tended to go to Hindus, and those of sweeper and water-carrier to the lowest castes. Anglo-Indian women generally agreed that native Christians, especially converts, were less trustworthy than Hindus or Muslims.[10]

After choosing the servants, the memsahib had to supervise them at their work. The relationship between the two parties reflected in exaggerated form the connection between the Collector and the population of his district: maternalist/paternalist and very commandant. A lot of shouting went on, but much kindness was also shown, both to servants and to their children. Anglo-Indians did not forget the loyalty that many retainers had shown during the Mutiny. Nor did they fail to appreciate the fidelity of their old bearer who, after a two-year furlough, would be waiting to greet them with garlands of marigolds at the Apollo Bunder at Bombay. Even if servants were 'occasionally irritating beyond measure', one Civilian confessed, 'the way they stick to you' redeemed everything.[11]

Like the District Officer, the Memsahib spent much of her time on inspections. She inspected the nursery and spoke to the ayah, a small smiling woman in a white sari whom she considered over-indulgent to the children. She inspected the garden and encouraged the mali to grow English flowers, although she realized there was nothing he could do to control the weeds in the monsoon or to keep the garden alive in the hot weather. On the veranda she sat in a cane chair, inspecting the work of the tailor and the goods of visiting tradesmen. She did not inspect the servants' quarters, which would have been considered intrusive before the First World War, but she examined very closely the kitchen, which was placed some way from the house. Although Anglo-Indians were impressed by the versatility of Indian cooks – and by the way they could conjure a quick three-course meal from a small charcoal fire in the jungle – they scolded them for their disregard for hygiene. The memsahib had to ascertain that the kitchen and the utensils were clean, that the milk and water were properly boiled, that the fish and meat had not gone bad, and that the fruit and vegetables were washed with a mixture of potassium and water. She also tried to check that the cook was not making more than the traditional profit from his visits to the bazaar.

The memsahib gave orders for the preparation of the food. She wanted plain 'nourishing' fare for the children, such as Irish stew and milk pudding, and she tried to limit the amount of spicy food cooked for her dinner parties. But she was often defeated by climate and conditions. In the hills she had good vegetables and familiar fruit such as apples and pears; in the cold weather she had game that could be hung long enough to be edible; and in the plains in their season she could enjoy mangoes and lychees. But for much of the year she was dependent on tasteless eggs, scrawny chicken and occasional hunks of very tough mutton. Good bread was a hopeless ambition, its achievement thwarted by the poor quality of flour, yeast, butter and indeed ovens. Fortunately Anglo-Indians acquired a taste for naan and chapattis. They also managed to give some flavour to their rather bland diets by the use of chutney and mild spices.

Anglo-Indian food is said to have improved from about 1840. 'Molten curries' and mulligatawny soup gave way to dishes that were lighter and more French and served as courses (*à la russe*) rather than all plonked together on the table.[12] Whether menus in French heralding tinned salmon or *potage à la julienne* were really a great improvement must be debatable. But at Christmas at least the fare was neither French nor native. Anglo-Indians agreed that they must try to make the festival as British as possible. They congregated in camps and stations and cities for the 'Week', bringing their racquets and cricket bats, their dogs and polo ponies. They ordered holly and mistletoe from the hills; they made real plum puddings with real brandy sauce. The chief problem revolved around the principal dish.

As turkeys, like farmyard ducks, did not thrive in India, the memsahib had to decide between tinned turkey, which rather missed
the point, and peafowl which, though real, could not be made very
succulent.

The British did not waste much time going through vintners' lists,
for India was not the place to lay down cases of claret. Victorians in
the Subcontinent drank very much less than their predecessors of the
eighteenth century, when Warren Hastings was almost the sole teeto-
taller – and managed to live, despite thirty years in Bengal, to the age
of 85. They seldom had a drink at lunch, except for a bottle of beer on
holidays and at Sunday tiffin, and rarely touched alcohol until the sun-
downer in the club or on their veranda after six o'clock. The Regency
favourites – madeira, sherry, port and other wines – had more or less
disappeared and had been replaced by beer, first by Hodgson's Pale
Ale and later by Bass and by brands brewed in India. In 1860, according to a Civilian in Madras, the only alternatives to beer were light
claret, from the French enclave of Pondicherry, and brandy and soda.
The image of Anglo-Indians lolling in rattan chairs with tumblers of
whisky and soda belongs to a later period. Until the late 1870s, when
phylloxera wrecked the French vineyards, a 'peg' meant brandy. Only
after then did blendied whiskies establish a hegemony which, despite
the invention of tonic (originally an anti-malarial medicine), they succeeded in defending against the challenge of gin.[13]

One of the main duties of the memsahib was to protect the health
of her family and servants. Large animals seldom entered a compound and were in any case unlikely to attack humans unless
wounded or threatened. Snakes were more dangerous, especially the
cobra and the krait, which appeared to be deaf and therefore more
prone to being trodden on. In hazardous places Anglo-Indians
defended their bungalows with wire netting over their drains and
broken glass across their paths; they wore gumboots in the long
grass and swung hurricane lamps at night. Yet they were seldom
bitten by poisonous snakes or indeed by rabid dogs. They were far
more likely to die of disease.

Civilians spent a good deal of their careers being ill, at times
feeling merely 'seedy' and 'liverish', at others suffering from prickly
heat, boils, dysentery, fever and headaches. The most virulent forms
of the latter were identified by locality such as 'Punjab head' or
'Peshawar fever'. Since wives and children suffered quite as much as

the men, families often went for months with at least one member suffering from fever or dysentery. Despite the precautions – the two grains of quinine each day – many also experienced malaria, the fever and shivering, the aching back and bones, the icy trickle down the thighs.

One of the consolations of India was the variety of pets that could be kept and the space which they could be kept in. 'What would life in India be without one's animals?' wrote Ethel Grimwood. Each morning in Manipur she and her husband went out to feed all the creatures – deer, monkeys, otters, even a bear and two cranes – that had made a home in their compound. Pets were regarded as important for children while they were there, and even more important for parents when they had gone. Apart from the obligatory dogs and horses, memsahibs were fond of squirrels and species of small deer; some also kept parrot houses and filled them with love-birds and parakeets. But menageries might contain less charming animals such as a porcupine or even an alien armadillo. Although not externally attractive, the bushy-tailed mongoose was a great favourite because it rushed about killing rats and snakes. Men sometimes adopted the orphaned cubs of wild cats until they were old enough to be released. Up at Chitral Armine Dew kept bears and a snow lynx; down in Burma R. Grant Brown specialized in gibbons and monkeys.

A Sense of Exile

Few Anglo-Indians in the Victorian age regarded India as home. The Subcontinent was a career not a colony, a place to work and move around rather than to settle in and put down roots. The British went out to Africa, Canada and Australasia to stay; they went to India to work for a specified period. 'We all feel', wrote Lord Minto, the Viceroy, 'that we are mere sojourners in the land, only camping and on the march.'[14]

Allied to the sense of alien impermanence was the sense of permanent vulnerability: Mrs Moss King, a Civilian's wife, always felt that she was living on a volcano 'with the elements of an eruption . . . seething below the surface'.[15] Allied to both these was the widespread feeling that Anglo-Indians were exhausting their health and their lives on a thankless duty. As Hunter put it:

Here we Englishmen stand on the face of the broad earth, a scanty pale-faced band in the midst of three hundred millions of unfriendly vassals. On their side is a congenial climate and all the advantages which home and birthplace can give; on ours long years of exile, a burning sun which dries up the Saxon energies, home sickenings, thankless labour, disease and often-times death far from wife, child, friend or kinsman.[16]

Civilians often died or became very ill or suffered mental break-downs in India. Even the survivors aged fast. Photographs of Lieutenant-Governors and Members of Council seem to portray men in their seventies and eighties. In fact nearly all the holders of these posts had retired by the age of 58.

Nostalgia for Britain was almost a constant of Anglo-Indian life. It was particularly acute in the late spring and summer when the contrast between the climates was at its most obvious. Young Civilians from Oxford recalled Magdalen Walk and the view across the meadow with the chestnuts and hawthorn in flower; they wrote letters to old tutors asking if they still took pupils on long Sunday walks and had lunches of beer and cheese in an inn near Blenheim.[17] Alfred Lyall got depressed in the summer because family letters from England were 'redolent of flowers, hay and innumerable babies' – not that he envied the babies. Nostalgia could be assuaged by furlough but was only increased by leave's end. Lyall felt 'the smart of exile' on his return voyage at Marseille: his arrival there produced 'a sort of rage at having to leave the pleasant lands which should be [his] habitation by birthright'. The rage quietened but the depression grew as he steamed eastwards. The view of Alexandria, with 'the peculiar smells and slovenly squalid look of the East', always gave him 'the despondent feeling' that he had left civilization.[18]

The return voyage was infinitely more depressing for Anglo-Indians who had left their children behind in Britain. Most accepted the custom of the time, which was to uproot their infants at the age of 6 or 7 and take them 'Home'; to eject them from a sunny paradise of pets and ponies and indulgent servants, and send them to a place of cold weather and school and unknown relations.

The stated reason for this brutal convention was climate. Like Britons of other ages, children were likely to be less healthy on the plains of India than on the south coast of England. But they could have been sent to schools in the hill stations, where children of poorer Anglo-Indians and Eurasians often went. It was a question of ambience and culture as well as of climate. The British in India wished to remain British. They did not want to be like their ancestors in the eighteenth century, who had absorbed and adopted so much of India, or like the Portuguese in Goa, whom they regarded as decadent and degenerate as a result of settlement and intermarriage. Bamphylde Fuller, the Lieutenant-Governor of Eastern Bengal and Assam, stated a popular belief when he claimed that the Indian climate was 'injurious to the European temperament' as well as to the European body. If children remained in the Subcontinent after the age of 7, they not only appeared 'to lose their energy of mind and body' but also began 'to experience sexual feelings earlier than is habitual with their race'.[19]

Anglo-Indians may not all have been convinced that their children would become sexually precocious in India. But they did agree that the ambience and conditions could be damaging to character. Mollycoddled by ayahs and often living in places with no contemporaries to play with, British children could become spoilt, languid, flabby and dictatorial. They might even acquire 'chi-chi' accents. As Fuller put it in his dramatic way, 'India enfeebles white races that cling to her breasts'.[20] It was much better, therefore, to send them 'Home', where they would become sturdy and rosy-cheeked, learn austere Victorian values and become thoroughly anglicized at boarding school. The process might even transform them into potential administrators ready to take their place in the 'exiles' line'.

Not all Civilians accepted the tyranny of this tradition. Maconochie took advantage of the climate of Bangalore to keep his children four years longer than was normal. Horsley delayed his furlough until he had been in India for sixteen years because he and his wife were 'in no hurry to bring on the inevitable separation'. His main preoccupation was to narrow the gap between his furlough, when he would feel obliged to leave his older daughters in England, and his retirement on the earliest date possible. Ultimately he could not face a separation until the very end. In 1889 the Horsleys returned from furlough with all four of their daughters and a governess. Criticized by his brother for keeping their children so long in India, Horsley felt nervous and guilty whenever they had fever and correspondingly relieved when he saw them 'well and jolly' in their garden in Sind. By the time the older girls did finally go to England, he had ensured that there was little more than a year before he could retire and join them.[21]

Most girls, however, were taken from their parents' Indian house to be placed in the homes of aunts or grandmothers and rotated among other relations in the course of the year. Boys were generally sent to preparatory schools when they arrived and to a public school later on; most were boarders who went to relations for their holidays. Eastbourne and other towns of the south coast were the favourite locations for early schooling. As Anglo-Indians were believers in 'bracing sea air', many of them settled along the coast of Sussex and Hampshire, thereby encouraging the establishment of good prep schools which in turn increased the influx from the Subcontinent. Favoured public schools had a more varied geography. While senior Civilians could seldom afford to send their sons to Eton or Harrow, they eagerly went for the second tier of such schools as Cheltenham and Rugby, institutions which promoted an imperial career to their pupils and did not spend too much time on Greek and Latin.[22]

Anglo-Indian mothers knew that at one stage they would have to choose between living with their children in England and staying with their husbands in India. It was 'a very unnatural state of existence', complained Jane Strachey, '& very odd that when by chance two perfectly congenial persons are joined together by holy matrimony they should be separated by devilish circumstance'.[23] Like her, a number of women attempted a compromise, sometimes by foregoing a season in the hills so that their husbands could afford to buy them a ticket home to be with their children in the summer holidays. Others, especially those in unhappy marriages, decided to go to England with their offspring and remain there with them. Most women, however, opted to take their children to England, settle them in schools and new homes and then return to their husbands in India. Poor Henry Cotton experienced the worst of combinations. After his parents left him at a 'dame's school' at the age of 6, he did not see his mother for eight years. As an adult he was abandoned again, this time by his wife, who took their two sons home after six years in India, gave birth to a third one in England and never returned. For the next twenty-eight years Cotton only saw his boys during his furloughs. His walking tour with them in Switzerland in 1891 must have been a holiday with strangers.

Anglo-Indian children sent to Britain have been described as 'orphans of the Raj, paying the price of Empire by a separation from parents'.[24] Children did of course pay that price, as Kipling described so evocatively in his story 'Baa Baa, Black Sheep', but so did parents, especially mothers. Memsahibs who were considered hard and frivolous were often women trying not to break down when they saw little children or heard baby voices, women whose most intimate moments were spent sighing over photographs or waiting for the post to bring misspelt and tear-smudged descriptions of experiences they could never share. Fathers also paid the penalty of Empire, though they could try to drown their sentiments in work. A paterfamilias naturally regretted his inability to play one of his most important roles – influencing his children's upbringing. Even that most reluctant of parents, Alfred Lyall, railed against a situation in which he could do almost nothing about his son who got into scrapes, seemed morally weak and was doing badly at Eton. 'The real drawback of Indian life', he told his sister Barbara, was that one could not 'train up a boy and decide, on full knowledge of his capacities and chances, what is best for him'. How could he, living in Allahabad, judge whether Alfred Junior was better suited to a career in the Army or one in business?[25]

One woman, Annette Beveridge, tried to avoid paying the price of Empire. After leaving her three eldest children (aged 7, 5 and 4) in England in 1884, she returned two years later and took them back to India, persuading her husband that they would be perfectly healthy in Bengal so long as they spent most of the year in Darjeeling. The arrangement did not work well. Separated by a vast distance, husband and wife saw each other for less than half the year, and both their sons nearly died of mysterious illnesses. After four years in India, Annette returned to Britain with the children and settled in Eastbourne. Their eldest son William survived to become the author of the famous report that shaped Britain's welfare state. Herman, their younger boy, did not. His death at the age of 5 was followed three years later by that of the eldest child, Laetitia, who died of influenza.

Family separations sometimes had happier sequels. Adelbert Talbot's three daughters all returned from England to join him in his last posting in the Kashmir Residency. But the reunion did not last long because, when their father retired and returned to England, they remained in the Subcontinent with their new Anglo-Indian husbands.

In any case such reunions were usually limited to daughters: Talbot's son started his ICS career in the month of Adelbert's retirement. Once again Henry Cotton was unlucky: having spent most of his childhood without his mother and most of his middle age without his wife, he was subsequently denied the company of his son, who served in Madras while he was in Assam. One of the few Civilians able to manage a successful family reunion in India was G.R. Elsmie, the Financial Commissioner of the Punjab.

> When we returned to India from furlough at the end of 1880, we left our ten children at home. In the following decade . . . they had been coming to India in detachments. In 1883, our two eldest daughters arrived. In 1885, our eldest son joined the army at Dinapore. In 1888, our four youngest daughters, then mere children, came out. In 1889, our second, and in 1890, our third son joined their regiments in India. In the latter year we all spent Christmas Day together, and filled three pews in the Lahore Cathedral . . . There were ten children, three grandchildren, and three sons-in-law.[26]

This remarkable gathering broke up after two days and was never reassembled.

Death in India

Before she lost two of her children in England, Annette Beveridge visited the Christian cemetery at Mussoorie and, in the words of her surviving son, 'found the tombs of so many children sending terror to her heart'.[27] There is an unbearable pathos in the British burial grounds in India, as much among the tombstones of small stations as among the neoclassical mausoleums of the Park Street Cemetery in Calcutta. Families can take a certain comfort from country churchyards in England, generations of their name side by side, old people as well as young, with relatives living close by to tend the graves and bring flowers. But in India nobody died old because there were no old people: the average age on the stones of a graveyard is often about 14. Nor can one find there the company of families, since two relatives seldom died in the same place except in the few towns where there was a settled business community. A couple buried their child and soon moved to another station, leaving a tombstone that never again received tearful visits or bunches of flowers. Salar Jung recalled how the Resident in Hyderabad, George Yule, went each morning to his child's grave and placed flowers upon it. But not long after the death he was transferred to Simla and never returned.

After a few years a child's gravestone had little meaning, except as a warning and a poignant reminder, to the new residents of a station. But of course the parents were never able to forget it. No relics of British India are more pathetic than the frayed yellow envelopes containing mementoes of a dead child: a lock of fair hair, some crumbling petals of a flower growing on the grave, designs and photographs of the tombstone, receipts for repair work and regilding of the inscription, letters sent to parents on their odyssey around India assuring them that the memorial was being looked after and the weeds had been cleared away. Sometimes one comes across a mother's letter enquiring about the state of a child's grave half a century after the burial.[28]

Babies often died of typhoid or cholera or other diseases that might have killed them (though less frequently) in Britain. Sometimes they died with their mothers in childbirth. Sometimes their mothers died alone, leaving their fathers with an agonizing decision. Widowed Civilians were usually given 'special leave on urgent private affairs' to take their children home and leave them with a relation. But unless they could combine this with furlough, they had to be back at their posts within a few months. Sometimes bereaved men could not bear to add to their loneliness by losing their children: after his young wife died in 1892, Hugh Barnes had to be more or less forced by Durand to take his babies home and 'to get away for a time and have a complete change'.[29] If a Civilian was senior enough to qualify for a pension, he might be tempted to give up his career. Henry Howard had just completed his twenty-five years when his wife Mabel died, leaving him with five children under the age of 9. Although he would have become a Member of the Viceroy's Council and perhaps also a Lieutenant-Governor, he decided to resign from the Service and bring his children up in England. Civilians who were not yet entitled to a pension almost invariably continued their careers following the death of their spouse. After his second wife died in Madras when he was only 32, Henry Stokes took their children to England to live with their grandmothers. As he had at least fifteen years still to go in his Indian career (twenty as it turned out), he was resigned to becoming a stranger to them. 'They must all grow up', he told his mother-in-law, 'without knowing or caring much for me.'[30]

Death could happen so abruptly in the Subcontinent that people who woke up with a headache often wondered whether it presaged a fatal illness. 'Everything is sudden in India,' observed one Anglo-Indian, 'the sudden twilights, the sudden death. A man can be talking to you at breakfast and be dead in the afternoon.'[31] Cholera claimed its victims in such a way: when it hit a station, the inhabitants began measuring their lives in hours. Even minor injuries and ailments, a cut toe or a septic boil, could become lethal. When a cart wheel ran over the foot of an Assistant Commissioner in Burma, the injury was not considered serious. But tetanus set in, and he died. Shortly after leaving India, Kipling wrote of a man who returns to his previous station after a season or so away to find that his closest friend has recently died. 'You are behind the times!' he is told. 'Dicky went out three weeks ago with something or other . . . I've forgotten what it was, but it was rather sudden . . . Poor old Dicky.'[32] Death in what-ever guise was so familiar that Anglo-Indians had to accept it as an event too natural and frequent for prolonged grief. When a man died, he was buried, mourned briefly and forgotten. As Kipling put it rather cynically in his poem, 'Possibilities',

> Ay, lay him 'neath the Simla pine –
> A fortnight fully to be missed,
> Behold, we lose our fourth at whist,
> A chair is vacant when we dine.

Thirty-four Civilians were killed in the Mutiny, and eight died of cholera and other illnesses incurred during the conflict. But over the remainder of the century few members of the Service came to a violent end. There was an occasional suicide. Flora Annie Steel recorded a meeting with a District Officer, 'tortured by gout and arthritis', who told her, as 'a sad joke', that he did not want to go to Heaven because he would be bound to have gout on his wings: 'Within a year he put the matter to the test, dying by his own hand.'[33] In Burma and Assam, as we have seen, a number of Civilians and Politicals were killed, usually in fights with dacoits and insurgents.

But murder was not common. As the young Harcourt Butler told his father, Indians 'don't often go for magistrates fortunately'. Although Rand in Poona was assassinated by Hindu opponents of his anti-plague campaign, Civilians were more likely to be victims of Muslims: a Collector of Malabar was murdered on his veranda by members of the Moplah sect, a Commissioner of Peshawar was killed by 'a religious fanatic' when hearing a petition, and a Resident of Tonk was shot dead while sleeping on his roof by a Mahsud sentry incited by one of his tribe's mullahs.[34] Political killings were more frequent in the twentieth century. In the early 1930s three successive Collectors were murdered at Midnapore in Bengal; and in 1940 Michael O'Dwyer, who had been Lieutenant-Governor of the Punjab at the time of the Amritsar massacre, was assassinated in London twenty years after his retirement.

Civilians were occasionally victims of wild animals. In Bengal a Collector of Tipperah was killed by a tiger which he thought he had shot dead the previous day. In Madras one Collector of Vizagapatam was mortally wounded by a cheetah, and a successor was killed by a tiger while he was trying to protect a village. Another Madras Civilian died from a combination of blackwater fever and wounds inflicted by a bear.

Earthquakes also produced their toll of casualties. Robert McCabe, Cotton's most efficient subordinate in Assam, was found crushed beneath the ruins of his house in Shillong in 1897. In the Dharmsala earthquake of April 1905 several hundred people were killed, including three Assistant Commissioners and the families of Civilians who were out on tour. In the course of that year the Punjab Commission lost eight of its officers to accidents and disease.

The mortality rate in the eighteenth century had been enormous, partly because Anglo-Indians had been so careless of their health: they ate too much and drank too much and went out in the sun without a hat. Although they had become more sensible by the middle of the next century, they still died in large numbers from smallpox, dysentery, enteric fever, sunstroke, tetanus, liver disease and other illnesses. Typhoid and cholera rivalled each other as the chief slayer of civil servants. Typhoid may just have had the edge in the quantity of Civilian victims, but cholera was a bigger scourge of the wider Anglo-Indian community: the disease could descend on a cantonment and wipe out half a regiment.

The death rate among serving ICS officers was naturally higher than was normal for civil servants at home. Three of the thirty who went out in 1878 were dead within twelve months, but 10 per cent was higher than usual for a single year. After two decades in India, a year's recruitment could expect to have lost about a third of its strength through death: by 1879 seven of the twenty who had joined in 1859 were dead, and nine of the thirty-two who had started the year after.[35]

Many Civilians died alone, in the jungle or in remote stations, without anyone to comfort them or even understand what they were saying in their last delirium. Harry Grigg, the Resident in Cochin, had sent his wife home to see their children before he realized he had typhoid. She heard of his illness at Suez, waited three days for a boat back to India, and heard of his death at Aden; she then returned to Cochin, via Bombay, to pack up their belongings.[36]

Among the most pathetic ends were those of Civilians who died just before or just after retirement. Some left their journey too late and expired even before they reached the steamer at Bombay. Between 1892 and 1896 three AGGs in Baluchistan died in office, all of them 'on the very eve' of demission. Sometimes they died on board ship a few days from British shores. More often the sick ones managed to struggle back to England in time to die there. Two of the ablest Civilians of the north-west, Ibbetson of the Punjab and Deane of the Frontier, were forced to relinquish office and return to London where they died within weeks of each other in 1908.

16

Pensioners

~

Repatriation

RETIREMENT WAS AN emotional experience for many Civilians.
They were given farewell dinners with toasts and speeches to
commemorate their work. If they were popular or successful, public
receptions were held in their honour while appreciative 'addresses'
were delivered from diverse parts of the province. On the day of
their departure leaders of the local community – Indian as well as
British – came to the station to see them board the train to Bombay.
It was a time for smiles and satisfaction and perhaps a little self-
importance.

Many Civilians, however, were prevented by ill-health from enjoying such moments of glory. Those who were sent home on medical
certificate in mid-career on half-pay often never saw India again. If,
after two or three years in Britain, a doctor pronounced them unfit,
they had to resign and accept a pension proportionate to their years
of service.* Richardson Evans, who was invalided out of the Service
at the age of 30, grumbled that he had 'to face life' with an annual
allowance of £250 from the Bengal Civil Fund. But as he was young

---

*If they had been in the ICS for five years or more, they received an annuity of £150 plus
£20 for each year of service in excess of five, so long as the whole annuity did not exceed
£450.[1]

enough to start a new career (as a journalist), and as he was still drawing the money in his eighties, it was not a bad deal.[2]

Although very few Civilians left the Service before they became eligible for a pension, many were determined to retire as soon as they had completed their twenty-five years. They counted the remaining days, planned their retirement homes and thought of all the things they were going to do once they were 'home'. In his solitude in the United Provinces, Joseph Goudge worked out which actors in London he would see, what music he was going to hear, and which Italian cities he was going to visit on holiday with his new wife.[3]

Yet for many, early retirement was a less straightforward matter. Some decided to take it because the fall of the rupee reduced the point of earning an Indian salary when they could be receiving a pension in sterling. Others retired when they realized that their aspirations for one of the top posts were going to be disappointed. And a few went because they could not work with their Lieutenant-Governor: the harsh temperaments of both Crosthwaite and MacDonnell in the NWP encouraged several talented subordinates to retire early.[4] Yet even Civilians with no further prospects sometimes found it difficult to leave India. Beveridge, who knew he would never be promoted to the High Court, thought longingly of 'a Scotch burn dancing down under the hawthorns'. But then he thought of the 'great turbid, rolling Hooghly' and realized that India had 'burnt itself into' him, making him 'dread the cold and wet country of [his] birth'. Finally deciding that he was 'transplanted rice' that should 'be harvested in the swamps', he stayed until a few months before compulsory retirement.[5]

Paul Scott's tragicomic novel *Staying On* has left the impression that Britons sometimes remained in India after their retirement. In fact Civilians almost never stayed on. Those who returned to India after the end of their service usually did so only if the Government offered them jobs as tempting as the viceroyalty (to John Lawrence) or the governorship of Bombay (to George Clerk). A handful did settle abroad, but usually in France or Switzerland where they could become Consul or Vice-Consul in places such as Berne and Cherbourg. In retirement John Rivett-Carnac gave up his post as an ADC to the Queen and, for reasons of economy, exiled himself to a Swiss château.[6]

Nearly all Civilians settled in Britain, a large majority of them in southern England. The most popular counties were Surrey and Devonshire, followed by Sussex and Hampshire. Few people chose an eastern county for their retirement, and it was very rare to find a Civilian in England north of Worcestershire. While Scotland was not the usual destination for the Scots, Ireland did attract many of the Irish. After London, Dublin and Oxford were the favourite towns, followed by Cheltenham, Camberley, Eastbourne and Hove.*

Civilians retired between the ages of 47 and 58. They were not – at any rate not then – doddery old men in straw boaters ensconced in south coast villas and boring the neighbours with Poona stories. Many of them, who had after all spent their careers moving about, found it difficult to remain in one place for very long. Like other people, they went to places where they were offered jobs. Henry Howard lived in Woking and Guildford before ending up as Bursar of a Cambridge college.

It was logical, therefore, for almost half the ICS pensioners to live in or near London, a proportion that would have been even higher among the recently retired. In the late eighteenth century the 'nabobery' was located south of Regent's Park in Harley Street and Wimpole Street. A hundred years later, its successors had moved westwards, both north and south of Hyde Park, to Bayswater (sometimes known as 'Asia Minor') and South Kensington (often referred to as the 'Anglo-Indian Quarter'). SW5 was the most popular postcode, the favourite streets situated near the Cromwell Road: Bramham Gardens, Cornwall Gardens, Southwell Gardens and Queensgate. The area became an élite 'Punjab corner' when three successive Lieutenant-Governors – Lawrence, Montgomery and Mcleod – all settled there. But Mcleod's retirement was cut short when he fell under a train at Gloucester Road Station.

Harcourt Butler was unusual in choosing to live in a small flat in Whitehall where he missed 'nothing of the East except the privilege of a governor to go to bed when he wants'.[8] Civilians who preferred not to live in the Anglo-Indian Quarter usually went further out, to the suburbs or to Surrey. Wimbledon attracted men who had jobs in

---

*This information comes from a 'List of the Retired Civilians who have sent half crowns' to a movement for increased pensions for the ICS in January 1921. The 200 annuitants who contributed and gave their addresses do not account for all the pensioners but are presumably representative. They had joined the ICS between 1869 and 1895.[7]

London but wanted some suburban peace. Surrey towns such as Dorking and Reigate were convenient for those who had part-time work in the metropolis.

Occupations

Since the 1820s Civilians had been receiving an annual pension of £1,000, regardless of what rank they had attained in the Service. If they died, their widows received an annuity of £300 and their children one of £100 each, boys until they were 21, girls until they were married. These were quite generous provisions: most Civilians who lived to a reasonable age got far more out of their pension fund than they had put into it. But since the cost of living increased while pensions remained the same, a man retiring in 1925 was much less well off than he would have been a century earlier.

Civilians were notoriously bad at saving money, spending much of their salary on school fees and entertaining, and often neglecting to make arrangements for their families when they died. Although Antony MacDonnell reached the highest rank of the Service and earned a good income in retirement, his contemporaries had to come to the rescue when his widow and daughter were discovered living together in a bed-sitting room. Although they paid off their debts and topped up their pensions, the daughter was found many years later trying to make a living as a London taxi-driver.[9]

Few Civilians had private means: not many would have joined the ICS if they had. So unless they wanted to vegetate on their pension in a resort like Bournemouth or Torquay, they tried to find some appropriate kind of work. In this respect, at least, Indians had better prospects. Among the few native Civilians who retired or left the Service during our period, Romesh Chandra Dutt and Behari Lal Gupta became Chief Ministers of Baroda while Surendranath Banerjea was both a President of Congress and a minister in Bengal after the introduction of the Montagu-Chelmsford reforms in 1921. Such options were not often open to Anglo-Indians, although in the 1920s after retirement Norman Seddon served as Revenue Minister in Baroda before becoming a lecturer in Persian and Marathi at Oxford.

Many Civilians retired with the thought that they should write a book about the Subcontinent while their memories were still fresh and their brains were still functioning. A profusion of 'Whither India?' books resulted; a still greater flood of 'Stories of My Life' or 'Ninety-five Years in Bengal' memoirs followed later (many of which failed to attract a publisher). Some repatriates went to Oxford or Cambridge and became dons, bursars and High Table pests. An obituary in the *Emmanuel College Magazine* records that Sir Evelyn Howell, after serving as Consul in Muscat, Governor of Baghdad (1918) and Resident in Kashmir, spent the last forty years of his life in or near Cambridge, bicycling along the towpath during boat races and correcting dons on abstruse points of philology at college dinners. 'He could exchange compliments by post in Latin hendecasyllabics or elegiacs.'[10]

Men who had left England at the age of 23 were not often well qualified for employment on their return thirty years later. Some, however, were able to match the skills acquired in their previous careers with the demands of postings to which they aspired. A Civilian who had served as Secretary for Education in Bengal might reasonably hope to become a Director of Education, even if only on the Isle of Man.[11] A skill that was clearly transferable was policing. Two Inspectors-General of Police in Bengal joined the Metropolitan Police in London and became its Commissioner. One of them, James Monro, had a row with the Home Secretary, resigned his post, returned to India and spent the next twelve years founding and running the Ranaghat Medical Mission.[12]

A few fortunate pensioners became directors of companies doing business in India. Railways were the main allurement in the nineteenth century, although subsequently ex-Civilians were drawn to electricity, telephones, banking and even the Tata Iron and Steel Company. In 1872, when he fell off the platform at Gloucester Road, Donald Mcleod was Chairman of the Sind, Punjab and Delhi Railway. In 1889 Richard Strachey resigned from the Council of India to become Chairman of the East India Railway Company and later of the Assam-Bengal Railway Company, posts which he did not relinquish until after his ninetieth birthday. And Lepel Griffin, although he failed to become an L-G or an MP, received some compensation with the chairmanship of the Imperial Bank of Persia and the Burmah Ruby Mines Company.

Retired Civilians sometimes opted to spend the rest of their lives in professions completely unconnected with their previous careers. Walter Lupton occupied his furloughs studying for a medical degree and doing clinical training so that he could begin general practice as a doctor as soon as he retired. Almost as unusual was the transition to a religious vocation. Nicholas Beatson-Bell retired as Governor of Assam to take holy orders, while William Dathoyt became an Anglican vicar and then, after getting rid of his wife, a Roman Catholic priest. One of the most eccentric Civilians was Frederick Tucker, who resigned after five years in the Service, joined the Salvation Army, married the daughter of its founder ('General' William Booth), changed his name to Fakir Singh to go begging in India, and later became Commander of the Salvation Army in the United States.

Civilians were often irritated by Westminster MPs who toured India in the cold weather and then wrote books and made speeches as 'experts' on their return. Some of them took a sort of revenge by standing for Parliament in retirement and making such dull speeches in the House that Indian debates were virtually unattended. Not that they were always elected. Retired Civilians were such unpromising candidates that it is difficult to understand why their local parties selected them. They were bound to be rather old and out of touch, ill-informed about contemporary politics and unfamiliar with their constituencies. Sir Charles Grant resigned as Foreign Secretary of the Indian Government to stand as a Liberal Unionist in Banffshire. His defeat by a Gladstonian Liberal was ascribed in the local press to his feeble campaign, his mediocrity on the platform and his talent for antagonizing his Conservative allies over every issue except Ireland. A more charitable correspondent blamed the result on the fact that the victor was a local man, while Grant, although Scottish, was a stranger.[13]

Former Lieutenant-Governors did not allow rebuffs to deter them from trying again. Thwarted in his attempts to represent Dumbartonshire and St Andrews, George Campbell eventually stood for Kirkaldy and served as its Liberal member for seventeen years. But he was not a success at Westminster. Henry Cotton, who had admired him as an L-G, observed that 'by training and temperament he was not fitted to take part in a deliberative assembly', that he was 'deficient in tact and deference to the environment of the House', and that, in addition to being 'afflicted with a voice like a file', he was 'also prone to the unwise habit of addressing the House on any and every subject'. In short, he 'fell into the category of parliamentary bores'.[14]

Campbell's successor in Bengal, Richard Temple, had a rather similar career after he resigned the Bombay governorship and rushed home to contest Worcestershire as a Conservative in the 1880 election. By his own admission he knew nothing of domestic issues and entertained his electors with speeches about Russia and Turkey. Yet he blamed his subsequent defeat on 'the suburbs of Birmingham' and the fact that hundreds of his supporters had 'ratted', going to the poll in Tory 'conveyances' and voting against him when they got there.[15] Five years later he was elected for Evesham and subsequently for Kingston in Surrey, which he represented until 1895. 'It cannot be said', observed Cotton, 'that he added to his reputation in the House of Commons.' Temple had the habit of reminding his listeners of his knowledge and experience of India, which perhaps explains the *DNB*'s comment that 'he was heard with impatience' by fellow-members. His parliamentary career was notable mainly for the assiduity of his voting, for which he set a record, and for the number of times he was caricatured in *Punch*.[16]

In spite of these unpromising precedents, Cotton himself was determined to retire to Westminster. Curzon warned him not to do so on the grounds that a retired Civilian 'inevitably gravitated into a parliamentary bore'. But Cotton pursued his ambition and entered the Commons in the Liberal landslide of 1906. He much enjoyed his new life, becoming 'a great devotee of the Members' smoking-room' and playing for the Commons chess team. But he spoke only in Indian debates and does not seem to have been interested in domestic issues. Like other Liberal MPs of the pro-Congress 'India Group', such as Donald Smeaton and C. J. O'Donnell, he lasted only one Parliament, losing East Nottingham in the election of 1910. By then in any case he had become disenchanted with a Government whose Indian policy showed none of 'the broad and sympathetic temper of Ripon'.[17]

Civilians seldom received peerages and never as a reward for their ICS career: Lawrence earned his because he had returned to India as Viceroy, while MacDonnell was given his after serving as Permanent Under-Secretary for Ireland. But repatriates were serious contenders for governorships outside India and received such diverse plums as

Canada, the Isle of Man and the Irish Free State. Two Lieutenant-Governors of Bengal, John Grant and William Grey, became Governors of Jamaica. After spending thirty-eight years in the East India Company, starting as a Writer at the age of 15 and ending as a Lieutenant-Governor, Charles Metcalfe became Governor of both Jamaica and Canada before dying of cancer at the age of 60. Not all Civilians, as Cotton would have put it, added to their reputations in such posts. Bartle Frere is less remembered for his success as Governor of Bombay and his suppression of the slave trade in Zanzibar than he is for provoking the Zulu War as Governor of the Cape in 1879.

Foreign postings were not reserved for former Governors. Mortimer Durand went from the Indian Foreign Office to Tehran, where he was Minister-Plenipotentiary, and thence to the embassies in Madrid and Washington; after leaving the United States, he turned down an offer to return to India as Governor of Bombay. No one, either Civilian or Political, enjoyed so varied a career as West Ridgeway, who started off in the Bengal Infantry, worked as a Political in Central India and Rajputana, spent the Second Afghan War with General Roberts, became Under-Secretary at the Foreign Office, was named Commissioner for determining the Russo-Afghan border, went to St Petersburg to conclude the consequent treaty, served as Under-Secretary for Ireland, was made Envoy Extraordinary to the Sultan of Morocco, was appointed Governor of the Isle of Man and then of Ceylon (where he was also Commander-in-Chief), and ended up as Chairman of the Committee of Constitution Enquiry for Transvaal and Orange River Colonies. Yet after all that he was one of the few Liberal repatriates to be defeated in the election of 1906.

The most popular posts for retired Anglo-Indians were in the India Office in London, where they could work either as full-time bureaucrats or as part-time members of the Council of India. It was logical for a man like Herbert Risley, an efficient Home Secretary in Simla, to become Secretary of the Judicial and Public Department at the India Office. Ex-Civilians aspired to the job of Permanent Under-Secretary, but this was long denied them by the presence of Arthur Godley, a wily and phlegmatic bureaucrat who held the post between 1883 and 1909 without visiting, or showing any interest in visiting, the area to which he dedicated his career. But three years after his retirement the post went to Thomas Holderness, whom Curzon had regarded as the best Secretary in India, and then to another Civilian, William Duke.

Secretaries at the India Office were sometimes appointed to seats on the Council of India, of which there were eleven at the turn of the century. These were usually filled, however, by former Lieutenant-Governors and Members of the Viceroy's Council. A seat was greatly coveted. Before his appointment as Viceroy, Lawrence preferred to remain a member of the Council rather than accept the governorship of Bombay. Yet a seat was not an automatic reward for retired L-Gs: difficult unclubbable men such as Charles Elliott were not offered one.

Members of the Council met once a week at the India Office under the chairmanship of the Secretary of State. They did not have much work but, under the Act of 1858, they had the power of veto over proposals of the Indian Government on legislation and financial matters. Although they were invariably distinguished men, it was illogical to give pensioners the right to overrule the decisions of a government. Their idea of India tended to be a static one, the India they had known rather than the India that was or might be. They were inclined to distrust a Viceroy like Curzon, who had energy and ideas, because, as Hamilton's Private Secretary observed, they thought he 'should be run by the bigwigs of the Civil Service'. The Secretary, Richmond Ritchie, exempted Lyall and Crosthwaite from his criticism but described their colleagues as played out and indolent. The maxim of Sir James Peile seemed to be that 'the most crusted Civil Service view is the right one'.[18] Frequently frustrated by such people, Curzon complained that it was 'too ridiculous that a batch of old gentlemen at home should casually stroll into the India Office and endeavour to upset the whole apple-cart' because they assumed that his reforms, which might be distasteful to them, must be equally distasteful to their successors in India.[19]

Lyall Venerabilis

Throughout his Indian career Alfred Lyall worried about his retirement. He admitted he was 'always inclined to despondency' over his 'future in England, having a dread of domesticity on small means, the actual fate of so many respectable [Anglo-] Indians'. He predicted that he would have few friends, no job and not enough money to live on. When he was 'an ancient Anglo-Indian in a small house in Westbourne Grove', he would have 'no associations to fall back upon', and people would think of him as an 'old fogey'. None of these anxieties proved well founded. Lyall's long retirement was the happiest period of his life.

He left India in the autumn of 1887. 'We went off honourably,' he reported; 'there were many sayings of regret, especially for Cora, who is very popular. In a month we shall be virtually forgotten.' Durand, who was travelling home on the same ship, saw him say goodbye to an old servant on the deck: 'the two men stood looking at one another in a silent life-long farewell that was very pathetic'. Then Lyall patted his servant on the shoulder 'with something very like a caress' before turning and going below. It was his goodbye to India.[20]

The Lyalls settled in Southwell Gardens in the 'Anglo-Indian Quarter' of South Kensington. The former proconsul liked the house but found the surroundings rather suburban and 'too distant from the social centres'. Yet within weeks of his arrival he found himself 'dining out a good deal', 'meeting various folk of interest' and being elected to 'two good dining clubs'. He was also given a seat on the Council of India, a post normally held for ten years but in his case for fifteen, an extension sanctioned by statute 'for special reasons of public advantage'. The worries about retirement evaporated very quickly.

Lyall told Walter Lawrence that work on the Council had the same savour as 'chewed hay'.[21] Yet he clung to his 'snug berth' there because it was easy and comfortable and kept him in touch with the life he had led for the previous thirty-two years. Although in Calcutta he had once aspired to become Governor of Jamaica, he now rejected the governorships of the Cape and New Zealand. He felt 'lazy about starting again on [his] wanderings', he told his brother James, and, besides, Cape Colony was 'well known to be the most difficult of the Colonial appointments'. Yet he would have wandered back to India if he had been offered Bombay or Madras, and he was disappointed not to be chosen to succeed Lansdowne as Viceroy in 1894. The view in Whitehall was that he was a brilliant man but not decisive enough for the post. The shy and very reluctant Earl of Elgin, Lord Lieutenant of Fife, was sent out instead.

Yet there was no lack of recognition of Lyall's talents and achievements. He was one of a handful of ex-Civilians to be made a Privy Councillor. King's College, Cambridge, made him an Honorary Fellow, and Manchester University gave him an honorary doctorate. He went to the Historical Congress in Rome, attended meetings of the Institut Colonial in Paris, and made speeches at the Girls' High School in Streatham. He became a trustee of the British Museum and President of the Central Asian Society, the Omar Khayyam Club, the Congress of Religions at Oxford and the Board of Dulwich College. Sometimes he felt he had to say no, as he did when telling the Literary Society that it needed a younger President.

Social life was very active. Lyall was surprised how popular he became, how many dinner parties he was asked to, how many weekend invitations he received. His sister Sybilla told their brother James, still out in the Punjab, that he had become very fashionable, that he was charming and distinguished-looking, and that 'all the great ladies' wanted him at their parties. 'One of Alfred's charms is the way he has of talking his best no matter to whom he talks. This flatters women immensely.' Cora was no doubt less flattered by his habit of spending almost every evening out of the house. His diary contains the occasional entry 'Dined at Home', underlined to indicate the rarity of such occasions.

One of the puzzles of Lyall's life is how he managed to do so much reading and writing, to get through so much official work and to lead such a full social life while giving the impression that he was rather lazy. In retirement he read more widely than ever and never travelled anywhere without books. When he fell over on a train going to Dresden, he panicked that he would run out of reading matter while he was recuperating from his consequent back injury. Fortunately he managed to borrow a Homer and get hold of Thiers's *Histoire de l'Empire* to supplement the Pascal and the pocket Virgil he had brought with him. Despite his mistrust of theories, he read philosophical works although, apart from Hume (a sceptic and empiricist like himself), he found it 'mostly a futile exercise'. Philosophers told one 'nothing, except that the Unknown Land is inaccessible, and Shakespeare knew as much as any of them'. The great poets were better at penetrating 'these clouds' and in a few lines could give 'the ultimate ideas, mostly negative'.

Although Lyall contemplated writing his memoirs, he decided in the end not to add to that most popular of Anglo-Indian genres. Yet he wrote regularly, dividing his subjects between the biographical, the literary and the Indian. While he wrote little poetry in retirement, he at last published *Verses Written in India*, a collection of most of his poems in a single small volume. He continued to be a master of the essay form, writing mainly in the *Edinburgh Review* but contributing occasionally to the *Quarterly* and the *Fortnightly* as well. He produced short biographies of Dufferin and Warren Hastings, a longer work, *The Rise and Expansion of the British Dominion in India*, and the second volume of *Asiatic Studies*, his best book. He also wrote a perceptive study of Tennyson and used to stay with the poet's son at Farringford.

Lyall became kinder and mellower as he got older, perhaps because he had much to be mellow about. People noticed that he was gentler and less cynical. His relationship with Cora may have become too distant for mellowness to make much of a difference, but at least he enjoyed the company of his children and the 'family bridge-parties'. When his second son Robert returned to India in 1905 to take up a post in the Political Department, Lyall wrote sadly in his diary that it was doubtful if they would meet again. They did, when Robert came back on leave in 1909, a visit which gave him 'much pleasure' but elicited a more prophetic diary entry: 'I hardly expect to see his face again.'*

A characteristic that Lyall never lost was his reluctance to take sides or see issues in black and white. At the first General Election in 1910 he voted Liberal despite his opposition to Home Rule and his dislike of Lloyd George's Budget, which he considered a socialist measure; for him these defects were outweighed by his suspicion of tariff reformers among the Unionists and the behaviour of the House of Lords over the Budget. By the time of that year's second election he had changed his mind, Asquith's plans for a Parliament Bill to reduce the power of the peers encouraging him to write a letter to *The Times* urging electors to vote Unionist. Yet he knew he should not get excited about such matters because he had a weak heart: he had already had to give up playing bridge because it brought on pain. A few months later, while he was staying with the Tennysons, he suffered the expected heart attack and died. He was 76.[22]

---

*Robert Lyall's final post was Consul-General in Chinese Turkestan.

Going Downhill

The preceding sections may have given the impression that Anglo-Indians habitually retired in pomp to the India Office, the House of Commons and Government Houses in the colonies. Yet of the thirty or so Civilians who retired each year, only three or four could aspire to such places. And even these seldom flourished outside the India Office. Writing in 1887, Lyall argued that Metcalfe had been the 'only Anglo-Indian who [had] made any sort of success in any time of life unconnected with India'. Frere's failure in South Africa had been 'very significant; and in parliamentary waters the Anglo-Indian only just manage[d] to swim'.[23] After 1887 a few names could be added to Metcalfe, notably Durand and perhaps MacDonnell, but the point remained valid.

Westminster, Whitehall and the colonies were simply not options for the Collector of Bogra and the Judge of Cuddapah. Britain changed so quickly during the nineteenth century that a man who pursued his career abroad was often equipped to do little on his return except sit on a parish council or become a Justice of the Peace. Some Anglo-Indians had taken steps to qualify themselves as lawyers by reading for the Bar during their furloughs; some had made contacts with the business world which led to directorships and other rewards later on. But Maconochie judged most repatriates to be fit only to become country squires, which was a pity because, unlike some of their predecessors, Victorian Civilians could not afford to buy country estates.

The withdrawal of so many Anglo-Indians into obscurity leaves a problem for historians. In India even unambitious Civilians like Horsley wrote letters or kept diaries, many of which have been preserved. But they did not write letters or diaries in Cheltenham – or if they did, their descendants have not considered them worth keeping. Occasionally one comes across a box in an attic with a few photographs, a fragment of a journal, a brief hand-written memoir by a granddaughter, a couple of letters from an old friend about the old days in India and the new ones at home with Britain/the Empire/the World all going to the dogs – mementoes which reveal that for many Civilians retirement led to almost total insignificance.

Britain could be a disappointing place for Anglo-Indians and their wives. Unlike Lyall, most had few friends who had not served in

India, which is why they tended to settle in clusters in southern England: a native of Kendal might pine for the Fells but would not settle near Lancaster when there were no Anglo-Indians nearer than Worcester or Edinburgh. Retirement was often lonely, expensive, alien and even inexplicable. One of the most difficult things for repatriates to adjust to was their reduction in status, their sudden lack of importance. Here were men who had governed millions of people and whose achievements had been recognized by decorations of the Star of India and the Indian Empire – Commanders, Knight Commanders and Grand Commanders according to their eminence. Yet no one in Britain seemed to care who they were or what they had been doing. As they used to grumble to each other, 'When we go home, we are nobody, we are utterly unknown.' Charles Trevelyan described how repatriates had to suffer the descent from 'a state of power to a state of absence of influence, from a state of mental activity to a state of inaction, and from a position of importance to insecurity and insignificance'. It was a 'severe trial', his son George Otto observed, 'for a leader of Calcutta society to become one of the rank and file in the pump-room at a watering-place; to sink from the Council-board to the Vestry, and from the High Court to the Petty Sessions'.[24]

In one of his novels Edward Thompson suggested that retired Civilians became either 'stagnant pastures of fat contentment or volcanoes of spouting impotence'.[25] Neither category seems quite fair or quite true. A more usual charge was that of becoming an 'old bore', one frequently feared and admitted by those Anglo-Indians who were not themselves bores. Maconochie began his memoirs with the sentence, 'The Anglo-Indian bore is an established character in fact and fiction', but decided to risk adding to the number.[26] A former Lieutenant-Governor in A. E. W. Mason's novel, *The Broken Road*, lived in Camberley and admitted that he was 'now nothing but a bore' at his club. Repatriates did indeed acquire a reputation for being unable to talk about any subject except India – perhaps a reaction to the fact that people seldom asked them questions about their careers. Richardson Evans began to worry when in old age he found himself saying nearly every day, 'When I was in India . . .'[27]

Another character in *The Broken Road* summed up thousands of repatriate feelings with the words, 'one misses more than one thought to miss, and one doesn't find half what one thought to find'.

It was remarkable how rapidly Anglo-Indians recollected India's good points and forgot the bad, how they recalled the sense of space and the favourite memories, the sound of frogs, the flame of the forest, the almond groves of Kashmir. Richardson Evans could never catch a whiff of burning wood without sensing that he was back in a village on the banks of the Ganges. Even Kipling, at the age of 23, could feel nostalgia after returning to England and experiencing London's 'greasy soup-tureen' of a sky.

> It's Oh to see the morn ablaze
>   Above the mango-tope,
> When homeward through the dewy cane
>   The little jackals lope,
> And half Bengal heaves into view,
>   New-washed – with sunlight soap.[28]

In their longing to return Home, Anglo-Indians often managed to forget such domestic defects as the fogs, the cold and the fact that rain was not limited to a single season. The reality of life on a pension made them regret that they no longer had a battalion of grinning servants to command. The reality of life in a suburb made them miss the neighbouring raja who used to invite them to go shooting in his jungle. They tried to compensate by setting up little Anglo-Indias in their houses, putting hunting trophies on the walls and Indian rugs on the floors, cluttering up their sitting-rooms with brass trays and furniture of teak and rosewood, using chutney and curry in the kitchen, sometimes even giving their new homes the name of their favourite Indian station. The crucial dates in the calendar were Service reunions such as the Burma (or other provincial) dinner and the Haileybury dinner, an event which lasted until 1898 (when competition wallahs were allowed to attend) despite the abolition of the college forty-one years before.

Only a rare spirit refused to put up with repatriation. Loftus Tottenham, a Madras Civilian who liked to sit cross-legged on a stool and 'was reputed to have progeny all down' the Malabar coast, found England a torture and returned to the southern Indian state of Pudukottai. He died there in 1946, bequeathing a large sum of money to feed the state's poor every year on the anniversary of his death.[29]

It would be nice to end with Lawrence or Lyall or Durand or Butler – or any of the ICS men who made a success of their retirement. But the wider reality is that of those former Collectors and District Judges, often depressed and usually disgruntled, who went downhill in obscurity, doing *The Times* crossword and muttering about the modern world. Barbara Rixon remembered her grandfather, Reggie Partridge, in retirement in Devon, 'very kindly – set in his ways and disliking everything new, modern or complicated'. Once a week 'he and Hinton [the gardener] would cut the lawn, Hinton pushing the mower and grandfather walking ahead and pulling a rope which was tied to the front of the mower . . . He wore a straw boater and was always formally dressed with wing collar and tie.'[30]

Such men grumbled to each other as they got older and iller, swapping news about their health, their pleurisy, the hospital operations which nearly 'wiped them out' or 'stopped their number'. They sat in armchairs witnessing developments in a world that seemed to have gone crazy. Many of their boys were killed in the First World War; both of George Smyth's sons were murdered by the Irish Republican Army. When Edwin Montagu, Lloyd George's Secretary for India, brought out plans for a 'dyarchy', a form of power-sharing between British Governors and provincial legislatures, they thought he was completing the 'destruction of Hindustan' which Ripon and Ilbert had begun thirty-eight years earlier.[31] In 1927 Walter Lawrence reflected on the repatriates and 'the pathos of the retrospect'.

> These splendid men working like slaves, their wives encouraging them, telling them it was the greatest of England's missions and endeavours, well worth the exile, the separation from children, and the certainty of the scrap-heap at an age when many are at their best – what must they feel in this strange new world, when they are told they were all wrong and sinners against the new-world Rousseau* and his law of self-determination.[32]

The youngest Civilians mentioned in this book began their careers at the beginning of the twentieth century, ended them just before the Second World War and lived on until the 1950s. Their adult lives thus

---

*President Woodrow Wilson.

stretched from the imperial high noon – Curzon's viceroyalty – to the imperial curtain, the withdrawal of Britain and the independence of India and Pakistan. As servants of the Crown, they carried on their duty while the Governments of Asquith, Lloyd George and Baldwin steadily eroded their authority until – after their retirement – Attlee's administration abolished their role altogether. To Indian nationalists, the road to independence may have seemed unnecessarily prolonged. Perhaps it was. But as a historical process it was not a very lengthy one. An Indian born in 1885, the year Congress was founded, would have been only 62 at the time of Independence. And for much of his life the nationalist movement had not even been advocating an independent India.

It is easy to understand the bewilderment of men who, recruited to do a particular job, saw their work and their significance repeatedly altered and reduced in the course of their career. Most of them knew their limitations; many recognized that their youthful idealism had soured and given way to aloofness and cynicism. But as Maynard, one of the most left-wing Civilians, privately wrote, they had managed to 'do great things in the very midst of their querulous discontents and unideal aspirations'.[33] They could not comprehend how now, after the years of labour and self-denial, they were ending up derided for their intentions and consigned by history to the role of oppressors. Some of them of course grasped the historical process, assisted it on its way and welcomed the dénouement. But for many raised within the Victorian ethos and imbued with the paternalist spirit of the District Officer, it was not easy to stand aside and make way for developments which they did not always understand and of which they often disapproved.

Although the tide of history was against them, and although the eventual winners (the Congress Party and its supporters) were rewriting the script so that they became historically marginalized and almost irrelevant, a few relicts tried to convince their children and others that they had done their best. After the massacres at Independence in 1947, they reminded their listeners that they had been able to keep 'law and order' by 'personal influence and impartiality – without troops and with only a few unarmed police'. There had been no such 'savagery and bloodshed', they pointed out, as was then taking place between Hindus and Muslims in the Punjab and Bengal. They had worked to further education, agriculture, sanitation and so on; they had preserved religious freedom; they had set India on the road to constitutional government.[34]

It was rather a forlorn exercise, a mainly private attempt to justify themselves at a time when the victors would only pay them the implicit compliment of modelling their successor, the Indian Administrative Service, very closely upon them. Yet although the ICS passed into history, its motives increasingly denigrated, its policies post-colonially mocked, revisionism has not destroyed the idea that it represented the British Empire at its best and at its most altruistic. Eleven years after its demise, Queen Elizabeth unveiled a memorial tablet in Westminster Abbey that does not say quite enough.

1858   1947

HERE

ARE COMMEMORATED

THE CIVIL SERVICES

OF THE CROWN IN INDIA

LET THEM NOT BE FORGOTTEN

FOR THEY SERVED INDIA WELL

What doth the Lord require of thee

but to do justly

and to love mercy

Notes

~

PREFACE
1. Hyde, *Stalin*, p. 397.
2. Moorhouse, *India Britannica*, p. 264; Morison (ed.), *The Letters of Theodore Roosevelt*, Vol. 2, p. 1052.
3. O'Malley, *The Indian Civil Service*, pp. 49, 173; Hübner, *Through the British Empire*, Vol. 2, p. 252.
4. Symonds, *The British and Their Successors*, p. 40; Strachey, *The End of Empire*, pp. 54, 57.
5. Bonarjee, *Under Two Masters*, pp. 122–3.
6. Kirk-Greene, *Britain's Imperial Administrators*, p. 87; Symonds, *The British and Their Successors*, p. 25; conversations with author.
7. Caine, *Bombay to Bloomsbury*, pp. 4–6.
8. Information from Partridge family.
9. Furbank, *E. M. Forster*, Vol. 2, p. 126.
10. Spangenberg, *British Bureaucracy in India*, pp. x, 336; Crane and Barrier, *British Imperial Policy in India and Sri Lanka*, pp. 56, 180–1; Metcalf, *Ideologies of the Raj*, p. 175.
11. Dewey, *Anglo-Indian Attitudes*, pp. 12–16.
12. Moore, *Paul Scott's Raj*, pp. 136, 198; Spurling, *Paul Scott*, pp. 362–3.

INTRODUCTION: QUEEN VICTORIA'S INDIAN EMPIRE
1. Queen Victoria to Salisbury, 25 May 1898, Curzon Papers.
2. Esher (ed.), *The Girlhood of Queen Victoria*, Vol. 1, p. 338; Vol. 2, p. 8.
3. Longford, *Victoria R.I.*, pp. 280–1; Moore in Porter (ed.), *The Nineteenth Century*, p. 425.
4. Hibbert, *Queen Victoria*, pp. 250–1; Longford, *Victoria R.I.*, p. 281.
5. Roberts, *Salisbury*, p. 140; Blake, *Disraeli*, pp. 562–3.
6. Northbrook to Queen Victoria, 14 June 1875, Northbrook Papers.
7. Curzon to Hamilton, 18 July 1900, 9 Apr., 20 and 27 Aug. 1902, Curzon Papers.
8. Lawrence, *The India We Served*, pp. 202–10.
9. Longford, *Victoria R.I.*, pp. 281, 509.
10. Longford, *Victoria R.I.*, p. 489.
11. The portraits are at Osborne.

12. Longford, *Victoria R.I.*, pp. 508–9, 535–41; Anand, *Indian Sahib*, pp. 45–6, 58.
13. Bradley, *Lady Curzon's India*, p. 126.
14. Queen Victoria to Curzon, 13 Apr. 1899 and 17 Aug. 1900, Curzon Papers; Cross to Lansdowne, 19 and 26 June 1891, Lansdowne Papers; Longford, *Victoria R.I.*, p. 509.
15. Curzon to Hamilton, 24 Jan. 1901, Curzon Papers; Lawrence, *The India We Served*, p. 241; Welldon, *Recollections and Reflections*, p. 263; Wilson, *Letters from India*, p. 223.
16. Loch, *The Family of Loch*, pp. 297–9.
17. Whitcombe, *Agrarian Conditions in Northern India*, Vol. 1, pp. 64–91; Cain and Hopkins, *British Imperialism, 1688–2000*, pp. 290–2; Stone, *Canal Irrigation in British India*, pp. 4–143 *passim*, pp. 278–80; Charlesworth, *British Rule and the Indian Economy*, pp. 23–37; Bayly, *The Birth of the Modern World*, p. 182.
18. Collingham, *Imperial Bodies*, pp. 52–3.
19. Moon, *The British Conquest*, pp. 426–8.
20. Hutchins, *The Illusion of Permanence*, p. 10.
21. Philips (ed.), *Historians of India*, pp. 219–37, 405.
22. Moon, *The British Conquest*, pp. 465–8; Bonarjee, *Under Two Masters*, p. 288.
23. Lyall's letters to his family 1857–9, Lyall Papers.
24. Lyall's letters to his family, 1857–9, Lyall Papers.
25. Metcalfe, *Ideologies of the Raj*, p. 45.
26. Lyall's letters to his family, 1857–60, Lyall Papers.
27. Lyall's letters to his family, 1859–61, Lyall Papers.
28. Bayly, *Indian Society*, p. 197.
29. Cunningham, *British India and Its Rulers*, p. 47.
30. Welldon, *Recollections and Reflections*, pp. 265, 291.
31. Pinney (ed.), *Letters of Rudyard Kipling*, Vol. 2, p. 75.
32. Pottinger, *Mayo*, p. 192; Cotton, *Indian & Home Memories*, p. 66.
33. Curzon to Hamilton, 20 Dec. 1900, and Hamilton to Curzon, 16 June 1899, Curzon Papers; Lawrence diary, Walter Lawrence Papers; Elgin to Hamilton, 27 Jan. 1896, Elgin Papers; *Civil & Military Gazette*, 28 Jan. 1887.
34. Grant Duff draft memo for Dufferin, 24 June 1885, Grant Duff Papers.
35. Koss, *John Morley at the India Office*, p. 128.
36. Gopal in Williams and Potts (eds.), *Essays in Indian History*, pp. 5–6.
37. Koss, *John Morley at the India Office*, pp. 140–1.
38. Gopal, *British Policy in India*, p. 120.
39. Banerjee, *Studies in Administrative History of Bengal*, p. 9.
40. Blunt, *India under Ripon*, p. 220.
41. Trevelyan, *Competition Wallah*, p. 451.
42. Anthony Hartley, quoted in *TLS*, 17 Apr. 1998; *The Times*, 4 Jan. 1878.
43. Woodruff, *The Guardians*, p. 224.
44. Symonds, *Oxford and Empire*, p. 32; Metcalf, *Ideologies of the Raj*, p. 54; Cromer, *Ancient and Modern Imperialism*, pp. 7–8.
45. Symonds, *Oxford and Empire*, pp. 31–4; Woodruff, *The Guardians*.
46. Cromer, *Ancient and Modern Imperialism*, pp. 19, 26–7; Lyall, *British Dominion in India*, pp. 340, 347–8.
47. Strachey, *India*, p. 13.
48. Curzon to Morley, 17 June 1900, Curzon Papers.
49. Strachey, *India*, p. 6.
50. Bayly (ed.), *The Raj*, pp. 253–9.
51. Seeley, *The Expansion of England*, p. 235; Strachey, *India*, pp. 3, 360–1, 390; Lyall, *Asiatic Studies*, p. 181.
52. Strachey, *India*, p. 390.
53. Roberts, *Forty-one Years in India*, Vol. 2, pp. 388–9.

54. Bonus to Phelps, 28 Aug. 1893, Phelps Papers.
55. Cromer, *Ancient and Modern Imperialism*, pp. 123–7.

CHAPTER 1: OLD BOYS

1. Bonarjee, *Under Two Masters*, p. 274.
2. Wedderburn, *Allan Octavian Hume*, p. xii; Ratcliffe, *Sir William Wedderburn*, pp. 13, 21; Brasted, 'Irish Home Rule Politics and India', pp. 76–7.
3. Holroyd, *Lytton Strachey*, Vol. 1, pp. 29–30; Strachey, *The Strachey Line*, p. 138.
4. Loch, *The Family of Loch, passim*.
5. Compton, 'Open Competition and the Indian Civil Service, 1854–1876', in *English Historical Review*, Vol. 83, 1968, p. 281.
6. Speech at Birmingham, 29 Oct. 1858.
7. Sengoopta, *Imprint of the Raj*, pp. 73–92 *passim*.
8. Temple, *The Story of My Life*, pp. 3–5; Rivett-Carnac, *Many Memories*, p. 64.
9. Dewey, *The Passing of Barchester, passim*.
10. Grierson, *The Letters of Sir Walter Scott*, Vol. 6, p. 489.
11. Campbell, *Memoirs of My Indian Career*, Vol. 1, p. 2.
12. Unpublished *ms.* by Archibald Macnab, Macnabb Collection.
13. Unpublished *ms.* by Archibald Macnab, Macnabb Collection.
14. *Who's Who.*
15. Danvers (ed.), *Memorials of Old Haileybury College*, p. 90.
16. Birdwood, *Competition and the Indian Civil Service*, p. 9; Beames, *Memoirs of a Bengal Civilian*, p. 60; Campbell, *Memoirs of My Indian Career*, Vol. 1, pp. 8–10.
17. Lee, *Brothers in the Raj*, p. 28.
18. Elsmie, *Thirty-five Years in the Punjab*, pp. 1–2.
19. Rivett-Carnac, *Many Memories*, pp. 12–13.
20. Durand, *Alfred Lyall*, p. 17; Lyall to his mother, 7 Apr. 1856, Lyall Papers.
21. Beames, *Memoirs of a Bengal Civilian*, p. 61; Elsmie, *Thirty-five Years in the Punjab*, pp. 5–6.
22. Campbell, *Memoirs of My Indian Career*, Vol. 1, p. 8; Danvers (ed.), *Memorials of Old Haileybury College*, pp. 85–6; unpublished *ms.*, Bowring Papers.
23. 'Languages of India' from the Statistical Office of East India House, 1852.
24. Unpublished *ms.*, Bowring Papers.
25. Campbell, *Modern India*, p. 265.
26. Ghosal, *Civil Service in India*, p. 319.
27. Beames, *Memoirs of a Bengal Civilian*, pp. 64–7.
28. Beames, *Memoirs of a Bengal Civilian*, p. 64.
29. Temple, *Story of My Life*, Vol. 1, p. 13.
30. Unpublished *ms.*, Bowring Papers; Beames, *Memoirs of a Bengal Civilian*, pp. 63, 75.
31. Dispatch to Northbrook, 24 Feb. 1876, L/PJ/6/24, file 1438, OIOC.
32. Rivett-Carnac, *Many Memories*, p. 81.
33. Griffin, 'The Indian Civil Service Examinations', p. 536.

CHAPTER 2: COMPETITION WALLAHS

1. Dewey, 'The Education of a Ruling Caste', p. 269; Moore, *Sir Charles Wood's Indian Policy*, p. 90; Symonds, *The British and Their Successors*, p. 44.
2. *Times & Standard*, 20 Apr. 1861.
3. *Oxford Magazine*, 15 Feb. 1893.
4. Unpublished memoir, Macnabb Papers; Hallam to Butler, 2 Aug. 1886, H. Butler Papers; unpublished memoir, Hayward Papers.
5. Birdwood, *Competition and the Indian Civil Service*, p. 7.
6. Birdwood, *Competition and the Indian Civil Service*, p. 7.

7. Jowett to Ripon, Mar. 1885, Jowett Papers; Monier-Williams, 14 Oct. 1884, Jowett Papers.
8. Banerjea, *A Nation in Making*, pp. 12–27; Nanda, *Essays in Modern Indian History*, pp. 68–74.
9. Singh, *The British Policy in India*, p. 19; Argyll to Mayo, 18 Apr. 1869, L/PJ/6/2, file 64, OIOC.
10. Misra, *The Bureaucracy in India*, p. 132.
11. Curzon to Hamilton, 11 Jan. 1900, Curzon Papers.
12. Misra, *District Administration and Rural Development in India*, pp. 346–7; Argyll to Mayo, 18 Apr. 1869, L/PJ/6/2, file 64, OIOC.
13. Cotton, *Indian & Home Memories*, pp. 28, 37.
14. Tikekar, *The Kincaids*, p. 247; Hill, *India*, pp. 7–8; Fryer 1862 diary, Fryer Papers.
15. Woodruff, *The Guardians*, p. 220.
16. Unpublished memoir, Hubback Papers.
17. Unpublished memoir, Caroe Papers; Pearce, *Once a Happy Valley*, p. 2; Mason, *A Shaft of Sunlight*, pp. 68, 129; Mason, *Kipling: The Glass, the Shadow and the Fire*.
18. Compton, 'Open Competition and the Indian Civil Service, 1854–1876', pp. 281–2; Spangenberg, *British Bureaucracy in India*, pp. 19, 153.
19. *India Office List*, 1880 and 1886; Dewey, *Anglo-Indian Attitudes*, p. 163.
20. Wenlock to Elgin, 6 June 1894, Elgin Papers.
21. Information from Anne Chisholm; memo in Maynard Papers; Sifton to father, 18 Oct. 1904, Sifton Papers.
22. Fry, *The Scottish Empire*, pp. 207–8.
23. Muir, *The Indian Civil Service and the Scottish Universities*, pp. 25–7.
24. Cook, 'The Irish Raj', pp. 510–11.
25. See articles by his granddaughter, Joy Rathbone, in the *Evening Echo*, Jan. and Feb. 1982.
26. Said, *Culture and Imperialism*, p. 275.
27. Cook, 'The Irish Raj', p. 515.
28. Fitzpatrick , 'Ireland and the Empire', in Porter (ed.), *The Nineteenth Century*, p. 505; Brasted, 'Irish Home Rule Politics and India', p. 584.
29. Lyall to his sister, 28 July 1879, Lyall Papers; O'Donnell, *The Irish Future*, pp. 13, 226.
30. Cook, 'The Irish Raj', p. 520.
31. L/PJ/6/11, file 11, and L/PJ/6/12, files 602 and 623, OIOC.
32. See articles by Joy Rathbone in the *Evening Echo*, Jan. and Feb. 1982.
33. Eardley-Wilmot to Cranbrook, 9 Jan. 1880, L/PJ/6/2, file 53, OIOC.
34. Partridge Papers; Godley to Curzon, 1 Jan. 1903, Curzon Papers.
35. Unpublished memoir, Portal Papers.
36. Grant Duff to Yule, 11 June 1885, Grant Duff Papers; Baker and Washbrook (eds.), *South India: Political Institutions and Political Change*, pp. 31–3; Elgin to Hamilton, 22 Jan. 1876, Elgin Papers.
37. Guha, *A Corner of a Foreign Field*, pp. 53–4, 68–72.
38. Spangenberg, *British Bureaucracy in India*, pp. 82–3.
39. Dawson to Phelps, 14 July 1895, Phelps Papers; Crosthwaite to Curzon, 3 Jan. 1902, Curzon Papers; Holderness to Butler, 1 Mar. 1917, H. Butler Papers; Butler to Scott, 28 Sept. 1922, Scott Papers.
40. White, *A Civil Servant in Burma*, pp. 7–8, 36, 84–5; Durand to Lansdowne, 4 May 1892, Durand Papers; Mackenzie to Elgin, 21 Feb. 1895, Elgin Papers.
41. Lawrence, *The India We Served*, p. 6.
42. Phelps Papers.
43. Maconochie, *Life in the Indian Civil Service*, p. 13.
44. Symonds, *Oxford and Empire*, p. 27; Bennett, *The Ilberts in India*, p. 35.

45. Potter, *India's Political Administrators*, pp. 68–71.
46. Speech at a banquet to honour Lansdowne, 1888, Jowett Papers; Asquith, *More Memories*, p. 187.
47. Griffin, 'The Indian Civil Service Examinations', p. 523.
48. Hall, *The Passing of Empire*, pp. 43–5; Hunter, *The Old Missionary*, pp. 9–10; Allardyce, *The City of Sunshine*, Vol. 1, pp. 171–2.
49. Brown, *The Sahibs*, p. 229.
50. Fergusson to Hartington, letters 1881–2, Fergusson Papers.
51. Ex-Civilian, *Life in the Mofussil*, Vol. 1, p. 42; Fergusson to Hartington, 5 Oct. 1881, Fergusson Papers; D. Macnabb letter, 5 Feb. 1871, Macnabb Papers; Northbrook to Muir, 26 July 1873, Northbrook Papers.
52. Grey to Lawrence, 26 Apr. 1866, and Lawrence to Grey, 27 Apr. 1866, J. Lawrence Papers; Trevelyan, *The India We Left*, p. 100; Steel, *On the Face of the Waters*, p. 41; Curzon to Hamilton, 21 May 1902, Curzon Papers; Blunt, *Ideas about India*, pp. 57–8; Wedderburn, *Allan Octavian Hume*, p. 102.
53. Bonarjee, *Under Two Masters*, p. 114.
54. Gupta, *A Foot in the Door of the Indian Civil Service*, p. 28.
55. Hall, *The Passing of Empire*, pp. 190–3.
56. Hunter, *Imperial Gazetteer*, Vol. 4, p. 44; Trevelyan, *The India We Left*, p. 139.
57. Elgin to Hamilton, 23 Dec. 1896, Elgin Papers; Curzon to Wedderburn, 17 Apr. 1900, Curzon Papers; Sifton to father, 20 Mar. 1904, Sifton Papers.
58. 18 Sept. 1866.
59. Hamilton to Elgin, 1 Apr. 1898, Elgin Papers.
60. Lawrence to Grey, 27 Apr. 1866, J. Lawrence Papers.

CHAPTER 3: GRIFFINS
1. Unpublished memoir, p. 89, Pearse Papers.
2. Lyall to mother, 23 Oct. 1857, Lyall Papers; Wilson, *Hints for the First Years of Residence in India*, pp. 10–16.
3. Beames, *Memoirs of a Bengal Civilian*, pp. 75–6.
4. Stokes to Stokes, 19 Nov. 1896, Stokes Papers.
5. Sifton letters to mother, Nov. 1902, Sifton Papers; Cotton, *Indian & Home Memories*, p. 58; Hill, *India*, p. 12; Lawrence, *The India We Served*, p. 14.
6. Beveridge, *India Called Them*, p. 37; Sifton letters to mother, Nov. 1902, Sifton Papers; unpublished memoir, Hayward Papers; Horsley to father, 24 Oct. 1889, Horsley Papers; unpublished memoir, 'Punjab Memories', Penny Papers.
7. Fryer diary, 1864, Fryer Papers; Thompson diary, 1897, Thompson Papers.
8. Steevens, *In India*, pp. 66–71.
9. Maynard to mother, 24 Nov. 1886, Maynard Papers.
10. Curzon to Brett, 20 Sept. 1878, Esher Papers.
11. Lyon to Phelps, 6 Feb. 1884, Phelps Papers; Maynard to mother, 10 Jan. 1887 and 6 May 1888, Maynard Papers.
12. Brown to Phelps, 16 June 1883, Phelps Papers.
13. Beames, *Memoirs of a Bengal Civilian*, p. 83.
14. Beames, *Memoirs of a Bengal Civilian*, pp. 81–2.
15. Montgomery, *Monty's Grandfather*, p. 9; Beames, *Memoirs of a Bengal Civilian*, p. 91.
16. Wilson, *Hints for the First Years of Residence in India*, pp. 7, 35.
17. Unpublished memoir, H. Butler Papers.
18. Thompson, *An Indian Day*, p. 21.
19. Unpublished memoir, pp. 87–8, Pearse Papers.
20. Unpublished memoir, p. 88, Pearse Papers; Cotton, *Indian & Home Memories*, p. 102; Darling, *Apprentice to Power*, p. 20.

21. Macleod, *Impressions of an Indian Civil Servant*, p. 136.
22. Ex-Civilian, *Life in the Mofussil*, Vol. 2, pp. 16–17.
23. Hutchins, *An Indian Career*, p. 45; Wilson, *Letters from India*, pp. 48–9; Lyall to sister, 12 Apr. 1877, Lyall Papers.
24. Horsley to mother, 23 July 1871, Horsley Papers.
25. Beames, *Memoirs of a Bengal Civilian*, p. 128.
26. Wilson, *Indian Embers*, p. 292; Welldon, *Recollections and Reflections*, p. 234.
27. Charter of the Unceremonials Club (British Library).
28. Darling, *Apprentice to Power*, pp. 51, 75.
29. Butler to uncle, 1 Jan. 1894, H. Butler Papers.
30. Kincaid, *Forty-four Years a Public Servant*, p. 42.
31. Horsley to father, 6 June 1873, Horsley Papers.
32. Kipling, *Something of Myself*, pp. 31–2.
33. O'Dwyer, *India as I Knew It*, p. 35.
34. McMillan, *Divers Ditties Chiefly Written in India*, p. 18.
35. Carstairs, *The Little World of an Indian District Officer*, p. 7.
36. Letter from 'Vermicelli' in *Pioneer*, 14 May 1897.
37. Lyall's letters to his family, 1855–8, Lyall Papers; Durand, *Alfred Lyall*, pp. 28–100 *passim*.

CHAPTER 4: DISTRICT OFFICERS

1. Fraser, *India under Curzon*, p. 260.
2. Whish, *A District Office in Northern India*, p. 9; Hunt and Harrison, *The District Officer in India*, pp. 77–8.
3. Maynard, 'A Day in the Life of a Civilian Officer', lecture in Maynard Papers.
4. Beames, *Memoirs of a Bengal Civilian*, pp. 223–5.
5. Carstairs, *The Little World of an Indian District Officer*, p. 57; Saumarez Smith, *A Young Man's Country*, pp. 4–6, 29.
6. Maconochie to Phelps, 23 Nov. 1891, Phelps Papers.
7. Hunter, *The Annals of Rural Bengal*, Vol. 1, pp. 222–55; Waley-Cohen, *A Young Victorian in India*, p. 118.
8. L/PJ/6/24, file 1462, OIOC; Carstairs, *The Little World of an Indian District Officer*, p. 156; lecture in Nottingham, Heald Papers; Mason, *A Shaft of Sunlight*, pp. 72–3.
9. Beames, *Memoirs of a Bengal Civilian*, pp. 246, 262.
10. O'Malley, *The Indian Civil Service*, p. 90.
11. Crooke, *The North-Western Provinces of India*, pp. 136–7; Strachey, *India*, pp. 310–11; O'Dwyer, *India as I Knew It*, p. 102.
12. Canning to Yule, 28 Aug. 1861, Yule Papers.
13. Crooke, *The North-Western Provinces of India*, p. 137; Butler to father, 6 Mar. 1897, H. Butler Papers.
14. Butler to uncle, 11 Feb. 1891, H. Butler Papers; Herschel to Commissioner of Revenue, 21 Nov. 1867, Herschel Papers; Bayly, *The Local Roots of Indian Politics*, pp. 154–5.
15. Butler to uncle, 11 Feb. 1891, H. Butler Papers.
16. Bayly, *Indian Society and the Making of the British Empire*, pp. 157–8; Tupper, *Our Indian Protectorate*, p. 294; Blunt, *The I.C.S.*, p. 232.
17. Butler to uncle, 1 Jan. 1894, H. Butler Papers; Crooke, *The North-Western Provinces*, p. 187; Ahmed, *The Bengal Muslims*, pp. 170–3; Pandey, *The Construction of Communalism in Colonial North India*, pp. 164–5, 174–6, 195, 200.
18. Forrest, *The Administration of Lansdowne*, p. 22.
19. White, *A Civil Servant in Burma*, pp. 236–7.
20. Butler to mother, 20 May 1891, H. Butler Papers; unpublished memoir, Hayward

Papers; Maynard to mother, 4 Aug. 1887, Maynard Papers; Mackenzie to Elgin, 31 May 1896, Elgin Papers.

21. Du Boulay to Phelps, 18 Jan. 1893, and Francis to Phelps, 3 May 1896, Phelps Papers.
22. Dufferin to Cross, 9 Jan. 1888, Dufferin Papers.
23. Horsley to father, 13 Feb. 1887, Horsley Papers.
24. Beames, *Memoirs of a Bengal Civilian*, pp. 159–61.
25. Butler to uncle, 11 Feb. 1891, H. Butler Papers; Beatson-Bell to Phelps, 10 Jan. 1891, Phelps Papers.
26. Horsley to father, 25 May 1890, Horsley Papers; Fryer to Elgin, 11 Oct. 1895, Elgin Papers.
27. Bonus to Phelps, 4 Nov. 1887, Phelps Papers; Lyall to mother, 12 June 1877, Lyall Papers; unpublished memoir, Bowring Papers; Kipling, 'The Judgment of Dungara'.
28. Butler to mother, 20 May 1891, and to father, 2 Oct. 1891, H. Butler Papers; Temple to Wyllie, 16 Aug. 1867, Temple Papers; Gandhi, *An Autobiography*, p. 46; Bonus to Phelps, 4 Nov. 1887, Phelps Papers; Curzon to Hamilton, 1 Apr. 1901, Curzon Papers.
29. Ex-Civilian, *Life in the Mofussil*, Vol. 2, p. 265; Sifton to father, 20 Aug. 1903, Sifton Papers; Lawrence, *The India We Served*, pp. 100–1.
30. Beames, *Memoirs of a Bengal Civilian*, pp. 148–50, 170–4, 182–4; Cotton, *Indian & Home Memories*, pp. 85, 157–8.
31. Kipling, 'William the Conqueror'.
32. Lyall to mother, 30 Aug. 1863, Lyall Papers.
33. Beames, *Memoirs of a Bengal Civilian*, p. 223; Mason, *A Shaft of Sunlight*, p. 104.
34. Hunt and Harrison (eds.), *The District Officer in India*, p. 135.
35. Francis to Phelps, 24 Sept. 1893, Phelps Papers.
36. Durand, *Alfred Lyall*, p. 92; fragment of Lyall letter, n.d., Lyall Papers.
37. Letters from Macnabb, 9 and 23 Apr. 1877, Macnabb Papers.
38. Maynard to mother, 22 Nov. 1891, Maynard Papers.

CHAPTER 5: CAMPERS
1. Blakesley to Phelps, 17 May 1894, Phelps Papers.
2. Maconochie to Phelps, 4 June 1890, Phelps Papers.
3. Unpublished memoir, Bowring Papers; Butler to uncle, 25 Dec. 1897, and unpublished memoir, H. Butler Papers; Butler to Scott, 15 Oct. 1922, Scott Papers.
4. Unpublished memoir, Hayward Papers; Wilson, *Hints for the First Years of Residence in India*, p. 52.
5. Wilson, *Hints for the First Years of Residence in India*, pp. 64–5; unpublished memoir, Hayward Papers.
6. Bonus to Phelps, 4 Nov. 1887, Phelps Papers; Maynard, 'A Day in the Life of a Civilian', lecture in Maynard Papers; Heald, 'A Lecture on Burma', Heald Papers; Mason, *A Shaft of Sunlight*, pp. 100, 137; Woodruff, *The Guardians*, pp. 86–7; Lawrence, *Indian Embers*, pp. 56, 89, 91, 161; Macleod, *Impressions of an Indian Civil Servant*, pp. 20, 23; Lawrence, *The India We Served*, pp. 50, 119; Lady Maxwell's unpublished memoir, Maxwell Papers; Chenevix Trench to aunt, 13 Dec. 1905, Chenevix Trench Papers.
7. Carstairs, *The Little World of an Indian District Officer*, pp. 89, 35; Bayly, *Indian Society*, pp. 108–9.
8. Unpublished memoir, Wingate Papers.
9. Mason, *A Shaft of Sunlight*, pp. 94–5; Lawrence, *The India We Served*, p. 92; O'Dwyer, *India as I Knew It*, pp. 52–8, 94–5.
10. Dewey, *The Settlement Literature of the Punjab*, pp. 21–3.
11. Lawrence, *The India We Served*, p. 152.

12. Butler letters to uncle, 1 Jan. and 30 Apr. 1894, and unpublished memoir, H. Butler Papers.
13. Penner, *The Patronage Bureaucracy in North India*, pp. 2–4, 101–2, 340.
14. Canning to Yule, 2 Mar. 1861, Yule Papers.
15. Butler to uncle, 12 Mar. 1891, H. Butler Papers; Crane and Barrier (eds.), *British Imperial Policy*, pp. 62–5.
16. Le Mesurier to Phelps, 7 May 1903, Phelps Papers.
17. O'Dwyer, *India as I Knew It*, p. 39.
18. Zinkin, 'ICS Revisited'; Mason, *A Shaft of Sunlight*, p. 74; Yalland, *Boxwallahs*, pp. 165–7; Dewey, *Anglo-Indian Attitudes*, p. 70.
19. Maconochie, *Life in the Indian Civil Service*, p. 63.
20. Moon, *The British Conquest*, pp. 806–7; Cotton, *Indian & Home Memories*, p. 69; Roberts, *Salisbury*, pp. 85–6.
21. Campbell, *Memoirs of My Indian Career*, Vol. 2, p. 324.
22. Moon, *The British Conquest*, pp. 841–3.
23. Arnold, *Famine*, pp. 113–14; Stone, *Canal Irrigation in British India*, p. 27.
24. Sifton to father, 21 May 1903, Sifton Papers.
25. Campbell to Salisbury, 6 Mar. 1874, Campbell Papers: Enthoven to Phelps, 5 Feb. 1900, Phelps Papers; Waley-Cohen, *A Young Victorian in India*, p. 149; O'Malley, *The Indian Civil Service*, p. 102; Blunt, *The I.C.S.*, p. 184.
26. Waley-Cohen, *A Young Victorian in India*, p. 26.
27. Woodruff, *The Guardians*, p. 99; O'Malley, *The Indian Civil Service*, p. 99; Carstairs, *The Little World of an Indian District Officer*, pp. 330–1.
28. Waley-Cohen, *A Young Victorian in India*, p. 25.
29. Northbrook to Queen Victoria, 8 May 1874, Northbrook Papers.
30. Elgin to Queen Victoria, 19 Mar. 1895, Elgin Papers; Curzon to Hamilton, 11 Apr. 1900, Curzon Papers; Crane and Barrier (eds.), *British Imperial Policy*, pp. 75–6.
31. Maconochie, *Life in the Indian Civil Service*, p. 81; Butler to father, 4 Apr. 1898, M. Butler Papers.
32. Fraser, *India under Curzon and after*, p. 292; Maconochie, *Life in the Indian Civil Service*, p. 127; Punjab Government reports in Hailey Papers; O'Malley, *The Indian Civil Service*, p. 101.
33. Arnold, *Colonizing the Body*, p. 217.
34. Arnold, *Colonizing the Body*, pp. 209–29.
35. Sifton to father, 3 Mar. 1903, Sifton Papers; Curzon to Hamilton, 29 Mar. 1900, Curzon Papers.
36. Curzon to Hamilton, 29 Mar. 1900, Curzon Papers.
37. Carstairs, *The Little World of an Indian District Officer*, p. 256.
38. 'Lecture on Burma', Heald Papers.
39. Horsley letters to father, 1870–81, Horsley Papers.

CHAPTER 6: MAGISTRATES AND JUDGES
1. Ex-Civilian, *Life in the Mofussil*, Vol. 2, p. 252.
2. Dobbs to Phelps, 26 Aug. 1893, Phelps Papers; Carstairs, *The Little World of an Indian District Officer*, p. 95; Mason, *A Shaft of Sunlight*, p. 99; Steevens, *In India*, p. 165.
3. Maynard lecture, 'A Day in the Life of a Civilian Officer', Maynard Papers; Allen, *Plain Tales from the Raj*, p. 185; Cassels to Phelps, 9 Sept. 1900, Phelps Papers; Temple, *Story of my Life*, Vol. 1, p. 44.
4. Sifton to father, 28 May 1903, Sifton Papers.
5. O'Dwyer, *India as I Knew It*, p. 45; Lyall to mother, 3 May 1857, Lyall Papers; Woodburn to grandmother, 21 Mar. 1865, Woodburn Papers.

6. 'Memories', Richardson Evans Papers; Zinkin, 'ICS Revisited'; Maynard to mother, 4 May 1889, Maynard Papers; Kincaid, *Forty-four Years a Public Servant*, p. 75.
7. Kincaid, *Forty-four Years a Public Servant*, p. 28.
8. Cassels to Phelps, 9 Sept. 1900, Phelps Papers; Carstairs, *The Little World of an Indian District Officer*, p. 192; Sengoopta, *Imprint of the Raj*, p. 156.
9. Ex-Civilian, *Life in the Mofussil*, Vol. 2, p. 65; Fraser, *Among Indian Rajahs and Ryots*, pp. 341–2.
10. Hunt and Harrison (eds.), *The District Officer in India*, p. 72.
11. Lawrence, *The India We Served*, p. 23.
12. Ex-Civilian, *Life in the Mofussil*, Vol. 1, pp. 264–5; Campbell, *Memoirs of My Indian Career*, Vol. 2, p. 69.
13. Lawrence, *The India We Served*, p. 37.
14. Lilly, *India and Its Problems*, p. 180.
15. Campbell, *Memoirs of My Indian Career*, Vol. 2, p. 113.
16. Moon, *The British Conquest*, p. 781.
17. Hunter, *The Old Missionary*, p. 68; Temple to Northbrook, 21 May 1874, Northbrook Papers.
18. L/PJ/6/50, file 1375, OIOC.
19. Horsley letters to father, 1883–4, Horsley Papers.
20. Kincaid, *Forty-four Years a Public Servant*, p. 32; Symonds, *The British and Their Successors*, p. 74.
21. Tikekar, *The Kincaids*, p. 26; L/PJ/6/63, file 118, OIOC.
22. Macleod, *Impressions of an Indian Civil Servant*, p. 67; Horsley to father, 21 Nov. 1886, Horsley Papers.
23. Bennett, *The Ilberts in India*, p. 35.
24. Gopal, *British Policy in India*, p. 147.
25. Bennett, *The Ilberts in India*, p. 56.
26. Beveridge, *India Called Them*, pp. 228, 248.

CHAPTER 7: BLACK SHEEP
1. Unpublished memoir, Hayward Papers.
2. Kincaid, *Forty-four Years a Public Servant*, p. 103; Tikekar, *The Kincaids*, p. 14.
3. L/PJ/6/17, file 20, OIOC.
4. L/PJ/6/2, file 67, and L/PJ/6/69, file 458, OIOC.
5. L/PJ/6/13 to L/PJ/6/193 *passim*, OIOC.
6. Grant Duff to Yule, 11 June 1885, Grant Duff Papers.
7. L/PJ/6/12, file 586, OIOC.
8. L/PJ/6/52, file 1530, and L/PJ/6/61, file 69, OIOC.
9. File 115, Grant Duff Papers.
10. Hutchins, *An Indian Career*, p. 55.
11. File 113, Grant Duff Papers; L/PJ/6/70, file 515, OIOC.
12. Brasted, 'Irish Home Rule Politics and India', p. 590.
13. 'The Black Pamphlet of Calcutta', pp. 7, 9, 63; Brasted, 'Irish Home Rule Politics and India', pp. 78–80, 418.
14. Durand to Northbrook, 25 June 1876, Northbrook Papers; L/PJ/3/79, file 1349, OIOC.
15. Eden to Northbrook, 19 Oct. 1880, Northbrook Papers; Bayley censure, L/PJ/3/79, file 1349, OIOC.
16. Brasted, 'Irish Home Rule Politics and India', pp. 300, 395.
17. 'The Ruin of an Indian Province', pp. 20, 33; Brasted, 'Irish Home Rule Politics and India', p. 396.
18. *The Times*, 25 Aug. 1880; L/PJ/3/79, file 1349, OIOC.

19. Brasted, 'Irish Home Rule Politics and India', pp. 410, 416.
20. O'Donnell, *The Irish Future*, pp. 13, 172, 208, 212–13, 224–6.
21. Cook, 'The Irish Raj', pp. 518–19; Brasted, 'Irish Home Rule Politics and India', p. 398.
22. Unpublished memoir, Wingate Papers; Du Boulay to Phelps, 11 Dec. 1893, Phelps Papers; Ibbetson note, 18 Dec. 1902, Curzon Papers; Sifton to father, 20 Feb. 1905, Sifton Papers.
23. Mackenzie Wallace to Maitland, 1 July 1887, Dufferin Papers.
24. Lyall to J. Lyall, 29 Aug. 1885, and File 48, Lyall Papers.
25. Letters between Elgin and Fowler and between Elgin and Elliott, Sept. 1894–Feb. 1895, Elgin Papers.
26. Cotton to Bayley, 18 Jan. 1895, Elgin Papers.
27. Cotton to Oldham, 22 Jan. 1895, and Elgin to Fowler, 23 Jan. 1895, Elgin Papers.
28. MacDonnell Papers, file 363.
29. *Tribune*, 7 June 1898.
30. File 14, Woodburn Papers.
31. L/PJ/6/27, file 1646, OIOC.
32. Letters between Northbrook and Hobart, Apr.–May 1874, Northbrook Papers.
33. File 108, Grant Duff Papers.
34. Bonus to Phelps, 10 Jan. 1889, Phelps Papers.
35. Ellis to Northbrook, 11 Apr. 1874, Northbrook Papers; Temple to Fergusson, 22 Apr. 1880, Fergusson Papers.
36. Copland, *The British Raj and the Indian Princes*, p. 197; Dufferin to Cross, 24 Aug. and 1 Oct. 1888, Dufferin Papers; letters from Lansdowne to Cross, Feb.–Mar. 1889, Lansdowne Papers.
37. Ibbetson note, 17 Dec. 1902, Curzon Papers.
38. Roberts to Kitchener, 27 Mar. 1903, Kitchener Papers; Curzon to Hamilton, 25 Mar. 1903, Curzon Papers.
39. Cross to Bombay Government, 4 Aug. 1887, L/PJ/6/201, OIOC.
40. Copland, *The British Raj and the Indian Princes*, pp. 195–7.
41. File 281, Curzon Papers.

CHAPTER 8: FRONTIERSMEN
1. O'Malley, *The Indian Civil Service*, pp. 56–8; Puri, *History of Indian Administration*, pp. 206–13; Elsmie, *Thirty-five Years in the Punjab*, pp. 293, 310, 337.
2. Lee, *Brothers in the Raj*, p. 321; Moon, *The British Conquest*, p. 623.
3. Lee, *Brothers in the Raj*, p. 145.
4. Unpublished memoir, Macnabb Papers.
5. File 7, Clerk Papers.
6. Lee, *Brothers in the Raj*, p. 300; unpublished memoir, Pearse Papers; Beames, *Memoirs of a Bengal Civilian*, pp. 102–3; unpublished memoir, Macnabb Papers.
7. Campbell, *Memoirs of My Indian Career*, Vol. 2, p. 8; Elsmie, *Thirty-five Years in the Punjab*, p. 98.
8. Moon, *The British Conquest*, pp. 624, 797–8; Bayly, *Indian Society and the Making of the British Empire*, p. 194; Lee, *Brothers in the Raj*, p. 403.
9. Meyer and Brysac, *Tournament of Shadows*, p. 109.
10. Meyer and Brysac, *Tournament of Shadows*, p. 156.
11. Curzon to Brodrick, 17 Apr. 1900, and Curzon to Chamberlain, 28 June 1902, Curzon Papers.
12. Gilmour, *Curzon*, pp. 196–8.
13. Masters, *Bugles and a Tiger*, p. 26.
14. Wilson, *Letters from India*, p. 215.

15. Metcalfe, *Ideologies of the Raj*, pp. 146–7.
16. *Emmanuel College Magazine* (1971–2); G.A. Anderson in Macdonald Papers; File 2, Dew Papers.
17. Warburton, *Eighteen Years in the Khyber*, pp. 126, 343.
18. File 200, Macnabb Papers.
19. Warburton, *Eighteen Years in the Khyber*, pp. 21–4, 40–1, 107–12; Elsmie, *Thirty-five Years in the Punjab*, pp. 175–6, 188–90, 207; Steevens, *In India*, pp. 167–8.
20. Kipling, 'The Story of Uriah'.
21. Note in Bruce Papers; Curzon to Roberts, 17 Mar. 1902, Curzon Papers; Dewey, *Anglo-Indian Attitudes*, p. 170.
22. J. Lyall to Bruce, 16 Jan. 1892, Bruce Papers.
23. Coen, *The Indian Political Service*, pp. 154–5; Woodruff, *The Guardians*, pp. 144–7; Durand to Lyall, 15 Apr. 1891, Durand Papers.
24. Coen, *The Indian Political Service*, p. 158; Woodruff, *The Guardians*, p. 147.
25. Warburton, *Eighteen Years in the Khyber*, p. 317.
26. Johnstone, *My Experiences in Manipur and the Naga Hills*, p. 30.
27. Cotton, *Indian & Home Memories*, pp. 143–4; Gait, *A History of Assam*, p. 316; Johnstone, *My Experiences in Manipur and the Naga Hills*, pp. 147–50, 274.
28. Johnstone, *My Experiences in Manipur and the Naga Hills*, pp. 19–20, 138–9, 190.
29. Grimwood, *My Three Years in Manipur*, pp. 2–49 *passim*.
30. Moon, *The British Conquest*, pp. 895–7; Roy, *History of Manipur*, pp. 136–7; Johnstone, *My Experiences in Manipur and the Naga Hills*, p. 278; Grimwood, *My Three Years in Manipur*, pp. 138ff.; Cotton, *Indian & Home Memories*, p. 253; Curzon to Hamilton, 21 Nov. 1901, Curzon Papers.

CHAPTER 9: RESIDENTS AND AGENTS
1. Curzon to Strachey, 25 July 1903, Strachey Papers.
2. Lee-Warner, *The Native States of India*, p. x.
3. Lee-Warner, *The Native States of India*, pp. ix–xii; Curzon to Edward VII, 19 June 1901, Curzon Papers; Godley to Curzon, 7 Nov. 1904, Godley Papers.
4. Curzon to Godley, 23 Feb. 1899, Curzon Papers; Northbrook to Strachey, 15 July 1874, Northbrook Papers; Elgin to Fowler, 17 Apr. 1894, Elgin Papers.
5. Durand to Reay, 13 Nov. 1887, Durand Papers.
6. Hill, *India*, pp. 135–6.
7. Copland, *The British Raj and the Indian Princes*, pp. 68–71.
8. Lee-Warner to Durand, 9 May 1887, Durand Papers.
9. Copland, *The British Raj and the Indian Princes*, pp. 66, 99, 104, 109–12, 187; Kincaid, *Forty-four Years a Public Servant*, p. 45; Maconochie, *Life in the Indian Civil Service*, p. 181.
10. Unpublished memoir, Hayward Papers.
11. Coen, *The Indian Political Service*, p. 37.
12. Kennion, *Diversions of an Indian Political*, p. 22; Chenevix Trench, *Viceroy's Agent*, p. 11; Lawrence, *The India We Served*, p. 38; Butler to father, 11 Apr. 1899, M. Butler Papers.
13. Copland, *The British Raj and the Indian Princes*, pp. 85–6.
14. Darling, *Apprentice to Power*, p. 146; Trevelyan, *The India We Left*, p. 158; Elgin to Mackenzie, 19 July 1895, Elgin Papers.
15. Lawrence, *The India We Served*, pp. 60–2.
16. Coen, *The Indian Political Service*, pp. 42–3.
17. Grigg to E. Grigg, 13 Feb. 1893, Grigg Papers.
18. Unpublished memoir, Dew Papers; Lawrence, *The India We Served*, pp. 128, 142.
19. Lawrence, *The India We Served*, pp. 66, 73.
20. Durand, *Alfred Lyall*, p. 183.
21. Kennion, *Diversions of an Indian Political*, p. 32.

22. Lawrence, *The India We Served*, p. 39.
23. Lyall to sister, 29 Apr. 1875, Lyall Papers; Coen, *The Indian Political Service*, p. 32.
24. Trevelyan, *The India We Left*, p. 154.
25. Jeffrey (ed.), *People, Princes and Paramount Power*, pp. 278–84; Copland, *The British Raj and the Indian Princes*, pp. 57–60.
26. Tweedie to Durand, 2 Aug. 1885, Durand Papers.
27. 1894 diary, Younghusband Papers; French, *Younghusband, passim*.
28. Chudgar, *Indian Princes under British Protection*, p. 7.
29. Meade to Durand, 10 May 1887, Durand Papers.
30. Malleson to Mayo, 29 Aug. 1869, Argyll Papers.
31. 'Method of work', Jan. 1902, note in Younghusband Papers.
32. Wylie to Durand, July 1885, Durand Papers.
33. Richardson to Phelps, 4 Nov. 1887, Phelps Papers.
34. Mangan, *The Games Ethic and Imperialism*, pp. 128–9, 133–5; Chudgar, *Indian Princes under British Protection*, pp. 9–11.
35. Curzon to Lamington, 4 Jan. 1904, Curzon Papers.
36. Lawrence, *The India We Served*, p. 111; Curzon to Hamilton, 28 Nov. 1900, Curzon Papers.
37. Curzon to Havelock, 14 July 1900, Curzon Papers.
38. Henvey to Durand, 17 June 1888, Durand Papers.
39. Curzon to Queen Victoria, 12 Sept. 1900, Curzon Papers; Martelli to Durand, 23 July 1887, Durand Papers.
40. St John to Durand, 20 Nov. 1885, Durand Papers.
41. Darling, *Apprentice to Power*, pp. 154–5, 224.
42. Notes for Minto, OIOC (Mss. EUR D.940); Curzon to Queen Victoria, 18 Nov. 1900, Curzon Papers; Lawrence, *The India We Served*, pp. 213–14; Scindia, *Princess*, p. 126; Tweedie to Durand, 2 Aug. 1885, Durand Papers.
43. Coen, *The Indian Political Service*, p. 69; Fuller, *The Empire of India*, pp. 247–8.
44. 'Method of work', Jan. 1902, note in Younghusband Papers.
45. 'Method of work', Jan. 1902, note in Younghusband Papers.
46. Durand to Henvey, 24 Feb. 1889, Durand Papers.
47. Durand to Griffin, 1 Sept. 1886, and to Cordery, 2 May 1887, Durand Papers.
48. Lawrence, *The India We Served*, p. 157; O'Dwyer, *India as I Knew It*, p. 135; scrapbook, Bayley Papers.
49. Jacob, *Diaries and Letters from India*, pp. 129–30.
50. Jeffrey (ed.), *People, Princes and Paramount Power*, p. 282.
51. Kipling, *From Sea to Sea*, Vol. 1, p. 52.
52. Jeffrey, *People, Princes and Paramount Power*, pp. 222–4.
53. Lee-Warner, *The Native States of India*, pp. 385–6; Fuller, *The Empire of India*, p. 246.
54. Copland, *The British Raj and the Indian Princes*, p. 305; Jeffrey, *People, Princes and Paramount Power*, pp. 35–6.
55. Trevelyan, *The India We Left*, p. 232.
56. Memo to Viceroy, 16 Aug. 1867, Temple Papers.
57. Durand to Bradford, 10 Apr. 1888, to Lyall, 3 June 1888, and to Plowden, 6 and 21 June 1888, Durand Papers.
58. Durand to Reay, 29 July 1887, Durand Papers.
59. Jain, *Concise History of Modern Rajasthan*, p. 63; Tupper, *Our Indian Protectorate*, p. 295.
60. Jain, *Concise History of Modern Rajasthan*, pp. 60–3; Moon, *The British Conquest*, p. 898.
61. Peile to Durand, 12 June 1887, and Reay to Durand, 10 Sept. 1887, Durand Papers.
62. Durand to Reay, 29 July 1887, Durand Papers.
63. Reay to Dufferin, Sept. 1887, Dufferin Papers.

64. Jeffrey, *People, Princes and Paramount Power*, pp. 112–13; File 13, Pelly Papers; Copland, *The British Raj and the Indian Princes*, pp. 141–52.
65. Lyall to mother, 11 June 1864, and sister, 2 Aug. 1865, Lyall Papers.
66. Beames, *Memoirs of a Bengal Civilian*, pp. 232–9; unpublished memoir, Macnabb Papers; Rivett-Carnac, *Many Memories*, pp. 125–6.
67. Temple, *The Story of My Life*, Vol. 1, p. 46; Elsmie, *Thirty-five Years in the Punjab*, p. 55; Beames, *Memoirs of a Bengal Civilian*, p. 107.
68. Cotton, *Indian & Home Memories*, p. 128; Rivett-Carnac, *Many Memories*, pp. 92–3, 135.
69. Temple, *The Story of My Life*, Vol. 1, p. 174; Temple to Cust, 2 July 1867, Temple Papers.
70. Dalrymple, *White Mughals*, pp. 348–9.
71. Temple, *Journals Kept in Hyderabad*, pp. 108–9.
72. Diary, Hyderabad 1867, and letters from Salar Jung to Temple, 1867, Temple Papers; Ray, *Hyderabad and British Paramountcy*, p. 59.
73. Diary, Hyderabad 1867, Temple Papers; Ray, *Hyderabad and British Paramountcy*, p. 169.
74. Jeffrey, *People, Princes and Paramount Power*, pp. 67–70; Digby, *Indian Problems for British Consideration*, pp. 27–8; Ray, *Hyderabad and British Paramountcy*, p. xiii; Raj, *Medievalism to Modernism*, pp. 11–15; Diary, Hyderabad 1867, Temple Papers.
75. Letters from Temple to Salar Jung, July–Oct. 1867, Temple Papers.
76. Northbrook to Clerk, 17 Jan. 1875, Clerk Papers.
77. Ray, *Hyderabad and British Paramountcy*, pp. 76–107 *passim*; Blunt, *Ideas about India*, p. 335; Lord, *The Maharajahs*, p. 81.
78. Northbrook to Davies, 2 Mar. 1875, Northbrook Papers.
79. *DNB* supplement, 1901–11.
80. Northbrook to Ripon, 6 and 13 Aug. 1880, Ripon to Northbrook, 21 Sept. 1880, Northbrook Papers.
81. Letters from Lyall to sister and brother, 1880–7, Lyall Papers; Dufferin to Cross, 29 June 1888, Dufferin Papers.
82. Khan, *The Begums of Bhopal, passim*; Ward to Durand, 24 July 1886, Durand Papers.
83. Khan, *The Begums of Bhopal*, pp. 134–6.
84. Durand to Griffin, 13 May 1886, Griffin to Durand, 27 May 1886, Durand Papers; Dufferin to Kimberley, 26 Apr. 1886, Dufferin Papers.
85. Henvey to Durand, 4 June 1888, Durand to Henvey, 12 July 1888, Durand Papers; Khan, *The Begums of Bhopal*, pp. 140–2; Curzon notes for Minto, OIOC (Mss. EUR D.940).
86. Dufferin to Cross, 23 Apr. 1887, Dufferin Papers; Lyall to sister, 22 Feb. 1887, Lyall Papers.
87. Henvey to Durand, 14 Aug. 1888, Durand Papers; Lawrence, *The India We Served*, p. 185; Curzon to Queen Victoria, 17 May 1899, Curzon Papers.
88. Dufferin to Cross, 14 July 1887, Dufferin Papers; letters from Griffin to Durand, May–Aug. 1887, Bannerman to Durand, 2 Sept. 1887, Durand Papers.
89. Lord, *The Maharajahs*, pp. 68–9.
90. Maynard to Eppes, 6 Sept. 1895 and 25 Dec. 1902, and File 67, Maynard Papers.
91. Maynard diary and letters to mother, 1889–91, Maynard Papers.

CHAPTER 10: MANDARINS
1. Maynard to mother, 31 Jan. 1892, Maynard Papers; Wilson, *Letters from India*, pp. 367, 413–14; obituaries in Yule Papers.
2. O'Dwyer, *India as I Knew It*, pp. 49–50.
3. Babington Smith to Buckland, 22 Feb. 1896, Elgin Papers; Howell to Northbrook, 1 May 1878, Northbrook Papers.

4. Files 1 and 2, Howard Papers.
5. Unpublished memoir, Hayward Papers; Waley-Cohen, *A Young Victorian in India*, p. 171.
6. Letters from Lyall to mother and sisters, 1873–4, Lyall Papers.
7. Kipling, 'The Conversion of Aurelian McGoggin'; Aberigh-Mackay, *Twenty-one Days in India*, p. 41.
8. Lawrence diary, 1902, Lawrence Papers; Curzon to Craigie, 17 Apr. 1899, Curzon to Godley, 26 Jan. 1899, Curzon Papers; Fraser, *India under Curzon*, pp. 376–80.
9. Curzon to Cuningham, 23 Jan. 1899.
10. Article by 'Vermicelli' in the *Pioneer*, 14 May 1897; Thorburn, *His Majesty's Greatest Subject*, p. 101.
11. Beveridge, *India Called Them*, p. 381.
12. Hunter, *The Old Missionary*, p. 67.
13. Letters from Butler to uncle, 1891–7, H. Butler Papers.
14. Hall, *The Passing of Empire*, pp. 63–4; Hamilton to Curzon, 20 Oct. 1899, Curzon Papers.
15. Ewing, 'Administering India', pp. 43–8; O'Malley, *The Indian Civil Service*, p. 113; Tupper, *Our Indian Protectorate*, p. 315.
16. 'Captain Cuttle', column in the *Englishman*, mid-Aug. 1901; Steevens, *In India*, p. 177.
17. Trevelyan, *The India We Left*, pp. 155–6.
18. Private Secretary to Money, 20 Apr. 1856, Money Papers.
19. Dufferin to Cross, 18 Oct. and 16 Nov. 1886, Dufferin Papers.
20. Fitzpatrick to Ilbert, 11 Mar. 1887, Ilbert Papers.
21. Letters from Lyall to sisters, 1877–8, Lyall Papers.
22. See correspondence in the *Pioneer*, Mar.–May 1897.
23. *Bombay Gazette*, 7 Nov. 1861.
24. Tweedie to Durand, 10 Aug. 1885, Durand Papers.
25. Jardine to Bombay CS, 21 May 1875, Hope Papers; dispatch from Bombay Government, L/PJ/6/50, file 1375, OIOC.
26. Waley-Cohen, *A Young Victorian in India*, p. 45.
27. Beames, *Memoirs of a Bengal Civilian*, p. 259.
28. Beveridge, *India Called Them*, p. 282.
29. Francis to Phelps, 22 Sept. 1892, Phelps Papers.
30. Butler to sister, 26 Dec. 1892, H. Butler Papers.
31. *Civil & Military Gazette*, 9 July 1885.
32. Lee, *Brothers in the Raj*, p. 392.
33. Price, *Ootacamund*, p. 38; L/PJ/6/63, file 114, OIOC.
34. Campbell, *Memoirs of My Indian Career*, Vol. 2, pp. 96, 207, 279–80; Waley-Cohen, *A Young Victorian in India*, p. 213.
35. Temple to Fergusson, 6 May 1880, Fergusson to Kimberley, 20 July 1884, Fergusson Papers; unpublished memoir, Hayward Papers.
36. Dufferin to Ilbert, 26 July 1888, Ilbert Papers; M. Curzon to Curzon, 6 Mar. 1899, Curzon Papers.
37. Wilkinson, *Two Monsoons*, pp. 195–6.
38. MacDonnell to Elgin, 2 Jan. 1895, Elgin Papers; *Naini Tal*, p. 95.
39. Waley-Cohen, *A Young Victorian in India*, p. 213; newspaper cuttings and note by Durand, 9 Mar. 1868, Clerk Papers.
40. Fraser, *India under Curzon*, pp. 471–2.
41. Lyall to sister, 17 Apr. 1873, Lyall Papers; MacDonnell to the *Englishman*, July 1884, MacDonnell Papers; Kanwar, *Imperial Simla*, p. 45.
42. Panter-Downes, *Ooty Preserved*, p. 11; Morris, *Stones of Empire*, p. 198.

43. Civilian, *The Civilian's South India*, p. 172; Wilkinson, *Two Monsoons*, p. 93; Lutyens, *The Lyttons in India*, p. 112.
44. Price, *Ootacamund*, pp. 69, 248; Civilian, *A Civilian's South India*, p. 171.

CHAPTER 11: LIFE AT THE TOP

1. Lutyens, *The Lyttons in India*, p. 27; Strachey, *The Strachey Line*, p. 162.
2. Dufferin to Cross, 3 Sept. 1886, Dufferin Papers.
3. Curzon to Godley, 23 Sept. 1903, and Curzon to Brodrick, 24 Mar. 1904, Curzon Papers.
4. Maconochie, *Life in the Indian Civil Service*, p. 90.
5. Garth, *A Few Plain Truths about India*, pp. 14, 19; Hunter, *Imperial Gazetteer*, Vol. 4, pp. 131–2.
6. Lyall to sister, 15 Sept. 1882, Lyall Papers.
7. Curzon to Selborne, 29 May 1901, Curzon Papers.
8. Bennett, *The Ilberts in India*, p. 27; Curzon to Godley, 27 Nov. 1899, Curzon Papers.
9. 31 Mar. 1866.
10. Campbell, *Memoirs of My Indian Career*, Vol. 2, pp. 193–7; Cotton, *Indian & Home Memories*, p. 118.
11. Seal, *The Emergence of Indian Nationalism*, p. 151; Dufferin to Kimberley, 2 July 1886, Dufferin Papers.
12. Griffin to Durand, 25 Apr. 1886, Durand Papers; Foster, *Lord Randolph Churchill*, p. 172.
13. Lyall to sister, 21 Sept. 1885, and to brother, 4 Oct. 1885 and 16 May 1886, Lyall Papers.
14. Dufferin to Cross, 3 Sept. and 18 Oct. 1886, and Griffin to Dufferin, 24 Sept. 1886, Dufferin Papers.
15. Dufferin to Cross, 25 Oct. 1886 and 23 Apr. 1887, Dufferin Papers.
16. Griffin to Dufferin, 26 Mar. 1887, and Dufferin to Cross, 2 Apr. 1887, Dufferin Papers.
17. Temple, *The Story of My Life*, Vol. 2, p. 5; Campbell, *Memoirs of My Indian Career*, Vol. 2, p. 203.
18. Butler to Scott, 1 Oct. 1920, Scott Papers; Elgin to Hamilton, 16 June 1896, Elgin Papers.
19. Kipling, 'On the City Wall'.
20. Maconochie to Phelps, 17 Sept. 1890, Phelps Papers.
21. Dufferin to Cross, 30 Jan. 1888, Dufferin Papers.
22. Lyall's letters to sisters, 1882–7, Lyall Papers; Durand, *Alfred Lyall*, pp. 251–319 *passim*.

CHAPTER 12: THINKERS

1. Goudge, 'Letters from Oudh', 2 Nov. 1917, Goudge Papers; Mason, *A Shaft of Sunlight*, p. 104; Furbank, *E. M. Forster*, Vol. 2, p. 129; Seal, *The Emergence of Indian Nationalism*, p. 136.
2. Butler to uncle, 12 Mar. and 29 Oct. 1891, H. Butler Papers.
3. Bosanquet to Phelps, 9 Jan. 1894, and Dobbs to Phelps, 26 Aug. 1893, Phelps Papers.
4. Letters to Phelps from various correspondents, 1889–91, Phelps Papers; Maconochie, *Life in the Indian Civil Service*, p. 39.
5. Various correspondents in Phelps Papers.
6. Goudge, 'Letters from Oudh', 23 Feb. 1917, Goudge Papers; Enthoven to Phelps, 27 Aug. 1893, Phelps Papers; Macleod, *Impressions of an Indian Civil Sevant*, p. 150.
7. Letters from Le Mesurier and Francis to Phelps, 1895–1900, Phelps Papers.
8. Darling, *Apprentice to Power*, pp. 31, 175, 192; Dewey, *Anglo-Indian Attitudes*, p. 120.

9. Howell to Northbrook, 1 May 1878, Northbrook Papers; Elliott to Elgin, 25 Apr. 1895, Elgin Papers.
10. Le Mesurier to Phelps, 10 Mar. 1895, Phelps Papers.
11. Goudge, 'Letters for Oudh', 7 Mar. 1917, Goudge Papers; information from Anne Chisholm.
12. Bayly, *Empire & Information*, p. 360.
13. Lyall to sisters, 15 Apr. and 12 July 1869, Lyall Papers.
14. McMillan, *Divers Ditties Written Chiefly in India*, p. 18.
15. Lyall, *Verses Written in India*, pp. 114–15.
16. Durand, *Alfred Lyall*, p. 152.
17. Lyall to mother, 1 Oct. 1869 and 9 July 1877, Lyall Papers.
18. Lyall, *Verses Written in India*, p. 17.
19. Darling, *Apprentice to Power*, p. 182.
20. Cotton, *Indian & Home Memories*, pp. 107–10; *Civil & Military Gazette*, 28 and 29 Jan. 1887.
21. Beames, *Memoirs of a Bengal Civilian*, pp. 184, 193, 202.
22. Whish, *A District Office in Northern India*, p. 5.
23. Brodie, *The Devil Drives*, pp. 293–8.
24. Dufferin to Cross, 8 Mar. and 23 Oct. 1887, Dufferin Papers.
25. Sengoopta, *The Imprint of the Raj*, p. 45.
26. Ramusack, *The Indian Princes and Their States*, p. 88; see critisicm of these views in Washbrook's essay in Winks (ed.), *Historiography*, pp. 600–4.
27. Sengoopta, *The Imprint of the Raj*, pp. 44–5.
28. Said, *Orientalism*, p. 11.
29. Northbrook to Dufferin, 8 Sept. 1884, Dufferin Papers; Maynard to Murray, 20 Mar. 1887, Murray Papers.
30. Lawrence, *The India We Served*, p. 157; Hose to Phelps, 10 June 1888, Phelps Papers; Symonds, *Oxford and Empire*, p. 202; Curzon to Ampthill, 17 Sept. 1900, Curzon Papers; Egerton to Phelps, 26 Sept. 1899, Phelps Papers.
31. Butler to uncle, 29 Oct. 1891, H. Butler Papers; Butler to Scott, 29 Nov. 1925, Scott Papers.
32. White, *A Civil Servant in India*, p. 25.
33. Reay to Rosebery, 3 Apr. and 14 July 1885, Rosebery Papers; Francis to Phelps, 24 Sept. 1893, Phelps Papers.
34. Conchman to Phelps, 30 May 1898, Francis to Phelps, 19 Aug. 1893, Phelps Papers; Butler to uncle, 29 Oct. 1891, H. Butler Papers; Kipling, *Letters of Travel*, p. 237.
35. Butler to Phelps, 12 Apr. 1893, Phelps Papers; Butler to uncle, 29 Oct. 1891, H. Butler Papers.
36. Fuller to Curzon, 29 July 1905, Curzon Papers.
37. Beveridge, *India Called Them*, pp. 96–9.
38. Cotton, *Indian & Home Memories*, pp. 136–7.
39. Temple memo for Viceroy, 16 Aug. 1867, Temple Papers.
40. Bayly, *The Local Roots of Indian Politics*, p. 56; Kipling, 'The Mother-Lodge'.
41. Northbrook to Queen Victoria, 11 Aug. 1872, Northbrook Papers; Cotton, *Indian & Home Memories*, p. 203.
42. Sifton to father, 19 Mar. and 10 June 1903, Sifton Papers; Beveridge, *India Called Them*, pp. 210–11.
43. Wilson, *Letters from India*, p. 140; Darling, *Apprentice to Power*, p. 180; King, *The Diary of a Civilian's Wife in India*, Vol. 1, p. 48; *Civil & Military Gazette*, 28 Jan. 1887.
44. Butler to father, 2 Nov. 1898, H. Butler Papers; Daniels to Phelps, n.d., Phelps Papers.

45. Lawrence, *The India We Served*, p. 140.
46. Curzon to Hamilton, 20 Mar. 1902, Curzon Papers.
47. Roberts, *Forty-one Years in India*, Vol. 2, pp. 387–8.
48. Ex-Civilian, *Life in the Mofussil*, Vol. 1, pp. 146–7; unpublished memoir, H. Butler Papers.
49. Owen, *Lord Cromer*, p. 168.
50. Lyall to sister, n.d. 1872 and 5 Nov. 1883, Lyall Papers.
51. Lyall to sisters, 16 June 1882 and 25 May 1883, Lyall Papers.
52. 'Method of Work', memo of Jan. 1902, Younghusband Papers.
53. Beveridge, *India Called Them*, p. 384.
54. Spangenberg, *British Bureaucracy in India*, p. 350.
55. Cotton, *Indian & Home Memories*, p. 277.
56. Cotton, *New India*, p. viii.
57. Bayley to Wallace, 5 Sept. 1887, Dufferin Papers.
58. Spangenberg, *British Bureaucracy in India*, p. 165; letter from Bombay Government to Sec. of State, 31 Jan. 1880, L/PJ/6/6, file 271, OIOC.

CHAPTER 13: PLAYERS
1. Elsmie, *Thirty-five Years in the Punjab*, pp. 121, 140.
2. Chettar, *The Steel Frame and I*, p. 57.
3. Durand to Ridgeway, 12 May 1889, Durand Papers; Crosthwaite to Ilbert, 29 Sept. 1886, Ilbert Papers; O'Dwyer, *India as I Knew It*, p. 48; Guha, *A Corner of a Foreign Field*, pp. xi–xii, 6, 104, 134.
4. Cotton, *Indian & Home Memories*, pp. 104–5.
5. Blunt, *The I.C.S.*, p. 229; Maconochie, *Life in the Indian Civil Service*, p. 26.
6. Price, *Ootacamund*, p. 401.
7. Simson, *Letters on Sport in Eastern Bengal*, pp. 6–10, 30.
8. Ex-Civilian, *Life in the Mofussil*, Vol. 2, p. 166; Calcutta Tent Club Rules, 1883–4.
9. Baden-Powell, *Pig-Sticking or Hog-Hunting*, pp. 72–3, 279; Blunt, *The I.C.S.*, p. 26.
10. Kincaid, *Forty-four Years a Public Servant*, p. 52.
11. Simson, *Letters on Sport in Eastern Bengal*, pp. 248, 250.
12. Book review by Howell, file 5, Howell Papers.
13. Cotton, *Indian & Home Memories*, p. 74; Durand, *Alfred Lyall*, p. 94; Lyall to mother, 3 May 1877, Lyall Papers.
14. Campbell, *Memoirs of My Indian Life*, Vol. 1, p 11.
15. Unpublished memoir, Moore Papers.
16. Maconochie, *Life in the Indian Civil Service*, p. 86; Mason, *A Shaft of Sunlight*, p. 122.
17. Maynard to mother, 23 June 1887, Maynard Papers.
18. Gilmour, *Curzon*, pp. 204–6; Lyall to sister, 10 June 1881, Lyall Papers; Dawkins to Curzon, 25 July 1902, Curzon Papers.
19. Lawrence, *The India We Served*, pp. 80–2; introduction to Lawrence diaries, Lawrence Papers.
20. Welldon, *Recollections and Reflections*, p. 219.
21. *Naini Tal*, p. 55; Blunt, *The I.C.S.*, p. 223; *Indian Daily Telegraph*, 24 Sept. 1901.
22. Allen, *Plain Tales from the Raj*, p. 132; unpublished memoir of Iris Portal, Portal Papers.
23. Du Cane to Du Cane, 30 May 1885, Du Cane Papers.
24. Unpublished memoir, Pearse Papers.
25. Curzon to Queen Victoria, 23 Mar. 1899, Curzon Papers.
26. Green, *Kipling: The Critical Heritage*, p. 40.
27. Conchman to Phelps, 30 Oct. 1894, Phelps Papers.
28. Diver, *The Englishwoman in India*, pp. 23–4.

29. Lutyens, *The Lyttons in India*, pp. 154–5; Longford, *A Pilgrimage of Passion*, pp. 152, 162.
30. Butler to Scott, 26 June and 1 Oct. 1920, Scott Papers.
31. Civil Service Regulations, 1900.
32. Official record, Beveridge Papers.
33. Letters from Horsley to father, 1886–7, Horsley Papers.
34. Buettner, *Empire Families*, pp. 208–30 *passim*.
35. Trevelyan, *Competition Wallah*, p. 153.
36. Aberigh-Mackay, *Twenty-one Days in India*, p. 87; O'Dwyer, *India as I Knew It*, p. 147.
37. Diary, 3 Mar. 1894, Younghusband Papers.
38. Unpublished memoir, Bowring Papers.
39. Hutchins, *An Indian Career*, pp. 38–41, 71; Elsmie, *Thirty-five Years in the Punjab*, p. 144.
40. Campbell, *Memoirs of My Indian Career*, Vol. 1, pp. 132–5, and Vol. 2, pp. 184–97.

CHAPTER 14: HUSBANDS AND LOVERS
1. Unpublished memoirs, Hubback and Hayward Papers.
2. Kipling, 'The Story of the Gadsbys'.
3. Lee to Phelps, 28 June 1890, Phelps Papers.
4. Hose to Phelps, 20 Dec. 1887, Phelps Papers.
5. Note by daughter in Maynard Papers; Beveridge, *India Called Them*, pp. 50–3.
6. Lee, *Brothers in the Raj*, p. 89.
7. Unpublished memoir, Bowring Papers.
8. L/PJ/6/2, file 67, OIOC.
9. Curzon's notes for Minto, 1905, OIOC *Mss*. EUR D.940; Lupton to daughter, 7 May 1950, Lupton Papers.
10. Unpublished memoir, Bowring Papers; Horsley to father, 23 July 1871, Horsley Papers.
11. Unpublished memoir, Dew Papers,
12. Unpublished memoir, Hayward Papers.
13. Note in Partridge Papers.
14. Wilkinson, *Two Monsoons*, p. 112.
15. Dalrymple, *White Mughals*, pp. 119–20, 182–3, 263, 337, 363.
16. Brodie, *The Devil Drives*, pp. 51–2.
17. Kincaid, *Forty-four Years a Public Servant*, p. 5.
18. Lecture on Burma by Heald, OIOC *Mss*. EUR D.688; Hyam, *Empire and Sexuality*, p. 108.
19. Hamilton to Curzon, 4 July 1901, Curzon Papers.
20. Crosthwaite to White, 5 Oct. 1888, and Mackenzie note, 3 May 1892, White Papers.
21. Fryer to Curzon, 1 June 1900, Curzon Papers.
22. Curzon to Fryer, 7 Apr. 1900, and to Hamilton, 24 July 1901, Curzon Papers; Fryer to Curzon, 24 Apr. 1900, Curzon Papers.
23. Ballhatchet, *Race, Sex and Class under the Raj*, p. 149; Curzon to Fryer, 1 June 1900, Curzon Papers.
24. Fryer to Curzon, 24 Apr. 1900, 17 Aug. 1901, 28 Nov. 1902, Curzon Papers; Fryer to Elgin, 11 Oct. 1895, Elgin Papers; Ballhatchet, *Race, Sex and Class under the Raj*, pp. 149–53.
25. Ballhatchet, *Race, Sex and Class under the Raj*, pp. 153–4; Hamilton to Curzon, 15 Aug. 1901, Curzon Papers.
26. Steel, *The Garden of Fidelity*, pp. 124–5.
27. Yalland, *Boxwallahs*, p. 187.
28. Caine, *Bombay to Bloomsbury*, pp. 70–1.

29. Lyall to sisters, 17 Oct. 1867 and 20 July 1883, Lyall Papers.
30. Lyall letters to sisters, 1865–87, letters from Rachel Holmes to Lyall, 1874–81, Lyall Papers.

CHAPTER 15: FAMILIES AND EXILES
1. Diver, *The Englishwoman in India*, pp. 8, 111.
2. Holroyd, *Lytton Strachey*, Vol. 1, p. 16; Caine, *Bombay to Bloomsbury*, p. 62.
3. Unpublished memoir, Hayward Papers.
4. Beames, *Memoirs of a Bengal Civilian*, pp. 185–6.
5. Jessie's diary, Sept. 1891, Partridge Papers.
6. Appendix C to ICS memo 1921, Indian Civil Service (Retired) Association Collection.
7. Dewey, *Anglo-Indian Attitudes*, p. 147.
8. Dewey, *Anglo-Indian Attitudes*, p. 158.
9. Beveridge, *India Called Them*, pp. 182, 195–8.
10. King, *The Diary of a Civilian's Wife in India*, Vol. 2, p. 145.
11. Du Boulay to Phelps, 26 Oct. 1890, Phelps Papers.
12. Burton, *The Raj at Table*, pp. 8–9, 27.
13. Burton, *The Raj at Table*, pp. 204, 208–10; Cotton, *Indian & Home Memories*, p. 85; Hutchins, *An Indian Career*, p. 18.
14. Golant, *The Long Afternoon*, p. xi.
15. King, *The Diary of a Civilian's Wife in India*, Vol. 1, p. 41.
16. Skrine, *Life of Sir William Wilson Hunter*, p. 68.
17. Letters to Phelps from India, Phelps Papers.
18. Letters from Lyall to Jackson and to sisters, 1866–77, Lyall Papers.
19. Fuller, *The Empire of India*, p. 195.
20. Fuller, *The Empire of India*, p. 196.
21. Letters from Horsley to father, 1882–92, Horsley Papers.
22. Buettner, *Empire Families*, pp. 151–78 *passim*.
23. Caine, *Bombay to Bloomsbury*, p. 52.
24. Brettner, *Empire Families*, p. 127.
25. Lyall to sisters, 27 July 1883 and 8 Feb. 1886, Lyall Papers.
26. Elsmie, *Thirty-five Years in the Punjab*, p. 352.
27. Beveridge, *India Called Them*, p. 394.
28. Files 6 and 7 in Nicoll Collection.
29. Durand to Barnes, 2 Oct. 1892, Durand Papers.
30. Stokes to Currie, 20 Sept. 1874, Stokes Papers.
31. Allen, *Plain Tales from the Raj*, p. 174.
32. Fryer to Elgin, 28 Mar. 1896, Elgin Papers; Pinney, *Kipling's India*, p. 285.
33. Powell, *Flora Annie Steel*, p. 63.
34. Butler to father, 2 Oct. 1891, H. Butler Papers; Wilkinson, *Two Monsoons*, p. 202; Warburton, *Eighteen Years in the Khyber*, pp. 37–9; note by Anderson in Macdonald Papers.
35. *India Office List*, 1880.
36. Grigg Papers.

CHAPTER 16: PENSIONERS
1. Civil Service Regulations, 1900.
2. Unpublished memoirs, Evans Papers.
3. Goudge, 'Letters from Oudh', 24 Aug. 1917, Goudge Papers.
4. See correspondence in the *Pioneer*, Mar.–Sept. 1897, MacDonnell Papers.
5. Beveridge, *India Called Them*, pp. 231–4, 248.

6. Rivett-Carnac, *Many Memories*, pp. 397–8.
7. File 9, Indian Civil Service (Retired) Association Collection.
8. Butler to Scott, 13 July 1928, Scott Papers.
9. Lupton to daughter, 7 May 1950, Lupton Papers.
10. Obituary in Vol. IV, 1971–2.
11. Note in Samman Papers.
12. O'Malley, *The Indian Civil Service*, p. 274.
13. File 54, Grant Papers.
14. Cotton, *Indian & Home Memories*, p. 115.
15. Temple, *The Story of My Life*, Vol. 2, pp. 85–9; Temple to Fergusson, 22 Apr. 1880, Fergusson Papers.
16. Cotton, *Indian & Home Memories*, p. 128; *Dictionary of National Biography*; O'Malley, *The Indian Civil Service*, p. 277.
17. Cotton, *Indian & Home Memories*, pp. 293–8, 334.
18. Ritchie to Curzon, 12 July 1901, Curzon Papers.
19. Curzon to Hamilton, 4 June 1902, Curzon Papers.
20. Durand, *Alfred Lyall*, pp. 318–19.
21. Lawrence, *The India We Served*, p. 267.
22. Lyall letters to siblings, 1878–88; S. Lyall to J. Lyall, 5 Nov. 1888; Durand, *Alfred Lyall*, pp. 318–457 *passim*.
23. Lyall to Grant Duff, 24 June 1887, Lyall Papers.
24. H. Trevelyan, *The India We Left*, pp. 61–2; G. O. Trevelyan, *Competition Wallah*, p. 154.
25. *An Indian Day*, p. 207.
26. Maconochie, *Life in the Indian Civil Service*, p. 1.
27. Unpublished memoirs, Evans Papers.
28. Kipling, 'In Partibus'.
29. Trevelyan, *The India We Left*, p. 133; Riddick, *Who Was Who in India*.
30. Partridge Papers.
31. Letters from King to Le Mesurier, 1918–22, Le Mesurier Papers.
32. Lawrence, *The India We Served*, p. 122.
33. Maynard to mother, 22 Nov. 1891, Maynard Papers.
34. Lupton to daughter, 7 May 1950, Lupton Papers.

Bibliography

~

ABBREVIATIONS
CSAS = Centre of South Asian Studies (Cambridge)
OIOC = Oriental and India Office Collections, British Library
PRO = Public Record Office

MANUSCRIPT COLLECTIONS

Ampthill, 2nd Baron, OIOC
Anderson, Gordon Hay (in Macdonald Papers), CSAS
Argyll, 8th Duke of, OIOC
Barnes, Sir Hugh, Bodleian Library
Barrow, Sir Edmund, OIOC
Bayley, Sir Charles Stuart, private collection
Bellasis, Augustus Fortunatus, OIOC
Beveridge, Henry, OIOC
Bowring, Lewin, OIOC
Bruce, Richard Isaac, OIOC
Butler, Sir Harcourt, OIOC (*see also* Lord Francis Scott)
Butler, Sir Montagu, OIOC
Calcutta Tent Club, OIOC
Campbell, Sir George, OIOC
Caroe, Sir Olaf, OIOC
Chenevix Trench, Charles, OIOC
Clerk, Sir George, OIOC
Cubitt, Major W. M., OIOC
Curzon, 1st Lord, OIOC
Dennys, Colonel W. A. B. (in Heaney Papers), CSAS
Dew, Sir Armine, OIOC
Dowdall, Lieutenant Thomas, OIOC
Du Cane, Sir Edmund, Bodleian Library

Dufferin, 1st Marquess of, OIOC
Durand, Sir Henry Mortimer, OIOC
Elgin, 9th Earl of, OIOC
Esher, 2nd Viscount, Churchill College, Cambridge
Evans, Richardson, OIOC
Fergusson, Sir James, OIOC
Foster, William, CSAS
Foulis, D., National Library of Scotland
Fryer, Sir Frederick, OIOC
Godley, Sir Arthur (in Kilbracken Papers), OIOC
Goudge, Joseph, private collection
Grant, Sir Charles, OIOC
Grant Duff, Sir Mountstuart, OIOC
Grigg, Harry, private collection
Hailey, 1st Baron , OIOC
Hamilton, Lord George, OIOC
Harris, 4th Baron, OIOC
Heald, Sir Benjamin, OIOC
Herschel, Sir William, OIOC
Hope, Sir Theodore, OIOC
Horsley, William, OIOC
Howard, Sir Henry, OIOC
Howell, Sir Evelyn, OIOC
Hubback, Sir John, CSAS
Ilbert, Sir Courtenay, OIOC
Jowett, Benjamin, Balliol College, Oxford
Keyes, Brigadier-General Sir Terence, OIOC
Kipling, Rudyard, University of Sussex
Kitchener, 1st Earl, PRO and British Library
Lamington, 2nd Baron, OIOC
Lansdowne, 5th Marquess of, OIOC and private collection
Lawrence, Sir John, OIOC
Lawrence, Sir Walter, OIOC
Le Mesurier, Sir Havilland, OIOC
Lee-Warner, Sir William, OIOC
Lowis, Cecil, OIOC
Lupton, Dr Walter, OIOC
Lyall, Sir Alfred, OIOC
Lyall, Sir James, OIOC
MacDonnell, Sir Antony, Bodleian Library
Macleod, Roderick, CSAS
Macnabb Collection, OIOC
Maxwell, Sir Reginald and Lady, CSAS
Maynard, Sir John, OIOC
Minns, Christopher, OIOC
Minto, 4th Earl of, National Library of Scotland
Money, William, OIOC
Moore, James, OIOC
Morley, John, OIOC
Murray, Gilbert, Bodleian Library
Nicholl, General Thomas, OIOC
Northbrook, 1st Earl of, OIOC

Bibliography

Parry, Mrs N. E., CSAS
Partridge, Reginald, private collection
Pearse, General George, OIOC
Pelly, Sir Lewis, OIOC
Penny, Sir James, CSAS
Phelps, Reverend Lionel, Oriel College, Oxford
Portal, Mrs Iris, CSAS
Prinsep, Edward Augustus, OIOC
Richards, H. Erle, OIOC
Ripon, 1st Marquess of, British Library
Rosebery, 5th Earl of, National Library of Scotland
Samman, H. F., OIOC
Scott, Lord Francis, private collection
Sifton, Sir James, OIOC
Stokes, Sir Henry, CSAS
Strachey, Sir John, OIOC
Temple, Sir Richard, OIOC
Thompson, Sir John Perronet, OIOC
Unceremonials Club, OIOC
Ward, F. W., OIOC
Wenlock, 3rd Baron, OIOC
White, Sir Herbert Thirkell, OIOC
Wingate, Sir Andrew, CSAS
Woodburn, Sir John, OIOC
Yeats-Brown, F., University of Texas, Austin
Younghusband, Sir Francis, OIOC
Yule, Sir George, OIOC

INDIA OFFICE AND GOVERNMENT OF INDIA FILES AND PUBLICATIONS IN THE OIOC

Census of India, 1871–1901
Crown Representatives' Records at Indian States' Residencies (R/2)
East India College Haileybury Records
East India Register and Directory, 1820–42
History of Services (V/12)
Imperial Gazetteer of India, 1881–1909
India List, Civil and Military, 1861–1895
India Office List, 1886–1922
India Register, 1843–1860
Indian Civil Service (Retired) Association Collection
Indian Home Department, *A Manual of Rules and Regulations*, 1885–1913 (V/27/212/1–5)
Languages of India (Statistical Office, East India House, 1852)
Procedures of the Public Service Commission, 1886–7
Public and Judicial Department Records (L/PJ/6)
Records of Pensions and Annuities (L/AG/21)
Records of Service (L/F/10)

Bibliography

BOOKS AND ARTICLES

Except for university presses, the place of publication is London unless otherwise stated.

Aberigh-Mackay, George, *Twenty-one Days in India*, Allen, 1881
Ahmed, Rafiuddin, *The Bengal Muslims, 1871–1906: A Quest for Identity*, OUP (Delhi), 1981
Alder, G. J., *British India's Northern Frontier, 1865–95*, Longmans, 1963
Allardyce, Alexander, *The City of Sunshine*, Blackwood (Edinburgh), 1877
Allen, Charles, *Lives of the Indian Princes*, Arrow, 1984
—— *Plain Tales from the Raj*, André Deutsch, 1975
—— *Soldier Sahibs*, John Murray, 2000
Anand, Sushila, *Indian Sahib*, Duckworth, 1996
Arnold, David, *Colonizing the Body: State Medicine and Epidemic Disease in Nineteenth Century India*, University of California Press (Berkeley), 1993
—— *Famine*, Blackwell (Oxford), 1988
Ashton, S. R., *British Policy towards the Indian States, 1905–1939*, Curzon Press, 1982
Asquith, Margot, *More Memories*, Cassell, 1933
Atkinson, George, *Curry and Rice*, Dakshin (Madras), 2001
Baden-Powell, Robert, *Pig-Sticking or Hog-Hunting*, Herbert Jenkins, 1924
Baker, C. J., and Washbrook, D. A., *South India: Political Institutions and Political Change, 1880–1920*, Macmillan (Delhi), 1975
Ballhatchet, Kenneth, *Race, Sex and Class under the Raj*, Weidenfeld & Nicolson, 1980
Banerjea, Surendranath, *A Nation in Making*, OUP (Calcutta), 1925
Banerjee, Sarmila, *Studies in Administrative History of Bengal*, Rajesh (New Delhi), 1978
Barr, Pat, *The Memsahibs*, Secker & Warburg, 1976
Bayly, C. A., *Empire & Information*, Cambridge University Press, 1996
—— *The Birth of the Modern World, 1780–1914*, Blackwell (Oxford), 2004
—— *Indian Society and the Making of the British Empire*, Cambridge University Press, 1990
—— *The Local Roots of Indian Politics: Allahabad, 1880–1920*, Clarendon Press (Oxford), 1975
—— (ed.) *The Raj: India and the British, 1600–1947*, National Portrait Gallery, 1990
Beames, John, *Memoirs of a Bengal Civilian*, Eland, 1990
Bence-Jones, Mark, *The Viceroys of India*, Constable, 1982
Bennet, Mary, *The Ilberts in India*, BACSA, 1995
Beveridge, Lord, *India Called Them*, George Allen, 1947
Bhanja, K. C., *Darjeeling at a Glance*, Oxford Book & Stationery Company (Darjeeling), 1941
Bhasin, Raja, *Simla*, Penguin (Delhi), 1992
Birdwood, George, *Competition and the Indian Civil Service*, Henry S. King, 1872
Blunt, Edward, *The I.C.S.*, Faber, 1937
Blunt, Wilfrid Scawen, *Ideas about India*, Kegan Paul, 1885
Bonarjee, N. B., *Under Two Masters*, OUP, 1970
Boxwallah, *An Eastern Backwater*, Andrew Melrose, n.d.
Bradley, John, *Lady Curzon's India*, Weidenfeld & Nicolson, 1985
Brasted, Howard V., 'Irish Home Rule Politics and India, 1873–1886: Frank Hugh O'Donnell and Other Irish "Friends of India"', Edinburgh University doctoral thesis, 1974
Brodie, Fawn, *The Devil Drives: A Life of Sir Richard Burton*, Eland, 1986
Brown, Hilton, *Parry's of Madras*, Parry (Madras), n.d.
—— *The Sahibs*, William Hodge, 1948
Brown, Judith M., and Louis, Wm. Roger (eds.), *The Twentieth Century*, OUP, 1999
Brown, R. Grant, *Burma as I Saw It, 1889–1917*, Methuen, 1926

Bibliography

Buck, Edward J., *Simla Past and Present*, The Times Press (Bombay), 1925
Buckland, C. E., *Bengal under the Lieutenant-Governors*, 2 vols., Lahiri (Calcutta), 1901
Buettner, Elizabeth, *Imperial Families*, OUP, 2004
Burton, David, *The Raj at Table*, Faber, 1994
Cain, P. J., and Hopkins, A. G., *British Imperialism: Innovation and Expansion*, Longman, 1993
Caine, Barbara, *Bombay to Bloomsbury: A Biography of the Strachey Family*, OUP, 2005
Campbell, George, *Memoirs of My Indian Career*, 2 vols., Macmillan, 1893
—— *Modern India*, John Murray, 1852
Cannadine, David, *The Decline and Fall of the British Aristocracy*, Yale University Press, 1990
—— *Ornamentalism: How the British Saw Their Empire*, Allen Lane, 2001
Caroe, Olaf, *The Pathans*, Macmillan, 1958
Carstairs, R., *The Little World of an Indian District Officer*, Macmillan, 1912
Chanda, Anuradha, *Public Administration and Public Opinion in Bengal (1854–1885)*, Bagchi (Calcutta), 1986
Chandra, Sudhir, *Enslaved Daughters: Colonialism, Law and Women's Rights*, OUP (Delhi), 1999
Charlesworth, Neil, *British Rule and the Indian Economy, 1800–1914*, Macmillan, 1982
Checkland, Sydney, *The Elgins, 1766–1917*, Aberdeen University Press, 1988
Chenevix Trench, Charles, *Viceroy's Agent*, Jonathan Cape, 1987
Chettur, S. K., *The Steel Frame and I*, Asia Publishing House, 1962
Chirol, Valentine, *Indian Unrest*, Macmillan, 1910
Chudgar, P. L., *Indian Princes under British Protection*, William & Norgate, 1929
'Civilian', *The Civilian's South India*, Bodley Head, 1921
Coen, Terence Creagh, *The Indian Political Service*, Chatto & Windus, 1971
Cohn, Bernard S., *An Anthropologist among the Historians and Other Essays*, OUP (Delhi), 1987
Collingham, E. M., *Imperial Bodies*, Polity (Cambridge), 2001
Compton, J. H., 'Open Competition and the Indian Civil Service, 1854–1876', *English Historical Review*, Vol. 83, 1968
Cook, Scott B., 'The Irish Raj: Social Origins and Careers of Irishmen in the Indian Civil Service, 1855–1914', *Journal of Social History* (Pittsburgh), Spring 1987
Copland, Ian, *The British Raj and the Indian Princes*, Sangman, 1982
Cornell, Louis L., *Kipling in India*, St Martin's Press (New York), 1966
Cotton, Henry, *Indian & Home Memories*, Fisher Unwin, 1911
—— *New India, or India in Transition*, Kegan Paul, 1885
Crane, Robert I., and Barrier, N. Gerald (eds.), *British Imperial Policy in India and Sri Lanka, 1858–1912*, Heritage (New Delhi), 1991
Cromer, Lord, *Ancient & Modern Imperialism*, John Murray, 1910
Crooke, W., *The North-Western Provinces of India*, Methuen, 1897
Cunningham, H. S., *British India and Its Rulers*, W.H. Allen, 1881
—— *Chronicles of Dustypore*, Smith, Elder, 1885
Curzon, George N., *British Government in India*, 2 vols., Cassell, 1925
—— *Leaves from a Viceroy's Notebook*, Macmillan, 1926
Dalrymple, William, *White Mughals*, HarperCollins, 2002
Danvers, Frederick (ed.), *Memorials of Old Haileybury College*, Constable, 1894
Darling, Malcolm, *Apprentice to Power: India, 1904–1908*, Hogarth Press, 1966
Das, M. N, *India under Morley and Minto*, George Allen & Unwin, 1964
David, Saul, *The Indian Mutiny*, Viking, 2002
Davies, C. Collin, *The Problem of the North-West Frontier, 1890–1908*, Cambridge University Press, 1932
Davies, Philip, *Monuments of India*, Vol. 2, Penguin, 1989

Bibliography

Davis, Mike, *Late Victorian Holocausts*, Verso, 2001

Dewey, Clive, *Anglo-Indian Attitudes: The Mind of the Indian Civil Service*, Hambledon Press, 1993

—— 'The Education of a Ruling Caste: The Indian Civil Service in the Era of Competitive Examination', *English Historical Review*, Vol. 88, 1973

—— *The Passing of Barchester*, Hambledon Press, 1991

—— *The Settlement Literature of the Greater Punjab*, Manohar (New Delhi), 1991

Digby, William, *Indian Problems for English Consumption*, National Liberal Federation (Birmingham), 1881

Dilks, David, *Curzon in India*, 2 vols., Hart-Davis, 1969–70

Diver, Maud, *The Englishwoman in India*, Blackwood (Edinburgh), 1909

Dodwell, H. H., *The Indian Empire, 1858–1918*, Cambridge University Press, 1932

—— *A Sketch of the History of India*, Longmans, 1925

Durand, Mortimer, *Sir Alfred Comyn Lyall*, Blackwood (Edinburgh), 1913

Edwardes, Michael, *High Noon of Empire*, Eyre & Spottiswoode, 1965

Elsmie, G., *Thirty-five Years in the Punjab*, David Douglas (Edinburgh), 1908

Esher, Viscount (ed.), *The Girlhood of Queen Victoria*, John Murray, 1912

Ewing, Ann, 'Administering India: The Indian Civil Service', *History Today*, Vol. 32, June 1982

Ex-Civilian, *Life in the Mofussil*, 2 vols., Kegan Paul, 1878

Faber, Geoffrey, *Jowett*, Faber, 1957

Farrell, J. G., *The Siege of Krishnapur*, Weidenfeld & Nicolson, 1973

Ferguson, Niall, *Empire: How Britain Made the Modern World*, Allen Lane, 2003

Fielding-Hall, H., *The Passing of Empire*, Hurst & Blackett, 1913

Fisher, Michael, *Indirect Rule in India: Residents and the Residency System, 1764–1858*, OUP (Delhi), 1998

Forrest, G. W., *The Administration of the Marquis of Lansdowne, 1888–1894*, Government Printing Office (Calcutta), 1894

Foster, R. F., *Lord Randolph Churchill*, OUP, 1988

Fraser, A. H. L., *Among Indian Rajahs and Ryots*, Seeley, 1911

Fraser, Lovat, *India under Curzon and after*, Heinemann, 1911

French, Patrick, *Younghusband*, HarperCollins, 1994

Fry, Michael, *The Scottish Empire*, Tuckwell Press (East Lothian), 2001

Fuller, Bamphylde, *The Empire of India*, Pitman & Sons, 1913

Furbank, P. N., *E. M. Forster*, 2 vols., Secker & Warburg, 1977–8

Gait, Edward, *A History of Assam*, Thacker, Spink (Calcutta), 1926

Gandhi, M. K., *An Autobiography*, Penguin (Calcutta), 2003

Garth, Richard, *A Few Plain Truths about India*, Thacker, Spink (Calcutta), 1888

Ghosal, A. K., *Civil Service in India under the East India Company*, University of Calcutta, 1944

Ghose, Indira (ed.), *Memsahibs Abroad*, OUP (Delhi), 1996

Ghose, N. G., *England's Work in India*, University of Calcutta, 1914

Gilbert, Martin, *Servant of India: A Study of Imperial Rule from 1905 to 1910*, Longman, 1966

Gilmour, David, *Curzon*, John Murray, 1994

—— *The Long Recessional: The Imperial Life of Rudyard Kipling*, John Murray, 2002

Golant, William, *The Long Afternoon: British India, 1601–1947*, Hamish Hamilton, 1975

Gopal, S., *British Policy in India, 1858–1905*, Cambridge University Press, 1965

—— *The Viceroyalty of Lord Ripon*, OUP, 1955

Green, Roger Lancelyn, *Kipling: The Critical Heritage*, Routledge & Kegan Paul, 1971

Greenberger, Allen, J., *The British Image of India*, OUP, 1969

Grierson, George, *Seven Grammars of the Dialects and Subdialects of the Bihari Language*, 8 vols., Bengal Secretariat Press (Calcutta), 1883–7

Bibliography

Grierson, H. J. C. (ed.), *The Letters of Sir Walter Scott*, 10 vols., Constable, 1932–6

Griffin, Lepel, 'The Indian Civil Service Examinations', *Fortnightly Review*, Vol. 17, 1875

Griffiths, Percival, *The British Impact on India*, Frank Cass, 1965

Grimwood, Ethel St Clair, *My Three Years in Manipur*, Richard Bentley, London, 1891

Guha, Ramachandra, *A Corner of a Foreign Field*, Picador, 2002

Gupta, S. K., *A Foot in the Door of the Indian Civil Service*, Papyrus (Calcutta), 1996

Hamilton, George, *Parliamentary Reminiscences & Reflections, 1886–1906*, John Murray, 1922

Hibbert, Christopher, *The Great Mutiny*, Penguin, 1980

—— *Queen Victoria*, Basic Books, 2000

Hill, Claude, *India – Stepmother*, Blackwood (Edinburgh), 1929

Holroyd, Michael, *Lytton Strachey*, 2 vols., Heinemann, 1967–8

Hopkirk, Peter, *The Great Game*, John Murray, 1990

Houghton, Bernard, *Bureaucratic Government: A Study in Indian Polity*, P. S. King, 1913

Hübner, Baron von, *Through the British Empire*, Vol. 2, John Murray, 1886

Hunt, Roland, and Harrison, John, *The District Officer in India, 1930–1947*, Scolar Press, 1980

Hunter, W. W., *The Annals of Rural Bengal*, 3 vols., Smith Elder, 1868

—— *Imperial Gazetteer of India*, 9 vols., Trubner (Calcutta), 1881

—— *The Old Missionary*, Henry Frowde, 1896

Hutchins, Francis G., *The Illusion of Permanence: British Imperialism in India*, Princeton University Press, 1967.

Hutchins, Philip, *An Indian Career, 1858–1908*, private publication, 1927

Hyam, Ronald, *Empire and Sexuality: The British Experience*, Manchester University Press, 1991

Hyde, H. Montgomery, *Stalin*, Hart-Davis, 1971

Imperial Gazetteer of India, Vol. 26 (Atlas), OUP, 1931

Inden, Ronald B., *Imagining India*, Hurst, 1990

Indian Mahomedan, An, *British India*, Pitman, 1926

Jacob, Violet, *Diaries and Letters from India,* Canongate (Edinburgh), 1990

Jain, M. S., *Concise History of Modern Rajasthan*, Wishwa Prakashan (New Delhi), 1993

James, Lawrence, *Raj: The Making and Unmaking of British India*, Little Brown, 1997

James, Richard Rhodes, *The Years Between*, Wilton (York), 1993

Jeffrey, Robin (ed.), *People, Princes and Paramount Power*, OUP (Delhi), 1978

Johnstone, James, *My Experiences in Manipur and the Naga Hills*, Sampson Low, 1896

Jones, John, *Balliol College: A History, 1263–1939*, OUP, 1988

Kaminsky, Arnold P., *The India Office, 1880–1910*, Mansell, 1986

Kanwar, Pamela, *Imperial Simla*, OUP (Delhi), 1990

Kapil, F. K., *Rajputana States (1817–1950)*, Book Treasure (Jodhpur), 1999

Keith, A. B., *A Constitutional History of India, 1600–1935*, Methuen, 1936

Kennion, R. L., *Diversions of an Indian Political*, Blackwood (Edinburgh), 1932

Khan, Shaharyar M., *The Begums of Bhopal*, I. B. Tauris, 2000

Kincaid, C. A., *Forty-four Years a Public Servant*, Blackwood (Edinburgh), 1934

Kincaid, Dennis, *British Social Life in India*, George Routledge, 1938

King, Mrs Robert Moss, *The Diary of a Civilian's Wife in India, 1877–1882*, 2 vols., Richard Bentley, 1884

Kipling, Rudyard, *Barrack-Room Ballads and Other Verses*, Methuen, 1917

—— *Departmental Ditties and Other Verses*, Methuen, 1904

—— *From Sea to Sea*, 2 vols., Macmillan, 1912 and 1914

—— *Letters of Travel (1892–1913)*, Macmillan, 1920

—— *Plain Tales from the Hills*, Macmillan, 1931

—— *Something of Myself*, Cambridge University Press, 1991

Kirk-Greene, Anthony, *Britain's Imperial Administrators, 1858–1966*, Macmillan, 2000

Koss, Stephen, *John Morley at the India Office, 1905–1910*, Yale University Press, 1969

Bibliography

Laurie, W. F. B., *Sketches of Some Distinguished Anglo-Indians*, W. H. Allen, 1887
Lawrence, John, *Lawrence of Lucknow*, Hodder & Stoughton, 1990
Lawrence, Lady, *Indian Embers*, George Ronald (Oxford), n.d.
Lawrence, Walter, *The India We Served*, Cassell, 1928
Lee, Harold, *Brothers in the Raj: The Lives of John and Henry Lawrence*, OUP (Karachi), 2002
Lee-Warner, William, *The Native States of India*, Macmillan, 1910
Lethbridge, Katharine (ed.), *Letters from East and West*, Merlin (Braunton), 1990
Lewis, Ivor, *Sahibs, Nabobs and Boxwallahs*, OUP (Delhi), 1997
Lilly, W. S., *India and Its Problems*, Sands, 1902
Loch, Gordon, *The Family of Loch*, privately published, 1934
Longford, Elizabeth, *A Pilgrimage of Passion: The Life of Wilfrid Scawen Blunt*, Weidenfeld & Nicolson, 1979
—— *Victoria R.I.*, Weidenfeld & Nicolson, 1964
Lord, John, *The Maharajahs*, Hutchinson, 1972
Louis, Wm. Roger (ed.), *The Oxford History of the British Empire*, 5 vols., OUP, 1998–9
Lutyens, Mary, *The Lyttons in India*, John Murray, 1979
Lyall, Alfred, *Asiatic Studies*, 2 vols., John Murray, 1899
—— *The Rise and Expansion of the British Dominion in India*, John Murray, 1906
—— *Verses Written in India*, Kegan Paul, 1893
Mackenzie, John M., *The Victorian Vision*, V & A Publications, 2001
Macleod, R. D., *Impressions of an Indian Civil Servant*, H. F. and G.Witherby, 1938
McMillan, Alec, *Divers Ditties Chiefly Written in India*, Constable, 1895
Macmillan, Margaret, *Women of the Raj*, Thames & Hudson, 1998
Maconochie, Evan, *Life in the Indian Civil Service*, Chapman & Hall, 1926
Mangan, J. A., *The Games Ethic and Imperialism*, Viking, 1986
Marriott, J., *The English in India*, OUP, 1932
Martin Jr., Brinton, *New India, 1885*, University of California Press (Berkeley), 1969
Martineau, G. D., *Controller of Devils*, privately published, n.d
Mason, A. E. W., *The Broken Road*, John Murray, 1907
Mason, Philip, *Kipling: The Glass, the Shadow and the Fire*, Jonathan Cape, 1975
—— *A Matter of Honour*, Papermac, 1974
—— *A Shaft of Sunlight*, André Deutsch, 1978
Massey, Montague, *Recollections of Calcutta for over Half a Century*, Thacker, Spink (Calcutta), 1918
Masters, John, *Bugles and a Tiger*, Michael Joseph, 1956.
Mersey-Thompson, E. C., *India of Today*, Smith, Elder, 1913
Metcalf, Thomas R., *The Aftermath of Revolt: India 1857–70*, Princeton University Press, 1965
—— *Ideologies of the Raj*, Cambridge University Press, 1997
Meyer, Karl E., and Brysac, Shareen Blair, *Tournament of Shadows*, Counterpoint (Washington), 1999
Mill, James, *History of India*, 6 vols., Madden, 1840
Minto, Countess of, *India, Minto and Morley 1905–1910*, Macmillan, 1934
Misra, B. B., *The Bureaucracy in India*, OUP (Delhi), 1977
—— *District Administration and Rural Development in India*, OUP (Delhi), 1983
Misra, J. P., *The Administration of India under Lord Lansdowne*, Sterling Publishers (New Delhi), 1975
Montgomery, Brian, *Monty's Grandfather: A Life's Service for the Raj*, Blandford Press (Poole), 1984
Moon, Penderel, *The British Conquest and Dominion of India*, Duckworth, 1989
Moore, Robin, 'The Abolition of Patronage in the Indian Civil Service and the Closure of Haileybury College', *Historical Journal*, VII, 2, 1964

Bibliography

—— *Liberalism and Indian Politics, 1872–1892*, Edwin Arnold, 1966
—— *Paul Scott's Raj*, Heinemann, 1990
—— *Sir Charles Wood's Indian Policy*, Manchester University Press, 1966
Moorhouse, Geoffrey, *Calcutta*, Penguin, 1988
—— *India Britannica*, Harvill, 1988
Morison, Elting E. (ed.), *The Letters of Theodore Roosevelt*, Vol. 2, Harvard University Press, 1951
Morley, John, *Recollections*, 2 vols., Macmillan, 1917
Morris, J., *Pax Britannica*, Penguin, 1979
—— *Stones of Empire*, OUP, 1987
Moulton, Edward C., *Lord Northbrook's Indian Administration*, Asia Publishing House (New Delhi), 1968
Mudford, Peter, *Birds of a Different Plumage*, Collins, 1974
Muir, J., *The Indian Civil Service and the Scotch Universities*, W. P. Kennedy (Edinburgh), 1855
Naini Tal: A Historical and Descriptive Account, Government Press (Allahabad), 1928
Nanda, B. R., *Essays in Modern Indian History*, OUP (Delhi), 1980
—— *Gokhale, Gandhi and the Nations*, Allen & Unwin, 1974
Naoraji, Dadabhai, *The Indian Civil Service*, Commonweal Office (Madras), 1917
Newton, Lord, *Lord Lansdowne*, Macmillan, 1929
Oaten, Edward Farley, *A Sketch of Anglo-Indian Literature*, Kegan Paul, 1908
O'Donnell, C. J., 'The Black Pamphlet of Calcutta', William Ridgway (Calcutta), 1876
—— 'The Failure of Lord Curzon', Fisher Unwin, 1903
—— *The Irish Future and the Lordship of the World*, Cecil Palmer, 1929
—— 'The Ruin of an Indian Province', Kegan Paul, 1880
O'Dwyer, Michael, *India as I Knew It*, Constable, 1925
O'Malley, L. S. S., *The Indian Civil Service, 1601–1930*, Frank Cass, 1965
Owen, Roger, *Lord Cromer*, OUP, 2004
Packenham, Valerie, *The Noonday Sun: Edwardians in the Tropics*, Methuen, 1985
Panckridge, H. R., *A Short History of the Bengal Club*, private publication, 1927
Pandey, Gyanendra, *The Construction of Communalism in Colonial North India*, OUP (Delhi), 1992
Panter-Downes, Molly, *Ooty Preserved*, Hamish Hamilton, 1967
Pearce, Roger, *Once a Happy Valley*, OUP (Karachi), 2001
Pearson, J. D., *A Guide to Manuscripts and Documents in the British Isles Relating to South and South-east Asia*, Vol. 1, Mansell, 1989
Penner, Peter, *The Patronage Bureaucracy in North India*, Chanakya Publications (Delhi), 1986
Philips, C. H. (ed.), *Historians of India, Pakistan and Ceylon*, OUP, 1961
Pinney, Thomas, *Kipling's India: Uncollected Sketches, 1884–1888*, Macmillan, 1986
—— *The Letters of Rudyard Kipling*, 4 vols., University of Iowa Press, Iowa City, 1990–9
Porter, Andrew (ed.), *The Nineteenth Century*, OUP, 1999
Porter, Bernard, *The Absent-Minded Imperialists*, OUP, 2004
Potter, David C., *India's Political Administrators, 1981–1983*, OUP, 1986
Pottinger, George, *Mayo: Disraeli's Viceroy*, Michael Russell, 1990
Powell, Violet, *Flora Annie Steel*, Heinemann, 1981
Price, Frederick, *Ootacamund*, Government Press (Madras), 1908
Puri, B. N., *History of Indian Administration*, Vol. 3, Munshiram Manoharlal (New Delhi), 1982
Raj, Sheela, *Medievalism to Modernism: Socio-Economic and Cultural History of Hyderabad, 1869–1911*, Sangam, 1987
Ramusack, Barbara N., *The Indian Princes and Their States*, Cambridge University Press, 2004

Bibliography

Ratcliffe, S. K., *Sir William Wedderburn and the Indian Reform Movement*, George Allen & Unwin, 1923

Rawlinson, L. H. G., *The British Achievement in India*, William Hodge, 1948

Ray, Bharati, *Hyderabad and British Paramountcy, 1858–1883*, OUP (Delhi), 1988

Ray, P.C., *India before and after the Mutiny*, Livingstone (Edinburgh), 1886

Ray, Rajat Kanta, *Social Conflict and Political Unrest in Bengal*, OUP (Delhi), 1984

Reed, Stanley, *The India I Knew*, Odhams, 1952

Riddick, John F., *Who Was Who in British India*, Greenwood Press (Westport, Connecticut), 1998

Ritchie, Gerald, *The Ritchies in India*, John Murray, 1920

Rivett-Carnac, J. H., *Many Memories*, Blackwood (Edinburgh), 1910

Robb, Peter, and Taylor, David (eds.), *Rule, Protest, Identity*, Curzon Press, 1978

Roberts, Andrew, *Salisbury*, Weidenfeld & Nicolson, 1999

Roberts, Lord, *Forty-one Years in India*, 2 vols., Richard Bentley, 1897

Roberts, P. E., *History of British India under the Company and the Crown*, OUP, 1958

Robinson, Ronald, and Gallagher, John, *Africa and the Victorians*, Macmillan, 1961

Roy, Jyotirmoy, *History of Manipur*, Firma K. L. M. (Calcutta), 1958

Roy, N.C., *The Civil Service in India*, Firma K. L. M. (Calcutta), 1958

Rutherford, Andrew (ed.), *Early Verse by Rudyard Kipling*, OUP, 1986

Said, Edward, *Culture and Imperialism*, Vintage, 1994

—— *Orientalism*, Routledge & Kegan Paul, 1978

Sarkar, Mahua, *Justice in a Gothic Edifice*, Firma K. L. M. (Calcutta), 1997

Sarkar, S., *Modern India, 1885–1947*, Macmillan, 1989

Satyanatha, Samuel, *Four Years in an English University*, Lawrence Asylum Press (Madras), 1890

Saumarez-Smith, W. H., *A Young Man's Country*, Michael Russell, 1977

Scindia, Vijayaraje, *Princess*, Century, 1985

Seal, Anil, *The Emergence of Indian Nationalism*, Cambridge University Press, 1968

Seeley, J. R., *The Expansion of England*, Macmillan, 1889

Sengoopta, Chandak, *Imprint of the Raj*, Macmillan, 2003

Sharma, Malti, *Indianization of the Civil Services in British India*, Manak (New Delhi), 2001

Simson, Frank B., *Letters on Sport in Eastern Bengal*, R. H. Porter, 1886

Singh, Dhananajaya, *The House of Marwar*, Lotus (New Delhi), 1994

Singh, Hira Lal, *The British Policy in India*, Meenakshi Prakasen (New Delhi), 1982

Skrine, F. H. B., *Life of Sir William Wilson Hunter*, Longmans, 1901

Smeaton, Donald, *The Loyal Karens of Burma*, Kegan Paul, 1887

Spangenberg, Bradford, *British Bureaucracy in India: Status, Policy and the ICS in the Late 19th Century*, South Asia Books (Delhi), 1976

Spear, Percival, *A History of India*, Vol. 2, Penguin, 1990

Spurling, Hilary, *Paul Scott*, Pimlico, 1991

Sristava, G. P., *The Indian Civil Service*, S. Chand (New Delhi), 1965

Steel, Flora Annie, *The Garden of Fidelity*, Macmillan, 1929

—— *On the Face of the Waters*, Heinemann, 1897

—— *The Potter's Thumb*, Heinemann, 1894

Steel, F. A., and Gardiner, G., *The Complete Indian Housekeeper & Cook*, Heinemann, 1898

Steevens, G. W., *In India*, Blackwood (Edinburgh), 1899

Stone, Ian, *Canal Irrigation in British India*, Cambridge University Press, 1984

Strachey, Barbara, *The Strachey Line*, Victor Gollancz, 1985

Strachey, John, *The End of Empire*, Victor Gollancz, 1959

Strachey, (Sir) John, *India*, Kegan Paul, 1894

Swinson, Arthur, *North-West Frontier*, Hutchinson, 1967

Symonds, Richard, *The British and Their Successors*, Faber, 1966

Bibliography

—— *Oxford and Empire*, OUP, 1991

Temple, Richard, *Journals Kept in Hyderabad, Kashmir, Sikkim, and Nepal*, W. H. Allen, 1887

—— *The Story of My Life*, 2 Vols., Cassell, 1896

Thacker's Bengal Directory, Thacker, Spink (Calcutta), 1863–84

Thacker's Indian Directory, Thacker, Spink (Calcutta), 1885–1900

Thomas, Henry Sullivan, *The Rod in India*, Thacker, 1897

Thompson, Edward, *An Indian Day*, Alfred A. Knopf, 1927

Thorburn, S. S., *The Punjab in Peace and War*, Blackwood (Edinburgh), 1904

Tidrick, Kathryn, *Empire & the English Character*, I. B. Tauris, 1992

Tikekar, Aroon, *The Kincaids*, Promilla, New Delhi, 1992

Trevelyan, G. O., *Competition Wallah*, Macmillan, 1866

Trevelyan, Humphrey, *The India We Left*, Macmillan, 1972

Trevelyan, Raleigh, *The Golden Oriole*, Secker & Warburg, 1987

Tupp, Alfred Cotterell, *The Indian Civil Service and the Competitive System*, R. W. Brydges, 1876

Tupper, Charles Lewis, *Our Indian Protectorate*, Longmans, Green, 1893

Tyndale-Biscoe, C. E., *Tyndale-Biscoe of Kashmir*, Seeley, Service & Co., n.d.

Waley-Cohen, Ethel (ed.), *A Young Victorian in India: Letters of H. M. Kisch*, Jonathan Cape, 1957

Warburton, Robert, *Eighteen Years in the Khyber*, John Murray, 1900

Ward, Andrew, *Our Bones Are Scattered*, John Murray, 1996

Wedderburn, William, *Allan Octavian Hume*, (new ed. by Edward C. Moulton), OUP (New Delhi), 2002

Welldon, J. E. C., *Recollections and Reflections*, Cassell, 1915

Wheare, K. C., *The Civil Service in the Constitution*, University of London, 1954

Whish, B. C., *A District Office in Northern India*, Thacker, Spink (Calcutta), 1892

Whitcombe, E., *Agrarian Conditions in Northern India*, University of California Press (Berkeley), 1972

White, Herbert Thirkell, *A Civil Servant in Burma*, Edward Arnold, 1913

Whitworth, George C., *An Anglo-Indian Dictionary*, Kegan Paul, 1885

Wilkinson, Theon, *Two Monsoons: The Life and Death of Europeans in India*, Duckworth, 1987

Williams, Donovan, and Potts, E. Daniel, *Essays in Indian History*, Asia Publishing House, 1973

Wilson, Anne C., *Hints for the First Years of Residence in India*, OUP, 1904

Wilson, Lady, *Letters from India*, Century, 1984

Winks, Robin, *Historiography*, OUP, 1999

Wolpert, Stanley A., *Morley and India, 1906–1910*, University of California Press, 1967

Woodruff, Philip, *The Founders*, Jonathan Cape, 1963

—— *The Guardians*, Jonathan Cape, 1963

Wright, W. H., *Muir Central College*, Government Press (Allahabad), 1886

Yalland, Zoe, *Boxwallahs: The British in Cawnpore, 1857–1901*, Michael Russell, 1994

Younghusband, Francis, *The Light of Experience*, Constable, 1927

Yule, Henry, Burnell, A. C., and Crooke, William (eds.), *Hobson-Jobson*, John Murray, 1903

Zaidi, Syed Zawwar Husain, 'The Partition of Bengal and Its Annulment: A Survey of the Schemes of Territorial Redistribution of Bengal, 1902–1911', doctoral thesis, University of London, 1964

Zinkin, Maurice, 'ICS Revisited', *Journal of Asian Affairs*, October 1994

Acknowledgements

WHILE DOING THE research for this book, I have accumulated many debts to the archivists and librarians who have acquired, preserved and catalogued the papers of the administrators of Victorian India. I also owe a good deal to a number of people who have faithfully conserved the letters, diaries and other memorabilia of their ancestors.

In the first category I would particularly like to thank David Blake and Richard Bingle, both formerly of the Oriental and India Office Collections of the British Library, and the archivists of the Bodleian Library at Oxford, the Centre of South Asian Studies at Cambridge, the National Library of Scotland, the Nehru Memorial Library in Delhi, the University of Sussex, and Balliol and Oriel Colleges, Oxford. In the second I am especially grateful to Anne Chisholm, Tam and Kathleen Dalyell, Antoinette Galbraith, Patsy Grigg, Jean Phillips and Xan Smiley.

The text has been read by my father Ian Gilmour, Jan Dalley, Ramachandra Guha and my brother Andrew, and the early sections were read by Professor C. A. Bayly. I am grateful to all of them for their sagacity and their advice. I would also like to thank the following for their various kinds of assistance: Sir Menzies Campbell, Keshav Desiraju, James Ferguson, Professor Roy Foster, Subinda Kaur, Professor Sunil Khilnani, Philip Mansel, Professor Arvind Mehrotra, Professor V. C. Pande, Shashi Sen,

Acknowledgements

Geetanjali Shree, Angus Stewart, Richard Symonds, Deirdre Toomey and Emma Williams.

I owe a special debt to Lord Dahrendorf and Sir Alistair Horne who, by electing me to a fellowship at St Antony's College, Oxford, allowed me to do much of my research in the most attractive and stimulating of locations.

My good fortune with publishers has continued on both sides of the Atlantic. I have benefited much from the wisdom and proficiency of Elisabeth Sifton at Farrar, Straus & Giroux, and of Roland Philipps and his new team at John Murray. As usual, I am particularly grateful to Gail Pirkis, the most skilled, perceptive and understanding of editors.

Finally, and once again, a special thanks to Sarah and my children for their own, more idiosyncratic, contributions to the project.

Edinburgh
March 2005

Index

Index